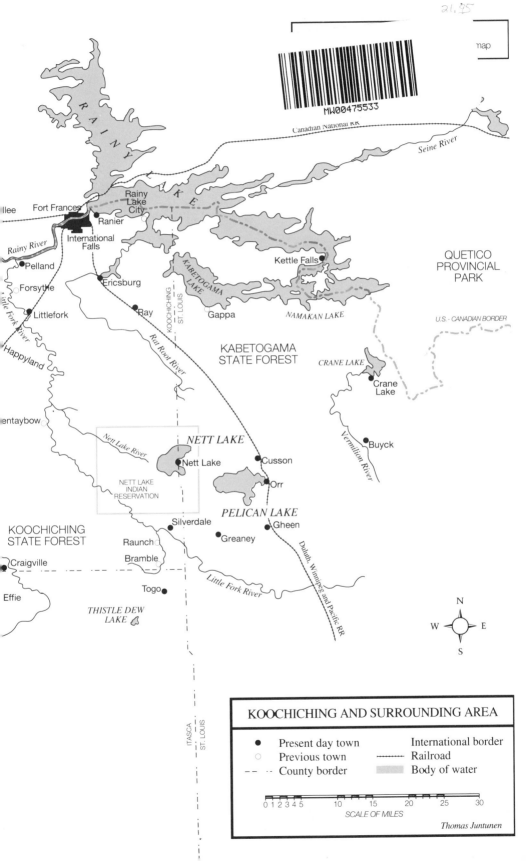

21,95

nap

RAINY LAKE

Canadian National RR

Seine River

QUETICO
PROVINCIAL
PARK

llee
Fort Frances
Rainy
Lake
City
Ranier

International
Falls

Rainy River

Pelland

Forsythe

Little Fork River

Littlefork

Ericsburg

Ray

KABETOGAMA LAKE

KOOCHICHING
ST. LOUIS

Gappa

Kettle Falls

NAMAKAN LAKE

U.S. - CANADIAN BORDER

Happyland

Rat Root River

KABETOGAMA
STATE FOREST

CRANE LAKE

Crane
Lake

Buyck

Vermilion River

entaybow

Nett Lake River

NETT LAKE

Nett Lake

Cusson

Orr

NETT LAKE
INDIAN
RESERVATION

PELICAN LAKE

KOOCHICHING
STATE FOREST

Silverdale

Greaney

Gheen

Duluth, Winnipeg and Pacific RR

Raunch

Bramble

Craigville

Togo

Little Fork River

Effie

THISTLE DEW
LAKE

N

W   E

S

ITASCA
ST. LOUIS

KOOCHICHING AND SURROUNDING AREA

- ● Present day town
- ○ Previous town
- – – ·· County border

International border
Railroad
Body of water

0 1 2 3 4 5   10   15   20   25   30
SCALE OF MILES

Thomas Juntunen

Taming the Wilderness

Taming the Wilderness

The Northern Border Country
1910–1939

HIRAM M. DRACHE
Concordia College

INTERSTATE PUBLISHERS, INC.
Danville, Illinois

Library of Congress Catalog Card No. 91-73161

ISBN 0-8134-2927-7

PRINTED IN U.S.A.

Dedication

TO RUDY AND RUBY ERICKSON
whose encouragement made this book possible

TO ADA
for her support, technical input,
and constant devotion

ABOUT THE BOOK

The purpose of the book is to describe several facets of life in this wilderness country in the three decades during which the region converted from a primitive to an industrial society. The story is of numerous struggles: harvesting the virgin forest; establishing the essential social institutions; challenging the soil to eke out a living; struggling to drain the swampland, which failed miserably and virtually bankrupted the counties involved; resisting the temptations of humanity; striving for harmonious labor-management relations; and competing with one another over the future of the wilderness.

The virgin forest disappeared, but the land would not yield to attempts to change it. When a new forest appeared, nature proved to be victorious, and the wilderness remained.

ABOUT THE COVER

Timber was the key to the economy of northern Minnesota. The logging industry provided work for those who cleared the land to prepare it for farming and settlement. Roads and railroads had to be built to make the timber accessible to the paper mill and sawmills, which were the basis for urban economy.

Entrepreneur E. W. Backus was responsible for the construction of the dam, the power plant, the paper mill, and various sawmills. Although not all of Backus' dreams were fully realized, his former enterprises are still the key to the area's economy.

The culture of logging was of primary importance and, therefore, dominates the drawing. The subjects all are taken from historical photos and represent the logging industry from the lumber camp of the past to the paper mill. But, except for a few isolated communities, the wilderness remains.

Foreword

How PRIVILEGED WE ARE to be able to pick up a book and get a look and a feel of a special place at a special time. Such journeys into yesterday leave a reader enlightened, inspired, and often entertained. *Taming the Wilderness* did all of this for me and more. It was a visit to the past that was both sad and heartwarming.

It is of the vast northern border country of Minnesota that Dr. Drache writes. Maps are silent regarding this huge empty space, but this respected educator and historian guides us to an understanding of the reasons for this unsettled yet productive area.

Although I have lived most of my life in Warroad, I spent my early years in Virginia, on the Mesabi Iron Range. Iron ore was king, but I distinctly remember my fifth-grade geography book stating that Virginia had the largest white pine sawmill in the world. I wish I had been able to connect the white pine with the lumber camps Dr. Drache so vividly describes and the development of the roads and railroads that brought the logs to their destinations, where they provided employment and materials for a rapidly growing nation.

As a teenager my father left Sweden with a dream of finding land he could farm. Fate lured him north to Virginia, where jobs were abundant, but he soon acquired a piece of land in Meadow Brook, 50 miles northwest of Virginia. With his wife and a daughter he lived on that farm by the Little Fork River for a year, when an irresistible employment opportunity arose in Virginia, so we moved back. The new job enabled Dad to subsidize the farm for years, but nothing could make it a winner. Dr. Drache discusses the agricultural challenges in this area and what life was like for the farm families who, in time, just quietly disappeared. The farms are gone and the wilderness has again taken over.

Warroad is not really a part of Dr. Drache's wilderness treatise, but as a neighbor of Lake of the Woods and Koochiching counties, it has shared many challenges and interests. The Backus enter-prises 106 miles to the east provided many small farmers a reliable market for their pulpwood. Drache spends considerable time portraying Backus' vision, energy, and influence. Pulpwood was shipped from Warroad to International Falls a year *before* the mill was completed. Starting around 1910, my father-in-law, George Marvin, served as a pulpwood broker for over 60 years. Today, pulpwood still rides the Canadian National to the Falls.

Reading about the hardships the wilderness residents endured is a moving experience, especially knowing that very few of them realized their hopes and their dreams. I felt frustration with the decision makers in St. Paul, who encouraged people to settle in the area without knowing anything about the soil; the isolation; the swamps; the mosquitoes; the extremes in weather; the lack of roads, medical services, and schools; and on and on. How I admired the clergymen who trudged many, many miles to hold services for small gatherings and who helped to a great extent with the construction of their churches.

The book has a real heroine in Annie Shelland Williams, who campaigned for good roads in 1912. She was deeply concerned that there were women who had never been more than 10 miles from their homes in 10 years. Above all, she worked for those roads so children could get to school.

However, all was not gloom and families were strong. Neighbors provided help and understanding and shared in simple pleasures. Dr. Drache interjects a bit of humor, such as his comments about the early cars, reminding us of the engines that boiled over, the flat tires that were part of even the shortest trip, the tool box with its tire-patching kit and pump on the running board, and the boiling sun and buzzing flies that did their best at tire-chang-ing time. He also quotes Billy Noonan, whose clever "Noonanisms" are still good for a chuckle.

The research done on this work is outstanding. With informa-tion from a variety of sources, the result is a very readable, honest, in-depth view of a special place in the not-too-distant past. What a treat it is for people like me who enjoy "touching" yesterday from time to time.

As harsh as the wilderness was in its treatment of those who tried to make it theirs, it prepared them well to succeed in their other choices. For those who chose to remain along the edge of the wilderness, progress came slowly but surely. Gradually the quality of their lives improved.

MARGARET W. MARVIN
Warroad, Minnesota

Preface

THIS BOOK is a continuation of the story found in *Koochiching*. It includes a larger area, extending from Kettle Falls on the east to the Beltrami Island State Forest on the west, and about 85 miles south of the northern border. It covers the years 1910 through 1939.

The area was still primarily wilderness in 1910, with only a few isolated settlers among the muskeg swamps and dense forest. However, it had been sufficiently scouted so that E. W. Backus and his associates could justify spending millions of dollars to harness one of the largest waterfalls on the continent, to build a state-of-the-art paper-mill complex, and to entice two railroads to penetrate the wilderness.

Backus, one of the last timber barons, had the country almost to himself. The international border meant nothing to him as he maneuvered to acquire stumpage (harvesting) rights on land from both the Canadian and the United States governments.

Backus had his way until the mid-1920s, when environmentalists campaigned and were successful in getting legislation to block his plans for more water power. Eventually, his unlimited ambition became his downfall, for he overextended himself financially, and in 1931 his $100 million empire fell into bankruptcy.

But this is not a story of one man—it is a tale about people who exploited the public domain for a few dollars and then left; about legitimate homesteaders, who came, settled, suffered, and often failed; about thousands of lumberjacks, who spent their winters toiling in the forest. Many were north European immigrants, who desired to escape the pre–World War I turmoil. They wanted to learn English and earn money for a better life. Others had reason to escape the more established communities of our nation, and often they recklessly squandered their earnings for booze, gambling, and sex. It is about missionaries, who endured countless hardships to spread the gospel; and it is about small communities and their citizens, who enjoyed a limited prosperity during an all-too-short boom period of the early logging days, only to learn that when technology changed the method of harvesting the forest, their way of life was over.

In some respects, this was the final land frontier in the contiguous 48 states, which served to draw many prospective homesteaders. It was one of the most brutal frontiers, because the natural conditions were such that to succeed in farming was nearly impossible. With few exceptions, most of these homesteaders failed; others survived only because there was no limit to their willingness to deny themselves. Unfortunately for those eager to farm, both the state and federal governments, through generous legislation, encouraged individuals to settle on land that should never have been opened. The bleak future ahead for the settlers stirred the government to conduct one of the most successful resettlement projects in our nation's history.

By the 1930s, all but the most obstinate settlers realized that this wilderness land was not meant to be farmed. The homesteaders willingly sold their farms and went to nearby lumber towns or left the area. Nature won the battle and the wilderness was not tamed, but those who believed in the future of the lumber and the paper industries have reaped their rewards because of continued reforestation.

HIRAM M. DRACHE
Professor of History
Concordia College
Moorhead, Minnesota

Acknowledgements

THE ORIGINS OF THIS BOOK, my second on wilderness country, date back to July 1973, when Rudy and Ruby Erickson confronted me with a challenge to write a history of the area where they had spent their lives. Rudy wanted a series of paperbacks like he had seen written about other frontiers.

Several students of Concordia College—Julie Hanson, Lori Lashbrooke, Lori Nornes, Rebecca Swanson, Signe Thompson, and Cindy Williams—did most of the newspaper research for this project while on campus. Lori Lashbrooke and Cindy each spent a summer working with me at International Falls in the 1970s. Three other Cobbers—Karen Borstad, David Drache, and Kay Drache—did months of research in the late 1970s in the archives of the Minnesota Historical Society. I know all of the above are anxious to see the results of their efforts.

Again, the total support of the Concordia administration, starting with President Dovre, has made the task of producing another book possible and easier. The wholehearted cooperation of Dr. Verlyn Anderson's excellent Concordia library staff, especially Mary Larson and Lola Quam, aided so much in locating the hard-to-find facts or securing data from other libraries. The special Drache button on the telephone is very flattering.

Tom Juntunen, computer specialist, created the first computer-designed maps in any of my books. How can one know history without understanding the geography? David Drache, Jon Frantsvog, Robert Hilke, and Ray Anderson, all amateur photographers, did professional-quality work reproducing hundreds of pictures to enable the fine selection we used.

This book profited from being edited a minimum of five times before the editors at Interstate saw it. That work fell on Ada, my severest and best critic, and Elva Bergseid, former student, whose keen mind has served me well for over two decades. In addition to editing, Ada did all the technical computer work, which freed me to supply the story.

Thanks to Marlys Hirst, of the Lake of the Woods County Historical Society; Carol Eberhardt, of the Beltrami County Historical Society; Dr. Terry Shoptaugh, of the Northwestern Minnesota Historical Center; and Mary Hilke, formerly of the Koochiching County Historical Society. Sandra Boen, director of the Koochiching County Historical Society, and her staff have earned a special thank-you for the many hours of digging and of replying to correspondence, but, more importantly, for the warmth and friendliness with which they did so. Researching is fun with such interesting people to work with.

Lester Pollard, who is a walking encyclopedia on the M & O woods history from 1927 into the 1960s, deserves my very special thanks, not only for the interviews, but also for verifying my facts and answering questions of every nature.

To the many individuals who consented to be interviewed, my sincere thanks, because without their input much of the human side of the story would be missing. My biggest regret is that so many who were interviewed are not here to see their names in print. I only hope that I have done them justice.

ABBREVIATED TERMS

AAA	*Agricultural Adjustment Act*
AFL	*American Federation of Labor*
CCC	*Civilian Conservation Corps*
CN	*Canadian Northern (later Canadian National) Railroad*
CWA	*Civilian Works Administration*
DW & P	*Duluth, Winnipeg, and Pacific Railroad*
DWRL	*Duluth, Winnipeg, and Rainy Lake Railway*
The Falls	*International Falls, Minnesota*
The Fort	*Fort Frances, Ontario*
IBT	*International Bridge Terminal Corporation*
IJC	*International Joint Commission*
ILC	*International Lumber Company*
IWW	*Industrial Workers of the World*
The Journal	The *International Falls Daily Journal*, *November 9, 1911–*
M & I	*Minnesota and International Railway Company*
M & O	*Minnesota and Ontario Paper Company (U.S.)*
M & RR	*Minneapolis and Rainy River Railroad Company*
MD & W	*Minnesota, Dakota, and Western Railway*
NP	*Northern Pacific Railway Company*
O & M	*Ontario and Minnesota Paper Company (Canadian)*
OBU	*One Big Union (Canadian branch of IWW)*
The Press	The *International Falls Press, to November 1911*
PWA	*Project Works Administration*
VRL	*Virginia and Rainy Lake Lumber Company*
VRLRR	*Virginia and Rainy Lake Railroad*
WPA	*Works Project Administration*

Table of Contents

Taming the Wilderness

CHAPTER I

Harnessing the Wilderness

THE NORTHERN MINNESOTA FRONTIER was one of the last areas of the contiguous 48 states opened to settlement. Only the western edge, which contains the rich agricultural lands of the Red River Valley, had received any great influx of settlers prior to 1900. Initially, the timber frontier east of the Valley was roughly along 96 west longitude and reached as far south as Fergus Falls, at which point it ran in a southeasterly direction toward the Twin Cities. From the 1840s on, this frontier receded steadily northward, but with only a few minor exceptions, by 1900 settlers had not yet entered any part of what is now Lake of the Woods, Koochiching, northern Itasca, or northern St. Louis counties.

Northward flowing rivers, dense forest, and considerable swampy land made it difficult to traverse the region and very costly to build railroads, which were necessary to transform the frontier from primitive to industrial. No major effort was made to penetrate the wilderness until E. W. Backus, one of the last of the Minnesota timber barons, recognized the area's potential and was willing to risk large amounts of capital.

In 1892 The Koochiching Company, whose principal officers were W. V. Winchell and C. J. Lockwood, purchased 127.5 acres from Joseph Baker, son of Alexander Baker, pioneer settler of Koochiching (after 1907 International Falls, hereafter the Falls). The Koochiching Company was unable to raise sufficient money to develop its plans until it became involved with E. W. Backus and W. F. Brooks in 1900. Backus, a well-established lumberman, and Brooks, a mechanical engineer, both were interested in the timber of the Rainy Lake and Rainy River region. They previously had secured riparian rights from the Canadian and United States governments.

In 1900 Koochiching had only 256 people and was still part of Itasca County, but with Backus in control, things were destined

3

to change. Cruisers scouted the woods, surveyors looked for the best railroad routes, and engineers scanned the power potential of the region. By 1902 plans were in motion for building the Minnesota and International Railway (M & I) north from Brainerd to the shores of Rainy Lake, where it was rumored that an immense water power project would be built.[1]

Cruising for Timber

By the time Backus had made projections for his dam and paper mill, his chief cruiser, Lyman Warren Ayer, the scout of the north woods, reported on the total supply of timber available within efficient range of harvest for the Falls and Fort Frances (hereafter the Fort). The cruiser's report was the first requirement of any timber operation, and no one skilled in the business proceeded without that information. Ross Slack, probably the first professional resident cruiser in the area, arrived in the Big Fork Valley in 1890. Other leading cruisers were Jesse Dow, of Virginia and Rainy Lake Lumber Company (VRL); Andy Gordon, of Crookston Lumber Company; Henry Graham, of National Pole Company; and Mark Hessey and Black Jack Wilson, of International Lumber Company (ILC).

Competition for timber in the north intensified as trees closer to the more settled and more accessible regions of the state were cut. Many firms, such as VRL, were primarily interested in lumber and did not look at the long-range potential of the forest industry as did Backus. VRL's purpose ended when the areas around Orr, Ericsburg, Ray, and the Superior National Forest were cut over in 1929. The same is true for many of the lumber camp towns that boomed and within a few years, once the timber was cut, started to die. Their reason for existing had come to an end.

Backus never stopped sending out cruisers to locate new sources of supply. After a hunting trip in 1922 he wrote to his son Seymour, "Our duck-hunt guide, Mr. Smith, remarked that he thought there was 15 million feet of quality hardwood in the Round Lake area, near Dunbar." He advised that a cruiser be sent there.

At the same time J. D. Twomey, forest manager for ILC, advised cruisers to go to all areas serviceable by railroads to determine the location of any hardwood stands. Backus was more emphatic; he advised that cruisers go through all areas "with fine-tooth comb" in search of hardwoods and contact all settlers informing them that the Minnesota and Ontario Paper Company (M & O; in Canada it is referred to as the Ontario and Minnesota Paper Company—O & M) was buying hardwood. He closed one memo, "We cannot afford to take up our rails and leave any timber of value standing." He also suggested that at least five cruisers, who were each paid $125 a month to look over all company land for signs of trespass, fires, blowdown, etc., were needed to spot any timber that ought to be cut at once.

Hessey was given special instructions in 1923 to survey all available land in Canada, especially in the Quetico Reserve tributary to Rainy Lake, for any sign of damage. Backus ordered this move while trying to decide on which 2,500-square-mile block of land to secure rights to from Ontario. In September he told Hessey that if he could find a block of 2,500 square miles that would yield seven cords of pulp per acre in addition to a total of 1.5 to 2 billion feet of pine, he would build a sawmill in the Fort. After Hessey had completed that project, he was instructed to re-examine four or five townships in St. Louis County owned by VRL which had suffered a forest fire. M & O considered buying the land to salvage the useable timber.

The cruisers were well paid by forest standards. On one special assignment in 1922 the cruiser was paid $8 per day and the other crew members $4. A normal crew included the cruiser, a compass man, and a cook/packer. On extended journeys the cook and the packer were separate individuals. Generally they worked quite distant from any settlement and spent long periods living in the wilderness. Their tents were of a silk-like fabric, double walled with an air space between the layers for warmth and to keep the snow from melting and dripping through, as was common with single-walled material. The cook/packer carried supplies for cooking and camp while the others surveyed. It was not uncommon for them to work during the winter, which usually was the best time to walk through the forest.

Most cruisers worked alone, but in the winter of 1938–39 a party of 4 cruisers, 4 compassmen, a cook, and Lester Pollard as packer spent 67 days surveying 46,570 acres—nearly half of M & O's timbered land in Minnesota. This $6,000 project was conducted to assess where the next logging operations should be located. Those 67 days consisted of 46 working days, 9 Sundays, 6 idle days, and 6 camp-moving days. The total cost was labor, $2,926; provisions, $450; lodging and board, $65; and car and miscellaneous expense, $300. A field cost of $3,741.00 equaled

$0.122 per acre. Each cruiser and compassman team averaged 174.03 acres per day.[2]

An International Paper Mill Complex

The history of the northern border country has been recorded as B.D. (Before Dam) and A.D. (After Dam), for more than any other single factor, the construction of the dam altered the course of events in that locale.

Residents of the twin towns of Fort Frances, Ontario, and Koochiching, Minnesota, rejoiced in December 1903 after the signing of an agreement between Backus and the province of Ontario, which gave Backus the right to develop water power on the Rainy River. The agreement stated that half of the power generated was reserved for Ontario, and work on the dam had to start by January 15, 1904. With a dam confirmed, Backus pushed hard to get a railroad or railroads completed.

Local newspapers described an immense complex that would make existing mills in either nation insignificant. It was reputed that Backus had the rights to 20 million acres of timber on both sides of the border, enough to keep a 200-ton-a-day paper mill in operation for 100 years. But Canadians were upset that a mill at the Falls was being erected before one at the Fort, and O & M was notified that no water could be diverted to the American side.

In 1907 the M & I and what was to become the Duluth, Winnipeg and Pacific Railroad (DW & P) were finished to the Falls and began delivering equipment, men, and materials for building the giant paper complex. Work had begun on the 35,000-HP dam, the key to powering a mill with a daily capacity of 175 tons of pulp, 100 tons of sulphite, and 200 tons of paper.

Not everyone was comfortable with the fast pace that Backus set. President Theodore Roosevelt vetoed a water grant bill when Backus applied for an extension to his construction time. Roosevelt said that power was worth money and that possibly a compensation clause should be included in any future bill. Congressman J. Adam Bede, of Minnesota, championed Backus' cause, and before the battle was over, Bede and Backus met with the President. Backus did not seem overly concerned, for he said that a patent of 1894 had given him control of the water rights. However, the government could deny him the right to develop the property.

Backus was not disturbed by the veto and continued to develop his plans as if everything were fine. He had building materials delivered to the Fort to appease the Canadians and was confident that the President would sign the new bill, although he realized that there might be some charge for the power. With that assurance he went to New York, where he met with the Knickerbocker Trust Company officers and arranged for up to $8 million in financing. The vote to override the President's veto was 240 to 5.

Soon petitions floated throughout the Rainy River Valley asking for the assurance of a supply of pulpwood and requesting concessions from the government to the capitalists so that they could justify their investment in a power plant and a mill at the Fort. After legal and financial matters were settled, construction on the project was renewed in late 1908.

In the meantime, the Watrous Island Boom Company, a subsidiary of Backus and Brooks, applied to the International Joint Commission (IJC) of the United States and Canada for rights to clear and straighten channels, close sloughs, build dams, erect booms, and make other improvements to enhance the driving of logs. The rivers affected were the Winter Road, Baudette, Rapid, Black, Big Fork, Little Fork, Ash, Vermilion, Namakan, and Rainy. The application stated that about $20 million would be invested in timber and mills capable of 200 million feet of sawed lumber each year at the Falls, Spooner, and Keewatin. In addition, ties, cedar poles, posts, 125 million feet of saw logs, and 50,000 to 60,000 cords of pulpwood would be processed.[3]

The people of the Fort had to be content while Backus completed the dam and then exported the power to the south shore of the Rainy to produce paper. When asked why he did not put the grinders on the Canadian side and export the pulp, Backus said that only raw wood could be imported duty free.

The first paper machine was put on line May 30, 1910; by June 6 it had produced 17.9 tons of paper. By October 17, four paper machines were in operation. The Falls mill, with a daily capacity of 164 tons of paper, was one of the largest paper mills in the world.

The citizens of the Fort were upset because Dominion officials had overruled an Ontario order-in-council and granted Backus the right to import 6,000 HP of electricity to run the Falls mill. Canadian Premier Wilfred Laurier visited the Fort and assured its citizens that, in June 1909, Backus had agreed to build and to operate a paper mill on the north side of the Rainy. Backus made a trip to Ottawa to convince the Premier that he would abide by the contract.

Soon 50 flatcars of pulpwood entered the storage yard at the Falls daily. Once all the camps were in full swing, 75 cars arrived daily. Ann Stone Fraser (Mrs. R. C.) at age 94 said, "The biggest event in this town's history was the building of the mill. It gave work and caused the town to grow. It is the source of wealth for the community."[4]

Other timber groups were interested in the area. During 1910 the Fort city council passed bylaws permitting Shevlin-Clarke and Company, the Weyerhauser group, and VRL to set up mills there. Everyone rushed to get in on the ground floor, but, except for the Shevlin firm, the other firms merged and left the area or were absorbed by the Backus interests.

In the meantime, O & M continued to delay its program at the Fort. Matters did not improve when it was announced that it owed $11,000 in taxes. A Minneapolis paper stated: "The Canadians cannot find words harsh enough to express their hostile feelings toward him [Backus]." But O & M continued to make eleventh-hour concessions and spent money freely in the Fort to buy time. In October 1911, it was announced that O & M was ready to build a mill of 100 tons daily capacity employing 250 men at the Fort in accordance with its contract of 1909. However, it was not until 1912 that a bylaw was passed giving permission to build. O & M obtained a concession that taxes would not be more than $25,000 a year for the first 10 years on a two-machine mill. Half of the power generated had to be used on the Canadian side, and the Fort would be entitled to purchase for municipal purposes up to 100 HP of energy at $14 per HP per year.

O & M purchased land in April 1912, and in May 1914 the long-awaited Fort pulp and paper mill was opened. This $2 million complex capable of 125 tons of newsprint a day was the first of its kind in western Canada.

At the same time business was booming in the Falls, and plans were announced for doubling the capacity of the mills there, but first a problem had to be solved. The paper machines rejected coarse fibers (shives) not suitable for paper making, and the product accumulated in the storage yard. A breakthrough appeared when a German scientist discovered how to recycle paper.

Carl Muench, a St. Paul scientist who had worked on using flax fiber as insulation in refrigerators, was hired. By February

1913 a material was produced from the coarse fibers of the pulp. Bror G. Dahlberg, one of the workers involved in its development, received the original patent on the product, which was named Universal Insulite. (Dahlberg later split with M & O and went on to found the Celotex Corporation, which nearly overshadowed the M & O firm, International Insulation Company.) Insulite, a by-product of paper making, became a very profitable part of the M & O operation. It was originally used for roof insulation and in refrigerator cars, but with the advent of World War I was in great demand for temporary barracks. Sheathing, siding, interior paneling, plaster base, and ceiling tile were some of its other uses.[5]

Once the main mill at the Falls started production, there seemed to be no limit to Backus' dreams. In 1913 he announced that plans were in progress to expand to 650 tons of various grades of paper per day, to make M & O the largest individual paper-producing company in the world. In addition to timber from floating logs down the rivers, once a forest railroad complex was completed, a "practically unlimited" supply of spruce and poplar for the manufacture of pulp would become available.

By 1916 an Insulite building was under construction, which, when finished, would require 100 workers. A kraft (wrapping) paper plant, which would employ over 200 people, was expected to be on line by April 1917, and a book-paper mill building, requiring 600 employees, was in progress. The demand for labor was strong. Many who had come to the area to farm soon realized the difficulties involved and were attracted by the high wages in the mills. Even Samuel Plummer, of Loman, who had earned $6 a day dismantling the original camp buildings used by the dam and mill workers in 1910, came back in 1917 to do carpenter work on 40 houses that the Koochiching Realty Company (an M & O subsidiary) was erecting.

In March 1918, the U.S. government placed an order for 3 million square feet of Insulite from M & O, the only manufacturer of that product in the world. The mill produced about 25,000 square feet daily, enough for two carloads to be shipped to military camps.

There seemed to be no long-term letup in demand after World War I, and another round of expansion took place in the early 1920s with the addition of a new paper mill at the Fort. At the Falls, the Insulite mill and the wrapping paper complex were expanded, 50 more homes were constructed, and the world's largest board machine for producing packing and shipping containers was installed. The demand for board-mill products peaked in the 1927–1929 era and then declined so drastically that the board mill was shut down and the machine sold in 1935. By 1925 M & O mills in the United States required 660 cords of pulpwood a day, made up of 20 percent poplar and 80 percent spruce. Insulite production had reached 65,000 square feet daily, and projections were made for expansion to 500,000 square feet.

With the Depression and the resulting bankruptcy of Backus, production dropped sharply. The demand for paper products remained irregular until 1933, when 1,200 people were again working in the mill and 327 at the sawmill in the Falls. However, the market for Insulite seemed to have no limits; by 1937 it was used even in airliners. But there was a change in the newsprint industry, and the original paper mills of M & O were no longer competitive. They were removed in 1938, and the company switched to the production of high-grade specialty paper. In October 1938, the Falls/Fort complex produced 409 cars of paper, 134 cars of Insulite, and 35 cars of lumber made from 11,176 cords of wood, which, if it had been brought to the mills on 12-foot stake trucks, would have required 3,792 loads.[6]

The Sawmill

Once the dam and the paper mill were completed, M & O took the next step in building its total complex—erecting a sawmill to provide lumber for the still expanding frontier communities of mid-America.

One of the most dramatic parts of the mill complex was the "high dive"—a 280-foot conveyor, 67 feet high, which overshadowed the Falls horizon from 1910 through 1938. It was located halfway between the city dock and the customs office (as of 1990). A smaller "high dive," on rails along the south shore of the Rainy, took logs from the hot pond (the catch basin for logs prior to entering the mill) and elevated them inland. Timber arrived at the mill in 8-foot or tree lengths and was manually unloaded and sawed into 4-foot lengths, which were elevated on the larger "high dive's" swinging boom onto a large pile that sometimes grew to 35,000 cords of wood. The 4-foot pulp logs then were pulled by submerged conveyor chains into the slashers located in the mill. The "high dives" were not part of the sawmill, but, like that complex, they were very visible and dramatic in contrast to the enclosed paper mill. Old-timers remembered that on clear days the sound of the falling 4-foot lengths from the larger "high dive" could be heard all over town. The larger "high dive" frequently was used as a means of committing suicide.

The International Falls Press (The Press) announced that a sawmill could double the town's population, because it would provide a market for timber that previously had had no value. It predicted that the Falls would surpass Bemidji and Brainerd in population as soon as the sawmill was finished. That did not come to pass, but the sawmill greatly increased lumber camp activity. Backus gave orders to start mill construction in December 1910 so it would be ready in time for the 1911–12 cutting season.

On August 7, 1911, a whistle announced completion of the sawmill, and a planing mill and drying sheds were under construction. On April 4, 1912, the sawmill, with a crew of 400 men using three band saws, opened to start a 24-hour-a-day run year around. This was not the typical seasonal sawmill operation.

The sawmill's normal capacity was 50 million board feet, but in 1917, 75 million board feet were cut from timber obtained from 23 lumber camps manned by 4,000 lumberjacks. Only a few work stoppages occurred during the mill's 27 seasons. After being shut down on November 15, 1932, probably no startup was more welcome than in March 1933, when the mill reopened and shipped 13 carloads of lumber, 8 of which were destined for Milwaukee to make cases for beer bottles.

Robert Fritz, Sr., a 40-year veteran of sawmilling, was put in charge of the mill January 1, 1916, and managed it until it closed late in 1937. The last of the large pine trees that fed the mill were used that year. The Falls' horizon changed when the 210-foot smokestack was tumbled July 8, 1939, making way for a new era in paper and lumber production.[7]

The Work Force

Once the area had been explored and the entrepreneurs had secured capital and started construction, the third ingredient necessary to tame the wilderness, labor, had to be persuaded to participate. Because of its severe climate and difficulty of access, the northern border country was not so appealing as other frontiers and was one of the last to be settled. It took a massive campaign by state and federal governments to entice people to come there to seek work or file for a homestead.

An early limited gold strike called attention to the region.

Trappers had long been active along Rainy Lake and River, and individuals had chopped trees near the rivers and floated them to the mills at Rat Portage, Ontario. Once the easily transportable trees were cut, these itinerant loggers collected their pay and moved to another frontier.

Fortunately for those who developed the area, worldwide events provided a steady supply of labor. Unstable conditions in Europe caused many people to emigrate to Canada and the United States in the late nineteenth and early twentieth centuries. Individuals who did not fare well in the industrial centers were looking for better opportunities, and others had personal reasons to escape the more settled areas.

In addition to workers to meet the demands of the mills and lumber camps, laborers were also needed to construct roads and judicial ditches during the years 1911 through 1917 in several of the northern counties. Northern Beltrami County (which became Lake of the Woods County in 1923) had 400 ditch and road workers in 1915. The numbers may not seem great to us today, but all labor had to be imported, because there was only a small pool of residents from which to draw.

Frank Alexander was two years old when his parents homesteaded south of the Falls in 1896. He decided that gypo (freelance) logging and farming were no way to make a living, so as a young man he went to work in the mill. He was paid about $0.18 an hour for a 12-hour day, soon received $0.30, and before he finished in the acid room, made $0.77 an hour. He received room and board at the Forest Inn for $6 a week, so he could do much better than he had in the past. However, he did not like working indoors surrounded by acid fumes, which prevented him from sleeping well.

Jennie Baker Rasmussen (Mrs. Fred) started working on the chippers in the woodsroom in 1915 at age 17. She earned $0.56 an hour for an eight-hour day, six days a week, and worked there for three years. She said that the work was not difficult, but she preferred being in other activities.

Alice Marie Peterson Tive (Mrs. Eric) started working in the mill in 1916, when many women were employed there. Her first job was carrying out slabs of Insulite; next she worked on the kraft machines that made large rolls of paper; and finally, after the big Insulite mill was finished, she weighed boxcars and sealed them for shipment. She had so much free time that she took her handwork with her. One night she got a crochet hook caught in her hand, but was too embarrassed to call the supervisor for help. She received the same pay as the men, $0.56 an hour, and had to join the union. Like her husband, she paid the dues, but otherwise paid no attention to the union. She said that the men referred to women as "foreigners." When they dated a girl they asked her whether she wanted to drink coffee or whiskey, and "they always wanted to test her virtue." "But," she added, "I worked on all three shifts and enjoyed the mill work. We had the most fun on the night shift."

Mary Curran Malerich (Mrs. Bernard) was 16 when she started at the sawmill in 1917, where she earned $3 for a 10-hour day. She worked the night shift, which ended at 6:00 A.M. She worked two weeks until her father found out what she was doing and made her quit.

Local papers reported that the number of girls employed at the sawmill increased daily. It was a common sight to see young ladies on the streets with their "overall suits." During World War I many young women worked in the mill, and most of them felt that they had satisfactory jobs.

The wartime labor shortage caused Canadians to place ads in the local papers asking for 50,000 farmhands from the United States and stating that they "are absolutely guaranteed against conscription." But the pressure from industrial firms and other sawmills was even more to be feared, because they had a much better wage scale than farming. O. J. Jones, superintendent of the Engler mill in Baudette, accepted a position with a mill in Idaho in July 1917 and took 76 men with him. The rail fare was paid by the hiring firm, and wages were higher than those paid locally. The Idaho mill also recruited in the Falls and hired eight families plus enough men to fill two train cars. Local mill operators said that they could secure replacements "without much difficulty."

The Industrial Workers of the World (IWW) and a series of strikes disturbed labor conditions after World War I, but their impact was lessened by the return of servicemen, who swelled the ranks of labor. By 1924 relative calm prevailed, and it was not until the economy took a downturn that there was any great degree of discontent. Plummer, who started delivering vegetables from his farm in 1923, generally commented on events in the Falls as he saw them. In 1931 he noted: "Took few vegetable orders. Money scarce. Business very poor. Mills down. Nearly 200 families on city relief." The mills were closed for nearly a year because of Backus' bankruptcy. Many old-timers said that people now realized how important the mills were to the economy of the area. For the first time in the memory of most of them, no one complained about the sulphite smell, and "The Falls was really dead."

Ray Schneider, who worked for the MD & W, said, "We had a pretty decent time during the 1930s. It's true our wages got down to $28 a week after making almost $50 a week in the 1920s, but our demands were less and we always had plenty of the essentials."

With the reopening of the mill in 1933, the Falls businessmen referred to the men's returning to work as the greatest event of the New Year, even if the work week initially was only three days. By April more workers were added at the sawmill, and a new wage schedule ranging from $0.225 to $0.45 an hour was announced. Because of a continued reduction in newsprint prices, M & O asked paper mill workers to take a cut. The company asked for a 10.75 percent cut, but after lengthy negotiations, the union agreed to a 9 percent reduction and the establishment of a new $0.35-per-hour minimum.

By August 1933, the mills were going at full schedule in the Falls, but it was not until early 1934 that the Fort had the same experience. By 1935 the economy had recovered sufficiently, and the county relief officer announced that 65 percent of those remaining on the rolls were 65 years of age or over. By December complaints were voiced that it was difficult to fill positions in the planned government projects that were created to reduce unemployment.

In May 1937, conditions were back to routine as the sawmill workers voted to go on strike. This led one interviewee to comment, "Our wage structure probably more than any other single factor discourages other industry from coming here."[8]

A Company Town

The debate has never been settled whether the Falls is a company town or a union town. The answer to that question has depended upon who was asked and what was taking place at the time. There is little doubt, however, that at all times in its history, the Falls has been faced with this dilemma. It is not clear if controlling the town was a concern of Backus. One long-time resident, who was not involved with either the unions or M & O, said, "It appears that he followed the logical steps—he built a dam to get power to run a paper mill, and then he built a town to provide the services necessary to support those who worked there."

Others in a similar position felt that to a degree it was inevitable that M & O was in control because of its sheer economic strength, but that it probably did not try to dominate. To an extent, the ability to do so was greater in the early days when Backus was around, and many employees who gained positions of influence in the company were, because of their long tenure in the Falls, able to exert influence on the community. However, many top-management people were very transient and were not really interested in what took place locally.

It appears that after Backus' bankruptcy, the receivership was very concerned about trying to be a "good citizen" and did all that it could to avoid conflict in the community. Company influence probably was minimized by union activity because "there has always been an anti-company mood by those people, even though they know that everyone's welfare is dependent upon the success of the company." It was suggested that this might just be the traditional "hate capital regardless" attitude that some individuals harbor.

It is possible that Frank Keyes, who was described as "a massive real estate owner" who "held mortgage on many properties and in other ways had many people beholden to him," had more influence over the affairs of the community than M & O ever openly exerted.

A neutral observer said that M & O and the unions have alternately exerted themselves. "Sometimes the company has secured legislative breaks, which have almost always benefitted the entire area." A company employee of many years said, "M & O looked after its economic rights, but the unions exerted their force for many reasons, giving them much more control in local affairs."

After the dam and the mill were under construction, M & O became a supplier of water and electricity to the Falls. Then it built The Forest Inn; provided steam heat to some homes; built company houses, the company store, the telephone service, the international bridge; and established the newspaper. From the very beginning the Koochiching Realty Company (sometimes called the Koochiching Improvement Company) controlled the development of much of the city property. Some people said that they knew that M & O never made money on most of the above subsidiaries, but it felt that they were necessary for the overall benefit of its business.

The company was blamed for the high cost of living by holding town lots for too high a price. On the other hand, it was charged with keeping wages down by providing living quarters and eating facilities for single men and women employed in the mill. It was accused of telling workers that if they wished to hold their jobs they should stay at The Forest Inn. This caused the hotel, restaurant, and rooming house owners to complain because their institutions "were being emptied." At the same time, several hundred more families came to town to work in the expanding industry. Married couples were not allowed to stay at the Inn, because the company was desirous of their becoming homemakers. To accommodate them, M & O provided coal at cost until it was prevented from doing so under protest from the Retail Coal Dealers Association.

When the company store opened, the complaint was, "This was done with the entire disregard to . . . the merchants . . . who were lured here under big promises of revenue from the payroll of the paper mill." It was rumored that the company issued vouchers to employees for supplies, rather than paying them in cash. M & O was accused of being too paternalistic, but probably used the above practices in an attempt to blunt the high cost of living caused by the shortage of good facilities.

People who lived at The Forest Inn generally were quite satisfied with their accommodations. The first manager was George White, who, with his wife, had 30 years of hotel experience prior to coming to the Falls. Later, Patty Walsh was in charge. He was a big man and was able to keep things quiet in the two three-story buildings, which could house about 60 men. Sometimes rooms provided for two shifts of workers. Those who worked on the night shift slept while day-shift workers were out. Women were not allowed to stay there, and Walsh saw to it that there was no liquor. The Inn was on Second Street just across from the mill. Originally, the weekly cost for room and board was $6; by 1922 it had risen to $8.

The company store, located on Third Street, was managed by Ken Speelman, assisted by Gerald Sutherland. Employees could get $10 books of tickets at the pay office against their wages. Tickets were removed as purchases were made at the store. Nick Raucher, an independent grocer, was forced to provide charge accounts at his store in order to compete. He also learned that he could buy the coupon books from mill employees at a 25 percent discount. Employees charged the coupon books at the pay office and then went to Raucher's store to get cash. Because many outsiders purchased coupon books from employees at a discount and then bought goods at the company store, this practice was soon discontinued.

Paul Anderson came to the Falls in 1934 to work for *The International Falls Daily Journal (The Journal)* for $80 a month. He was "thrilled to death" because the Falls seemed so alive compared to other communities. Anderson, who later became editor of *The Journal,* said that the company let those in charge of the paper have a free hand. To his knowledge, it never interfered with the operation of the Border Publishing Company, which had better equipment than most similar small-sized rural papers of that day. M & O made a decision to get good help and the latest technology, including teletype, so it could get news as soon as it was available and not have to wait to get it from big city newspapers like most rural presses did. Anderson noted that sometimes anti-company sentiment was as strong among the small business people as it was among many of the mill union workers.

One of the most direct intrusions of Backus into local affairs came after his bankruptcy, when he opposed the $230,000 bond issue to fund a new town water system. He wired from Baltimore: "I am sure this will be a serious mistake, even though the Federal Government pays part of the cost. . . . My Best Regards to All, E. W. Backus." M & O soon agreed to buy the necessary equipment to provide safer water and continued to serve the Falls.

Dr. C. C. Craig, who was mayor in the Falls during the 1930s, often opposed the company in local politics. The leaders of M & O let the word out that in the mayoral race they wanted everyone in the company to support C. O. Gustafson, the M & O paymaster. When the ballots were counted, Craig won by 30 votes—an indication that the company appeal and coercion did not work. A local historian said, "Individualism and equality of the frontier have remained strong here. Even the unions, which have been here so long and are openly accepted, are not always liked even by their own members."[9]

A Tax Dispute

Even before the mill was finished, M & O, Koochiching County, and the Falls officials were in a dispute over taxes. Richard

Liljeblad, the Falls assessor, had originally assessed the mill at $1,059,900, to which the village review board agreed; so the books were turned over to the county auditor. In the meantime, Councilman John Berg and Liljeblad reduced the assessed evaluation to $600,000. Backus and his attorneys appeared before the county board and stated that this amount was still too high, and the board agreed to cut it to $400,000.

The assessor claimed that M & O would not produce any figures to show actual value, so his evaluation was largely guesswork. After spending several days in the equalization process, and then not knowing what to do because of M & O's protest, the county board decided to appeal to the State Tax Commission. H. H. Harrison, a specialist in the field of taxation who had assessed throughout the nation, said that this plant was the largest of its kind in the United States. He reassessed it at $722,700, and the company immediately challenged the figure.

The Falls attorney appeared before the state commission to uphold Harrison's figure. The local community was not sympathetic, because Backus "and associates had been such consistent employers of the iron heel. . . ." In the meantime, Backus had become involved in a dispute with local political allies "because of the alleged double dealing of some of his subordinates" and had lost some clout in the process. The protest continued. Two years later, the council and the commission, in cooperation with the state and the attorney general, met to establish a fair tax policy.

All residents who paid more than $500 a year in property taxes in the county were asked what they thought was fair. They agreed that no one should be taxed excessively and that none of them would have anything if it were not for M & O, because the company had brought people to the area, provided employment, and was the key to the property values of everyone. In any case, everyone was anxious to see an end to the tax dispute.

The officials began to sense a real problem, because many citizens felt that if M & O did not have to pay taxes, no one should. On May 23, 1913, Plummer, who later became a leader in a tax protest movement, obtained the signatures of 11 people on a petition stating that they would not pay taxes until Backus did. This was the beginning of a prolonged dispute, which in part led to a major tax delinquency problem that virtually destroyed the financial structure of the county.

As long as Backus controlled M & O, property taxes continued to be in dispute, but the company's overall tax payment record was better than most of the county's taxpayers. The problem persisted under the trusteeship, which was in court nearly as much as Backus, attempting to secure reductions. In 1935 the state took M & O to court in an attempt to collect $1,726,000 in personal property taxes. The company was able to prove that most of its forest railroad equipment had been grossly overvalued. Due to changes taking place in the industry, it had no more than salvage value. It also proved that it was paying about three times as much taxes per ton of paper produced than the average paper mill in North America.

The company argued that it had paid $250,000 in taxes in 1934 and that if it had to pay the amount asked, the mill would have to close. Local citizens were sufficiently concerned that the city council appealed to county and state officials to suspend the proceedings against M & O. Judge Alfred L. Thwing ruled that the state figure was excessive because many items were improperly included and others were overvalued by "large amounts."

The company's position was supported by data that showed that during the six years 1929 through 1934, $4,995,874.17 in taxes had been levied in the county and $2,759,435.51, or 55 percent, had been collected. During those years M & O paid $1,529,044.78, or 55 percent, of the total paid. If all the taxes had been paid in those six years, M & O's portion still would have been over a third of the total.[10]

"King Ed"

In most communities, one person generally serves as the prime mover and catalyst to development. In the case of the northern border country, it was E. W. Backus, who saw the potential of this untamed wilderness and committed his life to harnessing it and to building a personal empire.

Edward Wellington Backus was born December 1, 1860, in Jamestown, New York. His parents moved to a farm near Red Wing, Minnesota, in 1862. Young Backus taught in a rural school to support his way through the University of Minnesota. In 1882 he became a bookkeeper with the Lee-McCullock Lumber Company, of Minneapolis, for $9 a week. By 1885 he had bought out both partners and formed E. W. Backus and Company. In 1889 he married Elizabeth Horr, whose father operated a sawmill which Backus took over. His company was now the second largest lumber firm in Minneapolis. In 1892 he sold 8 million feet of white pine to the stockyards at Kansas City, Missouri—the largest amount of lumber ever sold by a Minneapolis firm to that date.

In 1893 both of his mills burned in a 20-block fire, leaving him with $400,000 in insurance. He then joined a syndicate, which acquired an estimated 2 billion feet of saw logs in northeastern Minnesota. He helped start a logging railroad at Brainerd (later the M & I), which quickly was extended 60 miles toward Bemidji. About 1896 he bought an interest in the Columbia Gold Mining Company, which apparently paid him well. In 1899 he formed the Backus and Brooks Company, with William F. Brooks, and they began to acquire timber lands.

The two entrepreneurs soon realized that it was more profitable to secure water rights, because it was less expensive to buy timber from homesteaders than use company labor. They gained rights along the international border and by 1906 had gone as far north as Keewatin on the north shore of Lake of the Woods. The Canadians were very cooperative, for they wanted to develop the area. Backus conceived the idea of grinding the logs in Canada and finishing the product in the Falls. He told a congressional committee that by doing so he could save $1.66 a ton on paper production.

Backus showed either courage or audacity when he answered Congressman James R. Mann, who asked him if he had a permit from the government to do business: "I might say no and yes." When Mann asked for a direct answer, Backus replied firmly, "I don't care to say. . . ." Then Mann threatened to compel him to answer, and Backus retorted, "I don't believe you have the power to make public our affairs with a foreign government."

In any case, Backus proceeded as if he had the rights in Canada to the extent that he was referred to as "The Honorable King Edward W. Backus" and the Fort was called North International Falls.

A promotion booklet put out by the townsite company in 1909 spoke of the 35,000-HP dam to process the practically unlimited timber supplies and the ideal location to obtain wheat from the Prairie Provinces and Dakota. The wheat would be milled at the Fort and then transferred in bond to Duluth. This would be done at a considerable savings over shipping wheat to Minneapolis for milling and then to Duluth. The flour-milling idea was the first major scheme of Backus to fail, probably because it was contrary to the powerful Minneapolis Millers Association and it was not to the liking of Canadian interests. However, the paper mills expanded so rapidly in the two towns that they soon needed all the power the falls produced.

In 1917 five paper manufacturers, including Backus, were taken to court for conspiring to set the price of paper. *The Press* apparently did not comment on this matter, but *The Baudette Region* gave good coverage. It noted that if the homesteaders who received "starvation prices" from Backus for their pulp were the jury, they "would probably vote on the first ballot to hang him." Backus was fined $2,500.

While building at the Fort during 1912 to 1914 and erecting the international bridge between the two towns, Backus also added the Norman Dam on Lake of the Woods and the dam at Kenora. He then completed arrangements with Ontario to purchase the pulpwood forests along the English River north of Kenora. He negotiated for 2,500 square miles in the Quetico Reserve east of the Fort, taking advantage of the eagerness of the Ontario government to attract industry. His decision was based on the freedom to harvest pulpwood and pine at the same time. Eventually he gained control of an area in Ontario about 250 miles wide and 600 miles long.

Backus' ambition knew no bounds, for next he built generating facilities along the Seine and Little Turtle rivers to produce power for both the Fort and a new plant, the Great Lakes Pulp and Paper Company, at Fort William. All the while the expansion was taking place, he was being investigated by the U.S. government for unpaid taxes for 1917 and 1918 in the sum of $1,353,372.15 plus accumulated interest of over $1 million. By 1924 Backus contended that it was the interest bill that caused him to delay payment.

In early 1930 it was announced that M & O would build an Insulite mill at Karhula, Finland. At that time Backus was hailed as "one of this country's outstanding financial geniuses and business promoters." His partner was Mr. Ahlstrom, a Finnish capitalist, who owned more than a dozen paper mills and sawmills there. Little did Backus realize that the estimated $3 to $5 million project would be his last.[11]

Bankruptcy

The Fort William and Karhula projects caused him to be overextended at the wrong time. On February 28, 1931, entrepreneur Backus' empire fell into receivership with R. H. M. Robinson, managing trustee. His $100 million plus empire did not have sufficient cash flow to meet maturing bond payments, and, like the owners of many overextended firms of those days, he was unable to raise the money necessary to carry on. It is estimated that the Backus family, which held most of the common stock, lost $50 million, but they were not broke.

In 1934 Backus made a desperate fight to regain control by charging that the operation by the receivers had caused a $12 million loss. He listed the specific transactions that were responsible. The trustees countersued the family for $7 million. Backus also asked for an injunction prohibiting the sale of timber lands. In July federal judges granted a petition for reorganization and appointed S. M. Archer, C. T. Jaffray, and Robinson as receivers for the bondholders. Creditors and stockholders were enjoined by the court from instituting lawsuits against the company.

R. W. Andrews, chief engineer for M & O, testified that the company functioned more smoothly under the receivers than it had under Backus, because each department had "well defined lines and responsibilities known to all members of the organization. Under Backus . . . no department head was sure how far his authority went and might be overruled at any time."

On October 29, 1934, Backus died of a heart attack while in New York seeking $7 million in financial backing. He was at the Hotel Vanderbilt and had summoned the house physician, but it was too late. Police found 34 undeposited checks worth $37,000 and 213,500 shares of stock in 5 companies plus a small amount of cash. Elizabeth Backus was traveling in Europe, just as she had been in 1912 when their son E. Raymond was accidently shot by his own gun at age 21. Raymond was an honors graduate in engineering from Yale and was to assume a leadership role in M & O. In 1936 their other son, Seymour W. Backus, died at his winter home in Florida. Again, Elizabeth Backus, this time with her two daughters, was traveling in Europe.

At one time or other the original M & O firm had included the following:

> Border Publishing Company, including *The Journal*
> The Fort Frances Pulp and Paper Company, Ltd.
> The Great Lakes Paper Company—Fort William
> The Insulite Company
> The International Boom Company
> International Bridge and Terminal Company
> International Improvement Company
> International Lumber Company (ILC)

International Telephone Company
The Karhula (Finland) Insulite Mill
The Keewatin Lumber Company, Ltd.
Keewatin Paper Company, Ltd.
The Keewatin Power Company, Ltd.
Kenora Development Company
Kenora Paper Mills, Ltd.
Koochiching Realty Company
Little Turtle Improvement Company, Ltd.
Minnesota, Dakota, and Western Railroad Company
Minnesota Forest Products Company
Minnesota and International Railway Company
Minnesota and Ontario Paper Company
National Pole Company
The Ontario and Minnesota Power Company, Ltd.
The Ontario and Minnesota Pulp and Paper Company, Ltd.
The Rainy River Improvement Company
The Rat Portage Lumber Company, Ltd.
The Seine River Improvement Company, Ltd.
Watrous Island Boom Company

In addition, Backus had stock in the Columbia Gold Mining Company and several other mining companies, owned the Crookston Lumber Company, and was a director of the First National Bank at the Falls, the International Falls State Bank, Newsprint Manufacturers Association, the Northern Pacific Railway Company, and the Northwestern National Bank of Minneapolis. "King Ed" no longer is there, but the institutions that he developed have lived on to justify his dreams for the wilderness.[12]

ENDNOTES FOR CHAPTER I

1. *History of Koochiching County: Where the Trees Make a Difference* (International Falls: Koochiching County Historical Society, 1983), p. 11, hereafter *Hist. of Kooch. Co.*; interview of Robert Fritz, Jr., Fargo, N.D., January 30, 1991, hereafter Fritz interview; *Bemidji Pioneer*, October 25, 1902.

2. Annie Shelland Williams file, Koochiching County Historical Society (KCHS), hereafter Williams file; interview of Scott W. Erickson, Orr, Minn., July 20, 1976; International Lumber Company file, 1921–1948, KCHS, hereafter ILC file; E. W. Backus file, KCHS, hereafter Backus file; J. C. Ryan, *Early Loggers in Minnesota*, Vol. I & II (St. Paul: Minnesota Timber Producers Association, 1975), Vol. I, pp. 6–7, hereafter Ryan; F. L. Bussman file, KCHS, hereafter Bussman file. Bussman was forest manager for ILC.

3. Grace Lee Nute, *Rainy River Country* (St. Paul: Minnesota Historical Society, 1950), pp. 87, 88, hereafter Nute; *The Minneapolis Tribune*, May 3, 1908; *The Minneapolis Journal*, May 23, 1908; *Fort Frances Times*, June 9, 1910; *Chicago Daily Tribune*, April 13, 1908; *Duluth Herald*, no date; *St. Paul Pioneer Press*, April 16, 1908; *Duluth Tribune*, May 10, 1908; *Report to International Joint Commission (U.S. and Canada), 1909, in the Matter of the Application of the*

Watrous Island Boom Co. for Approval of Plans for a Boom in Rainy River, pp. 1–89, hereafter IJC Watrous.

4. *Toronto Globe,* February 10, 1910; *Overall Economic Development Program* (International Falls: Koochiching County, 1964), p. 17, hereafter *Econ. Dev.; Fort Frances Times,* April 19, 1906, April 18, 1912; *The International Falls Press,* February 23, 1911, June 20, 1912, hereafter *The Press.* This paper was continued as *The International Falls Daily Journal* after November 9, 1911, hereafter *The Journal.* Interview of Ann Stone Fraser (Mrs. R. C.), International Falls, June 3, 1976, hereafter Fraser interview. Mrs. Fraser was born March 23, 1882, and came to the Falls in 1898. R. C. Murchie and C. R. Wasson, "Beltrami Island, Minnesota: Resettlement Project," University of Minnesota Research Bulletin No. 334 (St. Paul: December 1937), p. 10, hereafter Bull. 334.

5. *The Journal,* May 23, 1912, June 4, 1914; *The Minneapolis Journal,* April 14, 1908; *Fort Frances Times,* September 10, 1914; International Joint Commission, hereafter IJC, *Hearing and Argument in the Matter of the Application of International Lumber for Approval of the Obstruction of the Waters of the Rainy River at International Falls, Minnesota,* Minneapolis, January 22–24, 1917 (Wash., D.C.: U.S. Government Printing Office), pp. 151, 152.

6. *The Paper Mill and Wood Pulp News,* March 29, 1913; *The Journal,* June 5, 1933, August 15, 1935; Samuel F. Plummer diary, hereafter Plummer diary. Plummer farmed, logged, and taught school near Loman and kept a daily diary from 1905 through 1948. Backus file; *The Mandonian: A Magazine for All Mando Employees,* Vol. I, July 1946, hereafter *The Mandonian.*

7. Plummer diary; interview of Alice and Eric Tive, International Falls, May 20, 1989, hereafter Tive interview; *The Journal,* June 5, 1933, July 8, 1939; *The Mandonian,* March–April 1947; interview of Lester Pollard, International Falls, June 25, July 20, August 13, 1976, August 3, 1989, April 11, 1990, hereafter Pollard interview.

8. *The Baudette Region,* September 9, 1924; interview of Frank F. Alexander, International Falls, June 11, 1976, hereafter Alexander interview. Alexander was born in 1893 and came to the area in 1896. *The Journal,* May 10, 1923, February 24, 1933, May 6, 1937, January 15, 1938; interview of Jennie Baker Rasmussen (Mrs. Fred), International Falls, June 5 and August 16, 1976, hereafter Rasmussen interview. Mrs. Rasmussen was born at Koochiching in 1898. Tive interview; interview of Mary Curran Malerich (Mrs. Bernard), International Falls, June 11, 1976, hereafter Malerich interview; interview of Mr. and Mrs. Ray Schneider, International Falls, June 11, 1976, hereafter Schneider interview; Plummer diary; Pollard interview; interview of Arnold R. Johnson, Littlefork, Minn., July 25, 1989, hereafter Arnold Johnson interview.

9. Interview of E. R. Gustafson, International Falls, June 10, 1976, hereafter Gustafson interview; interview of Fred Hendee, International Falls, August 12, 1976, hereafter Hendee interview; Arnold Johnson interview; *The Press,* September 29, December 1, 10, 1910; *The Journal,* January 17, 24, 1934; Schneider interview; Pollard interview; interview of George Hnatiuk, International Falls, July 26, 1976, hereafter Hnatiuk interview; interview of Paul A. Anderson, International Falls, June 8, 1976, hereafter Paul Anderson interview; interview of Leonard J. Kucera, Ericsburg, Minn., August 12, 1976, hereafter Kucera interview.

10. Proceedings of the Koochiching County Commission, August 4, 1910, hereafter Kooch. Comm.; *The Press,* September, 11, October 13, December 1, 1910; *The Journal,* March 20, 1913, July 11, 18, and 25, September 29, 1935, January 16, 1936; Plummer diary.

11. Backus file; *Associated Press*, October 14, 1908, Misc. clipping file, KCHS; *The Press*, November 24, 1910; *The Journal*, September 29, 1912, May 15, 1924, February 3, 1930, October 30, 1934, February 27, 1981; *International Falls, Minnesota: A Presentation of Its Commercial Future and Scenic Beauty* (Minneapolis: privately printed, 1909); *The Baudette Region*, April 26, May 17, December 7, 1917, October 15, 1920; *Hist. of Kooch. Co.*, p. 12; letter from E. W. Backus to Mark Hessey, September 14, 1923, ILC file, KCHS.

12. *Hist. of Kooch. Co.*, p. 13; Pollard interview; Paul Anderson interview; *The Journal*, January 9, July 13, September 1, 1934; Backus file.

CHAPTER II

Harvesting the Wilderness

AFTER BACKUS HAD DECIDED to build a paper mill, he needed to insure an adequate supply of pulpwood. The cheapest means of doing so was to purchase from farmer/loggers, but, unfortunately, only a few such individuals were in the area. Therefore, it was necessary to utilize the traditional labor-intense lumber camp system, which depended upon a large supply of transient workers. This system was near the end of its time, but it endured for three more decades until technology made it obsolete and a more economical method of harvesting the wilderness evolved.

Establishing the Lumber Camp

Once the cruiser had done his job, it was time to erect a "village in the wilderness"—a lumber camp in which the men would work and live from the time they arrived in the fall until they left prior to the log drive the following spring. Before forest railroads were constructed, the camps rarely contained more than 75 men and a limited number of horses. Transportation was too difficult to support a large community in the relatively hard-to-reach areas where most camps were located. The camps in this account generally were built post 1912. After forest railroads were constructed, they averaged from 150 to 200 men and from 30 to 50 horses.

J. C. Ryan, who spent his entire life in lumber camps and recorded much of their history in northern Minnesota, said that one of his pet peeves was hearing about the terrible living conditions of the old-time lumberjacks. He did not like the tendency of people to regard logging companies as exploiters of lumberjacks, working them 10 to 12 hours a day while providing poor housing, poor food, and meager pay and letting them die in the poor house. In one of his accounts he wrote, in italics, "This is far from the truth." Oliver Knox, who spent 26 years in

logging camps, said, "I really enjoyed camp life, and it appears
to me that most of the men I knew did too." The 92-year-old
Knox added, "And that was so even when we never got out of
camp from the first of November to the beginning of April.
International Falls was 50 miles away and hard to get to."

Even though the hours were from daybreak to dark, six days
a week, the quarters were as comfortable as possible and the
food was far above average for the time. Most people on the
American frontier lived in sod houses, log cabins, or flimsy frame
structures that were just as hot in the summer and cold in the
winter as any lumber camp bunkhouse. Probably because of those
self-inflicted discomforts, pioneers are seen as heroic rather than
exploited. Certainly the lumberjack had far more social contact
than most families living in remote areas on either the farm or
the forest frontier.

The pre-railroad camps generally were built of logs, and contained a kitchen, a root cellar, two small bunkhouses, a horse
barn, a blacksmith shop, a filers' shack, outhouses, and a combined office and commissary. In most of the camps discussed in
this history, the buildings were constructed with rough boards
covered with tarpaper and were far more roomy than earlier log
structures. Most camps had a large kitchen / mess hall capable
of feeding all the men at one time and two or more bunkhouses
that held at least 50 to 75 men each. Some had special wash
and laundry rooms, feed storage for grain and baled hay, and
warehouses, plus the usual other buildings—all considerably
larger than the earlier versions. By the 1920s tractor shops were
common at some camps.

The typical camp as described above could be erected during
the 1920s for from $3,000 to $5,000. The cost increased in the
1930s when modern bathing and laundry facilities were sometimes added. The duration of these camps varied from two to
five years, depending upon the timber supply and the ease of
moving to a new location. When they were abandoned, the doors,
windows, and frames of each structure were removed for use at
the next camp, and the rest of the building usually was burned.

The two largest lumbering operations south of the Rainy Lake–
Rainy River frontier from 1910 through the 1920s were VRL and
ILC. VRL started the 1909–10 season with about 15 camps and
2,800 men in the woods and a couple thousand more in mills at
Virginia and Duluth. ILC began operation a year later and did
not reach full capacity until 1912, when its first forest railroad

line was laid. By 1913 ILC had 3,650 men and 895 horses in 30 camps.

Each firm had a field, or railroad, camp that survived longer and became better known than most of its other camps. The VRL camp was at Cusson, and the ILC Camp 29 was about 32 miles south of the village of Littlefork. Both were more elaborate than the less permanent camps.

Cusson was built at a cost of $83,000. In addition to the headquarters buildings, it had a coal dock, icehouses, a boiler house, a large warehouse, a hay shed, a timber shed, a pump house, a doctor's office, family residences, a general store, a schoolhouse, a theater, a rooming house, a recreation building, a machine shop, and a railroad shop.

Camp 29 was not as elaborate as Cusson, but it lasted longer as a forest railroad headquarters. It was first established in 1912 as a logging camp, but railroad facilities were added as ILC penetrated other forests. It was rebuilt in 1920 after a fire, again in 1928, and had extensive remodeling and modernization in 1932 and in 1934. The original log buildings at Camp 29 were replaced by rough boards and tarpaper, later by Insulite, hardboard, drop siding, and white paint. In 1932 sewage facilities and walk-in refrigerators were installed, and propane stoves replaced the old wood cook stoves. In 1934 an electric light plant was added.

VRL had 15 camps in existence at any time in its 20 years of logging in the area, and ILC varied from a low of 2 in 1931 to a high of 45 in the early 1920s. However, the peak year for total logging output of ILC was 1917, when its 23 camps, 4,000 men, and 500 horses produced enough timber for the sawmill to cut 75 million board feet in addition to the paper mill's requirements. From 1910 through 1937, ILC operated 192 different camps within a 75-mile radius of the Falls but generally had 20 each year. After the mid-1950s, the work was shifted to independent contractors.

The typical camp had about 150 to 170 men with the following organization: a foreman, an assistant foreman, a clerk, a checker, a scaler, a cook, a second cook, 5 or 6 cookees, 2 bull cooks, a barn boss, a saw filer, a blacksmith with 1 or 2 helpers, a handyman, and a night watchman. The above varied from 20 to 30, depending upon the specific needs of the camp. The woods crew, whose numbers varied from 120 to 140, made up the other camp personnel.[1]

Administration of the Lumber Camp

As long as Backus was in charge, the camps, and all other phases of M & O, were tightly controlled either by him or his son, Seymour. Considerable correspondence took place on relatively small matters, such as replacing articles that employees had lost, which could not be approved until word came from headquarters in Minneapolis, where the top officers were located. Sometimes a decision was not made until one of the two appeared at the Falls office.

All camp purchasing was done at the Falls, except when fresh vegetables were available locally and went directly into the root cellar. Each week a supply train of two boxcars was hooked to the logging train and delivered to the camps. The supply clerk rode the train and checked with each camp clerk to make sure what was delivered to that camp. If a tote team was used to deliver goods, the supply clerk had to accompany it. The camp clerk, who was responsible for the weekly supply order, was instructed to prepare his list of needs on Sunday so it could be sent in the early Monday mail to the Falls for shipment of goods the following Saturday.

With so many people involved, care was taken to avoid loss through theft or time wasted through idleness. The clerks had a 21-page instruction manual plus an additional 8 pages of data on the cost of various items for payroll deductions. A separate ledger sheet was established for each person who showed up to work, "no matter for how short a time." The number assigned to the person was the ledger sheet number. Frequently men hired out through an employment office under one name and used another name when they arrived at camp to avoid having employment agency and transportation charges assigned to them. Clerks were ordered to charge all men with the above unless they could prove they had come without going through an agency. After a man had worked for a given time, his agency and transportation costs were dropped by crediting his account "Fares Earned." Ironically, the same instruction manual applied to all horses, each of which, instead of getting a brass tag, had its number burned into a hoof and was given other markings that properly identified the animal. Clerks "absolutely" had to make the rounds each day to see that both man and beast were working; if not, deductions were made. Men were known to "toss the axe" and go to another camp where they also registered for work, thereby earning at two camps at the same time.

All wanigan (supplies, sundries, etc.) secured by foremen, clerks, scalers, and others whose payroll was kept at the Falls office was telephoned in, and a letter confirming same followed. Any wanigan secured by the workmen, whose payroll was handled at the camp, was posted daily. A typical listing of such accounts varied from $2.40 for three rolls (30 tins) of snuff to $6.75 for three pair of canvas gloves, two suits of long woolen underwear, two pair of long woolen socks, and two rolls of snuff.

Clerks guarded against "jumpers"—those who left camp without a settlement, whether they had money due or owed. Their accounts had to be closed and transferred to profit and loss. Some men came to camp just to eat a meal or two before traveling on. To avoid this situation, each man was assigned a place at the table, or a ticket was required before eating.

Before a man was paid, the clerk required that the payee sign his name in a space provided in the left-hand margin of the check. That signature was the only evidence a banker had that the rightful owner was cashing the check. If the man could not sign his name, the clerk was given exact instructions as to the payee's placing an X in the space. The clerk then signed as witness. If a man had a difficult name, the clerk might assign an Americanized name or use a phonetic spelling for his convenience. All woodsmen were paid on a 26-day-month basis, and camp workers every 30 days.

The clerk took care of mail delivery, which, except for company business, was not heavy, because most of the men were not great letter writers, were single, or were immigrants with no relatives. He had charge of the commissary and was always given strict instructions never to leave the door unlocked, even if he were inside. The only other person allowed to enter was the monthly inspector. Because the clerk had first-aid supplies under his control, he also was responsible for their administration.

The work year for the basic personnel operating a camp consisted of more than the five to seven months that the woods crew was on hand. A watchman was on duty year round. During the summer, hay had to be either cut and stacked or (more commonly) purchased baled from farming areas and delivered when the rail line was fit to be traveled. Pollard, clerk at Camp 29 in 1927, arrived August 5 and did not leave until March 26 for a dental appointment. At first he was paid on a 10-month basis, but after M & O was reorganized, he went on a 12-month schedule. Joe Miller, who did maintenance work, said that he never got to town in the winter and got there only once a month in the summer. Alex Gerber, clerk at Cusson, started on July 5, 1913, and did not get out of camp until the next July.

Prior to the railroads, supplies were hauled during the fall months. In November the woods crew started to show up to clear and make roads and clear the forest where trees would be dragged to the skidways. If the demand for products was strong and the ground frozen, every effort was made to have a full crew by the end of November.

Once the full crew had arrived, the hand-crank siren blew, the iron triangle rang, or, if someone could play it, a bull horn was sounded at 5:30 or 6:00 A.M., with breakfast generally served an hour later. The teamsters arose a half hour earlier to curry, feed, and harness the horses. Sleigh work could start in the dark, but the woods workers had to wait until daylight. The cooks, who slept in separate quarters next to the kitchen, were up at least by 5:00. On Sundays everyone slept one hour longer. The cooks had no day off. If the blacksmiths were behind in their work, they also stayed on the job.

The bull cooks were the handymen of the camp, because they kept the buildings, especially the kitchen, the mess hall, and bunkhouses, clean. The kitchen and the mess hall were scrubbed daily, but bunkhouses sometimes were done only twice a week. The bull cooks never touched unmade beds or personal goods, except to place shoes and rubbers on the deacon seat (the center aisle bench) so they could scrub the floor. They were the "bosses" of the bunkhouse, because they made bed assignments, took care of the lamps and the lanterns, fired the stoves, heated the wash water, provided soap and towels, and oversaw the sink and the spittoons.

When he was finished with the bunkhouses, the bull cook carried in wood and water for the kitchen. Water usually meant at least two 50-gallon barrels, one for hot and another for cold. He filled bottles of kerosene for each sawyer to take as he left for the woods each morning. The kerosene was sprinkled on the saws to cut the pitch and to make the saws work more freely.

It was essential for the smooth operation of a camp that the foreman, the clerk, and the cook get along well, but not so well that collusion took place. In ILC Camp 8, five clerks quit in two months' time before Gust Holmstrom was able to get the foreman,

Joe Kennedy, to resign. As soon as he did, the fifth clerk withdrew his resignation and returned to work.

Even though clerks were screened closely, they did not always perform as expected. Quite often there was poor cooperation between the foreman and the clerk, which resulted in a virtual breakdown in administration. Such was the case in July 1923, when a new clerk was assigned to Camp 97 at Inger, in northern Itasca County. Lloyd Harris had been assigned as camp clerk but was unable to do the job and received no help from his foreman. C. W. Hammer was sent to take over as clerk. He wrote to C. H. Woodford, who was in charge of ILC camps:

> Everything here is in bad shape. Good records have not been kept. Lloyd Harris is keeping time but is not a clerk. Need Browman to come out to get me started. I do not think much of Ottoson [the foreman] and what I have seen of him it seems hard to get anything out of him.

The close watch on expenses in the camps is best illustrated by correspondence about the use of the telephone and the telegraph. A curt handwritten message to Woodford stated: "We must reduce the number of phones. Line will not carry and new phones will have to be added. Go over those with * mark and advise if they can be taken out." A memo was sent out over Seymour's signature requiring that a form be filled out for each long-distance phone call made, listing the time of call, details, department to be billed, and remarks. Individuals needed approval from their supervisors prior to making such calls.

A letter to Twomey, vice president for logging, from the comptroller's office stated that in November 1922, the telephone and telegraph bill for M & O was $863.49, of which logging's share was $15.90. Twomey was advised that a survey of telegrams received showed that many of them could have been reduced to within the 10-word limit, and letters could have replaced many of the phone calls. Twomey sent a general reminder to all camps and bulletin boards stating that the telephone was to be used only in case of accident, derailment, fire, or other emergencies.[2]

The Camp Work Force

The labor-intense method of lumbering typical of the lumber camp era, which lasted until the late 1930s, required massive numbers of men. This caused excitement when the sawmill and the paper mill were under construction, because for each worker processing the timber, at least two workers were needed in the woods. With that many woods workers, the land would be quickly cleared for farming, which would bring in even more settlers. In the meantime, local newspapers ballyhooed the need for manpower for harvesting timber.

As the paper mill neared completion, a boomer campaign started. In mid-1910 *The Press* began sensationalizing the need for men: "Five thousand lumberjacks will strike the International Falls lumber region within a month to set to cutting more than 100,000,000 feet of logs. . . ." A month later the headlines blazed: "The cry has gone up for lumberjacks and more than 6,000 of them are needed in the woods right now."

Each year thereafter the news was similar. In 1913 ILC reported that it needed 3,650 men and 895 horses for its 30 camps in Koochiching County. By 1915 the labor problem was compounded when 5,000 men were needed in the lumber camps, on forest railroads, for ditch digging, and for road construction. Of these, 3,000 men were needed in the 20 logging camps and for railroad construction, and several hundred were needed by Nord and Snyder, the chief contractor for ditch digging. World War I intensified the problem, and ILC placed a full-page bold-faced ad in *The Press* which read: **"MEN WANTED! 3000 EXPERIENCED MEN. . . . WOODS RAILROADS MILLS."** The ad continued requesting foremen, sawyers, filers, and cooks to replace those who had gone to France.

Scott Erickson, who started in the woods in 1919, said, "To me it seemed like there were always three crews, one coming, one working, and one going." *The Northome Record* reported that when one camp cut its wages in 1921, 50 men left in one day, and by the next morning an entire new crew was on duty.

James Webster, foreman at Camp 87 near Echo Lake on the eastern side of ILC territory, complained in early 1923 that men were moving all the time. He had placed his second order with William Moses, a contracted "man grabber" in an employment agency in Duluth. Webster need 18 general men, 4 gangs of sawyers, 2 cookees, and 4 teamsters in his camp of about 130 men.

Pollard felt that the location factor became less critical as transportation improved. He recalled the experience ILC had in five camps in the Togo area. He was clerk in Camp 149, which was manned by 150 men and in 1928–29 had a turnover of 1,700 men from August through May. He said that the unrest was caused by a wage cut during the winter. It was an area of mixed timber, and the men "didn't like the changing work." They came by the trainload from Duluth boarding houses, bringing with them the biggest lice problem ILC ever had.

Thomas Welsh, superintendent of logging for ILC during much of the 1920s, was in daily contact with the employment agencies trying to coordinate the flow of men into the Falls or directly to the camps, but the movement of men was always unpredictable. One day he canceled an order because "a nice bunch of men drifted into the Falls" from which about 40 were sent out to the camps.

Every ex-lumberjack interviewed had a different background or reason for joining the ranks of woodsmen. Alex Gerber said that he drifted north in hopes of finding a job and became a clerk. He was at the Cusson headquarters camp, which had better-quality men who returned for several seasons. He stated that a surprising number were family men and often very skilled at some other vocation. In that eastern part of the ILC region, many men were miners in the summer; in the western part, they were more likely to be farm workers.

Erickson had only a fourth-grade education but said that he had matured in the Navy during World War I and felt better equipped than most of the people he met. He was told to take outside work for health reasons, so he started north but ran out of money at Orr. He took a job with Rathburn-Ridgeway-Hare Lumber Company and after only 10 days had an accident. He recalled feeling very much alone and commented, "I even set my own leg after that accident." After his leg healed, he applied at VRL and, because of his naval experience, became a tow-boat operator.

In September 1922, R. V. Norbeck, secretary of the Northern Logging Association, wrote that members were having a difficult time getting men. Good weather and a strong economy kept men engaged in farming, building roads, and working in factories. He advised members to hold the line on wage increases, because only a cold snap or empty pockets would cause men to leave the Twin Cities (Minneapolis and St. Paul) for the woods. Idle men stood on the streets but would not take out-of-town or steady jobs.

The 1922–23 season ended with camps starting to shut down by mid-March, partly because a warm spell in February gave farmers spring fever and made them impatient to begin farm work. The season's production was about 85 percent of projections. The men had no particular grievances, but their restlessness caused a high turnover rate, which greatly reduced efficiency. Production per man was lower than at any time in logging history, largely because of the class of labor willing to work in the camps.

Leonard Costley, who spent nearly his entire working life in camps, said that "the mustard drive" (pulling weeds) was an important part of the work pattern of many lumberjacks. Some did not care to spend the entire summer season on the large farms west of the timber region, but because of the good pay, they would go out for a few weeks just to pull weeds. Some stayed in the woods for the log drives, and some went to other parts of the country where it was possible to log during the summer.

Hilford Johnson felt that the reason so many lumberjacks went to the Dakota harvest fields was for the drama and the adventure as much as for the cash. In his area along the Little Fork River, cedar logging was carried on from May through September, but many quit that work to go to the harvest fields just for variety. Winter logging and the river drive meant that in the early decades there was woods work nearly every month of the year. That changed in the mid-1920s as cedar became less abundant.

Writing from the Falls, Twomey cautioned the foreman of Camp 87 about hiring too many men from the Fort William–Port Arthur (now Thunder Bay) area. He said that those men were good pulpwood cutters but that there were many agitators among them who could cause trouble in the camp. He described the Finns as being "mighty good workers but hard to satisfy."

No one was ever asked for credentials or references when applying to work in a logging camp. Because the turnover was high, one could almost always get a job. Many of those interviewed often never got to know more than one or two people well during their stay in camp. That probably accounts for the wide variety of nicknames, such as Cast Iron for Carl Rindal, who never wore any underwear; Jippo John; Steel Hans; Pine Island Hans; Junk John; Muskrat Joe; Root Peet; Ten Day Slim, who never stayed in any camp more than 10 days; Poker Pete; Liver Lip Hoover, who had a big lip; Jim Heart, who was a soft touch; Sourdough Johnson, who liked sourdough pancakes; and Hungry Mike, who ate so much it was reputed that they took a 20-foot tapeworm from him.

C. M. Oehler wrote that the foreman often favored those of

his own nationality. Oehler did not see a large variety of nationalities represented until he got into a camp with an American-born foreman. Previously he had Frank Yankovich, a Croatian, as a foreman and, because he was camp clerk, as a roommate. Yankovich had been in America for 20 years but had learned little English and could neither read nor write it. Andrew Koski, who came from Finland in 1905, said that he could not speak much English, and his fellow workers preferred to use Finnish. That was still his preference for speaking or writing in 1976 at age 87. Scott Erickson recalled that most lumberjacks could speak some English and did not resist when the clerk Americanized the more difficult names.

All nationality groups were represented in the logging camps, but no lumberjack was able to recall ever seeing any blacks among those with whom he worked. Only John Ettestad and Elmer Henrickson remembered working with Indians, both of whom came from the Fort. "They were good workers and proud of their work." Except when work was done next to the Nett Lake Reservation, no reference was found of those Indians working at logging.

The general consensus of those interviewed was that many of the Americanized lumberjacks were professional people or those from otherwise good backgrounds who had lost their battle with alcohol or had other serious setbacks and wanted to get away from their problems. Unfortunately, these were the same people who left camp every time they had money.

Although ILC preferred not to hire local settlers, a large number of them, particularly sons of farmers who needed income during the winter, worked regularly in the smaller camps. Clarence and Joseph Mannausau, of Loman, spent many winters at small camps within five miles of their father's farm. These camps usually had 12 to 15 men, a cook house, and a bunkhouse. One cook was also the bookkeeper and operated the commissary. Every man took care of his own tools. Clarence said that these camps were cleaner and quieter than the big ones. A better spirit existed because all the men knew each other as local neighbors, and they went home to get fresh clothes every Saturday night. Joe added, "We only had lice in the camp once."

ILC advertised for workers in regional newspapers and distributed posters over a wide area, to get a steady stream of applications. Every personal inquiry was answered, because individuals who came on their own saved the expense of an employment agency, and they usually provided their own transportation. If no job was immediately available, the applications were placed on file.

A postcard (in pencil, but in good script) from Joe Clomes, August 31, 1922, read: "Please let me know how far from International Falls you expect to ship me and how much do you pay a Blacksmith (*sic*) let me know by return mail and I am ready to come if it hint to (*sic*) far."

A letter on commonplace, coarse, lined tablet paper from D. W. Shipley, Box 197, Big Falls, with no date, is as written: "Mr. Backes Dear sir I am writing to you to see if my wife and my Self could get a job of cooking in one of your camps I was told to write to you and they thought we could get a job so please let me heer by return mail and Oblige D W Shipley"

Thomas Welsh, superintendent of logging, replied on September 20, 1923, asking about the Shipleys' experience and specifically what each could do.

Shipley replied on September 23:

> my reply to yours of the 20 we never cooked in a lumber Camp but we have cook in a cook cer in N.D. and my wife has bin cooking at Van Norths Hotel this summer so we thought we could handle a Camp my wife would be cook and I would be cookee or help her if you can give us work how much would you pay per mouth and could you use a Black smith we have a soninlaw that wants a job so please let me hear by return mail Your Truly D W Shipley

The use of employment agencies and the advance of rail fare, which amounted to substantial business, is illustrated in Table I in the Appendix. ILC was happy that only 152 men did not arrive in camp to pay off their fare and agency fees, for a loss of $1,314. This was 75 percent lower than the loss for the previous season.

It was necessary to advance fare because so many of the men did not have the funds. ILC advanced fare money to the agencies and sometimes directly to the railroad agent, who issued tickets when requested to do so by the employment agent.

William E. Moses, chief "man grabber" for ILC in Duluth, worked closely with Joe Burke, manager of the State Employment Office there. Moses wrote Twomey that Burke always gave ILC preference in orders and did all he could in its interest. He reminded Twomey that ILC traditionally had given Burke a turkey for Thanksgiving and for Christmas, and suggested that since 1922 had been such a hard year and Burke had helped ILC so much, "maybe the Company would want to remember him in a more substantial way."

Twomey immediately wrote to Seymour Backus: "Now more than ever, we will have to depend on all sources for more men, owing to the present shortage. All circumstances considered—believe we could invest a hundred dollars to no better advantage."

The following February, Twomey received an urgent message from Webster at Camp 87 that he was short 10 gangs of sawyers and 10 general men. Twomey contacted Moses, reminding him that there was not much time left in the logging season, and closed, "Please go over our labor situation with Mr. Burke and see if it will not be possible to get us out a lot of labor within the next few days."

Frequently "man grabber" agencies sent men who were not ordered, and ILC was out the fare, or they sent men who they knew would never work after they got to camp. ILC advised that some men had pulled the same trick several times. Woodford wrote to Moses:

> You sent Joe Jeffries up and you know that he will never go to work after he gets up here. You should put this fellow on your blacklist as we have lost a fare on him several times before. You should be able to determine the bad actors among the bunch and steer clear of them. Avoid IWWs, several have been hired, who have been a loss to the Company.

The agencies were told never to send men who did not have baggage to be checked, because they would skip out as soon as they arrived at the Falls. The backpacks were called "turkeys" and were taken as soon as the men entered the train car and stored so they could not get at them. The packs were held by ILC until the men had worked out their fare and employment fees. Some men were skilled at filling their packs with stuffing and left as soon as they could escape the watchful eye of the ILC greeting party. Their names were placed on the jumper list, which was sent to all camps and employment agencies.

Sometimes men came to camp without adequate clothing, as Webster of Camp 87 experienced. He wrote, "I need eight general men but be sure they have enough clothes to work. We clothed two men that came with the last bunch and they only stayed two days."

The employment agents were told always to try to send three

to five men in each group, because the livery men charged $10 per trip, even if they had only one man. Pollard recalled that it was comical to see Pierce Arrows or Cadillacs coming down the road with up to seven men and their packs and "you knew they were all broke."

In January 1913, several men were arrested for refusing to work after their fare had been paid from Duluth and Minneapolis. Each was sentenced to 60 days of hard labor or to work for ILC long enough to pay the fare. The men all chose to work. In the same week 11 men were sent from Bemidji to an ILC camp at Littlefork, and when they arrived they professed that they knew nothing about cutting pulpwood. Each was fined $10.

At times agencies refunded the fare to ILC if the men did not arrive. Gustave Kulander, of Walker, notified ILC that he had sent 10 men, listed by name and ticket number, and asked that he be notified if any did not show, for he would refund the price of the ticket.

The Fargo, Thief River Falls, Crookston, and East Grand Forks agencies exchanged men moving back and forth between the bonanza farms and the lumber camps. Because these men tended to party in those towns when changing from field to forest or vice versa, the jails often became collecting points for them until they could be picked up by recruiters.

Despite the above comments, Alfred Johnson, who spent most of his life in the timber, said, "Lumberjacks were the most honest people I have ever met. When they were out of work they borrowed money, but as soon as they got back to work they paid it back. They helped each other. . . . If it wasn't for lumberjacks, we wouldn't have International Falls. . . . And you'll find very few lumberjacks ever got welfare."

Ryan agreed with Johnson and said that many men came to the same camp year after year, and when they no longer could produce, they were fed as long as they could walk to the table. He wrote, "It was not uncommon to see several old jacks working around camp—piling, splitting wood, filling lanterns and doing minor chores while they recuperated from illness or injury or [because they] were just too old to work in the woods." He cited the case of a Crookston Lumber Company camp that had 12 old lumberjacks who no longer were capable of a hard day's work. Pollard's parting comment about men was, "I doubt that you could find such a large number of men to work as well for equal pay today."[3]

The Lumberjacks' Work Day

Immediately after breakfast, the men left for their work spot to arrive at daylight. Work usually started between 6:45 and 7:15 A.M., depending upon how light it was. Lunch was eaten in the woods at noon, and the work day ended at 4:30 P.M., when the men returned to camp. The work week was six days, and the only time a camp shut down "was when the weather was too bad for the horses. Manpower could be replaced easier than horsepower."

The first person in the woods was the stripper, who marked off 90- to 100-foot strips in which the crews worked. Then came the notcher, or undercutter, who marked the trees to be cut. He notched the trees in such a way that they fell with the least damage and could easily be trimmed and sawed into proper lengths, if they were not moved from the forest in full length. He was followed by a two-man saw team, who generally used a 6-foot saw to cut the marked trees. These teams could saw from 100 to 200 logs a day. In most ILC camps, saw teams numbered about 50 men, or 30 percent of the total work force. As they worked, a swamper marked and cleared trails for the skidder.

Each day as the sawyers left for the forest, their saws were freshly sharpened. The company knew that saws lasted longer and were kept in better shape if one specialized filer did all the sharpening. Sometimes piece cutters paid the regular filer $0.10 to sharpen their saws, but usually they took a half hour out to do the job themselves, because they were using their own saws.

When freeze-up came, the horse skidder took the logs to the landing. There were times, such as the winter of 1919–20, when the skidders were not able to start until mid-December. Heavy, early snowfall had kept the swampy ground soft, and horses could not be brought into the woods until after the temperature had fallen to about 40 degrees below zero for a couple days and the ground finally froze.

A skidder and a helper could skid and load about 15 cords a day. Large logs were skidded one at a time, and small logs were loaded onto a two-bunk dray to be moved to the strip road. It was essential to get the logs skidded out as soon as possible after the trees were felled so they would not freeze to the ground or be covered with snow and lost until spring. The distance skidded to the strip road was never more than a quarter mile. The timber was sorted by species and for ties, pulp, or posts at this point. Skidders numbered about 40 to 50 men, a slightly smaller number than the cutting crew. This varied from time to time depending upon how fast or how slow the sawyers worked or if there was difficulty in keeping a full crew on hand.

Carl Dahlberg, who spent all of his life in the woods, said that skidding was his first job. He was given a big black horse and told to pick up all the stray logs. He said that it was such a boring job that he quickly asked for one with a little more variety and was assigned to a snatch team hauling logs to the spotting ground. Within two weeks he was promoted to the next step in log moving—a four-horse dray team.

Two men and a sled made up the dray team that hauled the logs to the landing, either by a river or, in the case of M & O after 1912, by a rail spur. Dahlberg said that his haul from the strip piles (or spotting-out ground) to the landing was six miles. He started in darkness at 5:45 A.M. in order to make two trips a day. The horses followed the road, so it was not essential that the driver see it well.

The roads from the spotting or strip piles to the landing were kept in condition by a five- or six-man crew referred to as road monkeys. The first work for these men each morning was to clean off the manure, which had a negative effect on the road surface. They also removed any fallen timber and checked the condition of the ruts. Hay was put on the downhill side of the road so the sleigh would not overrun the horses. Turnouts were provided so the returning empty sleighs could meet the loaded ones, which had to stay on the rutted trail.

During the night when the log teams were not hauling, the road monkeys used large sleighs, each laden with a water tank, to re-ice the road. Torches posted on corners of the sleighs provided light. After a heavy snowfall, large V snow plows made of logs were pulled down the trails to clear them. Sometimes the entire lumber camp crew tramped the snow to hasten freezing. Heavy snow meant many cut logs might be lost until it melted. It also meant that the sawyers cut the stumps higher to keep their saws out of the snow. In either case, this represented a loss.

At the rail landing was the loading crew, consisting of about 15 men in most ILC camps. The rest of the 150 men were in camp taking care of quarters and in administration. VRL camps were usually larger, averaging about 200 men, but the ratio of workers was the same.

Standard camp production was about one cord per person per day. Wages were $1.00 per day plus the cost of room and board. This brought the labor cost per cord of wood, prior to hauling to the mill, to $1.69. A good piece cutter made 1½ cords daily and could make more money than a monthly-paid lumberjack. It was cheaper to hire piece cutters because they were more efficient.

In the 1922–23 season, the average total cost per cord of wood varied by camp from a low of $4.04 to a high of $6.78. The cost of saw logs per thousand varied from $5.79 to $13.99. Some of the variation was caused by the supply of wood in any location, but the ability of the foreman to get the most out of a crew also was a factor. The same spread applied to the cost of poles, posts, and ties. The margin of profit was not great, so it was essential to determine whether or not it was feasible to enter a certain plot of ground to secure the timber. Piece workers were watched closely to see that they cleaned up their portion of the forest before they left.

VRL averaged 889 log feet sawed per man per day during the 1922–23 season. The cost of production for each item was broken down into 10 stages from the initial sawing to final delivery at the mill.

The crews' work was coordinated so the sawyers did not get ahead of the skidders or the haulers from the strip piles to the landings. No timber was left in the woods when the river drive was ready or when the railroads no longer could haul out of the forests with spring breakup. Sometimes sawyers were discharged early if the skidders, woods haulers, or the railroad was not able to keep up, because sawed lumber spoiled if it lay over summer.

Pollard determined that most sawyers were Finns, Norwegians, and Swedes, while the French, Irish, or Scots tended to be teamsters. The Germans were blacksmiths, and Slavs were likely to be cooks and mess hall helpers. There was always a cross section of older Americans who were either constant drifters or men, often from prominent families, who had "hit bottom."

The most depressing time for Pollard during his years in the woods was in late 1932 when the men, who were so happy to get back to work after not having much work in 1931 due to Backus' bankruptcy, were laid off and the camps closed because of court orders and a lack of capital. He recalled, "It was real gloom, because that is the first we really felt the Depression. What a depressing picture seeing the men with no place to go and no money. All the company could do was to offer to take them back to International Falls if they wanted to return to the emergency camps."

He contrasted that with early 1933, when orders were given by the federal bankruptcy court to clean up the forests and burn all the pulpwood that was not fit for paper making. Some old camps were burned and new ones were built with orders to start cutting all that could be brought out of the woods by late March. Pollard noted that it was good to see how happy the men were to get back to camp.[4]

The Lumberjacks' Food

When former lumberjacks were asked what they most remembered and liked about life in the camps, they all answered, "the food." Joe Miller said of his experience prior to World War I, "It was the best, oh yes. The beef and the pork, and even lamb. Five big pancakes every morning."

When John Ettestad looked back 50 years he remarked with a big grin, "The sourdough pancakes and pastries of all kinds were the very best treats." Elmer Henrickson agreed and added, "Plus those super good hams." Alex Gerber said that the food was "just great," and then recalled one old lumberjack from his first year in camp prior to World War I whose favorite slogan was, "Sugar three times a day and syrup all the time."

J. C. Ryan inspected over 70 camps in 1922 and wrote that with the exception of fresh fruit and milk, the food "was as good or better than food served in leading hotels." Pollard said: "The company tried to furnish really top food. Sometimes the cooks were not too good, but most did a fine job. Good food was the key to keeping men. For many this was their home."

Henrickson called poor cooks "belly robbers." He said, "Crews left fast if the food was not good, so the cooks had to be good or the camp could not function." Cooks probably were second only to the foreman in importance in maintaining a good camp.

Normally, each camp had a head cook, who was supported by a staff of one cookee for every 20 men. If the camp was larger than 150 men, a special meat and/or a pastry cook or both were added. Cookees set the tables, peeled the potatoes, washed the dishes, and kept the kitchen and dining room clean. In 1921 Carl Dahlberg was the only cookee for 55 men, under head cook Anton Carlson, in Camp Rattiborne, near Effie. Dahlberg recalled that he used lots of lye to scrub the eight-inch pine floor boards white. He peeled a 50-pound lard can full of potatoes each day six days a week, besides washing all the dishes. Dahlberg, who was a big man with a great deal of ambition, said that after two weeks he asked for a different job.

Since most of the logging in Koochiching, Lake of the Woods, and St. Louis counties was done after 1900, the lumberjacks had the advantage of canned goods, such as milk, apples, tomatoes, corn, and corned beef—all of which came in one-gallon cans. During the second decade of the century, canned fruits replaced dried fruits, except for prunes—the lumberjack's tonic—which remained a favorite over canned prunes.

The next change came in the early 1930s, when refrigeration and transportation improved enough so that fresh fruit was available. By the mid-1930s, fresh apples, beans, plums, berries, and grapefruit were commonplace. When grapefruit first appeared, some of the men thought they were green oranges and objected to them. Toward the end of the camp period, Kraft cheese, spinach, minced ham, turkey, salmon, and pineapple were added to the variety of food served.

A traditional breakfast menu might include five pancakes, most often of the sourdough variety but sometimes buckwheat; coarse pork sausage, up to 1½ inches thick; oatmeal, served with canned milk; hashbrown or American fried potatoes; salt pork; beans with blackstrap molasses; fried cakes (doughnuts); ham; bacon; fried pork; toast; and always coffee.

Except on Sundays, the noon meal was always served in the woods, regardless of whether the crew was one block or three miles from camp. The food was delivered in a well-insulated box on a sled—variously referred to as a swing-dingle, a junk wagon, or the lunch cart. The coffee or tea was boiling hot and helped to keep the insulated box and the food warm. Only slow eaters ever experienced having their food freeze to the enamel plates, but scalding hot coffee or tea took care of the problem. Pies sometimes were so hot that they had to cool before they could be eaten. Frequently deer followed the food sleigh because the leftovers were tossed along the trail on the return to camp.

The bull cook drove to the site where the men were to eat and lit a fire, which "was going good" by the time the men arrived. The men sat around if the weather was comfortable or, if it was too cold, stood close to the fire while they ate. The noon meal consisted of soup, roast beef, mashed or boiled potatoes and brown gravy, corn bread or muffins, at least one vegetable (such as string beans, beets, or rutabagas), a sauce, and at least one pastry. In the meantime, the horses, which had been covered with blankets, ate their oats and hay nearby.

The day ended at 4:30 or 5:00 P.M., and the evening meal was served at 6:00 P.M. It consisted of soup, a meat (either beef or pork), potatoes and gravy, and two vegetables—of which the most common were beans, rutabagas, canned corn, carrots, cabbage, or beets. Potatoes and rutabagas were abundant because they were grown locally. The most common soup was vegetable, followed by bean, pea, or tomato. Several choices of dessert were always available—cookies or doughnuts, cake or pie, rice or bread pudding, or a canned fruit. Every meal had its tea, coffee, and bread. The bread and pastries were praised by all those interviewed, which gave the impression that baking must have been a special talent of camp cooks.

In the days before improved transportation and refrigeration, all pastries were made without the benefit of eggs, which also explains why eggs were not standard fare until the 1920s. By the 1930s over 30,000 dozen eggs per year were used in cooking in ILC camps but were not a major part of the daily menu. Fortunately, the camps operated in the winter when frozen meat could be shipped without risk of spoilage. During the warmer seasons, the camps tried to purchase meat from the local farmers, but not enough meat could be reliably supplied in that manner. Farm animals were usually butchered and the meat brought to camp, but sometimes they were butchered in camp. Keeping animals in camp presented a real problem, because bears often chased the swine, and finding them took valuable time from other work. They were costly to feed since, except for limited table scraps, expensive feed had to be imported from distant places.

All meals were eaten in a 12- to 20-minute time span. Everyone had an assigned place on the bench at the long table, where talking was forbidden and the only noise was the chomping of jaws. Only the VRL headquarters camp at Cusson used chairs. On Sundays breakfast was eaten one hour later, and slightly less food was served at each meal. Afterwards, the dishes and utensils were scraped, put in a heavy burlap grain sack, thoroughly dunked and swirled in boiling, soapy water, rinsed, and then swung around to remove most of the water, after which the items were spread out on tables to dry. In spite of the impression that gives, the kitchens and mess halls were kept clean.

VRL had strict rules against females in camps, but relaxed the rules during World War I at Cusson, where it used female cooks and cookees. That camp contained entire families and had some husband-and-wife teams in its food service. However, when female help was tried later, there were so many battles among the camp members, pregnancies, and hysterical women phoning company headquarters during the middle of the night that women again were barred from camps. Alex Gerber told of the wife of a warehouseman at Cusson who used the fact that she had to eat in a dining hall with "uncouth lumberjacks" as part of the reason for a divorce.[5]

Even though surface water was abundant in the counties where ILC and VRL had camps, it was a standard practice to drill wells for camp needs. Lake and river water was believed safe to use, but the companies felt that they did not dare to risk the chance of water-related illness. In the days prior to forest railroads, the well often was the largest single expense of establishing a camp. Sometimes water was obtained by driving a sand point down a few feet. At other times deep holes were drilled only to hit rock, so the effort was repeated until water was reached. Most ILC wells were drilled by Ray Espe and were between 100 and 130 feet deep. No one connected with camp life recalled ever seeing water for a camp being taken from a surface source. In any case, the camps probably had a safer water supply than most of the farms and villages in the area at that time.

The foremen, clerks, and cooks always were on the lookout for freeloaders, who tried to get food and lodging without working. Sometimes transients got by for a week or so before they were detected. Some freeloading obviously was expected, but the total amount involved cannot be properly appraised.

For the years 1914, 1915, and 1917, board costs for the Cusson camp ranged from $0.64 to $0.80 per man per day—a sizeable sum considering that daily wages for that camp ranged from $1.27 to $1.52. The cost of various food items per pound was as follows: beef, $0.14; bacon, $0.31; frankfurters, $0.17; cod and herring, $0.085; flour, $0.055; carrots, $0.02; potatoes, $0.005; dried fruit, $0.095 to $0.14; coffee, $0.16; and oleomargarine, $0.24. Canned corn was $1.65 for a case of 24 No. 2 cans, and sauerkraut $5.00 for a case of 10 No. 10 cans. The daily cost of food and consumption are illustrated in Table II in the Appendix.

In 1930 crew members on the "Gator Rustler" (boats that towed log booms were called gators) ate 9.7843 pounds of food per man per day at a cost of $1.2952 plus $0.3925 overhead. Meat consumption over the years was about 1.5 pounds per man per day, and vegetable intake was about 2.2 pounds, while flour use averaged 1.13 pounds, and all forms of sugar, 0.58 pound. At one camp of 275 men, 104 dozen cookies were consumed in one day in addition to cake, pie, or doughnuts. The average camp used 40 pies and 48 loaves of bread per day.

Pollard, who served as camp clerk for seven years and studied all available records of the late logging period, determined that the average daily caloric intake varied from 5,500 to 5,745 per man. He added that the Canadian government recommended 5,200 calories in the summer and 5,800 in the winter, but the U.S. authorities insisted that 3,500 calories was adequate. This was a diet of abundant pancakes, pastries, meat, and vegetables, with limited fruits and cereal. Pollard emphasized that in his years as a camp clerk not one worker was taken from a camp because of a heart attack.[6]

The Lumberjacks' Quarters

No. 5 grade lumber was used in building the camps, which were intended to be used for as little as one season and almost never for more than five seasons. In spite of the temporary nature of these buildings, they were little different from most contemporary rural and small-town homes. Generally, they both lacked indoor toilet and shower facilities, but soap and hot water probably were more available in the camps.

The bunkhouses were heated by large stoves, which frequently were large steel barrels capable of holding 4-foot lengths of wood. They often contained a piping system to heat the water used for washing in a nearby sink, which contained up to 10 wash basins. Costley recalled that in spite of an adequate supply of water, often there were no more than three towels for the 100-plus men. Oliver Knox said that prior to World War I the Kettle Falls camp where he worked had a building for a sauna bath and a laundry.

In the bunkhouse, lanterns and lamps were located down the center over the deacon seat. Probably the only camp of either company that had electric lights and steam heat prior to the 1930s was the VRL camp at Cusson, which had them about 1910, when the camp was constructed. Sometimes a stove sat in the middle of the bunkhouse, and there was a little additional space where the men gathered to converse. It was an unspoken rule that no one ever sat on another's bunk.

A wire or a stringer of timber ran along the center of the building a few feet below the skylight, an opening in the peak of the roof that was opened and closed to control odors and temperature. Wet clothes and socks were hung there to dry during the night. Pollard said that "caused the air to be ripe by morning." Each person had an acknowledged spot on the wire for his clothes. Dahlberg said, "The lice and smell stories of the bunkhouse are true. Thank God for the skylight above the stove."

The double-decked wooden bunks were two wide, divided by a center board. Originally, the bunks had a solid bottom, which was covered with hay. Some men preferred to use pine boughs because they felt that gave more protection against insects. Costley said that the bunks running parallel to the deacon seat were referred to as "side delivery" bunks, and those perpendicular to the deacon seat were called "muzzle loaders." He preferred the muzzle loaders because "you slept with your head to the wall and were not bothered by any activity along the deacon seat." Some men changed the hay in their bunks frequently, while others did not bother until it was completely flat.

About 1920 the old wooden-bottom bunks gave way to steel bunks with springs and mattresses. Costley said that white sheets, pillow cases, and single bunks would have been almost unthinkable to those with whom he worked. "If a lumberjack had seen painted floors, a washroom, and a library in the camp, he would have fainted dead away."

Sanitation in the bunkhouses left much to be desired. Blankets were not washed all winter and were aired only on weekends. Some men were so lacking in good hygiene habits or were too stingy to spend money for extra clothing that others in the camp made them "shape up or ship out."

A running commentary in letters, in January and February 1923, gives a good insight on the problem of sanitation. Jim Sedore was a "roving undercover camp inspector," whose job was to note camp conditions and determine which men were trouble-makers. On January 26, 1923, he wrote from Camp 98. His spelling and punctuation were not unusual for one in his position:

> Friend Pit i have looked over 94 things are not looking bad. Say that Sleeping camp at 94 is Bad you see 65 or 70 men half of them with a bad cold Spiting on the floor hasnt ben Scrubed this winter from the way it Smells, there is some good men leaving there on account of it, only one bull cook, and he cant take care of it. i am not trying to tel how

things should be. just how they are. probly a line to the foreman Supposed to be from the State board of health would do a lot of good and Save Some Hospital bills. i wil go to 99 tomorrow and Stay over Sunday. i here there is plenty of Moose [appears to be a code for IWWs] around there. i have found a few bad ones they ar gon now. any instructions Sent to 98 wil get me as i wil look for it here. yours resp. Jim

On January 30, 1923, Twomey wrote to Gust Holmstrom, the head of all camps, at Camp 29: "I am advised that the sleeping camps at Camp 94 are in a dirty condition. Will you investigate same? Have some men put on to scrub out & clean them up so that a visit from sanitary officer will not result in criticism."

On February 9, 1923, Louis Bruce, foreman for Camp 94, answered Twomey: "I am willing to bet ten dollars that the sleeping camps [quarters] at this camp, are in as clean a condition as any other camp you have at any job on the company's operation and can see no reason for any criticism at this particular camp."

Bruce noted that both Holmstrom and Twomey had been through the camp and knew the sleeping quarters were clean. He closed, "Furthermore it is impossible . . . to keep logging camp floors snow white at all times." In contrast to the Sedore letter, this was beautifully written, as were many from the foremen and clerks.

Oliver Knox recalled that "lice and bedbugs were standard" but, contrary to most of the persons interviewed, said that even though his camp had a laundry building, there was not always enough hot water to clean out the insects. Ettestad and Henrickson laughed as they said, "More lice and bedbugs came from the poor hotels and cat houses than from the camps, which were kept far cleaner than the hotels and houses." Pollard agreed, adding that bedbugs came more by accident, because the men were checked quite carefully. A shy Andrew Koski said that bedbugs and lice were a problem but that what he disliked most was being in a bunkhouse all winter with a hundred other men.

Various means were devised to rid the bunkhouses of pests. Joe Miller reported that frequently after the bedding was taken to the outside lines to air, a steam hose was turned into the quarters. This method was used most often if the camp was near the forest railroad track so the locomotives could supply the steam. As a camp clerk, Oehler slept in separate quarters and put his bed posts in jar covers filled with kerosene to prevent bedbugs from getting into his bed. He explained that this method was not used in the "bull pen," as the bunkhouse was called, because the men would not keep their blankets off the floor, and so much kerosene presented a fire hazard. He added, "The men would just not feel at home in the camps unless there were a few bedbugs around." However, he was sure the bugs were not welcome because he remembered seeing the men sitting on rocks on warm nights trying to escape the bugs.

Tom Welsh, in charge of forest operations, wrote to the camp watch at Camp 94 (Ericsburg) on July 1, 1923:

> We are sending . . . a five gallon can of bed bug remedy and sprayer. . . . Now what I want you to do is move out the bunks from the wall and give the camp a thorough spraying. Also take the mattresses off every bed and spray the beds thoroughly and also spray the mattresses thoroughly, take the blankets and hang them on a rope or wire and give them a thorough pounding to knock all of the dust and dirt out of them and also give them a light spraying. . . . Go at this job and do it in a thorough way and try to kill every bug there is in camp. We will see what the result will be.

The men joked about the pests, but most were serious about preventing them or at least minimizing their impact. Sunday mornings were spent washing clothes at a nearby lake or stream, using boiling water in 50-pound lard cans with an abundance of lye soap, trying to get a "good kill." A clothing plunger was used to give the garments and socks a good "going over." The "boiling up" helped control the pests, and clean clothes, especially socks, were warmer than dirty ones. It was not until after World War II that chemicals were effective in controlling camp pests.

Fortunately, few men were needed in the camps during the summer, for there was little protection against mosquitoes and flies. Joe Miller said that it was summer work which encouraged him to look elsewhere for employment.[7]

The Lumberjacks' Health

Joe Miller, who worked at several occupations, preferred the woods to the mill because the former was more healthful. Most of the men were between 25 and 40 years of age and in the prime of life; those past the mid-50s worked around camp. The older ones were almost always single men who had nowhere else to go.

John Ettestad recalled that if the "'jacks came to camp in the fall with the snakes it took them about four days on the good camp food to get back to health, and then they were fit for the winter. Most of them went all winter without getting a cold." During the first few days of work, the biggest problem was muscular soreness, but the general consensus was that "sickness was really a minor problem," and very little time was lost because of it.

Any concentration of people in facilities like lumber camps was bound to have health problems, but Oliver Knox, who spent 26 years in camps, indicated that sickness was so infrequent in his time that if a man was sick he seldom was docked if he stayed in camp for a day or two. The camps where Knox worked were all more than 40 miles as the crow flies from medical help, but a doctor came once a month to check anyone with a problem. Career lumberjack Leonard Costley commented that frostbite was a regular occurrence for newcomers to the woods, and the cure was contrary to current beliefs. He said that when someone had a white nose or white tip of the ear, it was customary to rub the affected part with snow. In later years the spot was gently rubbed with a dry woolen mitt.

Costley felt that accidents were more of a potential problem than sickness. He said:

> Lumberjacking was a hazardous occupation . . . you had to be all man and half wildcat to stay on the job. A man working at that kind of work in those days was very quick and sure-footed and there had to be something really contrary to the ordinary work in order for a man to get caught. . . . One of the main hazards . . . was the big timber. When a tree fell, there was sometimes what was called a "widow maker." The widow maker was a limb that was broken off the tree when it was falling and it caught on another tree. The tree would bend over and send the limb back like an arrow.

Pollard referred to that as a snag. He vividly recalled the day that he and a strawboss were walking among the men in the woods. Just after they had alerted one man to the danger, he was killed by the whipping tree. In all his years as a camp clerk, Pollard never had a man lose a toe or a finger because of an accident with an axe or a saw. Costley noted that such accidents usually occurred among swampers, who, he implied, were losers in society and had no experience in woods work but were there because an employment agency had sent them. Ryan clerked a camp of 175 men one year that did not have any accidents. In his opinion, head injuries from falling limbs, or "dry tops," were more common than saw or axe cuts; sometimes a man slipped and cut his head with his double-bitted axe. Most accidents occurred during loading because of the swinging or hoisted timbers.

First-aid kits were almost unknown in the camps until the World War I era, when insurance companies required them as part of the workmen's compensation regulations. The commissaries carried home remedies, such as liniment, pain killer, castor oil, petroleum jelly, and carbolic salve. Pollard jokingly said that most camps had more medicine on hand for horses than for men, and added that if a man got a cut or a scratch he applied balsam pitch or tobacco juice.

In case of an accident, the only thing that could be done was to get the person to town. That took about two days, unless the log train happened to be in camp and was loaded and ready to go to the Falls. After the gasoline-powered speedsters were purchased in the early 1920s, the time from camps along the railroad was reduced to three hours. Oliver Knox noted that anyone injured or very sick was taken out by tote team over the ice in the winter and by boat in the summer. "Fortunately," he said, "I only remember one person with a broken limb in those 26 years."

Hospital insurance for ILC employees cost $1 per month per man. This entitled them to go to the Northern Minnesota Hospital (NMH) for complete medical attention without additional cost. VRL had its own hospital at Virginia and charged workers $1.35 a month for medical coverage. Starting in the early 1920s, ILC agreed to let employees of the independent contractors have hospital and medical coverage under their plan.

The NMH was owned by several medical doctors, who were quick to see a need for their services in the area. They built facilities in a number of communities where ILC had mills or camps. The public often associated NMH with ILC and felt that there was collusion between the two. Older men resisted going to NMH because they felt that if ILC did not want them any more, they would be given medicine from the "black bottle." Ettestad and Henrickson said that the "black bottle" myth persisted because quite often no one ever heard from a lumberjack once he entered the hospital.

Frequent outbreaks of communicable diseases occurred in the camps, as in the public schools, before the days of vaccination.

Smallpox probably was the most persistent plague. In 1916 three men with the disease were responsible for 150 being quarantined near Big Fork. In 1921 one man, who traveled around the camps in the Northome area, spread smallpox. ILC called in doctors to vaccinate everyone. C. J. Langham, of ILC, was put in charge of watching health conditions of the men and worked with medical professionals to keep things under control.

Another outbreak occurred in October 1923, at Camp 102. Langham immediately vaccinated 20 men; 16 did not need to be vaccinated and 4 refused. The camp was quarantined, and no one could leave without permission from a doctor. State law required that anyone refusing vaccination must remain in camp three weeks. Notice was sent to all camps that anyone complaining of a backache and headache should be given a hospital ticket at once. Langham added that the camp was very sanitary; the food was good and properly cooked.

The flu and measles were the next two most common illnesses. Again outbreaks closed schools about the same time the plague hit the camps. The flu outbreak that was practically worldwide after World War I affected the isolated camps and was remembered by several of the older individuals interviewed. Sometimes nearly all the men in a camp were ill with the flu.

Occasional cases of insanity were present. *The Journal* reported that an elderly man at a VRL camp cut his throat the second day of work. In the 1923–24 season, two double killings occurred at ILC camps when one crazed lumberjack killed a fellow worker by chopping off his head with an axe while the victim slept. Another man, crazed by liquor, shot the camp cook as he slept. In both cases the offenders were shot and killed while resisting arrest.

Ettestad recalled the year that everyone at Camp 186, near Nett Lake, had dysentery that lasted for three weeks. Several men died. He said that it probably was caused by the hot weather, the water, flies, and the meat that hung in the screened-in buildings.

ILC was careful not to hire men with physical problems and constantly warned employment agencies to be on the lookout for anyone who was disabled. Scattered reports of those who were classified No. 4 by the medics give an idea of the problem: "Man 55 with a very bad knee was discovered last year and reported, how did he get to a camp now? He can do no manual labor and must be let go unless he can get a job like signing checks." A

62-year-old man with a very bad heart spent considerable time in the hospital. He was given a No. 4 rating because he was incapable of manual labor.

Another report stated that a man had both first toes slightly frozen, which should not have prevented him from working except that he was 68 years old and had been in the woods only once before, 40 years previously. He was not fit for woods work because he was "too old and clumsy." Man No. 161 was simply marked "Brights Disease." J. J. Kelly was classified No. 4 because he was an alcoholic and was an industrial hazard. All employment agencies were notified accordingly, and the Bemidji agency was given a reprimand because it completely disregarded age and physical condition.

Many letters in the files directed camp clerks to administer immediate first aid when an accident occurred, get the person to proper medical attention, and be sure that a full report of the accident was made. The instructions were quite clear: "Any employee of the Company is entitled, on request, to receive a hospital ticket. The clerk should be satisfied, however, that the request is bona fide and that the employee is in probable need of hospital attention."[8]

The Lumberjacks' Wages

In the first decades of the 1900s, forestry, like farming, was a crude, labor-intense, low-technology industry with low labor returns. As in farming, wage rates in forestry did not change until the late 1930s.

The October 21, 1915, *Journal* noted that 5,000 men and many horses were needed to cut 400 million feet of lumber. To get that many men, ILC was willing to raise wages of piece workers to $4 a day for making poles, posts, and ties. Two-horse teamsters earned $35 a month plus room and board, while those driving four horses received $40. Pay for lumberjacks ranged from $26 to $40. Sawmill workers earned $2 a day and paid their living expenses. In one camp, at Cusson, the gross earnings per day for men on a monthly basis varied from $2.07 to $2.32, including room and board, during the years 1914, 1915, and 1916.

Independent, or gypo, loggers were sought for $1.50 a cord, or $1.00 a cord for pole wood. A strong, ambitious person who preferred to work on his own liked piece work because he could make more money. Generally, gypos could harvest timber at a lower cost than the monthly workers, but they did not always respond as well to regulations.

Wages rose during World War I and stayed at a relatively high rate up to 1920. Clerks earned up to $90 a month. Scott Erickson received $75 as a gator pilot for floating equipment and transporting men, horses, supplies, and food to camps. In 1919 Clarence Mannausau loaded pulpwood onto the rail cars at Camp 6 at Loman, while his brother Joe was a cookee; both made $75 a month. The following year they decided to cut wood for $2.50 a cord. Each man could cut about two cords a day, which was nearly double the rate per man per day in the camps.

In November 1920, ILC complained that its pay scale was too high. However, by January 1921, rates started to drop. At that time Billy Noonan, editor of *The Baudette Region*, wrote, "The lumber companies are surely playing Santa Claus to themselves these days, judging by the offers of $16 to $22 a month for men to work in the woods." But by July 1922, members of the Minnesota Loggers' Association complained about the outrageous pay scale of Wisconsin and eastern Michigan groups. The easterners paid $50.00 a month or $0.15 a log but complained that even at that level they were not able to get men at the "common labor rates," because those people were all doing road work.

The eastern group decided that, in order to hire men for woods work, the pay scale should more nearly equal that of the mills, which was $2.50 to $2.75 daily. For a 26-day month, this amounted to $65.00 to $71.50 a month. If $1.00 a day was deducted for room and board, this reverted back to $35.00 to $41.50 for woodsmen. These wages still did not attract workers.

In August 1922, the Minnesota Association decided to set a scale ranging from $30 for general workers to as high as $50 for six-horse teamsters but leaving the bulk of the 26-work-day-a-month men in the $30 to $35 range. The 30-day-month men were paid as follows: $65 for the straw boss, $85 for the blacksmith, $100 for a cook of a large crew, and $35 for cookees and bull cooks. Room and board were always included in woods wages. Foremen and clerks negotiated on an independent basis, and at least some foremen asked for up to $175. At that time, $0.40 an hour was the common labor rate in Duluth.

By November 1922, camps in the western part of the Minnesota Association territory were full, and some had to turn people away. The eastern part of the territory, which generally was east of

Koochiching County but included some ILC camps and all VRL camps, felt pressure from the higher wages paid by the camps farther east. The Association, therefore, approved a resolution that those camps could pay $5 a month more than the agreed upon schedule. The leaders of Camp 87, at Echo Lake, reported that as soon as VRL raised its base wage to $40, ILC men started "to do some kicking" and a few left to go to the Virginia camps. They said, "We will have to have some arrangements made . . . if we want to hold our men."

Twomey replied to Webster at Camp 87, "Go to $40 a month if necessary, but we do not propose paying this at any of our other camps." Twomey permitted a $5 increase as of December 1 for woods workers only, and only for those who stayed the entire month. He cautioned Webster that it would add $2,000 to the cost of operation for the winter for his camp alone and that he did not want that increase to affect the 2,500 men in any of the 14 other ILC camps.

As the holiday season approached, men started to leave camp, so the Association members decided that it was necessary to grant an increase to entice the men to return in January. Norbeck, the Association secretary, commented that most of the married men had stayed on the job because they did not want to lose any time but that the single men went to towns "for a little diversion." On January 8, 1923, he reported that the rate increase paid off because the men returned.

In March 1923, C. H. Woodford, auditor of camps, wrote to the clerk at Camp 80 asking where he had received permission to increase the wages of four-horse teamsters to $60. Twomey had authorized the raise after Gust Holmstrom approved it in a memo. Within a few weeks the members of the Association heard from Norbeck saying that the only thing holding men in the eastern camps was the big snowstorm. Prior to that, they were leaving for the steel mills and other industries, which paid $0.35 to $0.50 an hour.

Norbeck called for a meeting of the members. Seymour Backus replied, "The wages must be set at the proper basis and lived up to by all concerned or we are going to create a runaway market which will be detrimental to us all." Seymour was sure that his father would attend the meeting. In May 1923, a new wage schedule was adopted, but the members voted strongly against piece cutting. Seymour was particularly opposed to piece cutting when he learned that some men in Wisconsin had made "over $150 a month which they were not warranted in doing." But a new basic schedule of $50 a month was put into effect.

By November 1923, Seymour instructed Welsh to reduce the basic schedule to $40 or $45. He wrote, "The labor situation is easing off materially. . . . The Minneapolis and other markets are full of men; the Wisconsin people are reducing their wages." Twomey replied that the competition in Washington state "was paying $4.00 to $8.00 for an 8-hour day, providing 8-men shacks, charging $1.20 a day for board, which included all the vegetables, fruits, seafish, chocolate, powdered sugar, etc." that the men wanted. He said that the IWW still planned a strike.

Wages leveled off gradually for the next couple of years. By December 1928, the basic schedule started at $30; four-horse teamsters, $45; blacksmiths, $70 to $85; cooks for a small crew, $70; cooks for a large crew, $100; and cookees and bull cooks, $35. The gator crews, which averaged $3.33 per day, were an exception. For the 1927–28 season, VRL had an average cost for monthly men of $3.01 per day. Gerber, at VRL, made $150 as a camp clerk. He was quick to add that in 1930 he had started as a forester for the state of Minnesota at $80 a month and provided his own living.

By the fall of 1929, the base schedule started at $26, but as soon as the camps filled, it dropped to $20 for the "new hands." The old-timers were advised that if they stayed the full season they could earn as much as $35. By November 1931, all wages were cut from $25 to $100 a month, depending on the previous high, but the base scale dropped to $15. The mill had just reopened after reorganization, and only four camps and a few jobbers were operating.

When Ettestad started as a clerk for a contractor camp in 1935, he received $50 a month and within a year was raised to $65. That year 14 new clerks were employed. Because a supply of qualified men was available, potential workers were well screened. Marion Plummer and Adam Clement, both experienced woods hands, received $2.28 a day at Camp 6. Even though both men were married and lived nearby, they stayed at the camp six days a week.

Pollard said that "time checks" or "due bills," which technically were not negotiable, frequently were issued to men who wanted quick cash. Local firms, especially the bars, readily accepted them at discounts as high as 30 percent for holding them until they were due. This amounted to big dollars for some saloon keepers. The practice was used most frequently by contractors who were undercapitalized and were not paid until after the log drive was complete, even though the men were released in April.

Meager as the above wages seem, most of the men interviewed did not think that it was too little for that time. Many men sent most of their money home, others were able to make regular investments, and "there were always a few who blew it as soon as they received it."[9]

Social Life in the Lumber Camps

The evening meal was usually over by 6:30 P.M., which allowed the men some free time until "lights out" at 9:00 or 9:30. Nearly every former lumberjack remarked that there was always need to do some patching of mitts or trousers. Patches were a trademark of a lumberjack's clothes. Henrickson stated that well-patched pants could be up to an inch thick. Ettestad recalled that one spring Art Flohrs discarded his well-patched pants in the woods. When he returned the next fall, he picked them up to wear. A few men who could write and had relatives in this country wrote letters. Some time was spent drying clothes and getting ready for the next day. Occasionally men exchanged giving haircuts, but that usually was a Sunday project.

Some camps forbade card playing, such as penny-ante poker, smear, seven-up, or rummy, while others allowed it but regulated attempts at gambling. Costley, who traveled in more lumbering areas than any of the others interviewed, said that gambling was "strictly forbidden in 99.5 percent of the camps." Checkers and cribbage were allowed, and the stakes were never greater than a plug of chewing tobacco.

Reading was very limited, for few books were available, and the only newspapers and magazines were used copies from nearby communities. Conversation, the big pastime, generally was carried on in a subdued manner. It consisted of stories about personal experiences, with an occasional effort to see who could weave the biggest tale.

Most of the men made a trip to the commissary at least once an evening to purchase sewing material, clothes, toilet items, pencils, writing tablets, smoking needs, or candy. Pollard noted that it was "absolutely essential that there was always a supply of snuff on hand and that it was properly priced." The Camp 29 account book for one year indicates that 60,284 tins of snuff were sold in contrast to 247,900 packs of cigarettes, 197,760 candy bars, and 52,600 tins of smoking tobacco, of which Prince Albert was the leading brand, with 20,220 tins. Gloves, socks, insoles, and rubbers were the leading clothing items, in order of sales. Commissary sales for ILC from September 1, 1925, to May 1, 1926, totaled $42,640.20, with a margin of $14,582.06 over the cost of goods. Most items were priced at less than $0.15, and the highest-priced item was caulked driving shoes at $9.50 a pair.

Music in the bunkhouse came from harmonicas, violins, accordions, and even a tambourine. Washboards and washtubs might be used to round out the camp orchestra. Music was nearly always restricted to Saturday evening and Sunday afternoon. If the musicians were good enough, stag or squaw dances were held in which the follow partner was designated by a flour-sack apron or a white handkerchief tied around an arm. Costley said of those square dances, "Believe me, those fellows could tamarack. . . . Professional square dancers today are just amateurs alongside a lumberjack with caulk shoes on."

Liquor was strictly forbidden in the camps, but clandestine activity persisted. Pollard said that it was the camp clerk's duty to keep track of kitchen items that might provide the crew with alcohol. Lemon extract and vanilla extract were two favorites. One cook, who used raisins to make liquor, was fired after being caught the third time. Another cook was always under the influence, but it was not until a bottle fell out of the roller towel used by the kitchen crew that the source was found. Oehler related an experience in a VRL camp where a "snaky" logger danced a jig on top of a woodpile, stark naked. He was not dangerous but caused a large audience to assemble. After slivers were removed, he was sent to the company hospital.

Neither Ettestad nor Henrickson recalled that any of the camps where they worked had booze runners or women. Pollard, who saw the overall picture, felt that during Prohibition booze runners were one of the biggest problems within ILC camps. Oehler pointed out that because smuggled Canadian liquor was so expensive, it was profitable for local farmers to make corn whiskey. This was a deep brown liquid with small brown particles floating in it. The rumor was that Peerless tobacco had been added to give it the deep brown color and more kick. In any case, it was harsh and powerful. "The first couple of gulps were hair-raising, but after that it became fairly easy to take."

Moonshine usually entered camp in half-gallon glass jars from nearby towns or farms. It was occasionally brought in by newcomers to the camp. The companies wanted to prevent the use of liquor, but they realized that this was nearly impossible to enforce unless the foreman was very strong. Strict prohibition was apparently a reality in only a few camps of either VRL or ILC. At least one foreman, Lon Dailey, of Camp 53 near Northome, died after drinking a mixture of formaldehyde and wood alcohol, but foul play was suspected.

Webster, from Camp 87, wrote to Twomey in September 1922, stating that four or five of his men were "stewed from Saturday until they quit camp on Thursday." The camp was short 40 men at the time. He continued, "The moonshiners are getting worse around here and something will have to be done pretty quick." Webster advocated different investigators, because the previous ones had tipped off the moonshiners as to when the raid was scheduled.

The moonshiner problem was so bad that the Association asked federal authorities to intervene because moonshiners in the vicinity of the camps outnumbered the men working. F. L. Bussman, of ILC, informed all camp clerks and foremen that many camps were having trouble. Twomey contacted the St. Louis County sheriff's department. He then explained that if John Larson and Charles Peterson (the two farmers suspected of making the most moonshine) were caught, "it would save a great deal of trouble for the companies [*sic*] operation in that district."

At Camp 99 the foreman was replaced because he could not maintain discipline; the checker and the clerk were replaced because of drinking. On December 30, 1922, the buildings were not completed, and the camp lacked a full complement of men. Farmers had brought in moonshine, and the camp quickly became disorganized. Gust Holmstrom investigated and reported, "Not a stick of timber cut yet half of the winter gone. This does not look very encouraging."

On January 13, 1923, the sheriff's raid led to the arrest of two farmers and the confiscation of their still. Camps 87 and 99 continued to be a headache the rest of the season, for moonshine entered on a regular basis even though the worst producers were caught. Webster wrote that moonshine kept the crew thinned out, which hurt efficiency. He was worried that it would hold up the spring drive. On March 3, his complement of men was exactly two-thirds of what it should have been. When Camp 99 needed a watchman, Holmstrom reminded headquarters, "This is a bad place for moonshine and we must have a man who will stay sober."

Peddlers often asked permission to enter camps, but prior to the 1920s, ILC rules strictly forbade such activity. After that some tailors and even jewelry peddlers were allowed into camp but had to pay ILC a percentage of their sales. At least one tailor was able to work in a camp by bribing two cooks with suits.[10]

Conflicts with Settlers

A constant tug of war existed between the lumber camps and the adjacent homesteaders. Some conflicts were based on misunderstanding, others were caused by accident due to carelessness of camp employees, some occurred because ILC took liberties when it should have been more considerate, and others happened because many settlers looked upon the company as a big, wealthy institution, which was popular to attack, in hopes of gaining a concession as an appeasement.

C. H. Woodford, in charge of camps, wrote to George Enger, a settler near Camp 99, who held a hog that had strayed from the camp. Enger claimed that the hog had done $10 in damages. A camp employee, who was sent to retrieve the hog, learned that no damage had been done but that Enger had spent three or four hours trying to drive it from his premises and wanted ILC to pay for his time. Woodford declined the request because ILC employees always returned settlers' animals without charge. He warned Enger that ILC would not be responsible for the feed if Enger insisted on holding the hog. Six letters were written before the hog was returned.

Cutting timber on someone else's land and selling it was a practice carried on by roving individuals and would-be homesteaders as soon as a market for timber was generated. The sale of timber to Canadian firms before any U.S. companies were established in the region was the first of such affairs. The files are filled with letters about individuals, usually identified, who cut and sold timber from ILC or government land on which ILC had secured stumpage rights. On April 2, 1923, Twomey wrote to Martin Brothers, in Duluth, to stop payment on timber sold by Ross Walley, of Wirt, who had entered ILC land and removed the timber. Twomey advised that a cruiser would estimate the loss, and ILC would submit a bill. A second letter indicated that about four acres totaling 60 cords of spruce had been removed by Walley, "who is an old hand at this game." Fortunately for ILC, Walley had not received payment for the timber he had removed and sold.

On March 26, 1923, O. C. Everling, of Big Falls, wrote to Twomey advising that Everling had loaned his car to Arthur Kimbell, foreman of Camp 68: "They froze and bursted [*sic*] the radiator, broke the carburetor and tore the curtains and broke the top. I cannot get any satisfaction from him. . . . Gust Bromson and Walter Dickson are the men that run [*sic*] the car." The local garage wanted $30 to repair the car, and Kimbell told Everling that he was leaving ILC. This made Everling nervous about getting a settlement.

On March 27, Twomey replied: "We regret the circumstances in regard to the use of your Ford car. We will make the necessary repairs or adjust this matter with you. The writer expects to be in Big Falls within a short time and will be glad to have you take this matter up with him."

Joe Smith telephoned that 33,000 posts belonging to ILC had floated to his property a short distance from Craig. He informed Bussman that in the past Twomey had always provided Smith with employment in such cases. Smith was currently unemployed, and Bussman wrote, "He intimates that we should either pay him something for the use of his land or give him some kind of employment." Smith received a job, which is what he wanted.

Simon Palm, a farmer/logger from Loman, wrote to ILC in March 1923, advising that the company was building a dam on the Black River, which would cause considerable damage to his property and inconvenience him in many ways. Arthur Metcalf, also from Loman, telephoned to complain that the new dam was 2 feet 8 inches higher and would cause flooding. What was the company going to do about it?

Twomey replied: "It is difficult to anticipate the length of time during the summer we will be required to hold a head of water. . . ." He offered Palm $125 a year for each year the dam was used and said that ILC men would not be allowed to walk in Palm's planted fields.

Whenever possible, ILC refrained from employing settlers, because conflicts invariably resulted. For example, Elmer A. Peterson, Camp 53 clerk, reported that L. Penry, a local farmer, took two blankets home and said he was going to wash them. He did not bring them back. "This weekend he took more blankets, a hack saw, 12 blades, one new brace, a few bits, a new wood chisel, and a new screw driver." Penry told Peterson that he needed the tools to work on the Loman line. Penry previously had packed a box of boiler tools and wanted Peterson to send them to him. Peterson asked Twomey how to handle the matter. He closed, "I would rather have him pay for them than me."

One of the best known and most widespread conflicts between ILC and the settlers came in the late 1920s when 10 camps were opened in southern Koochiching County east of Northome. One individual securing right-of-way leases for the forest railroad from landowners "over promised the land owners by suggesting that ILC would haul their freight free, etc." When ILC ignored their complaints, homesteaders blew up a couple of crossings. This necessitated putting up shacks and keeping guards near the crossings. Fortunately, ILC was harvesting on state lands and obtained a court order requiring the homesteaders to stop their activities against the railroad.

Henry Anderson, town clerk, wrote for the supervisors of Plum Creek and Wildwood townships, near Northome, requesting that the rail crossings and the telephone lines be repaired. About two weeks later Twomey replied that he had investigated and found that the ILC lineman had been keeping the farmer lines repaired all year, even going out of his way a number of times to fix downed lines. He closed, "Would be very glad to have you call our attention to anything we may do in the future to make everything satisfactory." The settlers assumed that ILC needed the telephone lines and would keep them repaired.

These and other conflicts probably were inevitable. It was not until many settlers failed and left the area or were removed via the resettlement program that such conflicts in the wilderness ceased to be part of the daily routine.[11]

ENDNOTES FOR CHAPTER II

1. Ryan I, pp. 3, 24, 26, II, p. 36; Agnes M. Larson, *History of the White Pine Industry in Minnesota* (Minneapolis: University of Minnesota Press, 1949), p. 193, hereafter Larson; interview of Oliver Knox and Mary Knox Johnson, Crane Lake, Minn., July 26, 1976, hereafter Knox interview. Mr. Knox was born in 1884 and came to the area in 1903. *Hist. of Kooch. Co.*, p. 10; Nute, pp. 92, 93, 94, 96; *The Journal*, October 30, 1913; *The Mandonian*, September 1946, p. 15; *Econ. Dev.*, p. 17; ILC file; Pollard interview; Mary Lou Pearson interview of Lester Pollard, June 25, 1976, hereafter Pollard-Pearson interview.

2. ILC file; Bussman file; Camp Account Books, ILC file, KCHS; Pollard interview; *The Rainy Lake Chronicle*, March 24, 1974; letter from C. H. Woodford to camp clerks, September 7, 1923, ILC file; interview of Joseph Miller, International Falls, August 20, 1976, hereafter Miller interview; interview of Alex Gerber, Orr, Minn., July 21, 1976, hereafter Gerber interview; interview of John Ettestad, International Falls, August 4, 1989, hereafter Ettestad interview; interview of Elmer Henrickson, International Falls, August 4, 1989, hereafter Henrickson interview; "Instructions to Clerks in Logging Camps, Season of 1917–18," issued by ILC, hereafter "Instructions, 1917-18"; Ryan II, pp. 24, 25,

37; Pollard interview; C. M. Oehler, *Time in the Timber* (St. Paul: Forest Products History Foundation and the Minnesota Historical Society, 1948), pp. 8–11, hereafter Oehler; Knox interview; Larson, p. 177; letters in the Telephones file, KCHS, hereafter Phones.

3. *The Press*, September 22, November 3, December 8, 1910; *The Journal*, January 23, 30, October 30, 1913, September 16, 1915, February 7, 1918; *The Baudette Region*, October 21, 1915; *The Northome Record*, February 4, 25, 1921; Scott Erickson interview; ILC file; Bussman file; Pollard interview; Gerber interview; Northern Logging Congress file, KCHS; Minnesota Logging Association file, KCHS, hereafter Minn. Logging Assn. file; Costley interview; interviews of Hilford Johnson, International Falls, June 2, August 10, 1976, hereafter H. Johnson interview; Echo Lake Timber Company file, KCHS; Oehler, pp. 15, 16, 41; Ettestad interview; Henrickson interview; interview of Andrew Koski, International Falls, August 12, 1976, hereafter Koski interview; interview of Clarence and Joseph Mannausau, International Falls, July 21, 1976, and May 5, 1987, hereafter Mannausau interview; interview of Harold Barber, Littlefork, Minn., July 24, 1989, hereafter Barber interview; *The Rainy Lake Chronicle*, March 17, 1974; Ryan I, p. 3.

4. Gerber interview; Ryan I, pp. 4–5, 12–14; Ryan II, pp. 21–22; Pollard interview; Lester Pollard, "Logging and Forest History Development in Koochiching County," KCHS, hereafter Pollard, "Development"; Gust Holmstrom letters, ILC file, KCHS, hereafter Holmstrom file; Twomey letters, ILC file, KCHS; Camp Account Books, ILC file; *The Northome Record*, December 12, 1919; interview of Carl Dahlberg, Marcell, Minn., July 7, 1989, hereafter Dahlberg interview; Ettestad interview; Henrickson interview; T*he Koochiching Chronicle*, Vol. VI, No. 2, February 1980, hereafter *Kooch. Chron.*

5. Miller interview; Gerber interview; Ryan I, pp. 3, 15, 16, 42; Larson, pp. 193–197; Ettestad interview; Henrickson interview; Oehler, pp. 22, 37–38; ILC camp correspondence file, KCHS; Dahlberg interview; Bruce C. Harding interview of Leonard Costley, International Falls, August 3, 1957, hereafter Costley interview. Costley started working in the woods in 1903 at age 16 and continued woods work until 1937, when he entered the paper mill. Pollard interview; Pollard, "Development"; Knox interview; *The Rainy Lake Chronicle*, March 17, 1974.

6. Oehler, pp. 19, 23; Dahlberg interview; M & O Logging Camp Data file, KCHS, hereafter M & O Logging file; ILC file; Nute, p. 97; *The Journal*, April 20, 1935, May 6, 1937; Pollard interview; Pollard, "Development."

7. Miller interview; Gerber interview; Nute, p. 95; Larson, p. 195; Costley interview; Pollard, "Development"; Pollard interview; Pollard-Pearson interview; Dahlberg interview; Ryan I, pp. 3, 24, 26; Ryan II, pp. 37–38; Koski interview; Knox interview; Oehler, p. 21; *Newsletter*, Vol. VI, No. 3, March 1980; Holmstrom file; ILC file; Ettestad interview; Henrickson interview; *The Northome Record*, October 21, 1921.

8. Miller interview; Ettestad interview; Henrickson interview; Gerber interview; Knox interview; Costley interview; Ryan I, p. 11; *The Journal*, January 11, March 8, December 6, 1923, May 29, 1924; Pollard interview; Oehler, p. 11; Health file, ILC, KCHS; Labor file, ILC, KCHS; *The Northome Record*, February 4, 1916, December 27, 1918, February 27, 1920, February 18, 1921; "Instructions, 1917–18," KCHS.

9. *The Journal*, October 21, 1915, November 25, 1920, November 10, 1921; *The Baudette Region*, January 25, 1917; Oehler, p. 16; Scott Erickson interview; Mannausau interview; *The Northome Record*, November 12, 1920; Minn. Logging

Assn. file; Labor file, ILC; Bussman file; ILC file; Camp Account Books, ILC; Gerber interview; M & O Logging file; Holmstrom file; Ettestad interview; Henrickson interview; Plummer diary; Pollard interview; Pollard, "Development"; Costley interview.

10. Ettestad interview; Henrickson interview; Gerber interview; *The Northome Record*, July 9, December 24, 1920, January 7, 1921; Oehler, pp. 44–45; M & O Logging file; Ryan II, pp. 36, 38; Pollard interview; Pollard, "Development"; Bussman file; Northern Logging Congress file; Larson, pp. 198–199; Costley interview; Oehler, p. 26; "Instructions, 1917–18; letter from T. Welsh to S. W. Backus, December 27, 1923, ILC file.

11. Correspondence regarding trespass claims, ILC file; correspondence regarding conflicts with settlers, Bussman file; Pollard interview.

CHAPTER III

The Word in the Wilderness

Cⅼᴇʀɢʏ, especially of the Catholic faith, first traveled through the northern border country with *voyageurs* in the mid-seventeenth century. Their activity was limited because the *voyageurs* primarily were interested in furs, and the Hudson's Bay Company, which had been granted millions of acres in what is now Minnesota, North Dakota, Manitoba, and Saskatchewan, did little to foster religious activity. That changed in 1818, when the Catholics established a mission at Pembina, and in 1820, when the Hudson's Bay Company sent a Protestant chaplain there. Attempts at evangelizing the area from Lake Superior to Lake of the Woods were minimal because it contained few Indians, even fewer hunters and trappers, and no settlements and was very difficult to traverse. Except for the work of Catholic missionaries in Fort Frances and north, it was not until ca. 1887–1890 that a Reverend Johnston, an Episcopalian, worked south of the border, traveling as far west as Roseau.

A Man with a Mission

In 1902 a religious leader appeared who had a lasting impact and became a legend to people in Koochiching, Lake of the Woods, and western St. Louis counties. Near the end of his career, Everett Lesher, director of home missions, wrote a series of 10 articles about him and early Congregational activity. In an article entitled "A Prophet in the Wilderness," he wrote: "No one in all the Rainy River Valley is so well known, and none so much loved as this veteran missionary of the cross. For many years this man of God lived far away from his brother ministers faithfully preaching the word and, like Paul, also laboring with his own hands to make ends meet."

Thomas W. Howard was born in Polk County, Iowa, in 1856.

66

At age 12 he attended a meeting of a traveling missionary with his brother Mac, who planned to enter the ministry. Thomas had his mind set on becoming a medical doctor. However, when Mac died, he decided to become a minister.

He taught school in Iowa and in New York before entering the seminary in New York, where he was ordained in 1883. The following year he married Florence Eaton, whom he had known in Des Moines but who was teaching in Massachusetts. The couple served four congregations in the east and one in Iowa. They had four children—Penn, Earl, Florence, and Elizabeth. Elizabeth was sickly, and Mrs. Howard had contracted tuberculosis, so the family moved to Trinidad, Colorado, for health reasons. Florence Eaton Howard died December 9, 1896, leaving Howard to continue his work and to care for the young family.

In July 1898, Howard married Susan Culver, a teacher, who was active in one of his early congregations. They lived in Antlers, Colorado, where he served five preaching stations in an area 20 miles wide and 65 miles long, while the new Mrs. Howard raised her adopted family and was active in mission work. Howard wanted a more challenging mission field, one where he could support his family by living off the land. On May 25, 1899, they set out for Eugene, Oregon. Susan Howard, her mother, Florence (age 7), and Elizabeth (age 5) traveled by train, while Howard, with sons Penn (age 12) and Earl (age 9), left Antlers with six horses, a buggy, and a covered wagon. They arrived at Eugene on August 12, 1899. On December 7, John Thomas Howard was born.

Howard was disappointed with his new mission, because the frontier there had been closed to homesteading. When the opportunity arose the following year, he happily accepted a call to a mission congregation in Des Moines, Iowa. However, he was quick to learn that city mission work was not for him. On a business trip to St. Paul in the fall of 1902, he made a chance comment to Mr. Anderson, a banker, while cashing a check. Anderson was active in Congregational mission work and directed him to the Rev. Dr. George R. Merrill, superintendent of the Minnesota Congregational Missionary Society. Merrill's group was searching for someone to do home mission work in Rainy River country, especially near the Falls. Some land west of the village recently had been removed from the Indian reservation and was opened for settlement.

The 46-year-old Howard is reputed to have told Merrill, "I

want to go where the work is hard. Send me where no one else is willing to go." He spent October 1902 scouting the area and testing the climate. He learned that no religious work had been done outside of the Falls as far west as Baudette.

Howard had two goals in mind—to find a mission field with no roads or railroads, and to file on a homestead that would support his work and his family and provide a retirement income. He located a homestead about 50 miles west of the Falls on the south shore of the Rainy River. His homestead was called Howard's Landing until 1906, when it was renamed Birchdale.

After he had located his homestead, he spent the rest of the month "partly in a logging camp and partly doing missionary prospecting and preaching on Sundays." Outside of the lumber camp, the only inhabitants he found were those who had secured concessions from the government for logging operations and lived in small settlements along the rivers. The homesteaders included a few families, many single men, and "not a few unmarried women," whose major goal was to take the timber and then leave. Camp followers were numerous. Some were attracted by the prospect of free land with timber, others wanted to speculate in timber land, and a few adventurous ones had no particular goal.

It was clear to Howard that this was just the place he was looking for. Merrill was pleased with Howard's report, but told him that the Missionary Society could give him only a little financial support. That did not deter Howard, who expected to support himself from the sale of timber and produce raised on the cleared land.

In March 1903, Howard and 13-year-old Earl packed the household goods and supplies and left for the north country. The move was relatively easy, because the Canadian Northern Railroad (CN), which paralleled the Rainy River, had been completed from Winnipeg to the Fort in 1901. They left the train at Stratton, Ontario, about four miles northwest of the homestead, and hauled their goods across the still frozen Rainy. Howard and Earl cleared land, prepared a garden, and improved the log cabin, which a previous homesteader had erected. After paying his moving expenses, Howard had $4 left, which meant that he must sell timber to pay for moving the family from Iowa.

Worship services were held the first Sunday Howard was at the homestead, but not as he initially had planned. Two bachelors had consented to have services in either of their cabins, so Howard advertised the event. In the meantime, the bachelors "got cold feet," locked the cabins, and left. When Howard and a few parishioners arrived and found that they were locked out, they went to the partially completed one-room Howard cabin filled with unpacked furniture, boxes, and barrels. In the following weeks father and son continued clearing land, tending garden, and working on the cabin, but Howard never missed holding Sunday services or contacting prospective churchgoers.

On Elizabeth's eighth birthday, May 1, 1903, Susan Howard arrived with Penn, Florence, Elizabeth, and John, age four. The family of seven lived in the one-room cabin with one small window and a bark-covered roof that leaked like a sieve. Mrs. Howard later recalled, "Dreary were those first, cold May days, in the dark and crowded cabin. If I had had enough money to have gotten out of there, I would have done so at once." However, she had no choice but to make the family comfortable, for Howard started on his circuit at once. Fortunately, the burden was made easier "because game was plentiful, fish were plentiful and friendly Indians kept them well supplied." Log drives and occasional steamboats plying between the Fort and Lake of the Woods provided some entertainment.

Howard was popular with the Indians immediately. A 70-year-old Chippewa, Wishigin, came to him for many things. One cold morning he rapped on the cabin door to tell Howard that old Mrs. Sears was out of wood and in danger of freezing. The two men returned to the Sears cabin, where they sawed wood and started a fire. Mrs. Sears was well-to-do, but stingy. She did not want to hire Indians to cut wood, so she hid her saws. Later, Howard received a check for the mission from her and a box of clothes for Wishigin.

While Howard was on the circuit, Mrs. Howard improved the house and became acquainted with people in the neighborhood. Soon Sunday school was held in their cabin. This was the best way to get people interested in church and in public school, which ranked high with both of the Howards. The Sunday school soon outgrew the Howard home, and interest in public school increased, so a log building was erected in the summer of 1904 to serve both purposes.

On March 15, 1905, eight charter members organized the Congregational church, with services held in the schoolhouse. Because there was no official name for the community, it was designated as the church in Townships 159 and 160, Range 27,

Itasca County. In 1905 the interior was sealed to prevent snow from drifting through the cracks onto the pupils' seats.

While his home base was Howard's most active congregation, he also established mission stations at Indus, Border, and Loman during the winter of 1904–05. For the next 20 years he held services continuously at Birchdale, Indus, and Border. Although he preferred working in the wilderness, at the same time he was required to give a good deal of attention to the Falls. Its 600 inhabitants could not be overlooked.

Ann Fraser, a Catholic, at age 94 recalled that in 1905 at a service in the Falls led by Howard, the worshippers used hymnals from Methodist, Baptist, Presbyterian, Catholic, and Lutheran denominations while meeting in the newly erected Episcopal church. She said that it was so cold that the people squeezed their chairs around the stove, except the organist, Mrs. A. R. Wilson, and Howard, who stayed at their positions.

Denominational differences often were overlooked on the frontier, and people worshipped in union. Howard held services regularly near a concentration of French Catholics, which was referred to locally as "French Town." A Catholic family became interested in a series of winter meetings and attended regularly, but suddenly they stopped coming. After a few weeks Howard met the man and asked if someone had been sick, because they were not at the meetings. The Catholic gentleman replied, "Oh, no, Riverend! Ye see there's a law of our church that forbids us goin' to places of amusement durin' Lent. So we ain't bin comin'. But we'll come agin after Easter."

In 1904 Howard started preaching at Baudette on a regular basis and continued there for six years. The village consisted of a boarding house, a hotel, two stores, five saloons, three houses of ill fame, and a few family homes.

The Baptists had been in Baudette first but did not have much success. In the fall of 1904 the Baptist minister turned over what good will he had generated to Howard and left the area. Howard built on that foundation and in 1905 organized a formal congregation with regular worship and Sunday school. The schoolhouse was used until 1907, when a $700 church building was erected. Baudette became the western hub of Howard's mission field.

Within his first two years in the area, Howard established several preaching stations in the territory from the Falls to Warroad, a distance of 110 miles. This was all done on foot or by canoe until 1906, when he finally was able to afford a horse—

Charley. He rode horseback or used a sleigh, depending on the season, but many times when conditions were bad he walked or used his canoe. He slept in trappers' shacks, in Indian camps, or in the open.

In 1906, after being released from the responsibility of working at the Falls, Howard was able to spend more time in the woods and in the farm country west of the Rainy. There are no records to the effect, but his daughter Elizabeth recalled at the time of her father's death that he had established several congregations in the Black River area, where no towns ever existed. This area, parallel to the Rainy about 12 miles directly south of Birchdale, was known for its muskeg swamp and thick black spruce. It had a heavy influx of settlers late in the first decade of the 1900s.

Susan Howard often accompanied her husband, walking along the indistinct trails from one isolated cabin to the next. On one trip to the Black River region she recalled walking through about two miles of muskeg swamp, which meant wading in water most of the time. However, she knew what to expect and wore rubber boots. On this trip her boots became stuck, and she had to pull her feet out and then retrieve the boots. She did not catch a cold, even though her ankle-length skirt was wet to the waist.

Returning from another trip to the Black River just prior to Christmas, they left early Monday morning on a trail through the woods to Birchdale. After walking a short distance, they mistakenly took a deer path but did not realize it until much later. Howard reckoned that if they walked straight north they would hit the Rainy, so, even though they no longer had a path, he was not overly concerned. Because it was only 12 miles from the Black River to Birchdale, they had not brought any food. About mid-afternoon it began to storm, and snow obliterated the solid hummocks of unfrozen muskeg, making walking extremely difficult. Howard could hear his wife groan with each step she took. Night was coming and the storm had not abated.

They were lost, and Mrs. Howard suggested that he ought to practice what he preached and pray for help. Even before they had finished their prayers they heard the train whistle as it pulled into Emo on the Canadian side. They walked toward the sound and soon saw lights. After crossing the frozen Rainy, they spent the night at a hotel in Emo and walked home the following day.

After Howard had built a fairly solid base in Baudette, he felt that it was time to reach communities being established to the north and west. It was easier traveling to settlements along the

Rainy, so the trip to Baudette was almost a "breather" for him. The area west of Baudette along the CN was still unchurched but also was easy to reach. Between October 1907 and April 1908, he held regular services in Pitt, Graceton, and Cedar Spur. In April 1908, he organized his first church west of Baudette with 11 charter members, who came from 5 different denominations—not one of them a Congregationalist. Soon all three communities had organized churches.

In some respects the period from about 1908 to 1910 was a low point for Howard, but at least one good came out of those years. In 1909 Samuel Plummer, who attended Howard's services often and frequently invited him to stay at the Plummer house while on his travels, directed neighbors in building a new parsonage. Howard gave Plummer a .22 rifle for designing the house and overseeing its erection. Plummer's diary indicated that he felt he had been overpaid for his efforts. It was of this period that Elizabeth Howard wrote, "His heart outran his footsteps as he followed along the trails, roads, and rivers, on foot, horseback, boat, or horse and cutter with the snow swirling about and the thermometer hanging 30 to 40 below. . . . No place was too remote if there were people who would come to the services."

Howard wrote:

> I felt like a boy on the burning deck whence all but him had fled. There was so much to do and only myself to do it. It seemed that the Rainy River valley was isolated from the rest of the world. That no one cared for us—that we were in a forgotten country. Oh! how I longed to get out and tell the people of our need. The field was too important to be neglected and I was too busy with my work. It seemed that I could not be spared to get away.

Mrs. Howard said of those early years: "Many a time, when my husband came home from those long tramps so tired that he could hardly move I just broke down and cried and I determined that he must have help. He was working himself to death and the people in the churches in southern Minnesota must hear and know about the need of our country."

According to Ann Adams Hage, archivist for the Congregational church, the major reason for the indifference of church leaders was that they assumed that the topography from St. Cloud north was similar to that of southern Minnesota. The first recorded trip made by any Congregational leaders to the Rainy area was in 1907, when Dr. Merrill preached for the dedication of the new church at Baudette. But coming there from Winnipeg via the only railroad to the region and returning without seeing the primitive woods settlements did not give a true picture of conditions.

Two years after his statement about being on a burning deck, Howard reached a low point relative to feeling rejected when he attended the state Congregational Association's annual meeting at Crookston in the fall of 1910. He was disturbed and dismayed at the total lack of interest toward his mission field. Gathering his thoughts about the convention while returning to Baudette via the CN, he recollected, "No one at this Association seemed to take any interest in the work in the Rainy River valley, not even to make any inquiries concerning it."

A short time later, as the train neared Warroad, Howard learned of a vast forest fire in the area that had moved eastward for two days. It had already passed through Williams, only 17 miles west of Baudette. The train stopped constantly to pick up people fleeing the fire. At Baudette he found smoked-filled skies, a stifling atmosphere, and refugees pouring into town. A train following Howard's was filled with women and children with their cats and dogs. He immediately became involved in helping the victims who had lost everything and took them to his church, which served as relief headquarters.

By evening a fierce gale blew from the west, the sky was filled with fire, and it was expected to be in Baudette soon. Howard went to a saloon crowded with men drinking, "as though in perfect ignorance of the dreadful peril that threatened." He sounded the warning, and those in the saloon swelled the streets already filled with people rushing to the depot. Many carried litters with people who had typhoid. Those whom the train could not accommodate headed for the river.

Howard learned that a deacon from his church and one of his little girls were sick with typhoid. He found them just leaving their house—the father carrying the sick child, the mother carrying a baby. He grabbed the other child, and they headed for the Rainy. Baudette was already on fire, with flames leaping 100 feet into the air, and soon the Spooner mills were ablaze. In a short time only one house was left standing. This became a hospital as soon as the fire had passed, and 54-year-old Howard, suffering from physical strain and exhaustion, was confined there for several days. When he was released, he held services in a Red Cross relief tent.

After seeing the suffering, Howard decided that he must go to churches in Duluth, the Twin Cities, and Northfield to tell of the need. He collected $1,800 from those congregations and obtained a $1,000 grant from the Church Building Society. The members at Baudette raised $500 toward a new church. Exactly one year after the church built in 1907 had burned, a new structure was dedicated.

The fire made people aware of the northern isolated areas, but after the initial publicity, things settled back to normal, and Howard found himself alone once again. The Howards attended the annual State Association meeting at Northfield in October 1912. By then the Falls had 3,500 people, Baudette, 1,000, and Spooner, 700. Howard was the only English-speaking missionary in the entire Rainy district, with the exception of the Falls.

Superintendent Merrill seemed to be the only one who realized Howard's plight. When Howard was informed that his appeal for help before the gathering was restricted to five minutes, Howard was dumbfounded and replied that if he were to write a history of the United States, he would want more than one sheet of paper. He declined to speak and instead asked for an appearance before the Board of Directors, where he poured out his heart, pleading for three men at once—one for Baudette and Spooner, another for the Falls, and a third in the country. He sensed that for the first time some board members were made aware of the Rainy River field.

Board chair and Carleton College president Dr. D. J. Cowling and Carleton professor Fred B. Hill were sent to the area. They found the Falls businessmen indifferent and received no encouragement from the other clergy. They reported, "Church life had made little impression on the city as yet. The church buildings were all dilapidated shacks . . . evidently religious services and life were more or less on the same level." But results of the visit soon became apparent as clergymen were sent to the Falls and Baudette/Spooner, and three men were added to the missionary force. By 1915 there were five English-speaking missionaries besides the two men in the towns.

In 1913 a new $4,000 church was erected at Birchdale and another for $800 at Cedar Spur. On August 13 and 14, 1913, all five Congregational churches of the Rainy River region, which comprised an area from Lake Vermilion west to Kittson County and south to Red Lake, met at the new consolidated schoolhouse in Birchdale to form the Rainy River Association, with Howard presiding. Howard preached at the cornerstone laying of the church, Florence Howard sang a solo, and 10 people joined the congregation.

After 1913, with other missionaries in the area, Howard concentrated on the small, outlying informal congregations where he had preached over the years. A church was organized in 1914 at Border, which at that time had a store, a post office, and a schoolhouse. At Frontier, the Sunday school became so active that people wanted to erect a church building, but Howard warned that they were a disorganized group of many denominations—not one of them a Congregationalist. It did not take them long to agree to follow Howard, and 24 people became charter members at the meeting.

Howard continued to preach in at least four churches every week, which meant that his Birchdale congregation often had services during the week or that someone else filled the pulpit. He was known for his good sermons and usually attracted sizeable crowds, but on at least one occasion that was not true. In May 1917, *The Baudette Region* quoted him as he addressed a sparsely attended service in that village: "Enough people do not appreciate their opportunities and should turn out better and help to pay the rent." Howard was not alone in his feelings as the following indicates. Headlines in *The Baudette Region* in March 1917 read, "Salvation Army in town to Reclaim Sinners." The article continued that an old-time revival would be held and concluded, "There is no question that there is plenty of raw material in Baudette for a Salvation Army campaign."

In September 1917, when the Rainy River Association met at Border, there was a substantial increase in churches and in membership. What is probably a first for northern Minnesota occurred on August 30, 1917, when Florence Howard, home from her teaching position in Montana, took her father's place in the pulpit and reportedly did "fairly well."

In December 1917, the 61-year-old preacher met his match "when he was knocked down and trampled by a colt which he was endeavoring to catch for a neighbor." Although his condition was not dangerous, he was confined to his bed and recovery was slow because of his age.

Susan Howard died in 1920 and was buried at Birchdale, but the preacher continued his work. In August 1921, he became lost in the woods and spent the night with the Plummers—his final visit with them after 16 years in the area.

Everett Lesher described home missions as:

> A daring enterprise, demanding resourcefulness of character. It is no place for the anemic. The men and women who subdue the wilderness and make the desert blossom . . . are red blooded in soul as well as in body. Discomfort and privation do not terrify them. . . . The history of the Rainy River Association is largely the history of such a man, Rev. Thomas W. Howard.

The Baudette Region of October 5, 1924, reported that Rev. T. W. Howard, "a real pioneer in religious work along the border," had resigned to work in a mission school in Pleasant Hill, Tennessee. His replacement was expected to serve only the Loman, Indus, Bannock, and Laurel congregations, plus a consolidated school two miles from Loman, "and as many places along the Black River as he can attend to." Howard had organized 13 congregations and 20 Sunday schools and mission stations, and he had taken part financially and manually in constructing 9 church buildings. In 1919 he expressed his feelings, "We are grateful that we have been enabled to make so good a beginning, . . . but we realize that it is but a beginning . . . ," to which Lesher added, "Things are moving in the north woods. Northern Minnesota . . . is in the making. Development has just got started. . . . Forward is the watchword. . . . Northern Minnesota is not yet made morally and religiously. . . . The land is not yet possessed."

Howard wanted to go to the mountains of Tennessee to reach the poor people there. He told his superiors, "I do not feel I want to be put on the shelf for a while yet, and I hope I can carry on a while longer."

Howard died in 1930 while climbing a mountain in Arizona looking for former parishioners from northern Minnesota who needed his attention. As his daughter Elizabeth said in the eulogy, "He had a message of God's love . . . which was like fire in his bones and would not permit him to keep silent."[1]

Sodom in the Wilderness

Rev. M. C. A. Mueller, the Missouri Synod pastor at the Falls, 1912 to 1914, said bluntly, "International Falls was a Sodom." Judging from the struggle all the churches at the Falls had, probably most of the clergy felt the same way, for founding religious organizations there was a very slow process and was exceedingly hard on the ministers. The Catholics had the least difficulty becoming established because of their stronger national organization and the fact that they relied on celibate clergy. Frontier communities had a reputation for being crowded, ungodly, and unlawful, and stories about the Falls probably equaled or surpassed any others.

Records are vague as to which religious workers arrived in the Falls first, but it appears that the Catholics had that distinction. However, the Baptists and then the Episcopalians were the first to organize and to have their own buildings for worship. Howard, the cross bearer for the Congregationalists, did not make his first missionary calls in the Falls until early 1904, even though he had visited there in 1902. An early comment in Congregational archives—probably from Howard—stated that International Falls was "an immoral, rum-cursed gambler's paradise and a rendezvous for men coming out of the woods."

Sometime during 1904 to 1906, Howard preached on the parable of "The Foolish Rich Man." A lumberjack named Mike had heard the sermon, and as he walked by a saloon the proprietor asked what he had been doing. Mike replied that he had attended Howard's service. The proprietor bet Mike $20 that he could not relate the text. Mike repeated Howard's sermon and won the bet. He then entered the saloon and bought everyone drinks with the saloon keeper's money.

After two years the mission superintendent felt justified in sending Rev. W. R. McClane to take charge in the Falls, enabling Howard to concentrate his work in the wilderness. Fresh out of the seminary, McClane found the Falls to be a "real border town where lumberjacks were prominent, saloons and houses of prostitution held sway, and evil was rife on every hand." His congregation consisted mainly of single men. During his first summer there he organized a church, where he was ordained and installed. A shack, purchased for use as a parsonage, also served as a reading room with the best reading material available in the Falls. On Sunday the bed and the tables were removed, and camp chairs were provided for worship.

McClane's duties included being pastor, Sunday school superintendent, teacher, janitor, beggar for funds, sort of "YMCA secretary," librarian, and housekeeper. His efforts were received with little enthusiasm by the townspeople, who were more interested in liquor, gambling, and prostitution. One day McClane reported to the police that a lumberjack lay dead drunk in the street. The police did nothing, but the next day the boss saloon keeper as much as ordered McClane out of town. This motivated McClane to work even harder. However, after 18 months he could see little result from his hard work, so he resigned.

Rev. A. E. Merick replaced McClane, but because of ill health stayed less than a year. The Mission Society was unable to find people suited to the task of coping with the Falls inhabitants, and Howard was too busy with his congregations to return, so for a time no services were held there.

In March 1913, Rev. E. L. Heermance, assistant superintendent of the Society, was appointed to fill the position at the Falls. He found only one member of the original congregation, but he was "fired up" to improve the town's morality and make up for lost time.

The town site company had given the Congregationalists two lots on which to build, but they were deemed unsatisfactory. Heermance had no church organization or constituency; nevertheless, he set out to raise $15,000 to purchase lots in a choice location and to build and equip a structure. His efforts were impressive enough so that the Mission Building Society made a generous grant to help him reach his goal. The church was dedicated in September 1913. At the time of dedication, the new Bethlehem congregation had no members and no local contributors. Heermance targeted the 2,000 non-church-going residents as his mission field.

Soon after the dedication, Heermance organized a congregation of 12 members. He formed a Boy Scout troop and organized gymnasium classes, open to all who came. Then he established an outdoor lighted skating rink, again free to all. He became very active in the formation of cooperative creameries and a potato warehouse association. He was a county leader in the dry campaign of 1916, which resulted in a victory for the drys. He did what he could to help Howard in pushing mission work between the Falls and Baudette at a time when no other denomination was active in the area.

Probably the first resident Catholic layman was Joseph Baker, nephew of Alexander Baker, the first settler of the Falls. Joseph Baker came to the area in 1882. He and his wife were part of the original core of Catholics, who were joined by the Mertens, the Donahues, the Alexanders, and the Stones. These loyal people either attended services at the Fort or held them in the J. J. Stone Hotel or in the Stone home. Ann Stone Fraser recalled those regular meetings, always under the leadership of a priest from the Fort. Her father paid to have some rock from the dam moved to the future building site before they had any idea when a church would be built. By July 1905, the group was too large for the Stone home, so they met in the schoolhouse until February 1906, when their 26- x 36-foot church was ready. A larger church had been planned, but bids were too high, so a smaller, $1,040 structure was erected. Ann Stone Fraser, whose marriage in 1907 was the first in the parish, said, "It was such a little wooden building, but soon a 25-foot addition in the rear and a new front entrance were built."

On June 20, 1909, the congregation became a full-fledged parish under the leadership of Rev. Patrick J. Killeen, with 31 families consisting of 121 souls—by far the largest congregation in the Falls. It was not long before an Altar Society, the Knights of Columbus, and the St. Thomas League were formed. The Benedictine Sisters started St. James Hospital in 1912. By early 1913 it closed for lack of funds. However, in April 1913, construction started on a new church using the blue granite stone that J. J. Stone had paid to have hauled there in 1906. The new 600-seat-capacity, $25,000 building project was greatly aided by a $10,000 gift from Thomas Feigh, of Duluth—a friend of the Stones who wanted the building named St. Thomas.

The question of a parochial school plagued the congregation annually. In 1926 the 285 member families felt strong enough to build a school. In September 1927, the $70,000 building opened with 200 students. Even though the debt proved a substantial burden for the congregation, the student body increased steadily. The auxiliary organizations proved to be a real strength for the parish. As early as 1910 the ladies groups had raised $857.96 at a single event—more than the annual budget of some other churches.

In 1906 a group of Lutheran Church–Missouri Synod pastors from the Red River Valley visited the Falls and concluded that the field was ready for another church. The following year Rev. W. Hitzemann, a traveling missionary, was put in charge of the "northern section" between the Falls and Port Arthur. Hitzemann did his work well. In 1908 Rev. G. Winter was sent to cover the 110-mile-long parish, which already contained 12 preaching stations that could all be reached on foot or by canoe.

By 1910 the seven-member ladies aid had raised $187.20, which encouraged the mission board to recommend building a chapel. In June 1913, under Rev. M. C. A. Mueller's leadership, the structure was dedicated. Even though Mueller was able to attract an average attendance of 20 in the year that followed, he was not comfortable in the combined Falls/Fort parish and was replaced by Rev. Ad Trost. Trost also was assigned the congregations at Ray, Gemmell, Baudette, Graceton, Cedar Spur, Hay Creek, Warroad, and two groups at Sleeman, Ontario.

At the Falls/Fort parish, Trost held German services in the morning and English services in the evening on the first Sunday of the month and reversed the language on the third Sunday. The German services had an attendance of from 4 to 18, but when Trost switched to English for all the morning services, no one attended the evening German services, so they were dropped. On the other two Sundays of each month he held services at Warroad and at Sleeman.

Trost continued to serve the other seven stations during the week, but soon three of them were dropped due to "the hopeless situation of affairs, or the plain indifference of the people." When some members of the Warroad congregation left the area and others joined the Presbyterian church, the remaining few joined the nearby Hay Creek congregation.

Trost wrote that the 3,000 people in the Falls were served by 13 saloons "and the connected evils. It was an open town, and few took problems of life and eternity seriously. . . . It is true, there were eight churches there. But not one was self-supporting. . . . It was hard even to induce members from our own circles to attend services. This spiritual evil must be contagious."

Trost personally called on people who attended once or twice, then stopped coming or did not respond. He attempted to form a Sunday school, but only five pupils showed up. Fortunately, the ladies aid continued to function and by April 1917 had paid the final $175 debt on the church lots. When Trost tried to improve stewardship, he was only able to convince the members that they should pay at least $0.50 a month.

By 1913 the combined Falls/Fort congregation had grown to 44 confirmed members, 10 ladies aid members, and 3 in the first confirmation class. Considering that all 12 stations had only 54 names on the communion list when Trost first arrived, this progress was not bad. He received $500 a year and was allowed to live in the chapel; however, he had to eat at the hotels owned by two members. His salary was paid by the mission board, except when the collection exceeded expenses; then the mission board reduced its paycheck. He left November 15, 1917.

Dam and power houses at the end of construction, Fall 1910. Fort Frances in background; Emperor Hotel three-story building on right. (Koochiching County Historical Society, hereafter KCHS)

Fourth Avenue, the Falls, looking north toward M & O office. Building on left with tower is city hall and fire station. (KCHS)

Falls volunteer fire department banquet, April 11, 1911. (KCHS)

The Falls, 1911, from the paper mill. L-R: Rainy River, sawmill and storage yard, roundhouse (four white stacks), M & O office, Forest Inn (two dark buildings). Second schoolhouse at extreme R. (KCHS)

Licensed ferry at dock, Summer 1912. Fare varied from $0.05 to $0.15 between the Falls and the Fort. (KCHS)

ILC sawmill at opening, 1910. Fort Frances in background. Note yard paved with plank. Smokestack is 210 feet. Storage yard on right. (KCHS)

The Falls, 1911, looking west. L-R: depot, courthouse, school, city hall, paper mill, high dive, dock. (Eleanor Bloom)

Holler Confectionery, the Falls, 1915. L-R: Mrs. Holler, Mrs. J. J. Lloyd, Irving Robideau, Mary Keyes. (KCHS)

August 1, 1912, opening of international train, auto, and pedestrian bridge, looking toward the Fort. (KCHS)

Chicago Cafe, 1914-1946. Open 24 hours a day 7 days a week; seating capacity 148. Mr. and Mrs. James Serdaris, after remodeling, 1936. (KCHS)

City bus, 1921, Oscar Neveau, driver. Round trip between the Falls and Ranier, $0.50. (KCHS)

Living quarters, South International Falls, 1937. (KCHS)

River storage yard east of the Falls, 1910-1937. Logs were unloaded from cars and stored on shore until they were floated to the mill. (KCHS)

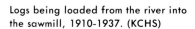

Logs being loaded from the river into the sawmill, 1910-1937. (KCHS)

Steam-powered crane unloading pulpwood into storage yards. Cranes of this type were used from the 1920s to the early 1950s. (KCHS)

ILC pulpwood storage yard, Winter 1935-36; sawmill in background. (KCHS)

Large logs being sawed into dimension lumber, ILC sawmill, 1927. (KCHS)

ILC sorting chain, where each man took a specific dimension board and loaded it onto his wagon for storage, 1936. (KCHS)

Loading green and untreated railroad ties in storage yard, 1912, for shipment to treating yards. Ties had to be 9 inches across and weighed from 100 to 150 pounds. (KCHS)

Stacking rig and crew at storage yard. Horses were used from 1910 to 1934, when replaced by Caterpillars. (KCHS)

Caterpillar "20" pulling lumber buggy with 3-inch planking from the sorting chain to the storage yard, 1936. (KCHS)

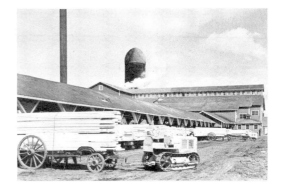

Unloading pulpwood onto conveyor to the paper mill, 1936. (KCHS)

The 67-foot high dive with 28,600 cords of wood pulp in pile, March 1937, its final year. (KCHS)

Slasher, which cuts 8-foot lengths of pulpwood into 4-foot lengths, 1937. (KCHS)

Conveyor taking pulpwood from the slashers to the chippers within the paper mill, 1936. Men are sorting species for different uses. (KCHS)

Hand feeding the grinder, where the pulpwood is ground into wood pulp, 1940. (KCHS)

Pulp vat with beater, where the pulp "stock" is mixed with dyes and chemicals for different blends of paper. Beating time for 20,000 to 40,000 pounds of stock was from one to five hours in 1936. (KCHS)

Pulp grinding room prior to start up, October 1910. Jack Weiner, in hat, superintendent of the installation crew. (KCHS)

Paper machine room at initial test, June 1910. These four machines were the fastest and made this the world's largest-capacity mill. Jules Jager (white shirt and bow tie), engineer of installation. (KCHS)

A 1914 view of the Falls. L-R: M & O office, paper mill, 36,000 cords of pulpwood, the Falls power plant, customs office at the bridge, hot pond with pulp, dam, the Fort power plant, and mill. (KCHS)

Storage and paper production room, 1936. Cutters vary from 72 to 144 inches. Overhead crane takes rolls to basement. (KCHS)

Packing room, 1936. Tables have different types of paper. Train loading doors in rear. (KCHS)

Enclosed loading dock for 12 rail cars, M & O, 1936. (KCHS)

Knut Braaten, homesteader and trapper, Faunce, 1920. (Marian Peterson)

L-R: Grace, Ellen, Nellie, Samuel, Marion Plummer, with bear, at Loman, June 12, 1923. The bear's hind quarters were sold to Camp 6 for $8.00. (Plummer)

Winter's meat supply. L-R: Earl Kleppe, Mrs. Pieper, Mrs. J. Frahm, J. Frahm, Miss R. Frahm, L. Wilson, R. Johnson, A. Dickhous, of Ray, November 18, 1936. (KCHS)

Hand-powered stump puller called "knuckle buster," in Beltrami County, 1910. (N.W. Minn. Hist. Center, Haakon Bjornaas Collection, hereafter NWMHC)

Steam-powered well driller, ca. 1915. (Lake of Woods Co. Hist. Soc., hereafter LOWCHS)

Mowing hay at Caribou, 1915. (Minn. Hist. Soc., hereafter, MHS)

Ox team, Ole Wold Farm, Ericsburg-Ray, ca. 1910. Load of hay in deep snow. (KCHS)

Cutting oats, J. O. Gowan farm, Baudette, August 7, 1911. The first crop after the big fire. (KCHS)

Clark and Kelley threshing rig, Williams, ca. 1912. Probably clover for seed. (Elizabeth Rippey Clark)

Stacking hay, Erick Sundin farm, Ray, 1916. (KCHS)

Cocking clover for curing, Littlefork area, 1920s. Littlefork was a prime hay seed producing area for several years. (KCHS)

Digging potatoes, Erick Sundin farm, 1919. Art Enzman in World War I uniform driving horses. Four people could dig and pick about one-half acre a day. (KCHS)

Sam Plummer in 1925 GMC truck with a load of cabbage and Jim with Kinkade garden tractor, September 1926. (Plummer)

Marion Plummer on 20-inch brush breaker plow and Jim on tractor, August 1937. Stumps were blown off in 1936. Field seeded to oats-alfalfa in 1938. (Plummer)

Cream separator in kitchen of farm home near Northome, September 1937. (Chester Fritz Library)

Preparing pancakes in farm home, Northome, September 1937. (Chester Fritz Library)

Erecting a home for O. O. Bjornaas, Rapid River, 1910. (NWMHC)

Homestead in Rapid River area, 1911. (NWMHC)

Harold Johnson homestead, Faunce, ca. 1922. The frozen carcasses are of animals Johnson had shot or trapped for their pelts. (Marian Peterson)

Joe H. Rogers homestead, Ericsburg, after additions. A family of 14 lived here from 1914 to 1928. Black mark on roof is from a 1908 fire. (Rogers)

Tosten Johnson homestead on Nett River, southwest of Littlefork, ca. 1915. (KCHS)

Mike Daley home south of Littlefork, 1920. (KCHS)

Sam Plummer home, Loman, 1928. Built in 1907, with bath in lean added in 1923. Water from roof eaves ran into tank in the lean. (Plummer)

Marion and Emily Plummer plowing their yard for seeding, Indus Township. House built in 1934 by Marion and Jim Plummer. (KCHS)

Meat storage shed at lumber camp south of Rainy Lake. Meat stored on second floor to keep it safe from animals. (KCHS)

Bull cook at Camp 188, Galvin Line, 1934-35. The bull cook chopped wood and carried water, wood, and ashes, but did no cooking. (KCHS)

Farm home near Northome, September 1937. Boards are for catching water. (Chester Fritz Library)

Jack Danielson (L), Big Fork, saw filer and helper, Camp 188 on Galvin Line, Winter 1935-36. (KCHS)

Logging camp blacksmith. Typical M & O facility until the motorized era. (KCHS)

Headquarters Camp 185 for Nett Lake operations, 1936-37. Wanigan, where men bought clothing, tobacco, candy, etc. Seated L-R, Neil McDonald, a senior camp clerk, and Charles Hess, camp auditor. Standing, Frank L. Bussman, superintendent of M & O logging operations. (KCHS)

Slashing being burned, Camp 187, Nett Lake, May 1937, to reduce fire danger and to speed regrowth. (KCHS)

Sunday morning bath and laundry, VRL Camp 90, Ash River Falls, February 1921. Underclothes and socks boiling in water in lard pail while lumberjack washes his feet. (KCHS)

Putting caulks in boots, Hans Pomersberger camp, Littlefork. A good pair of boots cost $12 to $15 in the 1930s. (KCHS)

A spacious bunkhouse built of logs, indicating a permanent facility. Note iron beds, lanterns, writing table, deacon's seat, and barrel stove. (KCHS)

Bunkhouse at M & O Camp 6, Loman. Hoist camp with 60 men, July 1937, the last year of operation. (KCHS)

Lumberjacks enjoying a drink in a bunkhouse of an independent contractor's camp, Effie, September 1937. (Chester Fritz Library)

George Bartz, cook at Camp 188, Galvin Line, Winter 1935-36, making pastries. (KCHS)

Mess hall, with kitchen in background, at Camp 6, July 1937. This was a camp of only 60 men. (KCHS)

Cookee sounding mess call, Nett Lake area, 1920s. (KCHS)

Noon lunch in the woods, Little Fork River area, 1920s. (KCHS)

Mess hall, Camp 188, 1934-35 season. Seated 192, with a kitchen crew of a cook, six cookees, and a bull cook. (KCHS)

Supper time at a contractor's camp, Effie, September 1937. (Chester Fritz Library)

August Gilchrist lumber camp, Ray, 1915. (KCHS)

M & O Camp 186 on Nett Lake Indian Reservation, December 1936. (KCHS)

Lumberjacks with 6-foot crosscut saw, Camp 186, February 1937. After a tree this size was notched, it could be sawed in five minutes. (KCHS)

Arthur Metcalf sawmill, Loman, 1915. L-R: Tom Taylor, Metcalf, ——, ——, ——. (KCHS)

Henry Keyes camp on Rainy Lake, 1924. Oswald Johnson and Ed Zimmerman were teamsters. (Leona Zimmerman)

Albert Palm's portable sawmill. L-R: Ellen, Grace, Jim, and Marion Plummer, Palm, Sam Plummer. Loman, June 1927. (Plummer)

Harold Bromley, farmer/logger, Loman, ca. 1926. (Plummer)

Shacker John Swagger making stew in his one-room shack. Koochiching County, ca. 1920s. (KCHS)

Shacker and home in tall timber, Littlefork area, 1920s. (KCHS)

Klabunde's Bar, the Falls, 1915. (KCHS)

Modern shackers in shack made of Insulite, Loman, February 1938. (KCHS)

Saloon at Craigville, September 1937. (Chester Fritz Library)

Saturday night at a Craigville saloon, September 1937. (Chester Fritz Library)

Poker game at Craigville saloon, September 1937. Electricity furnished by a locally operated generator. (Chester Fritz Library)

Team skidding a log to jammer to be loaded onto a sleigh for haul to rail landing, Camp 186, January 1936. (KCHS)

Pulpwood from harvesting strips waiting to be skidded to collecting point. Estimated yield 12 to 16 cords per acre. (KCHS)

James Plummer with half-cord skidding drag, hauling to highway assembling point, Loman. (Plummer)

August Gilchrist loading crew, Ray, 1915. M & O scaler on left. Ox used to roll the log from the sleigh. (KCHS)

P. A. Erickson, farmer/logger, hauling logs from woods to the rail landing, Ray, 1924. (KCHS)

One-horse drags being unloaded to sleighs by power jammer at woods collecting point for trip to river landing, 1920. (KCHS)

Steamer pulling one water sleigh and eight sleighs of logs in southern Koochiching County, 1910-1920 era. Front skis made steering questionable. (KCHS)

Ed Zimmerman, operator of a converted-to-tracks Fordson, Henry Keyes camp, Black Bay, January 1924. (Leona Zimmerman)

It was not until September 14, 1919, that Rev. H. A. Mayer accepted the call to the Falls. On the day he was installed, 17 people were in church, but only 7 the next Sunday, and for the rest of his first year often only 3 attended. Mayer also served stations as far east as Port Arthur and as far west as Graceton. He was able to make his circuit in 10 days traveling by rail. To enable him to have weekly services in the Falls, he introduced Saturday school, whose surprising growth caused attendance to increase enough so that by 1922 he held services every Sunday. He conducted morning and evening services to accommodate the shift schedule at the mill. Evening services became an effective missionary institution by attracting men off the street.

A Young People's Society was founded, and a monthly bulletin was sent to all homes from which anyone had ever attended church. The growth in membership necessitated hiring a supply pastor to take care of the outlying preaching stations and to help at the Falls. By 1923 the original chapel was used so often that Mayer no longer could live in it, and the congregation spent $5,000 for a new house. The next year a $2,500 addition was put onto the chapel.

During Mayer's last four years at the Falls, the annual congregational budget grew from $98.40 to $843.00. In his six years there he averaged 3.55 sermons a week, 634 people communed, 58 people were confirmed, and he performed 29 marriages, 168 baptisms, and 15 funerals.

Many times in the early years the clergy appealed to city officials to have the Unique [vaudeville] Theater closed during Sunday evening services in an effort to improve church attendance. At other times they petitioned the saloon keepers, asking them to close during either the morning or the evening worship hour to encourage the young men to attend church. No records are available to determine if the pleas were honored, but the churches grew. By 1913 the Catholics, the German Lutherans, and the Congregationalists were building new churches.

By 1914 the Falls boasted having 13 saloons, but it also had 13 churches, including the non-denominational People's Church Society. The members met in the original schoolhouse, which a group of women had purchased and remodeled, without the help of any outside group.

The Norwegian Lutheran Church, later called Zion Lutheran, probably was the last of the mainline churches to be organized. On May 27, 1912, a group of eight families and three individuals met for that purpose. They paid the Methodists $1 per meeting for the privilege of holding services in their church. In 1913 a lot on the corner of Sixth Street and Sixth Avenue was purchased for $1,000. Because the church board had passed a resolution limiting debt to $500, no action was taken. The ladies aid assumed the payments and paid for the lot. Then the ladies agreed to fund the new church, which was completed in January 1916. However, for the next 30 years the church relied on fixtures from other congregations.

During the congregation's first 13 years it had no parsonage. When Rev. Rudolph Evans asked that one be built, he was told by the board that he would have to get a wife first. The race was on. When the new bride arrived January 30, 1926, the paint had barely dried on the new $4,150 house, complete with a full basement.

Evans spent 38 years at Zion, during which time he also served 21 other congregations and for several years served the Civilian Conservation Corps (CCC) camps. The congregations were as far west as Baudette or as near as Littlefork. If the roads to Littlefork were impassable, he walked the 25 miles on the railroad tracks Saturday evening. After Sunday worship and Sunday school, he walked back to the Falls for evening services.

Evans was not one to shirk physical work. On several occasions he was the first to volunteer to work in the woods to obtain fuel. In 1937 he bid $10 for the recently closed ILC sawmill, which was to be dismantled. The bid included clean-up and removal. After all the work was completed, Zion had 60 cords of wood at a cost of $0.58 per cord—about one-tenth the market price.

From those meager beginnings congregations in the Falls continued to struggle and to grow. The 1930s was not an easy decade, but the local economy was sound after the mill was reorganized, and the churches remained to serve.[2]

The Church in the Countryside

The sparse population between the widely spaced settlements of the northern border region limited the ability of missionaries to contact many prospective church people. Gina Finstad Erickson (Mrs. John), who lived on a homestead with her mother and siblings while her father worked in Duluth, said that except for the Catholic church in Buyck, the only religious activity was an occasional visit by a traveling missionary. Gina's mother was "a real church woman and read the Bible whenever she had a break." The family held their own services every Sunday and had daily prayers.

Marian Crabtree Peterson (Mrs. Frank) said that her family, who homesteaded near Faunce, on the western edge of the timber territory, saw no external evidence of religion. Like Mrs. Finstad, Marian's mother was a very devout person, and the family received their religious training from her. After the family moved to Faunce in the late 1920s, the only church activity they experienced was when the "Holy Rollers" came to town one summer and held meetings in the schoolhouse. When the Crabtrees moved to Baudette about 1933, Marian, her sister Lillian, and her father were baptized at the same service.

According to Owen Gorden, who spent his entire life in Big Falls, the Mission church was the only denomination in town that ever had a full-time minister. Gorden was the town justice for many years and operated a hardware store. One day he summoned his wife to the store to serve as a witness as he married a couple standing by the nail counter. Those in the area who attended services regularly generally went to Littlefork after roads were improved.

Joyce Kohlhase, who grew up in Mizpah, said that the town died rapidly after the lumber camp era passed. The active life of that community did not last more than about two decades. The only church he recalled was the Presbyterian, which was attended by all the Protestants, while the Catholics went to Northome, only five miles away.

An in-depth study in the 1930s about the future of the region, headed by O. B. Jesness, of the University of Minnesota, revealed that most churches—whether in the country or in the villages—received 10 to 50 percent of their income from home mission funds. Jesness concluded, "Despite considerable subsidization from outside sources, the religious institutions of the rural areas of the north were inadequate."

Except for Buyck and Faunce, the communities named above were on main roads, but their religious institutions did not thrive. Annie Shelland Williams, first Koochiching County superintendent of schools, lamented the lack of religious opportunity. Specifically, she referred to the southeast corner of Koochiching and adjacent St. Louis and Itasca counties, which she said did not have any religious activity until 1923, when Rev. Julius Fadum walked from Virginia to Silverdale (about 80 miles) to hold services in private homes. When churches were built at Celina,

Bear River, and Silverdale, Fadum, like Howard, did much of the carpenter work. Williams wrote in 1913 that there were only three missionaries in an area two-thirds the size of Massachusetts. Other ministers were present, but they did not care to leave the railroad line. Young people who had lived in that area for 10 years had never attended any social gathering other than rural school.

By 1911, along the Duluth, Winnipeg, and Pacific Railroad (DW & P) for 90 miles from the Fort to Virginia, the only two places that had ever had any religious services were Ericsburg and Ray. Rev. W. L. Sutherland, head of the Minnesota Congregational Missionary Society, was sent to organize Sunday schools in seven locations and preach in the lumber camps. Sutherland said that the villages were only about three years old and were "raw and ragged," with unpainted tarpaper-covered shacks.

In 1913 a missionary on the Cook Circuit stopped at a cabin where 10 children played in the yard and 4 women visited inside. After introducing himself, he asked if they had any Sunday school or preaching service. The lady of the house replied, "No . . . that boy will be nine years old his next birthday and there isn't one of them that know what a church or Sunday school is. They wouldn't know when Sunday comes only for the Saturday night dance. There isn't one of these ten children that has ever been in a church."

In April 1914, Rev. R. W. Downing was put in charge of the Cook Circuit and was joined by Everett Lesher on a trip to Meadow Brook, 15 miles west of Cook, where services had been requested. They left Cook at 3:00 P.M., walking down the muddy road through the "unbroken canyon with walls of green" and crossing rushing torrents and rugged terrain. At sundown they stopped at a cabin for a drink of water and discovered that they still had nine miles to go. It was nearly 11:00 P.M. when they reached Meadow Brook. The lady of the house asked if either man could play her little cabinet organ. When they answered affirmatively, the lady "rang up" all the neighbors on the party line. The two men were requested to sing several hymns and encores before the Friday service was announced.

G. P. Netherly was assigned to be resident preacher in that area in 1916. His first funeral was that of a young Finnish mother, who had lived several miles from town and died leaving a family of little children. It was terribly cold, and the snow was deep, but the husband brought her body to town in a box on a sled with two women sitting on the box. After a long wait to obtain a burial permit, the group continued about a mile out of town toward the cemetery. Netherly and one other person followed the sled carrying the body, the two women, and the husband. They met the gravediggers, who did not want to return to the grave site to help bury the woman. The grave was too short and had to be lengthened below the frost line; even so, the coffin had to be lowered in endwise. Netherly concluded, "Poor dear folks! But this is life and this is death in the north woods."

St. Michael's Catholic parish, of Northome, probably was the second Catholic congregation in the region. In 1905, Northome had 500 people. Father Murphy held services in the hall over the Pine Tree Saloon, later in a feed store, and finally in the Northome Hotel dining room, all the while encouraging the construction of a church. During the first year, bazaars were held, a doll contest was tried, and chances were sold on a donated cut-glass dish, all of which brought in $123. In 1906 a solicitation of townspeople was held. Non-Catholics gave from $3 to $10, while some Catholics gave as much as $25. By 1908 a building was finished, but it was not until 1919 that Father Costious, a native of France and under the Canadian Oblate, was assigned as resident priest to St. Michael's. At that time an addition to the church provided sleeping quarters for Father Costious. As in most other congregations, it was the work of the ladies aid that provided necessary funds. Throughout the 1920s and 1930s, sheep raffles, bazaars, dinners, fancywork sales, Keno games, candy sales, and fishpond events brought in from $13 to $18 per month.

Father Costious also served congregations at Effie, Big Falls, Littlefork, and Cingmars during his 25 years at Northome. The Cingmars worshippers did not have a regular facility until 1932, when they bought the local schoolhouse for $80 on a contract-for-deed. Mass was said twice a month when Costious came to Littlefork. The Cingmars and Littlefork congregations rotated between 8:00 and 10:30 A.M., early enough for him to eat dinner at a parishioner's home before going to Big Falls for afternoon services and then returning to Northome for evening services.

Hilford Johnson, whose family were members of the Nett Lake Lutheran Church, said that the congregation never had a church building but always used the schoolhouse and held confirmation classes at the Johnson home. The minister came out the night before and stayed with the Johnsons. The first pastor was Rev. Thompson. Once in a while Bill Saas, a mission pastor who traveled up and down the M & I, walked to their home for services. On one cold Thanksgiving Day, Saas waded the Little Fork holding his clothes above his head.

In 1928 newly ordained Peter O. Onstad was assigned the home mission parish at Littlefork, which also contained Nett Lake Lutheran, 18 miles southeast, and Sturgeon River Lutheran, 35 miles southwest. He was expected to preach at Cross River, Big Falls, Waukanha, Loman, and Lindford and, from 1935 to 1937, at the CCC camps at Effie and Pine Island. The only church building he had was at Littlefork. All the other services were held in private homes. His salary was $1,400 a year, of which $1,000 was paid by the home mission board. He paid his living and travel expenses. Fortunately, the M & I gave him a pass good anywhere on the Northern Pacific.

During Lent, the pastors exchanged pulpits. Onstad preached at Cass Lake, Bemidji, Walker, Sebeka, Remer, Kelliher, Northome, Blackduck, Mizpah, and the Falls before returning to Littlefork for Sunday services. All were on the railroad line, so travel was not a problem; but that was not the case with his regular preaching stations. Onstad recalled traveling to the Nett Lake congregation early one spring when his car became stuck in a mud hole. He tried to curl up and sleep, but it was too cold. He commented, "Fortunately, I always wore good boots, so I walked seven miles to the nearest settler and spent the night there. The next day he pulled me out. . . . This was during mud vacation that we had each spring for the schools." His most unique method of transportation was used when he preached at the Pine Island CCC camp. He drove his car on a ditch-bank road to the Sturgeon River, where he switched to a handcar, provided by the Twomey-William-White logging railroad, for the remaining 11 miles.

The first three years Onstad stayed with a family. In 1931, when he married Alice Olson, a teacher at Littlefork, the congregation bought an old two-bedroom house and remodeled it for the parsonage. It was very cold and required 25 cords of wood a year for heating and for cooking, but the parishioners joined Onstad in cutting bees to provide the wood.

By 1930 the mission board cut his salary, and by 1935 it was only $800. However, the members were always good about giving the Onstads turkey, beef, or pork or garden produce:

> No one seemed to sense the depression because they did not have anything before the depression. They had subsistence living, raised most of their food, all of their fuel, so I never felt badly for them during the so called hard times. I

had several chances to go elsewhere during those years but we liked it, even though at my three main congregations I never had more than 8 or 10 families that were the real backbone. At Sturgeon River and Nett River if there were 20 people in attendance it was a good crowd, and in Littlefork I felt so happy when I could count 75.

Like Howard, Costious, and Onstad, Rev. S. E. Gregg, who preached from 1912 to 1925 in the area, found that there were always too many miles to cover and no efficient way of doing so. On a September Sunday in 1912, Gregg preached at Meadowbrook School at 9:30 A.M.; Lindford, 1:00 P.M.; Riverdale, 3:00 P.M.; and Loman in the evening. None of these points were closer together than six miles, and all were reached by walking. On his next preaching tour he visited 9 locations and covered 187 miles, of which he walked 106. Two days after arriving home he went to Craigville, where he had Sunday school and services in an ILC section house. The next day he was at a logging camp, with 250 in attendance, and then on to 13 other locations in adjacent Itasca and Beltrami counties for services before returning to Loman. On that trip he covered 184 miles, of which 154 were on foot.

In February 1913, Rev. F. D. White was sent by the Congregational church to serve the congregations at Spooner, Baudette, and Graceton and continue the work started by Howard. That spring he was asked to investigate the needs of people in the Rapid River area, about 25 miles south of Baudette. White and two college students, one of whom was Walter Beach, left Baudette at 6:00 A.M. They drove a team of horses for 8 miles and then took their backpacks to walk the next 17 miles. White's pack contained a comforter, four loaves of rye bread, a pound of butter, a pound of cheese, two pounds of rice, four pounds of bacon, two large onions, sugar, condiments, and pans, but "best of all," a loaf cake his wife had made especially for the trip. The pack weighed 30 pounds.

At the end of the first day they had traveled about 16 miles. They prepared for the night by laying tarpaper on the ground to keep their comforters dry. One student had gone to Carp for supplies and on return was unable to locate the others before dark. He spent the night on a haystack and rejoined his partners on the North Branch of the Rapid River. Here the group built a raft to cross the river and then walked eight miles to a site where they erected a crude shack of poles and tarpaper and picked high bush cranberries, black currants, raspberries, and huckleberries to complement their food supply. White returned to Baudette. Within a few months the two students had located about 300 people, most of them within a few miles of the river. By November they held their first worship services at Carp.

Besides having preaching stations at Dutchie, Fruitland, and Rapid River, Beach also served Cedar Spur, Graceton, Pitt, Williams, and points along the Rapid River, including lumber camps. One of his first services was at Dutchie, 12 miles north of Williams. He had written that he was coming to hold evening services; apparently his letter went astray. When he arrived he found that everything was prepared for a dance, and the crowd was in no mood to cancel it. The people could not go home after the dance and return the next day for church, because they all had too far to walk. A compromise was reached wherein the crowd danced all night and then prepared the hall for worship at 8:00 A.M. Beach was pleased that 16 people stayed for church. He had been invited to stay for the dance but declined and stayed with a family who did not dance. By February 1916, he had formed a congregation of 12 members, which grew to 36 by March 1919.

On another occasion Beach arrived at Williams during a ball game, and everyone was concerned that he would try to stop the game to hold services. He made it known that he was happy to wait until after the game, at which time he had a "good crowd." A congregation of 14 charter members was organized, which grew to 27 by the summer of 1916.

For his services from 1913 through 1917, Beach received no guaranteed income, only what was collected after expenses were paid. He left the Cedar Spur Circuit anxious to attend the seminary.

Local clergy were not the only ones who found it difficult to travel throughout the district. Church officials left Baudette at 9:00 A.M. to visit the Rapid River congregation. The newly built drainage-ditch roads were so muddy that the men had to walk because the horses could pull only the empty buggy. They arrived at the flooded Rapid River one hour before sunset, 15 miles from their starting point. They found a leaky flat-bottom boat, which they used to cross the Rapid. It was 10:00 P.M. before they were able to conduct services, but they had a "full crowd" that stayed until midnight. The next morning they were up at 5:00 A.M. to recross the Rapid, this time on a newly built raft. They spent the entire day returning the 15 miles to Baudette.

A contemporary of White and Beach was Rev. E. E. Thompson,

of the Baudette Methodist Church. In one of his more exciting sermons entitled "Making Insanity Pay, or the Movie Craze," he depicted the influence of moving pictures on the minds of children and adults. However, movies were not a problem for most of those who lived in the wilderness.

Probably the most unique congregation in the region was the Russian Orthodox Church at Bramble, which was organized on May 15, 1932, at the home of William Lucachick. The eight members present agreed that any one who wanted to join should pay $0.25 per month. For that fee, at death, candles were furnished, the grave dug, and a free cemetery lot given. Every member who failed to attend a funeral was fined $2. If any of the three top officials failed to attend a funeral "without any reason whatsoever," they were fined $4. The president of the congregation was empowered to appoint a policeman for their meetings to see that no member smoked, that if a member had any argument of importance it would be heard by the members, and that members did not talk or disturb the meeting. Any member disturbing the meeting was asked to leave and was fined $0.25. If an argument arose between any two members, three members were selected to act as judges to settle the argument. If three judges could not settle the dispute, three more were chosen. When the six judges made their decision, the offender was fined accordingly.

If a non-member was buried by the organization and the church was used, $25 was charged to cover the cost of candles, the use of the church, the Orthodox banner, the cemetery lot, and the labor of the gravediggers. A $5 charge was levied for any baptism or marriage of non-members. Today the Bramble church stands alone [see photo]—another symbol of those who had hopes of a bright future in the wilderness.[3]

The Sky Pilot

Religious activities were a regular part of lumber camp life. Ministers, lay preachers, and gospel teams were always well received. Religious groups from nearby towns came to the camps because they were a good place to evangelize and a good source of revenue. Singing groups were especially popular, and the nearer a camp was to a town, the more visits it received. The mission division of all mainline churches made a special effort to hold evangelistic campaigns in the camps. Lester Pollard recalled that the only women he ever saw in camp were those associated with religious activities.

Leonard Costley was quick to point out that one reason the men were so happy to see the gospel groups and the sky pilots, as the camp missionaries were called, was that they "were like walking newspapers. They could tell you where all the other lumberjacks were, and who was hurt, in the hospital, and who had died."

Rev. Howard was one of the earliest sky pilots in northern Minnesota. In 1903 he started working in camps from Baudette to Lake Kabetogama and spent considerable time in small camps along the Black and Rapid rivers. He enjoyed visiting them because he "always found a hearty welcome and a respectful hearing." Camp foremen were advised that the sky pilot was to receive a place to sleep, meals, transportation, and whatever else he needed. It was one of the few times that camp clerks were permitted to make out checks for men who wanted to contribute but had no cash.

The true sky pilot did most of his work in the remote camps, getting there in any possible manner—by walking or by tote team, the forest railroad, or river boat. Alex Gerber, who spent part of his career as a locomotive engineer, said that he enjoyed having John Sornberger, who covered a large territory from his Duluth base, ride in the cab on his way to the camps.

Rev. H. Test, who lived at Mizpah and worked along the M & I rail line and east and west of Northome, carried a portable organ as he walked from camp to camp. Frank Higgins was thought of as "the greatest of the sky pilots," probably because he was both a fine preacher and a singer. He worked along the M & I and also the Minneapolis and Rainy River (M & RR) line between Deer River and Craigville. Higgins carried song books, Bibles, and pamphlets in his backpack, which was reputed to weigh 75 pounds.

Rev. Channer, of Duluth, usually had someone along to help carry a portable organ. Channer preached for an hour, took an offering, and then visited with the men as long as they were interested. John Ettestad and Elmer Henrickson enjoyed Channer, but preferred Higgins and Alrich Olson, a lay preacher. Hilford Johnson recalled John Hysten, a lay preacher/homesteader, who distributed American Bible Society literature. Hysten often got into arguments with the lumberjacks because he was "very aggressive but not persuasive" and relied too much on using emotions.

One of Howard's most attentive visits came on a Saturday night when he told the men that after his sermon he would read

Ralph Selkirk's novel, *The Black Rock*. After he began reading, some who had not been paying particular attention to his sermon came to listen. He read more on Sunday morning, had a larger crowd for his afternoon sermon, and then finished the book in the evening.

The Northwestern Bible and Missionary Training School, of Minneapolis, and the Moody Bible Institute, of Chicago, regularly sent missionary trainees to work in the camps during their Christmas vacation—a particularly lonesome time for the lumberjacks. The Moody Institute volunteered as many as 20 trainees per vacation period. Letters from ILC usually mentioned that the trainees should use tact when dealing with the men. During the period of IWW activity, they were cautioned not to make any reference about labor.

Reuben C. Larson, who worked for Moody, wrote of his experience: "Wherever I went the men came out of their way to express their appreciation and pleaded with me to come back as they said it was the same story every day out there, and no one seeming to care."

Hungry Mike Sullivan, a Catholic camp foreman, was once asked by a Protestant missionary if Sullivan objected to a Protestant working in his camp. His reply was, "We are all headed for the same landing."

Whether the average lumberjack was concerned about his life beyond the immediate is not for us to determine, but every person interviewed and all accounts researched were positive about the work of the sky pilots. Lumber firms knew that their work produced a wholesome response in the camps and always encouraged them. While the final results of their intangible work cannot be measured, they were universally welcomed by men desperate for relief from their daily toil.[4]

ENDNOTES FOR CHAPTER III

1. Hiram M. Drache, *The Challenge of the Prairie* (Fargo: North Dakota Institute for Regional Studies, 1970), p. 248, hereafter *Challenge*; Hiram M. Drache, *Koochiching* (Danville, Ill.: Interstate Publishers, Inc., 1983), pp. 211–212, 280, hereafter *Koochiching*; Everett Lesher, "Congregational Pioneering in Northern Minnesota: A History of the Rainy River Association," *Congregational Minnesota*, XII, No. 4 (December 1918), pp. 5–9; Everett Lesher, "Congregational Pioneering in Northern Minnesota: Lost in the Muskeg," XII, No. 6 (February 1919), pp. 7–9; Everett Lesher, "Congregational Pioneering in Northern Minnesota: Humor and Tragedy on the Frontier," XII, No. 7 (March 1919), pp. 3–6; Everett Lesher, "Congregational Pioneering in Northern Minnesota: They That Sow in Tears," XII, No. 8 (April 1919), pp. 4–8; May St. Lawrence Smart (Mrs. George), "Rev. T. Howard, Other Sky Pilots Brought the Gospel to First

Settlers," in Community Clipping File, KCHS, hereafter May Smart file; Lake of the Woods County Historical Society, "A Brief History of Lake of the Woods County, Early 1900s: Early Churches and Missionaries" (privately printed), p. 13, hereafter LOW Co. Hist.; Elizabeth Howard tribute to Thomas Howard, May Smart file; conversation with Ann Adams Hage, Minneapolis, October 5, 1989. Mrs. Hage is archivist for the Congregational Church. Everett Lesher, "Congregational Pioneering in Northern Minnesota: The Old Guard," *Congregational Minnesota*, XIII, No. 2 (October 1919), pp. 4–5; *The Baudette Region*, March 8, 29, May 1, 24, June 14, September 6, 9, December 14, 21, 1917, January 22, 1926; Florence Howard Brown, Memorial Letter, May Smart file; Everett Lesher, "Congregational Pioneering in Northern Minnesota: A Prophet in the Wilderness," *Congregational Minnesota*, XIII, No. 2 (October 1919), pp. 5–8; Sylvia Kohlhase, *In the Shadow of the Spruce: Recollections of Homestead Days on the Black River* (International Falls: privately printed, 1974), p. 37, hereafter Kohlhase, *Spruce*; Plummer diary; *The Baudette Region*, September 19, October 5, 1924; Everett Lesher, "Congregational Pioneering in Northern Minnesota: The Harvest," *Congregational Minnesota*, XIII, No. 3 (November 1919), pp. 5–7.

2. *Koochiching*, p. 281; Everett Lesher, "Congregational Pioneering in Northern Minnesota: The Romance Days of the Lumberjack, *Congregational Minnesota*, XII, No. 5 (January 1919), pp. 5–8; Lesher, XII, No. 8, pp. 5–7; Fraser interview; *The Journal*, May 1, 1913, July 16, 1914, July 3, 1924, April 30, 1925, May 14, 1976; "St. Thomas Parish, International Falls," a typed manuscript, no date, KCHS; *The Press*, November 24, December 15, 1910, July 27, August 31, October 5, 1911; H. A. Mayer, "History of St. Paul's Evangelical Lutheran Church, International Falls," a typed manuscript, no date, KCHS; "History of Zion Lutheran Church," no date, KCHS; Tive interview; letter to Rev. Rudolph Evans, October 9, 1924, in possession of his son, Rev. Robert Evans.

3. Interview of Gina Finstad Erickson (Mrs. John), Ranier, Minn., June 3, 1976, hereafter Gina Erickson interview; interview of Marian Crabtree Peterson (Mrs. Frank), Ranier, Minn., May 20, 1989, hereafter Marian Peterson interview; interview of Owen L. Gorden, Big Falls, Minn., July, 24, 1989, hereafter Gorden interview; interview of Joyce Kohlhase, International Falls, August 13, 1976, hereafter Kohlhase interview; Oscar B. Jesness and Reynolds I. Nowell, *A Program for Land Use in Northern Minnesota: A Type Study in Land Utilization* (Minneapolis: University of Minnesota Press, 1935), p. 103, hereafter Jesness; Williams file; Everett Lesher, "Congregational Pioneering in Northern Minnesota: The Cook Circuit," *Congregational Minnesota*, XIII, No. 1 (September 1919), pp. 6–9; Organization and By-laws of the Russian Orthodox Church, Bramble, Minn., May 15, 1932; "History of St. Michael's Catholic Parish, Northome, Minn.," a typed manuscript in KCHS; "The Sacred Heart Chapel in Cingmars," a manuscript typed by Joan Barkovic, KCHS; H. Johnson interview; interview of Rev. Peter E. Onstad, Moorhead, Minn., May 24, 1989, hereafter Onstad interview; Plummer diary; Everett Lesher, "Congregational Pioneering in Northern Minnesota: The Rapid River Mission," *Congregational Minnesota*, XII, No. 10 (June 1919), pp. 2–6; Everett Lesher, "Congregational Pioneering in Northern Minnesota: The Cedar Spur Circuit," XII, No. 9 (May 1919), pp. 4–7; *The Baudette Region*, February 22, 1917.

4. *The Northome Record*, March 19, 1920; *The Journal*, February 15, 1930; Costley interview; Ryan, II, pp. 27-29; H. Johnson interview; Gerber interview; ILC camp file; Ettestad interview; Henrickson interview; Jim Sedlaw correspondence, ILC file; Twomey file, ILC; Pollard interview; Lesher, "Congregational Pioneering in Northern Minnesota: The Romance Days of the Lumberjack," *Congregational Minnesota*, XII, No. 5 (January 1918), pp. 5–6.

CHAPTER IV

Surviving in the Wilderness

PROBABLY NO LEGISLATION by a benevolent government caused as much suffering and heartbreak as the Homestead Act of 1862, and few people who took advantage of that act suffered more than those who came to the north country. Later legislation by state and federal governments only served to compound the problem.

In its natural condition, the land contained a crop of trees that could readily be harvested. The potential profit enticed many people to use homesteading as a pretext for selling the timber and then leaving. Filings at the Duluth, Cass Lake, and Crookston land offices, verified by the book of original entry and newspaper accounts, indicate a virtual flood of settlers to the area. In addition to those who came only to harvest trees, many others left as soon as they realized the hardships involved, often even before the first winter was over. They abandoned their claims, happy to be alive.

Homesteading

In the early 1900s, *The Farmer*, Minnesota's major farm magazine, carried a large number of boomer articles and ads describing the virtues of this last agricultural haven. A 1909 article by a homesteader's wife proclaimed that the region had 7 million acres of swampland which, when drained, would be transformed into the richest farms in the world. The sale of trees would pay for the clearing and often for the land. The writer claimed that the region would lead all others in stock raising and dairy products, because clover grew wild and timothy pasture would handle twice as many animals per acre as less favored localities.

The article advocated draining the land, establishing agricultural schools, and starting 1,000 farms. It was suggested that the only way to reduce the "high cost of living" was to reverse the migration from the country and make the people "producers instead of consumers." The writer recommended "Northern Minnesota as the very best place in which these city people [going back to the land] might settle."

Ironically, the 1913 annual report of D. B. Jewell, the first county extension agent for Koochiching County, stated that he doubted that people could make a living farming even though production did not meet local demands. He continued in an almost prophetic note, "Most settlers work in the woods in the winter." Jewell noted that potatoes should receive special attention because the country was "naturally adapted to them and they did exceptionally well." He suggested that they would be the money crop and boasted about the ability of cows and chickens to thrive, giving the inland farmer a good living.

An early *Journal* article stated that 40 acres with half under plow would comfortably support a family. At that time the 200 farms in Koochiching County included 1,600 acres of crop land and about 1,000 acres of wild hay. An early agri-businessman suggested that "many had been failures elsewhere and had come to the north to start again. So it was a case of lots of poor farmers coming to a marginal farming area at best. These people naturally turned to logging and eventually worked their way out of farming."

A March 1912 *Journal* article reported that A. J. McGuire, superintendent of the Northern Minnesota Experiment Station at Grand Rapids, claimed that potatoes were second only to dairying as a money maker for farmers. He claimed that a profit of $75.00 an acre had been realized from a 250-bushel crop at a sale price of $0.50 a bushel. McGuire was a persistent promoter of local agricultural potential, and his estimates were considerably better than most farmers ever realized.

In 1911 the Crookston land office had 1,203 homestead filings, up from 707 in 1910; Cass Lake had 816, up from 750; and Duluth had 654, up from 596. In addition, the state had sold 156,171 acres of school land at an average price of $6.71 per acre, up from 70,242 acres in 1910 at a price of $6.20. This land was offered at 15 percent down, 4 percent interest, and 40 years to pay.

For those who could not afford the above terms, the so-called Borah Homestead Act made it possible to prove up in three years and permitted being absent from the land five months each year. Only 1/16 of the land had to be cultivated the second year, and

⅛ the third year. That legislation started a flood of land filings, which exceeded 50 or more each week for several years.

According to the extension report for 1928, farming was becoming more stable. Farm buildings no longer were made from old lumber camp buildings, and the supply of saleable timber was nearly depleted. Farming was at a critical point in its development.

The Mannausau brothers said, "It was our impression that the country was going to go to farming. Dairying, clover seed, potato seed, and flax were all good in our area. The grass seed era was our best farming time. It started about 1929 and lasted until 1940."

The 1929 extension report indicated that it was time to overcome the belief that timber products were inexhaustible and concentrate on dairy and livestock enterprises. The agent claimed that he had witnessed a change from a timber area to an area with unlimited potential in agriculture. Clover seed was profitable, and low timber prices caused many farmers to consider dairying to better utilize their labor.

The trend toward agriculture continued in 1930, for many people who worked in the paper and logging industries were unemployed. They realized the need for agriculture, which the agent predicted would result in a stable population and more desirable and profitable employment. When the industrial depression continued into 1931, more mill workers started cultivating small tracts of land. Clover seed was still the best crop for low labor and high return, but livestock was needed to balance income.

Ironically, 1933 was a boom year for northern agriculture. Conditions were dry enough to permit good harvest conditions, the CCC camps provided enlarged markets for vegetable and animal products, and prices improved 40 to 50 percent over the previous year. Forest fires had cleared "many thousands of acres of very fertile soil, opening the way for helping the county to become more self-sufficient in agriculture." New settlers entered the area as more land was cleared, and good yields gave a false impression as to the profitability of the area.

Many farmers from southern Minnesota and Iowa, who were dried out in 1933 and 1934, moved in. One of those who came and succeeded was Melvin Johnson, who sold out near Harmony, Minnesota, took his household goods and $740 in cash, and moved to Forsyth, north of Littlefork. The county agent said that Mr. Johnson was "a particularly aggressive and innovative farmer."

Events of the next 30 years proved the county agent's evaluation of Johnson. He drove a log truck while he sized up the agricultural opportunities and soon purchased some of the better cleared land. By working double shift between the woods and the farm, he expanded his operation to 400 acres with a grade A dairy and with beef, seed potato, clover seed, and tree-farming enterprises. This diversity provided a stable income and a good standard of living for the family. Despite his success, Johnson was active in the resettlement project of the 1930s, because he saw that most homesteaders could not make a living from farming.

Many people were convinced that once the trees were gone, agriculture would prevail and farming would become the dominant occupation in the northern border region. In retrospect, it is difficult to understand why the hope of farming persisted for so long and how much the government misled prospective homesteaders. With the exception of those who came only to harvest the trees and leave, no wholesale abandonment occurred until it was obvious that the massive ditching projects of 1913 to 1919 were a failure. The next out-migration came when homesteaders could not meet the tax obligation that resulted from those ditching projects. The third out-migration took place when homesteaders were removed by the resettlement projects of the 1930s.

Despite the realities, agriculture, or at least the dream of agriculture, was so strong that *The Journal* published a special farmers' newspaper each week until the late 1940s. By that time the dream of the area becoming a great hay and seed potato producing region had faded. After the collapse of dairying, only trees were left.[1]

Clearing the Land

After the trees were removed, the homesteader faced the task of clearing stumps and roots. Mark Abbott recalled that when he started as county extension agent in 1918, most farmers had only a few acres cleared and added about one acre each year. By the time he resigned in 1925, the rate of clearing had increased to about five acres annually for those who were serious about farming.

Many boomer articles made it sound as though the roots and the stumps practically disappeared on their own. One article stated that trees cut off within 2 inches of the ground "will not grow and will soon decay." Seeding clover or timothy and "working it in with a spring tooth harrow" would produce a "fine field of grass." In only five months five acres of plowed land would produce enough for 1 cow, 1 horse, 25 chickens, and 2 hogs, with some hay to spare. Obviously, the writer had neither cleared land nor farmed.

A 1921 extension bulletin recommended that the financial condition of the settler determined what method should be used to remove stumps. The quickest way was to use plenty of dynamite. If funds were short, it was necessary to hand grub first and finish the job with dynamite. A third method used hand-operated stump pullers, known as "back breakers." Horse-powered pullers had some early "enthusiastic supporters," but soon most of them were discarded. Ettestad and Henrickson said that a horse-powered puller could remove about four 18- to 40-inch stumps per day. Normally, there were about 50 such stumps per acre. The final method was to clear out the underbrush, seed the area with clover, and turn cattle in to tramp the seed. As the clover improved, more cattle were turned in as conditions warranted. This kept the underbrush down while the stumps dried out for easier dynamiting. It was stated that this method would yield $10 per acre income the first year after seeding.

Probably not much of the above advice was heeded, but soon after World War I the extension service held land clearing demonstrations, since the state had millions of acres of northern land for sale. It was reputed that 24 state-sponsored demonstrations in 1920 drew a total of 10,000 farmers. The banks cooperated with the extension service, and several carloads of surplus World War I dynamite were distributed. By pool buying through the extension service, substantial price discounts were realized. Martin Pearson said that he purchased dynamite for as little as $8 a hundred pounds. He used 1 to 2 pounds to blow an 8-inch diameter stump.

Plummer started using dynamite in 1912. In one day he used 8.5 pounds on 40 stumps on one-fourth acre. After a day of dynamiting, he often felt ill and assumed that it was from the smoke fumes. By 1914 he had 50 acres cleared and 12 acres plowed. Plummer was a workaholic. Every day that he was not occupied with essential work, he cleared.

In 1915 Plummer contracted to clear 24 acres of burned-over land for Mac Loman for $350. He hired four men, and they averaged about six man days per acre on the job. Plummer paid them a dollar a day and board, so he realized a good return for his management time. Regina Krost, who homesteaded seven miles southwest of Baudette on land that had been well burned by the 1910 fire, boasted that she cleared 12 acres her first year. She cleared only eight acres her second year.

The farmers interviewed averaged from 80 to 174 acres of cleared land in addition to several acres of native hay land. The 1926 extension report indicated that the 4 largest alfalfa growers in the county had 12, 14, 20, and 20 acres, respectively, and the other 39 registered growers had an average of 3.2 acres each.

Low snowfall, a fairly dry summer, many fires, and the lack of opportunity for woods work made 1931 the peak year for acres cleared. At the end of 1931, a total of 22,450 acres were cleared on 925 farms—about 1.1 percent of the land in the county. By 1937, a total of 45,000 acres had been cleared on 1,300 farms.

The extension experiment on 69 farms at Blackduck and 67 farms at Grand Rapids had an average of 140 and 103 stumps per acre, respectively, which required an average of 107 and 133 man hours and 57 and 74 horse hours per acre for stump removal. At $0.30 per man hour and $0.20 per horse hour, using an average of 46 pounds of dynamite at $0.22 a pound, the cost of clearing was $54.99 an acre at Blackduck and $68.93 at Grand Rapids. The obstacle of clearing the land kept many settlers from becoming overly excited about farming.

Sylvia Hafdahl Kohlhase, historian of the Fairland area along the Black River, wrote that when her family arrived in 1902, only three families had settled there. By 1910 there were 47 other homesteads, including 4 single women. In 1920, when her father, Simon Hafdahl, had their land logged off, he decided it was time to relocate on better land more accessible to a school. It was a sad day for the children as the family packed all their possessions in a wagon, tied the cows behind, and waved to the few remaining settlers. In a few years none were left.[2]

Drudgery, Sweat, and Toil

Even though this area was one of the last agricultural frontiers in the contiguous 48 states, with very little farming carried on until after 1910, it is amazing how primitive it was. Slick promotion campaigns by realtors, newspapers, and the government drew unsuspecting would-be farmers to "the last garden of Eden." Probably the best thing that can be said about the challenge is that it was so difficult most of the farmers failed within the first decade.

The first seven settlers along the East Black River arrived

during 1907 and 1908. Others followed, and by 1911 the Wayland school, post office, and store had been erected. Hopes were high in Wayland, because a survey team for railroad builder James J. Hill had traversed the area, and it was rumored that a rail line would be built.

About the time the virgin trees were logged off, the settlers learned that there would be no railroad and lost their desire to cultivate the land. The first to leave were the single men and women, for without the unpaid labor of a family, there was virtually no chance for a farm to survive. This signaled a rapid exodus, and Wayland soon disappeared from the map.

Malkor Finstad wisely retained his job in Duluth while his wife and children fulfilled the requirements on their homestead, about seven miles from Buyck. Daughter Gina Finstad Erickson recalled that they had a cow, a horse, a buggy, a cutter, and only enough hand tools to maintain a garden and put up wild hay. She said:

> Using homemade ropes slung over our backs we carried hay ¾ of a mile to our barn. The two animals kept us busy all winter carrying water and caring for them because they seldom got out of the barn. Besides those chores, getting wood, milking, and making butter, plus doing the normal housework, mother found enough duties to keep us busy most of the time.

Sylvia Hafdahl Kohlhase disliked haying. Her father scythed hay in every available meadow. The children followed, raking and shocking it. The family's horse, Paddy, hauled the hay on a stoneboat with a rack to the yard, where Mrs. Hafdahl made the "best stacks in the area." In a few years the abandoned cabins of former neighbors were used to store hay. The girls had the "miserable job of stomping the hay down" to get all the hay possible under cover. "Dust, stickers, and grasshoppers" were her memories of haying.

The Sam Plummer family, near Loman, was one of the earliest pioneer farm families in the north country. Plummer expected his family to do their share as soon as they were old enough. Jim Plummer, the eldest of four children, in his late eighties, and Grace Plummer Austin, the youngest, in her mid-seventies, related with some bitterness the seemingly endless tasks they performed to keep the farm going. Jim was large for his age, and by the time he was 11, he did tasks expected of any mature hired man. His father assumed that Jim was there to work.

The Plummers had one of the finer homes in the area. They were considerably better off than most of their neighbors and lived on a main artery of travel with easier access to supplies and markets. Plummer worked hard and seldom complained. He sensed the potential offered by the mill opening for both logging and farming and, much to his wife's consternation, quit teaching in 1910 to become a full-time farmer and logger. Because the farm was only a few miles from the Loman railroad, Plummer marketed produce in the Falls and took advantage of the expanded demand for pulpwood. From 1910 on he always hired at least one man to work in the woods in the winter and on the farm in the summer. As the family grew, they were fully involved in market-gardening and with farm chores.

Because most farms in the area were too small, it was difficult to justify machinery; so primitive tools, not very different from those of the early nineteenth century, were used. For over two weeks in August 1911, Plummer cradled his few acres of oats or wheat. One "very hot" day he cradled "about" 50 dozen bundles of grain, and shocked them after supper. At the same time the cows kept getting out, so he had to hunt for them and then fix the fences. One day the entire family wasted time pulling Pat, their only horse, out of a sink hole.

On November 29, 1911, Ernie Helmer arrived with his two-man machine, powered by an 8-HP engine and pulled by horses, to thresh Plummer's grain. To rush things along, Helmer and his men helped a neighbor thresh 33 bushels of wheat in 3 hours in the forenoon. In the afternoon they threshed 58 bushels of oats and 12 bushels of wheat for Plummer. The next day they threshed another 58 bushels of oats—a total yield of 116 bushels from 4 acres of oats—and 12 bushels of wheat from three-fourths of an acre. Threshing Plummer's crop required 16 people hours, and the machine bill was $7.45.

After 1915 Plummer had his grain cut by neighbors using a binder, but he cradled some every year until 1919, when he purchased a new 6-foot binder for $205. After that he cradled only to open fields, when the ground was too soft for the binder or he was short of horses. It was not until 1923 that he switched to shock threshing from the field. The new machine required a crew of six, but threshed 326 bushels in six hours. By 1929 a crew of four threshed 1,063 bushels of oats, barley, and wheat in 16 hours.

The Ericksons, at Forsyth, and the Rogerses, near Ericsburg, moved to their areas in 1910 and 1912 respectively. They did not have access to a threshing machine, so they fed the oats to their chickens and cows in bundles. They flailed wheat during the winter as it was needed for flour. In 1913 the Ericksons bought a binder and gained access to a thresher. The Rogerses did not secure a binder and a thresher until 1915.

Plummer had only one horse for skidding logs in the winter and often exchanged with a neighbor, who also owned a horse. He purchased a 5-foot hay mower in 1912 for $35, but he still scythed his hay, unless he could borrow a horse or an ox. In 1914 he purchased a yoke of oxen for $200, but they walked so slowly that the mower did not work well, and at times he cut only one acre a day. In addition, mosquitoes and blue dog flies were so bad that the oxen often refused to work.

Late in 1914 his oxen became lame, and he had to finish with a scythe. For three weeks he and Nellie worked until dark every day putting up hay. Plummer was particularly irked with the oxen because he had received a black fly bite on one finger and it affected his scythe grip for two weeks. They finished haying August 24, but after a hard frost it was necessary to cradle the wheat. While Plummer cradled, Nellie and 13-year-old Jim used a new $18 breaking plow to open more land. His diary entry read: "Nellie and Jim can do a fine job of plowing alone."

By 1912 Plummer produced several acres of potatoes in addition to large quantities of other vegetables for the market. He started the plants and/or seeds each year in a hothouse to avoid frost and be ready for the early fall market. To mark the field for planting, a furrow was opened by pulling the front end of a farm sled over the soft ground. The seed was hand dropped into the opening and covered by pulling a harrow over the field. It required about 2½ days per acre, cutting and seeding only. After one of those days Plummer wrote: "We got very tired."

Two entries in the Plummer diary shed light on how well family members were paid for their labor. In 1915, Jim, age 14, received $40 for his work up to September 20. In November 1930, Marion, 19, and Jim, 29, each received $160 for their wages up to November 1. The old adage that family farms survived on the unpaid wages of the women and children was proved true many times over.

With the advent of the tractor, a settler had to decide whether to become a full-time farmer and expand or whether to stick to logging and part-time farming. The three Mannausau sons wanted to farm, so they purchased a Fordson with a two-bottom plow in 1924. It was not fast enough for them, so in 1929 they secured a model "L" Case with a four-bottom plow for $1,800. To help pay for it they custom plowed for $2.50 to $4.00 an acre at the rate of 10 acres a day.

Melvin Johnson purchased a good used tractor, a plow, a mower, and a side delivery rake in 1936 for about $600. He said that the tractor was the "difference between success and failure, because I could get work done on time." He did custom clover mowing for $1 an acre and plowing for $2 to $3 an acre.

The greatest difficulty with most farms in the area was that they were too small to justify the investment in a tractor. The lack of power machinery put them at a competitive disadvantage with mechanized farms in better farming regions.[3]

Too Little to Live On

Most farms in the area produced only a subsistence living. Plummer's total production in 1911 was wheat, 88 bushels; oats, 232; barley, 31; flax, 7.5; alsike clover, 7; potatoes, 100; rutabagas, 100; and several bushels each of beets, carrots, onions, and other vegetables. His inventory consisted of 28 hens, 2 roosters, 1 horse, 1 cow, 1 yearling heifer, and a 7-month-old heifer, with ample hay and straw to compensate for the small amount of grain available for feed. At that time his farm was 320 acres, with 30 acres cleared, plus a good house (the Plummers' second), a poor barn, 85 cords of pulpwood sawed, and 16,000 feet of logs ready for sale.

Despite Plummer's very best efforts, Nellie's fears materialized on January 23, 1933, when he received notice that the Minnesota Rural Credit Administration would foreclose on their farm. By voluntarily signing the deed over to the Rural Credit, he was allowed to buy the original homestead back at any time he could repay the loan.

Minnesota Rural Credit permitted farmers to rent the farms they had lost, but in Plummer's case, Nellie did not feel that it was worth the effort and refused to allow him to operate their homestead. It was difficult for Plummer to ask the Mannausaus to rent it. Steve Mannausau and his three sons agreed to rent the farm on a two-thirds–one-third share basis. That fall Plummer collected $8.44 an acre rent from a 12.5-bushel-per-acre flax crop, which was as well as he had ever netted, except for the few acres of vegetables.

The original Plummer homestead eventually was sold for $20 an acre, and the Plummers purchased a neighboring farm. In 1940 they had 8 cows, 3 heifers, 70 hens, 5 roosters, 2 horses, and 5 cats. They were denied credit to buy a model "H" IHC tractor, but the old tractors were good enough to seed 16.5 acres of grain and 10.8 acres of potatoes, plus about 40 acres of hay. Yields were normal that fall, and prices had improved, but the big gain in income came from the increased wages in off-the-farm opportunities. Plummer's farm, like most, was still "too little to live on."

Ettestad and Henrickson said that their families always "made their tax money" and refused to borrow, which forced them to "live without." They consumed the milk and eggs that were not sold to pay bills.

Despite dismal production figures, county farm numbers increased from 944 in 1920 to about 1,400 in 1936, when the extension report indicated that the 40,319 acres of crop land in the county had yielded 14 bushels of wheat, 165 bushels of oats, 49 bushels of barley, 91 bushels of potatoes, and 17 tons of hay per farm. This came from an average of 28 acres of crop land per farm, far from enough to support a family under the very best conditions. Even the top 31 farmers who belonged to the registered sire circuit had only 5.2 cows per herd.

Apparently only Riverdale Farm and G. A. Murray's farm were large enough to be considered full-scale commercial farms. Both of these farms were subsidized by outside sources, which gave them a definite advantage over the undercapitalized homesteads. Murray farmed at Drayton, North Dakota, and in 1914 opened at least 1,280 acres west of Birchdale as a cattle, horse, and/or sheep ranch to supplement his home farm. He purchased cattle, horses, or sheep from the western range and brought them to Birchdale, where drought was less likely. But in the 1930s, the drought forced him to reduce the number of livestock at Birchdale. This brought financial problems, and on May 8, 1933, he solicited Plummer for a loan from the Federal Land Bank.

Riverdale Farm was well known because it was close to the Falls and was well publicized as a showplace of the Koochiching Company. By 1912 it was heralded as a possible site for a state agricultural experiment station. In 1914 *The Journal* boasted that it was "one of the largest, best equipped and most modern privately owned dairy farms within the state." Riverdale, managed by C. B. Kinney, consisted of 500 acres, of which 300 were under cultivation. It had 75 Holstein milking cows, 25 heifers that were in line for production, and 150 Duroc-Jersey hogs.[4]

Logging to Live

The greatest influx of settlers came between 1910 and 1920. Most of them settled along the Big Fork, Little Fork, Rat Root, Rapid, Black, and Rainy rivers and in a small area near Northome. The opening of the mill in 1910 created a demand for pulpwood, which gave the homesteaders immediate cash and appeared to be the logical way to enter farming. Forest products produced between 10 and 40 percent of Plummer's gross income each year. His New Year's resolution for 1913 was to sell at least $1,500 worth of timber, clear at least 10 acres, put up enough ice for all summer, and secure a passable summer road. Only $220 was earned that year from the sale of farm produce, which was far overshadowed by timber sales.

Simon Hafdahl cut and sold $150 worth of timber his first winter and used the money to buy Paddy, the family's only horse for many years. Roy, the oldest son, did not attend school beyond the eighth grade because his labor was needed at home. Each day father and son left home in darkness and returned in darkness, cutting rail ties, posts, and logs.

From the first year on his homestead, George Watson always hired a small crew and independently logged. Emma Watson said, "We were better off than most homesteaders, because our farm was larger than most, we did more logging than most, and I received $4 to $6 a week for at least 20 years from [boarding] teachers." She was quick to add that as soon as the children were old enough to work out they did so to help with high school expenses for three of the children.

Gina Erickson, whose parents left the homestead after they received clear title to it, recalled that when she was married, her father sold $1,800 worth of pine from the land. Part of the money paid for her wedding and a wedding gift, and the remainder was put away for other family events.

Tosten Johnson always hired three other men to earn extra income by logging and to clear land for farming. But he soon gave up the idea of farming and purchased land as he needed it to continue logging. His son, Hilford, said that during most of the 1920s and 1930s it was possible to gross as much as $2,800 a year using three workers and two family members. But most homesteaders preferred to rely only on family labor and grossed only about $1,000 annually.

Emma Watson recalled that the best year her family ever had in logging was 1922, when they grossed $4,000 from the sale of mining timber from a virgin stand. Martin Pearson said that without his sawmill he never would have made it on the homestead. He purchased a Case steamer, which provided cheap power because it ran on slabs, but it was a fire danger.

Leonard Kucera's family specialized in cutting firewood, which they delivered to families in the Falls for $4 a cord. If they had no buyers, the school paid a set price of $3. For several years Plummer supplied wood for the school near his farm. By cutting it to stove length, delivering it, and stacking it at the schoolhouse, he sometimes received as much as $6.50 a cord.

Whenever there was no local market for pulp or timber, farm youth went to Wisconsin or Michigan to find work. In the winter of 1925–26, Adam Clement, the Plummers' son-in-law, earned enough driving a truck in the Michigan woods to purchase 80 acres next to the Plummer farm, and made it his home. When the mill closed in the 1930s, comments in Plummer's diary were terse: "No woods work, boys gone."

Arvid Peterson used a different approach to make his farm pay. He worked chiefly as a lumberjack and added land until he had "too much land" to handle on a part-time basis, so he quit lumberjacking. His future wife, Elsie Rustfelt, enlarged her homestead at the same time she taught school. After she quit teaching in 1924 to get married, the couple purchased tax-forfeited land for $1.50 an acre. They eventually acquired 640 acres but never cropped more than 40 acres of hay land plus what was needed for a garden. They pastured the cut-over land to graze sheep, which provided a stable income during the 1920s and 1930s.

For a few years the Petersons had a small herd of milk cows, but it was 8 miles cross country, or 18 miles by road, to the Loman creamery. Arvid Peterson often carried the cream, because he and his wife did not want to use the horses "just to take five gallons of cream to town." Each winter he cut cedar poles, posts, and ties and sold them across the Rainy at Barwick, Ontario. Peterson enthusiastically added that his wife was a great walker and an excellent farm worker.

Oscar Bergstrom said that his father was fortunate to own a good woods-working team of horses and that he always was in demand by the homesteaders who had timber but could not afford horses. Johnson and Bergstrom thought that if there had been enough homesteaders in the wilderness to provide a steady supply of products, Backus would never have set up lumber camps.

A study by the extension service published in 1920 indicated that the best way for families to survive at farming was to do it in conjunction with logging. By 1920 many of those who tried farming had reached the same conclusion.

It is also clear that financial agencies felt much more comfortable lending money against contracts for delivery or accounts receivable from the mill for timber sold than they did for more traditional agricultural operations.[5]

Alternative Agriculture

Alternative income was absolutely necessary for farmers to survive in the northern border country. Plummer's 1912 New Year's resolution implied that they should try to do without luxuries until the land was paid for, to sell enough timber to pay current expenses, to do carpenter and other well-paid work to meet expenses and buy machinery, to study architecture and to try to make it pay, and to make a careful test of the poultry business to determine if it could pay.

Plummer thought of farming as a business, was aware of the shortcomings of the area, and from the beginning sought ideas on alternative agriculture. In 1911 he started raising potatoes and other garden produce for commercial sale. He constructed a large root cellar to store vegetables for the winter and spring markets. That fall he shipped produce by riverboat, and after freezeup hauled wagonloads of potatoes, rutabagas, cabbage, beets, and carrots to Loman for rail shipment to the Falls or lumber camps.

He operated in that manner until 1923, when he acquired a secondhand Buick pickup, which he used to deliver 1,200-pound loads to restaurants and homes in the Falls. In 1925 he purchased a new GMC truck, which hauled 2,500 pounds. From August 21 through October 15 he hauled 47 loads to the Falls for $45 to $67 per load. If he had more orders than he could fill, he purchased from other farmers and resold the same day.

Plummer raised chickens, turkeys, and beef cattle and also bought them from other settlers to butcher for retail sales. In one eight-day period the Plummers butchered and delivered five cows and three pigs. The family also dressed as many as 50 chickens and/or turkeys a day. This provided a cash flow in the winter, when Plummer could not deliver vegetables. When the mill was closed in 1930 he wrote: "Very hard selling. No money." On that day he had taken 15 quarters of beef to the Falls and sold only 5. After the M & O reorganization in 1933, he noted that "activity revived." His sales included 8,500 pounds of cabbage for $0.025 a pound, 300 bushels of potatoes for $0.90 a bushel, and 4,000 pounds of beets at $1.45 a hundred—all far better prices than he had previously received. He starred a note in his diary to indicate that he had received a check for $602.29 for an order he had filled.

The Ericksons, of Littlefork, hauled potatoes to the Falls by wagon. The potatoes were loaded into a bed of straw and were well covered with blankets to keep them from freezing. The Ericksons left the farm at 4:00 A.M. to make the 38-mile round trip and return home by 10:00 P.M. Fortunately, there were five lumber camps within a few miles of their farm. In the early years the demand for meat and vegetables far exceeded the supply.

Those who lived closer to the Falls turned to dairying to capitalize on the milk market. In 1912 Matt Donahue installed what was probably the first farm telephone in the area so he could take orders for milk, cream, butter, and eggs. The Rogers family got into commercial dairying in 1924, when Joe Rogers paid $250 for a used Model T pickup to deliver milk to Ericsburg. By 1926 he had a home route in the Falls. In addition to cream sales, he delivered about 130 quarts of milk a day, at $0.15 a quart.

Extension personnel were so enthusiastic about the Rogerses' dairy business that they helped finance a new dairy barn in 1928. Instead of relying solely on selling milk for $20 a day, the Rogerses decided to hold barn dances from which they grossed $100 a night by selling tickets at $0.50 each. Frank Alexander, deputy sheriff at the dances, said that gambling, moonshine, and drunks were prevalent.

Farmers in the Ray area survived the 1920s and 1930s by selling meat, butter, eggs, and milk to tourists and people in the Falls. When licenses were required, the farmers quit because they could not comply with the regulations.

ILC lumber camps needed as many as 1,000 horses in addition to those at the sawmill, which created a demand for oats and hay. To save on freight, ILC paid a premium for local products. For example, in 1922 ILC offered to buy 35 tons of hay for Camp

87 from a settler in Buyck for $14.50 a ton delivered, when the price elsewhere in the state was $9.20.

Newspapers reported that a settler near Mizpah harvested 300 cases of strawberries from three-fourths acre. Others supposedly grossed $200 to $300 an acre raising cucumbers, causing rumors that a pickle company would soon invest in the area. From 1933 to 1942, several CCC camps provided an improved market opportunity for vegetable and dairy products. Government regulations, however, did not permit the purchase of meat from farms.[6]

Odd Jobs

Determined homesteaders sought outside work to supplement meager farm income. In a study conducted by the extension service, the following jobs were listed as those commonly performed by farmers in forest regions: road worker, harvest hand, logger, blacksmith, section hand, miner, carpenter, brick layer, member of town board, auto liveryman, switchman, school bus driver, barber, sawmill operator, assessor, and paper-mill worker.

One settler considered himself a farmer, even though he taught school, was an attorney, and was also a logger. Besides teaching school, until 1910 Plummer had a notary commission and collected regularly for notarizing papers, writing wills, and writing letters for others. For many years he was the local secretary/treasurer for the Farmers Loan Association (Federal Land Bank), from which he collected for each transaction he completed, was paid to attend meetings, and also received a small monthly payment. Later, he was involved with the Agricultural Adjustment Administration, the Farm Security Agency, and the Soil Conservation Service—all of which paid a daily wage and expenses. This represented a significant portion of his cash income and provided a far better life style than he earned from farming.

Plummer served as assessor and also did ditch digging and graveling for his township. He earned $0.30 to $0.35 an hour for building schoolhouses and houses in Birchdale, Loman, and the Falls—far more than he could make teaching. He earned a 10 percent commission selling stock in the Loman Cooperative Creamery, which paid well for the time it took. He also sold casualty and life insurance, a job which he probably secured because he was far better educated than most people in his community, was an excellent writer, and owned a typewriter—a rarity on the frontier. In some years he earned up to $1,200 in non-farm or non-woods income.

Many homesteaders worked in the Minnesota iron mines and were gone for months at a time, while their families worked on their homesteads. Others went to the Red River and Dakota harvest fields for as much as two months each year.

The farmers surveyed by the extension service averaged $344 a year from outside income, which was considered necessary to maintain a farm. Extension personnel strongly recommended that starting farmers spend a large portion of their time in non-farm work. Many of these new farmers soon learned that farming alone could not support the family and quit trying to farm. Others looked at farming as a way of life and were willing to pay the price to continue.[7]

False Hopes

Area agriculture got off to several false starts before most residents realized that their future was in trees. Initially, federal and state governments and commercial interests promoted agriculture. In May 1913, the Koochiching County Commission reluctantly appropriated $1,800 at the urging of the Minnesota Extension Service for partial support of a county agricultural agent, effective August 1, 1913. D. B. Jewell, the Falls superintendent of schools, resigned to take the new position, for which $2,920 was appropriated by the county, the state, and the school district. He was to oversee the teaching of agriculture in all county schools and to run a countywide agricultural program.

Jewell decided that teaching agriculture to the school children and creating Farmers Clubs would be more effective than individual contacts. Because farmers were suspicious of the county agent, he thought they might be more willing to listen in a club setting. In his first year he organized 27 clubs and concentrated on social and financial problems—the greatest immediate concerns of farm families.

After his initial success in organizing the clubs, Jewell realized that the people were not overly concerned about the business of farming. By the fall of 1914, he expressed discouragement because he saw little desire among the people to better themselves. They were not inclined toward cooperation, and they could not agree on how things should be done. He resigned in disgust in 1915, and the office of county agricultural agent remained vacant for three years.

In early 1918 the state again pressured the county commissioners to hire a county agent. They objected as a matter of economy and decreed: "Whereas, we believe that the appointment of such a county agent would be an unnecessary expense inasmuch as there is no demand or need of any such agent at this time." At their next meeting the commissioners had a directive from the university dean of agriculture ordering that, effective April 1, 1918, $1,000 be set aside contingent upon the organization of a county Farm Bureau of at least 100 members with a fund of $200 for agent work. All commissioners voted against the directive, but the state prevailed.

The extension service promoted cooperatives. The area pioneer was the Cloverdale Creamery, founded in Baudette in March 1913. By 1920 it operated year round and in 1940 paid out more money than any other business in Lake of the Woods County.

A creamery was proposed at the Falls in 1912, again in 1915, but it was not until 1917 that the Koochiching Dairy and Produce Association opened with $2,925 in capital. Most of the 65 stockholders were blindpiggers and gamblers, which, some jokingly said, gave the impression that the creamery was for producing moonshine. Since the biggest run barely exceeded 300 pounds of cream—hardly enough to dirty a churn—the operator pushed the churn aside and turned the building into a boarding house.

The creamery opened again in 1922. While many creameries dumped their buttermilk down the sewer, at the Falls it sold for $0.20 a gallon, because it was good for sobering up the drunks. By 1924 the firm produced 1,200 pounds of butter per week and had a contest to select a name. A total of 987 names were submitted, and $5 was paid to the person who suggested "Kooch-Minn Butter." Late in 1927 the county agent was asked to investigate after the creamery lost $2,000 in six months. He found that no records of purchases were kept, there was no inventory control, and the firm paid over market price to get cream from other communities. A new manager was hired.

In March 1916, a creamery was organized in Northome boasting all new equipment and a "first class" buttermaker. A price of $0.43 a pound for butterfat was promised, but the 44 patrons had to be satisfied with $0.28. The name was changed from Northome Cooperative Creamery to The Farmers' Cooperative Creamery to appeal to the farmers, but even that did not bring in the cream. The local bank made loans on dairy cattle at 7 percent interest to encourage dairying, but that did not help the cause.

The cooperative struggled, and it survived only because of inflation. Production increased in 1927 after the county agent spent a great deal of time in the Mizpah, Gemmell, Big Falls, Dentaybow, and Sturgeon River communities motivating farmers to produce cream and support the cooperative. Membership grew to 69. Over 200 people attended the annual meeting, where they learned that their cooperative had lost $1,100.

When the Northome State Bank failed, the local creamery board had to cope with outstanding bills, an overdraft, and a mortgage. The sale of another 128 shares to raise $3,200 was made easier by the removal of the double liability clause. The following year the creamery again lost $1,000. Miraculously, the firm continued and in 1937 showed a profit of $2,612.

The Loman Cooperative Creamery was organized in 1916 and experienced several false starts before it produced its first butter in May 1921. But it had problems. For example, George Peggar, the cooperative's secretary, wrote to Hayes Young, a farmer who complained because his cream tested too low: "Just because you tightened up the cream screw one-fourth turn and did not get 5 to 10 percent more results on your test the first jump out of the box, your [sic] up in the air about it . . . for my part I don't care a whoop what happens to the creamery."

The Loman creamery was at the closing point in the spring of 1925, but the farmers rallied to save it by increasing the volume 50 percent. In 1927 it was again on the verge of failure when impassable roads prevented the sale of its butter. By joining the Land O' Lakes Creamery Association in 1928, the creamery improved its outlet for butter and was able to buy supplies more advantageously. In 1931 the members donated the ice and wood necessary for the creamery to operate. When the Loman creamery, the last in the county, closed in 1962, it marked the end of an era.[8]

By 1917 the area was promoted for growing potatoes, and yields of 300 bushels per acre and prices of $1.50 a bushel were talked about, indicating a potential far beyond what any other crop was capable of producing. Growers around Littlefork formed an association and built a warehouse. In 1919 the county agent worked to upgrade potato production "because," he said, "Koochiching county is one of the best potato belts in the U. S. It has good soil and is well adapted toward production of seed potatoes." The county had 21 cooperating farmers, 4 of whom grew certified seed.

In 1922 Frank Kiene, a large grower from Kennedy, Minnesota, purchased seed potatoes from four different locations. The seed obtained at three of the locations yielded from 150 to 169 bushels per acre, while that purchased from Ole J. Wold, of Ray, yielded 208 bushels. Within a few years as many as 10 carloads of seed were sold annually to growers as far away as California, Michigan, and North Carolina.

That year the Lake of the Woods County Extension Service offered 25 sacks of seed potatoes to farmers in the Graceton area, but because labor requirements to produce seed for certification were so intense, only one farmer, C. R. O. Sorrels, agreed to grow the potatoes. It was 10 years before a second grower accepted the challenge, and the following year Kiene purchased all the foundation seed produced in the county.

Growers were cautioned not to attempt production of potatoes for table consumption, because transportation to the large centers of population was costly, but seed potatoes were another matter. Isolated fields, cool climate, freedom from disease and insects, low land cost, and cheap building material all served to overcome the transportation costs. But for seed to pass certification, farmers had to rogue the fields (hand-pulling weeds) and remove any infected plants. This they were reluctant to do, and the area lost its claim as a seed potato producer.

By World War I producing hay seed was heralded with stories as exaggerated as those on producing seed potatoes. "Profits" of $175 to $275 per acre above all expenses were boasted by local newspapers. Plummer's yields for clover and alfalfa seed varied from 150 to 600 pounds per acre, and the price ranged from $0.097 to $0.272 a pound. His gross income per acre varied from $21.00 to $95.30, making hay seed his most profitable crop after vegetables, with far less labor.

Yields of up to 600 pounds on as many as 45 acres on a single farm, with gross income up to $143 an acre throughout the 1920s and 1930s, were not uncommon. Some of the highest income years were 1934, 1936, and 1937. When other parts of the nation suffered from drought, this area's reduced rainfall made it ideal for haying. For many farmers those were the "golden years," because a national seed shortage kept the price up. Leonard Kucera's parents were able to build a large new house for $3,600 "because yield and price were both good." Because most farmers had only a few acres of hay seed, no big fortunes were accumulated, but some farmers' children had money for college.

Baudette and Littlefork were the major shipping points for alfalfa and clover seeds. By the early 1920s, as many as 15 carloads of clover were shipped from each community. In the 1930s, 18 buyers for national seed firms worked out of Littlefork. In 1937 seed buyer Aad Tone shipped 265,000 pounds.

Even though 200 to 300 people turned out at every whistle stop to view the M & I and extension service sponsored "cow and hen" special in 1929, it was already evident that top-level agriculture was not to be part of the future. Farmers were not interested in providing the level of management required to produce clean seed. Tone felt that farmers were careless about weed control and replanted in the same fields because they wanted to produce as much seed as possible without clearing more land. Some farmers would not let beekeepers put hives on their land, which would have aided pollination, and they were no more willing than the potato farmers to rogue their fields.

Even the dairy farmers lost their enthusiasm. In 1932 the local dairy herd improvement association was discontinued. Martin Pearson said that in his area "when night clubs came in, farmers' clubs died out." The 1933 county extension report was clear about the problem: "The pioneer spirit of rugged individualism is sometimes not the best for developing cooperative enterprises." It was the agent's impression that farmers hurt themselves by not buying pure seed, by not using a good seed cleaner, and by taking a discount for impure seed instead of putting forth the effort to produce a top-quality product. They were unwilling to secure good breeding animals and to provide proper nutrition for the best milk production. In their defense, it must be concluded that their attitude was partly shaped by the country they lived in—it would not be tamed.[9]

ENDNOTES FOR CHAPTER IV

1. Paul Anderson interview; Mrs. William M. Liggett, "The Needs of Northeastern Minnesota," *The Farmer*, XXVII, No. 4 (February 15, 1909), pp. 142–143; G. G. Hartley, "Northern Development Association Meeting," *The Farmer*, XXIX, No. 24 (June 17, 1911), p. 785; Koochiching County Agricultural Extension Records, County Extension Office, Koochiching County Courthouse, International Falls, annual reports for 1913, 1914, 1928, 1929, 1930, 1931, 1933, 1934 (all records from August 15, 1913, through December 31, 1937, were researched), hereafter Kooch. Ext.; *The Journal*, January 11, March 7, April 4, May 30, August 15, 1912, September 7, 1916; interview of Aad Tone, International Falls, July 24, 1976, hereafter Tone interview; interview of Melvin and Pearl Johnson, Littlefork, Minn., August 12, 1976, hereafter Melvin Johnson interview; Mannausau interview; *Hist. Kooch. Co.*, p. 168.

2. "Building a County's Agriculture," *The Farmer*, XLIII, No. 21 (October 17, 1925), p. 627; Paul Anderson interview; "Clearing Land in Northern Minnesota,"

The Farmer, XXIX, No. 3 (January 21, 1911), p. 82; *Farm Development Studies in Northern Minnesota,* University of Minnesota Agricultural Experiment Station Bulletin No. 196 (St. Paul, August 1921), pp. 14–15, 33–34, hereafter Bull. 196; *The Journal,* July 8, 1920; *The Northome Record,* June 4, 1920; Kooch. Ext. 1921, 1926, 1931, 1937; interview of Martin Pearson, Littlefork, Minn., June 12, 1976, hereafter Pearson interview; Ettestad interview; Henrickson interview; Plummer diary; *The Baudette Region,* July 12, 1917; Kucera interview; Dahlberg interview; interview of Oscar Bergstrom, Loman, Minn., July 22, 1976, hereafter Bergstrom interview; Kohlhase, *Spruce,* pp. 7, 42.

3. Community file for Wayland, KCHS; H. Johnson interview; Gina Erickson interview; Kohlhase, *Spruce,* pp. 3940; interview of James Plummer, International Falls, August 1, 1979, August 2, 1989, April 12, 1990, hereafter Plummer interview; interview of Grace Plummer Austin (Mrs. Harold), Emo, Ontario, April 12, 1990, plus several letters about family events, hereafter Austin interview; Plummer diary; interview of Anna (Mrs. Harold), Harold, and James Erickson, Littlefork, Minn., June 10, 1976, hereafter Harold Erickson interview; interview of Clarence H. and Ernest E. Rogers, Ericsburg, Minn., June 4, 1976, hereafter Rogers interview; Mannausau interview; Melvin Johnson interview.

4. Plummer diary; Bergstrom interview; Ettestad interview; Henrickson interview; Kooch. Ext.; interview of Arvid Peterson, Birchdale, Minn., June 23, 1979, hereafter Arvid Peterson interview; *The Journal,* July 16, 1914, May 26, 1921, April 16, 1925, March 5, 1936.

5. *Econ. Dev.,* p. 14; H. Johnson interview; Plummer diary; Plummer interview; Austin interview; Kohlhase, *Spruce,* pp. 6, 39; interview of Emma Andersen Watson (Mrs. George), Ericsburg, Minn., June 20, 1976, hereafter Emma Watson interview; Gina Erickson interview; Pearson interview; Kucera interview; Arvid Peterson interview; Melvin Johnson interview; Bergstrom interview.

6. Plummer diary; *The Journal,* July 18, 1912, July 1, 1920; *The Northome Record,* October 28, 1921; Plummer interview; Harold Erickson interview; Rogers interview; Alexander interview; *The Baudette Region,* January 4, 1917; Bussman file; Pearson interview.

7. Bull. 196, p. 41; Plummer diary; Tone interview; Mannausau interview; *The Northome Record,* August 6, 1920.

8. Kooch. Comm., May 24, 1913, February 7, March 7, 1918; Kooch. Ext.; *The Baudette Region,* July 9, 1914, May 13, 1915, May 9, 1919; LOW Co. Hist.; *The Journal,* August 3, September 14, 1916, June 14, 1917, August 8, 1918, July 21, 1921, August 24, 1922, March 27, 1924, March 17, 1927; Mark M. Abbott, C. A. Anderson, Clarence Rogers, a typed copy of "A Presentation to the Rainy Lake Women's Club, 1967," KCHS files, hereafter Abbott, 1967; *The Northome Record,* February 25, August 25, 1916, June 4, 1920; Tone interview; Plummer diary; letter from George Peggar to Hayes Young, August 23, 1923, on Loman Cooperative Creamery Association stationery, Loman file, KCHS; Bergstrom interview.

9. *The Baudette Region,* March 1, 1917; *The Journal,* September 13, 1917, November 27, 1919, March 6, 1924, February 12, 1925; Kooch Ext.; Plummer diary; Pearson interview; Kucera interview; Tone interview.

CHAPTER V

Living in the Wilderness

TRADITIONAL FARMING was not destined to be profitable in the northern border country, but many homesteaders were determined and paid dearly in an attempt to succeed. If they had known in advance what that price was, would they have stayed?

Nature's Bounty

At times settlers survived on what nature had to offer. Family members were trained at an early age to hunt, fish, trap, and pick berries, for often it meant the difference between subsistence or eating well.

Laura Pelland's family never really knew hard times, for even though their income was low, they always had plenty to eat. Both she and her husband were good shots with a .22 rifle and killed ducks, partridges, rabbits, and other animals whenever necessary, but never needlessly.

Moose were common in the virgin forest. Because the Buyck area had not been touched when the Malkor Finstad family settled there, moose were readily available and became their main source of meat. The steaks were stored in brine crocks, or the meat was made into meatballs with gravy and canned. Sandwich meat was salted, soaked, and dried on racks above the stove before it was stored.

Moose meat was so prized that homesteaders recalled exactly how many animals they had shot. Steve Mannausau, who first lived in the virgin forest at Hibbing and later at Loman, claimed 37. Arvid Peterson bagged only two moose the 69 years he lived in the woods. Both times he shared with his neighbors and with the game warden.

The Hafdahls shot only one moose in the 10 years they lived on the Black River. Eight-year-old Thelma spotted a bull moose on her way home from the Fairland store and ran to tell what she had seen, but no one believed her. To satisfy his daughter, Simon went to look. He spotted the tracks and spent the next several days tracking the moose before he was close enough to shoot it.

Deer were far more common in the cut-over woods. Venison was the most abundant meat enjoyed by the settlers, who kept a rifle handy—whether milking, clearing land, plowing, making hay, or cutting timber. It was satisfying to bag a deer under such circumstances, because it saved taking time to go hunting. Several days could be spent tracking deer without any luck. Plummer hunted from October 29 to November 5, 1911, before he bagged a five-pronged buck on his second try of the day. The next day he got a 150-pound fat buck "with a good head for mounting." On September 29, 1935, after more than 30 years of hunting, he shot a 310-pound buck, the biggest he had ever seen.

When boys reached the age of 12 or 13, they often were given rifles as gifts so they could contribute to the food supply. Hunting season was whenever meat was needed. Sylvia Hafdahl carried the bait as her brother, Roy, made his rounds on their trap lines. If they caught anything, she carried that also, for Roy had to carry his gun and watch for game. He was 14 and she was 10 when he shot his first deer, which they skinned, quartered, and carried home.

Rabbits and partridges were the most common meats when venison was not available. Many women were good shots, had their own trap lines, and often hunted for the evening meal. Children bagged partridges with slingshots and caught rabbits with snares made of copper wire. When snares were used, the lines were walked twice a day, often on the way to and from school or when getting the cows. Owen Gorden was instructed always to carry his rifle when he went for the cows. Because rabbits were easy to catch and everyone in the family liked them, the Finstads ate them often—roasted, baked, fried, in stew, or in soup.

For those who lived near water, fish was a staple. Children learned how to fish at a young age with homemade equipment. Net fishing was the most common, and it was expected that there would be fish every time a net was put out. During the spring run, walleyes were caught in gill nets. They were gutted with heads and tails removed, but with the skin and scales left, and salted down in wooden barrels. The Mannausaus put four lines in the Rainy River each night and nearly always had four walleyes the next morning. If the fish did not average 3 to 4 pounds, they were thrown back.

Walleyes, pike, northerns, red horse, black suckers, and sturgeon were the most common fish. One spring evening Owen Gorden and his friend, August, made 45 casts into the Big Fork and got 45 walleyes that averaged 2.5 pounds. The two boys made three trips to carry them to Owen's mother, who canned them as fish balls. On another occasion Owen's father caught a 158-pound sturgeon 5 feet 10 inches long, and Mrs. Gorden canned 21 pints of eggs from it. Sturgeon of 50 to 100 pounds were common. Unfortunately for the settlers, the days of unrestricted, free fishing came to an end. In 1935 Plummer paid $0.50 for his first fishing license.

If the season was right, the woods were full of berries, which were prepared in various ways for eating throughout the year. In berry season every family member capable of carrying a pail and fighting off insects was expected to take part. The amount picked depended upon the age of the picker and the abundance of the berries. Six to eight quarts for each picker per day was common. In one day Plummer, his son Jim, and Adam Clement picked 126 quarts of blueberries, and Marion and Ellen Plummer canned them. Each fall the eight Mannausau children picked a 55-gallon barrel of low-bush cranberries, which were kept in the family's root cellar until the following summer, when they were canned.

Low-bush cranberries, high-bush cranberries, lingonberries, cherries, plums, and blueberries were the most prevalent varieties. Many families picked and canned from 300 to 550 quarts annually. The Hafdahls were so proud of all that they had harvested and canned one year that they carried it out of the root cellar and took a picture of it.

When berries were plentiful, families from other areas took their vacations to join in the harvest. Each season hundreds of cases were shipped daily by rail, in addition to large volumes sold to independent truckers. Many Indians came and picked berries to sell to local retailers and shippers. The price most commonly quoted through the years was $0.08 to $0.10 per quart.

Trapping and hunting provided yet another source of income for the settlers. Mrs. Malkor Finstad and children earned most of their cash income from trapping mink, weasel, and muskrat. Mrs. Hafdahl was the only one in her family to trap a timber wolf. From 1907 through 1912, the most common price was $4.00 for mink and $0.50 for weasel and muskrat. Marion Plummer caught a "fine cross-fox" and sold the pelt to Montgomery Ward for $20. In addition to the price of the pelt, a bounty of $7.50 was paid for full-grown wolves and $2.00 for cubs. Later, as livestock became more common, the bounty increased to $15. Some individuals collected bounty on as many as 8 to 10 wolves a season. Most families took trapping and hunting seriously, for this was an important addition to their income.[1]

A Hostile Environment

Billy Noonan, the colorful editor of *The Baudette Region*, wrote, "This section has a good climate, although the weather spoils it occasionally." Homesteaders soon learned that "occasionally" meant far too often for good farming. Frost was possible every month of the year. On July 16, 1911, Plummer lost a half acre of potatoes to frost. The following year on September 2, he wrote, "No frost yet, this is the latest in 9 years." In 1915 the Northern Beltrami County Fair at Baudette was canceled after frost had damaged most vegetable crops on August 25, and the county extension demonstration plots "were almost a complete failure."

The demonstration plots in 1920, which compared corn with sunflowers for use as silage, gave the advantage to sunflowers, because the corn was "damaged by frost every month, and the sunflowers were only slightly damaged." Planting corn was discouraged, except along rivers. After the hard frost of August 20, 1934, which killed both corn and potatoes, the extension service recommended that "hardier crops, possibly legumes, should be planted in the future."

Emma Watson was very emphatic that, in her family's farming experience, flooding of the Rat Root River every spring was a much greater hardship than frost. After their first flood, the Hafdahls built a huge raft and attached it to their cabin to serve as a back porch. When the river rose, all the bedding and clothing were tied to the rafters, the cows and horses were left to seek high ground, and the chickens were placed on the barn roof with a supply of feed. As soon as the "porch" floated, the family got on, cut it loose, and poled to safety. During the flood they stayed with neighbors or at the Woodman Hall in Fairland. After 10 to 14 days it was safe to return to the cabin, which normally received about 3 feet of water.

In 1916 and 1919, many of the first highway bridges were washed out, either by water or log drives. In 1916 Kajeten Niedzwiecki was returning home from Baudette. After walking

12 miles he came to a bridge washout. He turned back only to discover that he was cut off when another bridge had also washed out. He went to a nearby farm and was happily greeted by the farmer, who needed help to move his cattle, which were knee deep in water in the barn. On another occasion he was forced to use a raft as he returned from working in the mill carrying supplies to last the family three months. He decided to quit farming and work full time in the mill; it was more profitable.

In the Caldwell Brook settlement, farmers used a launch each spring to transport cream and eggs out and supplies in. After the first bridge was washed out by a log drive in the early 1920s, it was never rebuilt, causing the community to decline.

The Journal reported that it was "no small job fishing potatoes out of the mud" after a flood at Loman the fall of 1926. The following April the Rainy flooded and mail was carried "in relays with Fords, boats, and barges. Business was completely paralyzed, merchants could not replenish their stocks . . . and had plenty of time to measure the rising waters," which were 12 to 14 feet above normal summer stage. On June 30, Minnesota Highway No. 11 into Loman was still under 4 feet of water.

The heavy winter snows of 1936–37, with 8- to 12-foot banks along main roads, caused extensive spring flooding. Schools were closed for three weeks in April. There was no travel, and bridges were destroyed, isolating many communities. The Lindford Farmers' Club did not meet until after freezeup in the fall. Most crops were not planted until June and were flooded out by heavy rains in July. The highest waters ever seen by Plummer came in 1938. On May 5 the Rainy rose 1 inch per hour, Loman streets were again under water, and students used rafts to get to school. An abundance of moisture was good for the trees in the wilderness, but it was too much for farming.

The climate of northern Minnesota is best described as continental—a land of extremes with long, cold winters, wet springs and falls, and short summers with long days. On January 3, 1912, Plummer complained for the first time about the cold. "Cut six logs in A.M. and got froze out. (-40 degrees)." He left the woods and helped Nellie put deadening felt on the upstairs walls. For the next two days the temperatures were minus 40 to 50 degrees. On January 6 the temperature was 52 degrees below zero, but Henry Berg, a hired man, came to work, so Plummer and he went to the woods and cut 90 logs. In the evening they walked to the neighbors for a visit.

In December 1916, the temperature ranged from 15 to 42 degrees below zero for 13 consecutive days; nevertheless, the children went to school, and the men worked in the woods daily. On January 14 through 26, 1917, the temperature ranged from 15 to 55 degrees below zero, yet the men did not miss a day in the woods. When the cold snap broke, Plummer shaved for the first time in two months. Livestock consumed a great deal more feed during prolonged cold snaps, so farmers often ran short before spring arrived.

Although floods caused extensive damage and minus-50-degree temperatures made life miserable, forest fires were more feared than either floods or cold. After the initial fright of fires subsided, a second wave of homesteaders moved in starting in 1912—partly because newspapers described the benefits of a fire for those who wanted to farm. Many fires were set deliberately by prospective farmers to ease the burden of clearing the land. Unfortunately, they sometimes got out of hand and destroyed timber on public and private lands, as well as farmsteads, communities, and lives. The prevailing attitude was that timber was so abundant that its loss did not matter, because in the long run the land would be used for farming. This resulted in a needless waste, for it was realized later that greater profits could be made from timber than from farming.

The Baudette area experienced a second fire in 1917, which destroyed more than 2,000 acres of timber and the Engler mill. In 1922 a fire that destroyed several square miles of timber south of Littlefork temporarily endangered the village and burned several more sections of cut-over land that was being prepared for farming.

Marian Crabtree Peterson recalled a fire in 1924 in the Faunce area. Birds and animals came out of the woods as the fire moved toward her grandparents' home. While her father worked in Baudette, Marian (age four), her sister, Lillian (age two), and her mother stayed with "Grandpa Gustafson." Although the fire jumped the swamp, which they thought would protect them, the Gustafsons had land well cleared around their farmstead and had a good root cellar, so they were not overly concerned. Harold Johnson, a neighbor, sought safety with them after his buildings were destroyed. While surveying the following year, Marian's father narrowly escaped a fire that burned over 5,000 acres, consuming 6 to 10 million feet of pine lumber belonging to ILC, several million pine trees, and many farm buildings.

The demand for explosives was down in 1929, because the season had been dry and over 2,000 acres were cleared by fire. Farmers needed permits to burn, but many fires were started by "unknown cause." The county agent said that if it had not been for the difficulty of securing permits, at least 10,000 acres would have been cleared. He criticized the State Forestry Department for not allowing the burning of partly cleared land.

In April 1931, when over 40,000 acres burned in the Mizpah, Northome, and Wildwood areas, only a few tracts benefitted, and much valuable timber was lost. The forestry department outlined a burning program that would avoid endangering thousands of acres of forest, "but most refused to cooperate with the plan so nothing was accomplished."

A 77-year-old homesteader from the Rapid River area wrote to Annie Shelland Williams in 1954 that he "had lost a considerable amount in the 1910 fire and a fortune in the 1931 fire." In September 1931, 38 families, totaling 165 people, lost their homes, 102 farm buildings, 325 cattle, and 2 lives. John Ettestad said, "The 1931 fire, which covered part of Lake of the Woods and Koochiching counties, was so complete that you could rake off the land and plow it." In Lake of the Woods County, 1,600 acres were made available for farming in the Hay Creek–Rapid River fire, which was more than in the 1910 fire. Backfires, which were started as fire control, sometimes got out of hand and caused more damage than the main fire.

According to Ed Richards, long-time forestry department employee in the Littlefork area, local people often set fires to get paid for putting them out. In the 1920s the rate of pay for such work was $0.25 an hour; by the 1930s it had dropped to $0.15. This practice continued for many years throughout Richards' extended career. The most common way to start such a fire was to place a lighted candle on a hollow stump that had dry material around it, and let it spread from there. Some individuals set fires to watch for large deer, which they shot and sold to people from the Twin Cities.

Hardly a year passed that Plummer did not write about area fires in his diary. The following comments are examples: "everybody out fighting fires"; "fires very bad"; "fires all over the northern part of the state, nearly everybody helping to fight them"; "people digging fire line"; "everyone moving lumber from the path of the fires"; "lots of fires both sides of the [Rainy] river"; "all threshing in the area stopped to fight fires"; "many dead from fires and more are missing." One year every member of the family spent 12 consecutive days working to put out fires at home or for others, until a heavy rain gave relief.

Most communities were endangered by forest fires; several were completely destroyed. Fire approached the Falls in 1934 and was not brought under control until 400 acres were destroyed on the south edge of the city.

In 1938 a fire started after the first killing frost. The Falls, Ericsburg, Ray, Gemmell, and Margie were completely surrounded by fire and thick smoke. North of the Rainy, the Fort and nearly all the villages to the west were in danger. Embers floated into the Falls and the Fort, setting buildings afire. Cars were not permitted to leave or enter either city. M & O management drafted an emergency plan under the direction of forester Vic Lofgren and J. H. Hubbard, the regional fire prevention coordinator. In the Falls, a large number of volunteers helped the regular firefighters for three days and nights to save the city. Ten families near the city lost their homes. Others abandoned theirs in a fire that covered at least 150,000 acres in northern Minnesota and an even greater area in Ontario. A family of nine was buried in one grave at Devlin, Ontario—the greatest single tragedy out of "nearly a score" who lost their lives. Nine others were hospitalized.

In May 1939, the Falls was again in danger when muskeg fires from the previous fall, that had smoldered all winter, were whipped up by spring winds, bringing fire to within 200 feet of homes on Thirteenth Avenue. From that time on, officials were given no rest until plans were laid, in cooperation with state and federal agencies, to build a safety belt around the city.

In addition to the fires experienced by settlers and the communities, M & O had its annual share of loss, which ran from a few hundred to several thousand acres. A large sum of money was spent for special portable firefighting equipment that could be moved on the rail lines with Fairmont gas cars. Ironically, an article in the forestry department files indicated that in 1940 only 12 percent of the fires were caused by lightning, while smokers caused 24 percent; incendiaries, 26 percent; campers, 6 percent; railroads, 4 percent; debris burning, 15 percent; and lumbering, 2 percent. The origin of 11 percent was listed as miscellaneous or unknown. The more people moved into the wilderness, the less safe it became.

By all outward appearances, the north country had an abundant supply of water. Certainly water was a major obstacle for those who first penetrated the area, but for some settlers the old phrase "water, water everywhere but not a drop to drink" applied. Even though there were many streams and rivers and the ground was normally saturated, water for household purposes was not always easily available. Melting snow for washing clothes in the winter and using river water in the summer was standard procedure. One homesteader, whose well went dry in summer, walked three miles to the river to wash clothes.

Plummer had serious problems securing water. By 1912 the well that he had dug in 1907 started to go dry, so he dug and cribbed as he went down to hit a more reliable supply. In December 1921, that well went dry, and this time he augured down, but kept hitting rock. After four days of working in 30 degree-below-zero weather, he got down 41 feet, and water came to within 14 feet of ground level.

In 1935 he hired the Espe brothers to drill a well. At 74 feet they hit rock, so they reset, went down 64 feet, and hit rock again. Nineteen days and several tries later, they left without hitting water. Water witching was commonly used to locate underground water veins. Unfortunately, this method did not indicate how much rock was between ground level and the water supply.

The well drillers tried again in 1936, but that well went dry within a week, so the Plummers were back to driving the animals down to the river's edge to drink and to carrying water for the house. Carrying water up the steep river bank and driving cattle to drink on a June day with the temperature at 107 degrees was as trying as in the cold winter, except the cattle were more willing to go on a hot day. It took three people to get the cows to water on cold winter days. It was dangerous for man and beast when ice started to break up in the spring.

In July 1937, Plummer augured a well and struck water at 35 feet, only to have it fail the next winter. The following summer the Erickson brothers drilled eight wells as deep as 100 feet. Plummer paid $80 for dry holes, and they left.

Not all settlers had such difficulty locating water. In 1920 Martin Pearson augured down 18 feet and hit a flowing well that was still good in 1976. The Tosten Johnson family, on the Little Fork River, dug and cribbed a 3-foot-square hole down about 3 feet and had adequate water. They felt safer using a well that shallow than drawing water directly from the river.

Those who lived farther away from the Little Fork had to dig down about 12 feet to reach a reliable water supply.

At Ruth Gowdy McLinn's home on the Big Fork, water was always obtained from the river. In the winter, the livestock were watered out of the same hole that the family used to secure their drinking water, which was normal for settlers who relied on river water.

Adam Clement, son-in-law and closest neighbor of the Plummers, had a cow fall into his cribbed well. It took the entire Plummer family most of one day to pull it out. The Clements continued to use that well for another year, when they drilled a 183-foot well.

Long cold winters and swampy land made attempts at raising poultry and livestock more hazardous than in most agricultural regions, but the wilderness presented yet another problem—an abundance of predators. On December 13, 1912, Plummer had 27 traps out. He commented, "Foxes and wolves everywhere but they seem to know how to steal the bait without getting caught." The same was true of weasels and skunks that invaded the yard and the chicken coop.

After sheep were introduced to the area in 1913, losses to predators were constant. The Metcalfs, at Loman, lost 12 sheep in one evening to wolves. In the 1930s, large numbers of sheep were shipped in from the drought-stricken western states. Sheep had great profit potential, except for the danger from wolves and bears. Farmers protested to the Minnesota Department of Conservation, which took the position that the danger was exaggerated. After cattle herds were attacked, the department agreed that farmers could shoot or trap bears and wolves if they seriously menaced livestock.

Less damaging than predators, but a greater nuisance to most animals and people, was the intense irritation from mosquitoes, no-see-ums, and flies. Billy Noonan's weekly column in *The Baudette Region* for April 26, 1917, warned: "The mosquito fleet will soon be with us." There was no escaping the pests. Farmers worked their horses early in the morning or late in the evening to minimize the problem. In fly season, animals were kept in barns or straw sheds during the middle of the day, because the insects seldom entered dark places.

The worst fly was the bull dog. Its bite drew blood and could affect the victim for as long as two weeks. The horse fly and the deer fly were not as bad, but they had a longer season. The extension report said of the pests: "In summer, pastures are good but flies and mosquitoes are almost unimaginable." During the early 1930s, high-quality insect repellant became available at a relatively low price; however, farmers showed little interest in it.

During the fly and mosquito season, people protected their heads by covering their hats with netting, which was gathered at the neck by a drawstring. In the evening, smudges were created by starting a small fire in a pail and, once it was burning well, smothering it with green grass or leaves. This made a dense smoke with no visible fire and lasted for several hours. The pail was placed outside the doorway so the smoke could enter the house.

Indoors, a teaspoon of "Buhach," a yellow powder, was put on a flat surface and ignited. As it smoldered it gave off fumes, which killed flies and mosquitoes. During the peak of insect season, people often carried smudge pots as they worked outdoors.[2]

The Farm Home

The lack of good housing, always a problem on the frontier, was even more serious in the northern border country because of the severe climate. Extension service personnel felt that the lack of social life and well-planned homes was critical. In 1924 agent Mark Abbott observed that "good health required a good comfortable home, but not many were." An extreme case was illustrated by Carl Dahlberg, whose parents came to the Effie area in 1901 with four other families. A 16- × 20-foot two-story log house was built. All five families lived there until four other identical houses were built. Dahlberg's family lived in their original house from 1902 until after he was born in 1905, when they added a lean-to, which sufficed until it burned in the winter of 1923–24.

On December 31, 1910, when the Simon Hafdahls and their six children moved into a 16- × 20-foot single-story log cabin, Mrs. Hafdahl broke down and cried. Simon put his arms around her and assured her that they would live in the small cabin for only a few months, but that was their home for the next decade. All the furniture except the stove was homemade. Nails in the walls and rafters served as clothes hangers. As the family increased to 12 children, double beds and trundle beds with straw-filled mattresses were added, as were lean-tos. The Hafdahls nearly always had at least two hired men, and for a few years a neighbor boy roomed and boarded with them. The hired help and older boys slept in one lean-to, while the girls and younger boys slept in another, where they sometimes were "forced to sleep crosswise to gain more space."

The lack of insulation enabled frost to penetrate the walls, and if there was no cellar, the cold from the ground came through the floor. A few homes were banked with manure piled up to the bottom of the windows to provide some protection. Children often were late to school on cold mornings, because the water in the drinking pail was frozen. They could not wash because the ice melted slowly as the room heated up.

On cold days thick frost covered the single-pane windows, which were common in most homes. To reduce the heat loss, rugs or blankets were put over the windows at night, and sometimes oil-soaked paper was placed over the windows to act as a transparent insulator. The 16- × 24-foot Bergstrom log house had one small four-pane east window, two windows on the south, and a small window in the door that faced north toward the woods. As lean-tos were added, a similar window was placed in each.

Normal fuel requirements, even for such small houses, ranged from 8 to 12 cords per year. The lowest amount used was 3 cords in a 22- × 26-foot log house, insulated in the walls and ceiling, covered with siding over felt paper, and with a full basement. Prior to remodeling, this house took 8 cords annually for heating, plus an additional amount for cooking. Heating stoves took pieces of wood up to 3 feet in length, while cooking stoves used wood about a foot long and split into pieces that were smaller in diameter. Normally, it took two days of labor to prepare a cord of wood.

Generally, floors were rough-hewn boards laid over logs. Homes with tongue-and-grooved floors were preferred for dances. Emma Watson's second home, built in 1915, had birch floors that cost $60, in contrast to the remainder of the house, which cost $300, exclusive of home-sawed lumber.

Tin stovepipes instead of chimneys caused many roof fires. If the occupants were home and a ladder and a barrel of water were handy, the cabin possibly could be saved, but in most cases the cabin was totally consumed. In homes with chimneys, chimney fires, caused by heavy accumulations of soot in the flue from burning wood, were common. These fires were extinguished by dangling a log chain in the chimney to knock the soot down where it could be cleaned out or by pouring salt down the flue.

Many homes had a loft, which was entered via a trap door in the ceiling reached by a ladder attached to the side wall or hinged at the floor joist and dropped down when needed. If such a loft was used for sleeping, mattresses were laid on the floor. One family of 11 lived in a 24- × 28-foot three-room house in which the second floor was never finished. This house had a large combination kitchen/living room with a pull-out sofa, where the parents slept. The other two rooms were bedrooms for the children, with tip-down beds stored vertically against the wall in the daytime.

Household conveniences were few. In 1919 the Plummers purchased a chemical toilet, which was a real oddity. In 1923 they added a lean-to with bathroom facilities, which used water from a tank under the roof of the lean-to that was filled with water from eaves on the main part of the house. Cooking and drinking water was pumped from a well located under the kitchen floor. This was one of six rural homes recorded by the county extension service as having a water system in 1923. Most homes did not have built-in cupboards or linoleum on the floor.

Emma Watson said it for all when she commented, "Washing clothes on the scrub board was the worst job that the pioneer housewife had." Washing often was done on Saturday, when the children were home to help. Mrs. Hafdahl carried two 12-quart pails of water at a time from the river and heated it in a copper boiler. The clothes were scrubbed on a scrub board, boiled, rinsed twice, wrung by hand, and hung on the fence to dry. In the winter they froze dry. Even if their backs ached and their hands were blistered and bleeding from washing, the women used the leftover hot water to scrub the floors, benches, and tables. A lye solution from wood ashes was added to bleach the floors and the woodwork.

The Plummers did not have easy access to river water. On one occasion when the well was dry, Nellie resorted to dipping water from puddles for washing clothes. She discarded the scrub board when they purchased a new Igoo hand-operated machine in 1912. A diary entry after its first use tersely read, "It is fine." A clothes wringer was soon purchased, but it was not until 1931 that an engine-powered Peerless washer was obtained. Nellie and Ellen practiced getting it started as soon as it was set up. About a week later the diary read, "Did first big wash with new Peerless, works fine."

In 1928, when the Ericksons got a new tractor, the salesman

suggested that Mrs. Erickson should have a new Fairbanks Morse gasoline-operated washer. He hinted that it could be financed on the same note as the tractor. Mrs. Erickson got rid of her scrub board and hand-cranked wringer that day.

Besides operating hand-powered washers, many children cranked hand-powered sewing machines and butter churns and pumped water for house and barn needs. Children disliked cleaning and filling the lamps because of the oily soot and the risk of breaking the chimney. Carrying in the wood and carrying out the "slop" pail were other daily tasks. Everyone was expected to help with livestock chores.

In 1912 Plummer purchased a typewriter for $50. He paid $1 down and $3 a month. If he could sell three other typewriters, his was free, and what he had paid would be refunded. He sold the three machines to local business people and received a $25 refund.

The Plummers also had an organ, which was purchased when Nellie vacationed in Wisconsin and said she would not return until Sam bought one. For Christmas 1919, the family got an Edison phonograph with a dozen records. The next day they ordered 12 more records from Sears for $6.13. By 1923 they had 50 records. Occasionally they took the phonograph and records with them when they visited neighbors. Not all rural families had the luxury of organs, phonographs, or typewriters to relieve the boredom of their daily routine.[3]

Loneliness

In this day of television, direct-dial telephones, fax machines, hard-surfaced roads, and automobiles, it is difficult to realize the isolation experienced by those who attempted to tame the wilderness. Any visitor—whether it was someone following the trail past the farmstead, the lumber company scaler, the assessor, the traveling missionary, the Watkins or the Union Tea dealer, who "managed" to leave packs of gum for the children—helped to break the monotony of the daily routine. As one woman wrote from her tiny isolated community as the geese flew over, "Our world was pretty small . . . and we couldn't imagine where they [the geese] were going or why."

A homesteader, whose wife was the first woman in their township 18 miles south of Baudette, wrote that it was "considerably more than a year before she saw another woman." Ed Pelland's mother probably holds the record for isolation. She arrived at their homestead along the Little Fork River in 1895 and did not get to the Falls until 1920, when the family purchased their first car. Mrs. Pelland did not like riding in a canoe, so she contented herself with her family and occasional walks to the neighbors.

Clover Sabin, the home demonstration agent, wrote of a sewing demonstration meeting at Bescemar in April 1924, that neither impassable roads nor stormy weather prevented the women from attending. Some came in wagons or pungs, others walked, and some rode a gasoline speeder on the logging railroad. They were as desperate for companionship as they were about learning to sew. At a three-day Women's Recreational Camp, sponsored by the Farm Bureau in 1930, 60 women paid $0.25 a day to attend. One woman said that it was the first time in 20 years that she had any time for recreation.

The shock of coming to an isolated homestead in the wilderness caused more than one woman to cry for the first week before she realized that she could not go back. Oscar Bergstrom said that his mother had come from a substantial home in Sweden to settle along the Black River, about nine miles by canoe from Loman. When the Bergstroms arrived in the fall of 1910, they had $0.35 in their pockets and still had it the following spring.

One day a neighbor stopped by the Vic Lindstens, who lived along the Black River, to suggest that Mrs. Lindsten come with her to visit another neighbor. Mrs. Lindsten had started to bake bread, but they decided to take the pan of dough with them as they rowed down the river. They stopped on the way to knead it and then continued. By the time they arrived, the dough was ready to bake, so they visited until the bread was finished and then rowed home.

"Pack and paddle days" was a phrase used to describe the days prior to roads and railroads. Before a store opened at Fairdale, the Hafdahls traveled 12 miles through the woods, across a bottomless swamp, to the store at Birchdale. When Hafdahl went to the store he took a backpack, a can for kerosene, and a rifle and put mosquito netting over his hat and face. He returned with 50 pounds of flour, salt, sugar, yeast, coffee, a plug of Climax tobacco, a roll of Copenhagen snuff, and a "hidden" package of peppermint candy.

Arvid Peterson's home was isolated from 1912 until 1918, when a logging road was built to it. He added that it was 12 miles to the store, "so I just carried 60 pounds. . . . That was about all I could carry through the woods."

Plummer often purchased 100-pound sacks of feed and other provisions at the Loman store. He took half the feed and the provisions, so his load was not more than 75 pounds for the 3½-mile walk home through the woods. Jim's Sunday chore was walking to Loman for the mail and provisions, which generally took about four hours. In 1919, after a road was built by the Plummer farm, he biked it in 45 minutes.

No bridge ever was built to the township where the Gowdys lived west of the Big Fork River. It was 16 miles walking to Big Falls if they crossed the river on their homemade ferry. If they went by boat, it was 30 miles. The only people who ever came near their farm were those who wanted to see them.

Mary Malerich and her mother took the *Itasca* down the Little Fork River to visit the McClouds. They expected to return in a few days, but all boat traffic stopped when the river froze the first night they were there. It was six weeks before the ground froze hard enough for them to walk back to the Falls.

The region north of the border from Rainy River, Ontario, to the Fort was settled earlier than that to the south, because its soil was better drained and it lay along a major east-west artery of travel for Canada. Rainy River, Emo, and LaVallee, Ontario, were all larger than corresponding American settlements, so most settlers canoed across the river to trade, socialize, or catch the CN.

Rainy River and LaVallee had the only flour mills in the region, until one was built at Emo about 1920. LaVallee was 20 miles from the Plummers. It took two long days to make a round trip to the mill there to get wheat ground.

For a few years Douglas Kennedy, who operated the store at Indus, also served as U.S. customs officer. Later, when Jess Rose held that position, he lived with a family at Emo, because there was no place to live south of the river. Groceries were shipped to Loman, Indus, and Birchdale from Duluth, via Emo. Rose helped the storekeepers on the U.S. side haul their goods across the river. The customs officers virtually ignored daily transactions of petty items that were purchased north of the border, but levied fines if large items were not declared.

Socializing across the border was commonplace. Laura Pelland was in a group of six American and four Canadian couples who met regularly for all-night dances with music provided by one fiddler. At the Mannausaus', the party was about equally divided between Americans and Canadians. Canadian Red Rose tea was available all night. After a breakfast of pancakes, everyone returned home. Nearly every family on the American side had one or more families of relatives on the Canadian side. The Plummers visited almost as much with Canadians as with Americans, and two of their children married Canadians.

There was no serious obstacle to cross border traffic until the Canadian government passed a law, effective May 31, 1917, requiring a passport for anyone leaving Canada "even for an hour." When the United States passed prohibition legislation in 1920, the border became an exciting challenge.[4]

Rural Free Delivery was provided as soon as the population justified it and often before roads were built. Those who were extremely isolated picked up their mail at the nearest post office, which was nearly always at the local store. In addition to the local papers, most homes received a farm magazine, a ladies' magazine, several catalogs, the *Youth's Companion*, and sometimes the newspaper of the community the family had left. Many homes did not receive more than two or three letters a month. Other reading material consisted of the Bible, perhaps a set of encyclopedias, and a few classics. Sam Plummer was an avid reader and received many books as presents. He purchased a bookcase in the 1920s which held only about half of his books.

Probably no single innovation other than the automobile and electricity so changed the life of the homesteader as did the telephone. As ILC constructed its logging railroads, it also built telephone lines along them, and homesteaders were allowed to connect to those lines. The forest service also let settlers connect to its lines, if they agreed to help keep them operating.

After World War I, the extension service took an active part in forming rural telephone associations. Settlers turned out en masse and generally all bought shares and helped build the lines.

The largest rural telephone association in the area was the Border Cooperative Telephone Company, organized February 21, 1914, with "central" in Birchdale. Its purpose was to provide service from Loman to Clementson "along the state road and further if practical." Each member bought one share for $33.55, which was charged as follows: $5.00, when signing up, for purchasing equipment; $17.00, when needed, for wire and other material; and $11.55, when the telephone was installed. In 1916 each patron was assessed an additional $17.50. Members provided and set the poles, but the cooperative paid for wire, insulators, telephones, and the switchboard. The total cost of wire from Loman to Clementson was $450.

The by-laws stated that no person was to use the line for more than five minutes at one time. Anyone who refused to stop talking when requested to do so by someone wishing to use the line was fined $0.10 for each offense. These provisions were essential because there were up to 23 homes on some lines. Any non-member wishing to make a call paid $0.10 for each call. If the person called had to be sent for, an additional $0.10 was charged. No profane language or playing of a musical instrument over the phone was permitted. Offenders paid a $1 fine. Calls could be made to members on the party line 24 hours a day. For other calls, the central was on duty six days a week from 6:00 A.M. to 9:00 P.M. and from 8:00 A.M. to 9:00 A.M. and 4:00 P.M. to 6 P.M. on Sundays. Sickness or fire calls were free at any time, but other calls in "off hours" were charged $0.25, payable to the central operator.

"Rubbernecking," as listening in was called, was forbidden but was common practice on party lines because it provided so much entertainment. Even the central operators were known to listen in on conversations. To discourage this practice, people often switched from English to German, French, or another native tongue. As the receivers were hung up, the power increased. On one occasion a listener overheard two people talking about the virtues of a cow that one wanted to buy. The rubbernecker was so impressed that he hurried to the owner's farm and bought it. Patrons notified central if they were going to be gone so that the operator could inform anyone calling them in their absence.

Each member was instructed to provide 11 poles, 25 feet long with 5-inch tops, and to place them along the public road as designated by the lineman. Next, the member set 20-foot poles with 5-inch tops along the driveway leading to the farmstead. Then wire was furnished to connect the main line with the house. When the final assessment was paid, the lineman installed the telephone and linked it to the line. After the installation was completed on July 14, 1915, Plummer noted, "We talked."

After construction was finished on the original project, members wanted to reach the outside world, so a switchboard was installed in the Hinckley store, at Loman, to connect to the International Telephone Company line (a Backus company) at the Falls.

Border Cooperative, with 75 charter members, grew slowly to a peak of 175 in 1935 and declined gradually until it became part of another system in 1970. The phone bills of four accounts, taken at random, covering from 1914 through 1939, show that the telephone was used sparingly in the early days. After the initial shares were purchased, annual phone bills per patron ranged from a low of $3.00 to a high of $24.85.

Not many years after telephones were installed, an even more novel innovation helped to reduce the isolation. On October 25, 1922, Plummer spent an evening in the Falls and wrote, "I listened to a radio concert for the first time." In 1925 their neighbors, the Peggars, purchased a radio, but the Plummers did not get one until November 1929. They had good reception without an external aerial and heard "a fine sermon from Shreveport, Louisiana."

In 1932 the Plummers got a radio for Christmas, which worked better than their first one, but it was much harder on batteries. Marion and Jim built a charger using the rear housing of a Model T, mounted 12 fins on each wheel, and put it up on poles to catch the wind and run the charger. After working for nearly three weeks, they found the proper angle for the fins, which ran the generator up to 200 RPMs to keep the battery charged.

On January 25, 1939, the Plummers and some neighbors listened as Joe Louis knocked out his opponent in 2 minutes and 29 seconds. A few days later they heard a speech by Adolph Hitler. They still lived in the wilderness, but with a radio the rest of the world did not seem so far away.

For those who lived along the Rainy River, isolation never was quite as severe as for those who lived farther inland. During the summer, riverboats provided frequent service to the Fort for a one-way fare of $0.90 from Loman. The ferry to the Falls cost $0.15, but in 1912 a bridge put an end to that service. Crossing the river gave access to the CN, which had several trains daily each direction. One-way fare was $0.85. Each Sunday the ILC's logging railroad made a round trip between Loman and the Falls. The fare was the same, but the only seats were in the caboose.

The telephone and the radio were great improvements for those who lived in the wilderness, but it was the automobile that broke the grip of isolation. It is very clear from Plummer's diary that a whole new world opened to his family after they purchased a used Buick pickup in 1923. The immediate difference came in shopping habits. They passed through Loman on their way to the Falls to deliver produce and while there nearly always made some purchases. As settlers broke the shackle of being tied to their small community service center, they started its demise—a process that had commenced in the more developed areas by the mid-1800s.

We will never know the price that was paid by those who tried to tame the wilderness but failed, for most of them disappeared without leaving a story. But many did not survive to try elsewhere. Plummer frequently commented in his diary about suicides. Each winter the newspapers carried accounts of such tragedies. Many of those interviewed recalled individuals who had lost their minds or took their lives. The suicide rate was highest among single men, although the women bore most of the sheer drudgery. One woman who lived in the wilderness said it best: "I never thought my life was hard, but I was always glad when each day was done. . . . My hardest time was when the twins were born and I had one at home who was two and a half. We were one mile from the nearest neighbor, and there was only a path through the woods to town."

Living in the wilderness took courage, stamina, and a willingness to overlook the sacrifices required to establish a farm. Those who "stuck it out" were a hardy lot. Generally, they survived because they became good loggers and let farming become secondary.[5]

ENDNOTES FOR CHAPTER V

1. Interview of Laura Moulton Pelland (Mrs. Elmer), International Falls, August 11, 1976, hereafter Laura Pelland interview; Gina Erickson interview; Mannausau interview; Kohlhase, *Spruce*, pp. 40–41; Plummer diary; Plummer interview; Arvid Peterson interview; H. Johnson interview; Gorden interview; *The Journal*, January 18, 1912, June 12, 1924, February 18, 1930, August 29, 1935; Ettestad interview; Henrickson interview.

2. Plummer diary; *The Northome Record*, February 28, 1919; *The Baudette Region*, August 26, 1915, January 4, May 17, April 26, 1917, September 27, 1917, July 4, 1919, May 29, 1925, September 18, 1931; Emma Watson interview; *The Journal*, January 9, 1913, April 27, 1916, May 24, 1917, December 22, 1921, October 21, 28, 1926, April 28, June 30, 1927, July 16, August 13, 1936, May 13, 1937, October 11, 12, 13, 1938, May 3, August 15, October 9, 1939; Kooch. Ext.; Kohlhase, *Spruce*, pp. 31–32; interview of Mr. and Mrs. Kajeten Niedzwiecki, by Pauline Musetta, of KCHS, August 10, 1978, in KCHS files, hereafter Niedzwiecki interview; Tone interview; Kooch. Comm., March 15, 1911; H. Johnson interview; Marian Peterson interview; Gina Erickson interview; letter from Gust Palm to Annie Shelland Williams, April 11, 1954, Williams file; Ettestad interview; Henrickson interview; LOW Co. Hist.; interview of Ed Richards, Big Falls, Minn., by Arnold R. Johnson, for KCHS, October 9, 1985, in KCHS files, hereafter Richards interview; Gorden interview; Bussman file; Camp Account book, ILC file; "A History of Zion Lutheran Church," no date, International Falls, KCHS; Pearson interview; Rogers interview; interview of Ruth Gowdy McLinn (Mrs. George), International Falls, July 26, 1976, hereafter McLinn interview; *Hist. of Kooch. Co.*, p. 250.

3. Kooch. Ext.; Dahlberg interview; Kohlhase, *Spruce*, pp. 6, 26, 27, 32, 39; Bergstrom interview; Emma Watson interview; Pearson interview; interview of Ellen Carlson (Mrs. Ernest), International Falls, August 19, 1976, hereafter Ellen

Carlson interview; McLinn interview; Mannausau interview; Plummer diary; Harold Erickson interview.

4. Kohlhase, *Spruce*, pp. 38, 39, 42; letter from Gust Palm to Annie Shelland Williams, March 4, 1954, in Williams file; interview of Ed Pelland, International Falls, June 8, 1976, hereafter Ed Pelland interview; Kooch. Ext.; Bergstrom interview; Plummer interview; H. Johnson interview; Gina Erickson interview; letter from Mrs. Vic Lindsten to Annie Shelland Williams, Williams file; Arvid Peterson interview; Plummer diary; Malerich interview; McLinn interview; Mannausau interview; interview of Jess A. Rose, International Falls, June 7, 1976, hereafter Rose interview; Laura Pelland interview; *The Baudette Region*, May 31, 1917.

5. Ellen Carlson interview; Gina Erickson interview; Plummer diary; *The Journal*, November 21, 1912; *Hist. of Kooch. Co.*, p. 17; Kooch. Ext.; Dentaybow Community file, KCHS; records of the Border Cooperative Telephone Company, KCHS; F. L. Bussman, "The Days That Were," a brief history of the Border Cooperative Telephone Company, in Bussman file; Harold Erickson interview; Forsyth Telephone Company, records in possession of Harold Erickson; Ettestad interview; Henrickson interview.

CHAPTER VI

Rails and Roads to the Wilderness

Northern Minnesota long remained one of the most inaccessible areas of the contiguous 48 states, although the area was first penetrated by *voyageurs* in the late 1600s and early 1700s on their way to fur-producing regions farther west. As long as an abundant supply of timber was available elsewhere, there was little reason to enter this region of dense forest, muskeg swamps, and northward flowing rivers. It was not until Backus and associates saw the potential of the forest that people had a reason to settle there. This made roads and railroads essential.

The M & I Railway Company

As Backus worked north from Minneapolis, he developed railroads as needed to fulfill his dreams of an empire. On May 17, 1892, the Brainerd and Northern Minnesota Railway Company was organized, which served Backus until his woods operations drew him farther north. On July 1, 1901, the Minnesota and International Railway Company (M & I) assumed the assets of the Brainerd and Northern when it was extended to the Falls. By 1903 Northome was the northern terminus, and preparations were made for extending the line as easily available timber was harvested and as funds were available.

In November 1903, W. H. Gemmell, general manager for the M & I, and John Swan, chief engineer, were asked if completion of the railway was conditional to the construction of the power dam. Gemmell replied, "Not necessarily, but at the same time the building of the dam would be a *big factor* to be considered in the early completion of the road." He announced that the line would be extended to the Big Fork River in 1904. Gemmell and

Swan walked the survey line from the Falls to Northome looking for potential construction problems. Although there already was objection to railroads in the northern part of the state on the grounds of cruelty to animals, the Falls editor commented, "We are willing to exchange our game for railroads."

On December 29, 1906, the Big Fork and International Falls Railway Company (BF & IF) was organized to complete the final 33.77 miles to the Falls. It had the same officers as the M & I, and until May 18, 1910, it had no assets, but on that date it was advanced $871,991.52 by its parent company, the Northern Pacific Railway Company (NP). The M & I was owned 30 percent by Backus and 70 percent by the Northern Pacific.

Minneapolis and St. Paul interests watched with eagerness and encouraged early completion of the M & I for fear that the Duluth, Virginia, and Rainy Lake Railway (DVRL) might reach the Falls first and shift business away from the Twin Cities. On September 26, 1907, headlines in *The Minneapolis Journal* read, "Last Rail Laid to Rainy River—International Falls Now Out of the Woods." At 5:00 P.M. on September 27, Backus drove a silver spike to signify official completion of the road.

On September 29 the first freight car arrived with a small consignment for nearly every merchant in the Falls. The first passenger train arrived on October 7, but it was not until November 29 that the first through passenger train arrived from St. Paul. A number of Littlefork citizens boarded that train for the Falls, accompanied by the local band to help celebrate the occasion.

On January 30, 1908, mail service was transferred from the CN to the M & I. The train left the Twin Cities at 7:00 A.M. and arrived in the Falls at 11:00 P.M. for next day delivery— 24-hour mail service, which was far quicker than on the CN via Winnipeg.

The M & I listed 5 passenger engines, 15 freight engines, and 2 switch engines, 7 passenger cars, 430 flatcars, 100 freight cars, and 5 baggage/postal cars in its 1910 inventory. That year it hauled 14,774 tons of cement, brick, and lime, chiefly for construction of the paper mill. Timber products, 182 tons in 1908 for construction purposes, skyrocketed to 55,035 tons in 1911, the first full year of operation of the mill. In 1908, the M & I's first full year of operation, it carried 14,319 passengers. In 1911 that figure rose to 50,827. (See Table III in Appendix for the scope of operation of the M & I.)[1]

Construction and Operation of the M & I

Walter E. Paul spent his entire working career with the M & I. His first job, at Big Falls in the winter of 1906–07, paid $50 a month and consisted of keeping inventory of rails, ties, bolts, and spikes. The light-weight rails and bridge material had come from other NP lines that needed upgrading. The castoff equipment and rolling stock resulted in many breakdowns. The best and largest engine was used on the night passenger run, while the smallest and poorest engines were used on the logging trains.

After the survey crew had completed its work, men with wheelbarrows dug a ditch on each side of the right-of-way and hauled the dirt to the center of the surveyed area to form a roadbed. When they hit a granite ledge near Margie, which necessitated blasting a cut about 12 feet deep, work halted because teams could not haul in supplies after the tote roads broke up with the spring thaw. Much of the land was swampy/muskeg with virtually no drainage, so the men had cold, wet feet from walking in water, which caused them to "quit in droves."

The area from Waukanka, north of Big Falls, to Happyland was deep muskeg, which made for difficult working conditions. Reputedly the men were so happy when they hit a sand beach that they called it Happyland. A second story states that they were happy because the drinking water was much better than what was available in the muskeg area.

After the roadbed was finished, the construction crew of 20 to 30 men used a special engine with three pair of driver wheels and no flange on the middle drivers so it could travel with greater ease over rough and crooked track. A caboose was immediately behind the engine, and five flatcars, loaded with tools, ties, rails, and track fasteners, were pushed ahead of it. As the lead men walked on each side of the first flatcar, each took the end of a tie and placed it on the ground ahead of the train. When 40 feet of ties were properly laid, other workers carried a length of rail and placed it on the ties. The next men spiked in just enough fasteners to hold the rails in place while the train slowly moved ahead. At the train's rear, a second crew properly spaced the ties, aligned the rails at 56½ inches, and finished spiking them down.

Some track was laid during the winter, which meant that the ties and the rails were on top of frozen ground. After the frost left the ground the following spring, the ties and the rails sank so that the rails were under water as the train passed over. Ballast was inserted to stabilize the roadbed.

Roadbeds were not always well built. Within a couple years the M & I experienced trouble when the dirt gave way and logs piled in squares were exposed. The grading contractor had covered logs with dirt, which was much faster than making a bed entirely of dirt. This was first discovered when stray livestock broke through the top layer of dirt as they walked along the track. Inspectors walked the tracks and poked holes into the bed wherever they suspected it was not solid.

The first passenger train arrived at Big Falls each week day from the south at 8:15 P.M. and returned from the north the next morning at 4:30 A.M. with the same crew. The train consisted of a small engine with two sets of drivers pulling a combination mail/baggage car, a baggage and express car, two smoking cars, and a "clean" coach.

A telegraph line was built as the railroad was extended. At first there was only a single wire from Big Falls to the NP shop at Brainerd, from which messages were relayed to their destination. After the railroad was finished to the Falls, a telephone line was added to the telegraph line. When major events, such as prize fights and presidential elections occurred, the M & I was often asked to run a telegraph wire to a saloon and provide an operator to take messages, which were recorded on a large blackboard.

For many years there was sufficient telegraph business to justify night operators at North Bemidji, Blackduck, Funkley, Big Falls, Littlefork, and the Falls. They were especially busy in the winter when woods work was in full swing. To avoid congestion with the freight and passenger business, empty flatcars were delivered to the logging sites, and full trainloads of logs were picked up to be pulled to the mills at Bemidji or the Falls during the night. Full trainloads of finished products from the mills generally moved at night also.

From Bemidji to the Falls, junctions at Tenstrike, Blackduck, Funkley (the Bullhead branch to Kelliher, which contained many spurs), Gemmell, Margie, Big Falls, Waukana, Wisner, Happyland, and Littlefork made connections with the logging railroads. Each spring the head pumper, with an engine and a crew, traveled to each of the six communities that had water tanks to melt the ice inside the tanks to prevent it from breaking loose and crashing through the tank bottoms. This was done on Sundays to avoid congestion with the regular traffic. Normally, two tanks could be steamed per day.

When water taken on at Northome foamed in the engines, it was discovered that the local creamery dumped its excess buttermilk into a ditch that ran by the M & I well. The buttermilk seeped into the water, which was pumped to the tank that supplied the engines.

When Paul's brother, Andrew, was station agent at Blackduck, a woman purchased a ticket for Bemidji. After she was told that the passenger train was late and not due for six hours, she announced that she would take the freight train. She was informed that lady passengers could not ride freights, but she persisted and climbed into the caboose. She doubted the crew when they announced that they would leave the caboose, but the brakeman and the conductor unhooked the caboose and climbed into the engine cab, and the train slowly pulled out. As the freight rounded a curve, the brakeman jumped off and walked back to see what the woman would do. When she realized that the train had left without the caboose, she departed and walked up town. The freight stopped, backed up, rehooked the caboose, and left for Bemidji without its lady passenger.

A passenger train on the way to the Falls stopped when it came to the swamp at Wisner. Paul and others got off to see what the problem was. When the conductor saw them coming he yelled, "All aboard," but the train did not move. Ten minutes later other passengers decided to see what was wrong, and again the conductor yelled, "All aboard." After another five minutes, the train started. Paul's suspicions were verified when the conductor passed through the train and whispered, "That sure is a fine buck, . . . meat not hurt at all." The crew had completely butchered the deer and put some of the meat in the mail car, some in the baggage car, and the remainder back of the engine tank.

Bill Bush was conductor on a night train out of the Falls, which contained one smoker filled with lumberjacks. By the time the train pulled out of Big Falls, one of the lumberjacks became quite noisy. Bush told him several times to sit down and be quiet and then left the car. As he returned he peered through the dense smoke and saw the lumberjack hitting at other passengers. Bush told him to behave or he would put him off the train. When the man talked back, Bush gave two "sharp pulls on the signal cord [to stop the train], grabbed the 'jack by the collar, pulled him off his seat, and headed down the aisle." The brakeman opened the vestibule and outside doors, and after Bush kicked the lumberjack into a snowbank, he pulled the cord to restart the train. As he was collecting tickets, Bush overheard a friend of the discharged lumberjack say, "I'd like to see that ___ and ___ put me off this train." Bush pulled the cord again and tossed out the second lumberjack. After the train restarted, he roared, "Is there anybody else . . . who wants to see this so and so put them off?" The car was quiet for the remainder of the trip.[2]

Operational Problems

The M & I was a busy railroad from 1910 through the 1920s. On the line from Mizpah south, including the Kelliher branch, traffic peaked between 1914 and 1923. In August 1923, 617 cars of timber products, an all-time high, were shipped out of Kelliher. From Mizpah north, business remained strong until 1928, which was the peak year for logging railroads of the ILC.

The M & I was a relatively small division of the NP, and there was a great deal of flexibility in its operation. When a lumber camp needed workers or released them, passenger cars were quickly provided to move them. Even for a station as small as Gemmell, seven times in one month in 1917 additional coaches had to be provided to take care of as many as 80 extra men on one train.

Various problems occurred in the daily operation of the M & I. A mail pouch might not be dropped off because it was mislaid by the sorters, or sometimes it was carelessly kicked off the train and run over by the train wheels. In at least one case the mail car sorter put the mail bag on the dock and another person put it back into the mail car. Occasionally the postmaster did not arrive in time to place the outgoing mail on the train. A train was delayed 20 minutes at Kelliher because the ticket clerk was not at the depot. The agent wired to Superintendent Gemmell: "Alarm clock failed to go off, missed the train, will not happen again."

A settler, who lived nine miles out of Kelliher, wrote to Gemmell that his shipment of five rolls of roofing material lay at the depot for seven days. He did not get to town often and was upset when the agent charged him $5 for storage. Later, this same farmer wrote to Gemmell that a cat, shipped to him from Big Falls on April 15, was put off at Blackduck. When he called for it, the agent said he had shipped it to Kelliher on the 16th, but the cat was not there. The man had hired a team for $8 to get the cat from Kelliher. His letter continued, "so you se [*sic*] it is very much trouble for me, now I want to ask you who is going to pay for it I am not to blame . . . I sure like to hear from you Sir you are the General Manager." Eight telegrams were exchanged between Gemmell and the agents at Big Falls and Kelliher regarding shipment of the cat, which traveled 52 miles on the M & I and arrived at Kelliher on the evening of the 18th. The agent at Kelliher wired, "No delay here."

The storekeeper at Orth purchased his bread from a baker at Bemidji and complained that the town had to go without bread when the train crew did not leave it at the siding. There was no agent or depot at Orth, and the train man replied that he could never "see his way clear" to put off perishable goods, even at the owner's risk, when there was no one there to collect them.

Several letters were exchanged between Gemmell and C. C. Murphy, the agent at Kelliher, in December 1923 and January 1924, because Murphy was late to work and did not keep the station and the warehouse neat and clean. Gemmell protested that Murphy had two helpers and was not doing enough work himself. After the log shipments were taken care of each day, there was not much other work. The end result was the loss of a helper.

Snowstorms occasionally stopped traffic on the M & I. One passenger recalled that in March 1923, he was on the evening passenger train out of the Falls that got as far as Littlefork and was snowbound until the next morning. The northbound train was stopped at Bemidji, and it took from 8:30 A.M. to 4:00 P.M. to travel the 100 miles to the Falls because it was stuck in snowdrifts several times.

Major operational problems were caused by people, not equipment, even though much of it was cast off from other divisions. One of the most serious problems resulted when logs, laid on top of the chains of the flatcars to round out the load, often rolled off the fast moving trains and sometimes damaged switch stands and even flew through depot walls. After each winter's logging, it took a special crew using a steam derrick two weeks to pick up and reload onto flatcars the thousands of logs that lay along the tracks.

Workers sought positions with M & I because those jobs offered security and a better than normal salary. In 1917 the monthly salaries at the Kelliher station were: agent, $100; clerk, $75; helper, $60; and night clerk, $60. The salaries were based on a 9-hour day, 26 days a month. About the end of World War I the work day was cut to 8 hours, but sometimes that was spread out over a 12-hour period to insure that someone was always at the station when a train arrived to help passengers or to handle mail or freight. The method of pay was changed from a monthly basis to an hourly rate at the same time, even though there was no major change in the amount received.[3]

A Logging Railroad Network

To anyone unfamiliar with the many problems of floating logs downstream, it might appear that everything favored using rivers to transport timber to the mill. For the timber coming from the east, down Rainy Lake toward Koochiching Falls, floating worked well for M & O. However, this was not true for production from the south and west of the Falls, for the rivers in that area ran into the Rainy River, which flowed away from the Falls. That timber either had to be processed at Baudette, Spooner, or Kenora and Rainy River, Ontario, or it had to be loaded onto the CN and hauled back to the Fort or the Falls. Backus could not tolerate the advantage competitors had at those four more westerly locations, so he constructed a network of forest railroads to reduce his dependence on the rivers and to control the production in most of Koochiching, northern Itasca, and northern Beltrami (after 1922, Lake of the Woods) counties.

The Minnesota, Dakota and Western Railway

The Minnesota, Dakota and Western Railway (MD & W) was organized in 1909 to corner the timber supply south and west of the Falls and eventually to connect with the wheat fields of the Red River Valley and North Dakota. It was an unfulfilled dream of Backus to make the Falls a flour-milling center. On October 31, 1902, Backus had formed the International Bridge Terminal Company (IBT) as a Canadian concern. The purpose of this wagon, foot, and railroad bridge was to connect the mills at the Fort with those at the Falls. After the MD & W was organized, the IBT became a subsidiary of it. In the meantime, the MD & W also built three miles of line connecting the M & I with the Duluth, Winnipeg, and Pacific (DW & P), which crossed into Canada at Ranier, giving the Falls access to rail transportation to Duluth and east. Once the IBT bridge was completed in August 1912, M & O mills in both towns had access to three major railroads. The public paid a toll to use this bridge, which proved a great boon to tourism into Canada as well as to the local citizens, who previously had relied on ferries to cross the river.

During 1910 the MD & W constructed an 18-mile line to Loman. Before it was finished, Backus argued with officials of the M & I over proposed rates to handle their cars from Nakoda to the Falls and threatened to build a parallel line between those points. However, the M & I yielded. Rumors continued until about 1930 regarding extending the Loman Line west, but no railroad was built.

Another part of the Backus railroad dream involved the Minneapolis and Rainy River Railroad Company (M & RR), which built as far north as Turtle Lake, near Marcell, in 1890, to Big Fork in 1906, and finally to the Big Fork River, south of Craig, in 1910. The Deer River Line, which was part of the MD & W, was extended 18 miles south from Littlefork to Camp 5 in 1912–13, and in 1914, 16 additional miles to Craigville, on the north side of the Big Fork River. The bridge was never built across the Big Fork and a two-mile gap existed between the M & RR and the Deer River Line (sometimes called the Craig Line). Camp 29 became a headquarters camp and the rail terminus for the Deer River Line. Later, a 20-mile branch was built west toward Northome, followed by a 25-mile branch southeast toward Thistledew Lake.

Another branch of the MD & W was the Galvin Line, (sometimes called the Nett Lake Line), which was built off the M & I at Nakoda. Backus intended that it was to continue south, connect with the Holmstrom spur, and then on to Pengilly to link with a major railroad. Three or four other spurs branched off the M & I at various times, all of which reached into different sectors of the woods. In 1928, the peak year for the logging railroad network, the Loman Line consisted of 20 miles; the Galvin Line, 22.75; the Bear River Line, 9.5; the Grand Falls Line, 5; the Craig Line, 37.75; the Holmstrom spur, 10.5; and the Cutfoot Sioux Line, 46—for a total of 151.5 miles. Another 70 miles of spur track ran from these main forest lines to sites where timber was being harvested. There were 172 switches, 91 of which were on the 18 miles within the yards at the Falls. Between 1932 and 1940, the total network, except the Deer River Line, was taken up.

The cost of building main woods lines, which used 72-pound

rails, ran between $10,000 and $30,000 per mile, depending upon the amount of ballast needed and how many bridges were required. Flood damage to bridges was a big cost factor in maintenance once the roads were finished. Annual upkeep averaged about $300 to $350 per mile, if no major bridge repairs were required.[4]

In the 1928–29 season, over 19 million feet of logs, nearly 73,000 cords of pulpwood, plus thousands of ties, poles, posts, and pilings were hauled out of the woods. The total train expenses for the MD & W were $96,178.45, or $0.224 per carload mile. It took on the average 13 tons of coal for a train of 40 cars, loaded with 20 cords each, to make a round trip from Camp 29 to the Falls.

The forest railroad network was very fluid. From 1910 through 1932 a total of 192 different lumber camps were built with a spur to each. These temporary spurs replaced the traditional sleigh roads and were inexpensively built and easy to move. Sometimes the ties and the rails were laid over poles on the frozen ground, but most of the time the track consisted only of ties and rails, and, therefore, could be used only on frozen ground. A 20-foot path was cut through a 40-acre stand of trees in such a manner that no logs were skidded more than 650 feet to the spur. The road cutter filled the low spots with logs. When winter came, a flatcar loaded with ties and rails was pushed ahead of an engine, and a six-man crew laid the track.

Once the spur track was finished, lumberjack crews were assigned a 99-foot strip along the track, back 650 feet. They cut and skidded the timber to the rail siding, where it was piled according to species. A checker then determined the amount cut by each team of men. When there was enough timber cut, flatcars were pushed into position and loaded by steam-operated jammers, which could load 15 to 20 cars a day.

In addition to the Backus network of forest railroads, the Twomey-Williams Line branched off the M & I at Big Falls and extended 50 miles northwest. This road was built in 1924 by three former M & O employees—J. D. Twomey, Curt Williams, and Joe Lloyd—to tap the virgin white and Norway pine in the Pine Island district of western Koochiching and eastern Lake of the Woods counties. Most of that timber was cut in the 1927–28 season and sold to M & O.[5]

Even though the hours were not as regular as in the mill or in the lumber camps, many individuals liked working on the

MD & W. Eric Tive started working for the road on June 26, 1916, for $0.26 an hour. His job was to fix boxcars, which often had their ends pushed loose by the big rolls of paper shipped in them. By 1922 he was earning $0.40 an hour. Boilermakers, the top wage earners in the MD & W shop, received $0.635 per hour.

Ray Schneider worked in the shops as a machinist for $0.65 an hour 10 hours a day 6 days a week and thought he was "riding high," especially when he received time and one-half for extra work on Sundays. Alfred Johnson started work as a section hand on the line from Thistledew Lake to Camp 29 in 1928 for $45 a month, the best "anyone 16 years old could make." Next, Johnson was promoted to running the jammer loading cars at Thistledew.

Tive soon became car inspector and checked all cars in the MD & W centers at the Falls and at the Fort. Other than the loose ends, the main problem with cars was leaks in the top seam under the walking planks, which allowed water to drain onto the paper products. The leaks were patched with tar and tarpaper. If cars were too badly damaged, they were sent to the NP car shop at Brainerd. Tive's business card showed his sense of humor. It read: "Looking for loose nuts and hot boxes." He liked the work because he had to turn in a report only once a week. On cold days he wore two pair of underwear and extra large shoes so he could wear liners inside of them. Outdoor work must have appealed to him, for he never missed a payday in 50 years and 2 months. The only problems he encountered were sick people in the boxcars. They never caused trouble, but they refused help because they did not want people to know who they were. Tive retired in 1966 and was still going strong in 1989, at age 97. He felt that outdoor work was his right choice.

The rate of accidents on the MD & W because of equipment failure was enhanced by reckless operation by the crews and by lack of supervision. In an effort to reduce downtime, the woods personnel wanted gasoline-powered speeders instead of handcars. They would save time, improve service, speed up mail service to the camps, and hasten getting the injured or sick to the hospital. It was argued that the section men could not cover their territory with handcars. Therefore, in the fall of 1922, Seymour Backus was asked for permission to purchase ten Fairmont section cars with 6-HP engines to replace the handcars. The next spring train crews protested that the tracks were not safe for travel. After extra section crews were required to restore the tracks to safe operating condition, Backus agreed to purchase the Fairmont cars. Next there was discussion about a gasoline-powered rail car for passenger service and for transportation of labor and supplies in the off season, when logging trains were not operating. The leadership was not always willing to accept changing technology, even though it reduced operating costs and improved conditions for the workers.[6]

The DW & P and the VRLRR

While Backus was working out of Minneapolis and projecting railroads north from Brainerd and Bemidji, other individuals, including W. H. Cook, were planning railroads out of Duluth to the Falls. The Duluth, Virginia, and Rainy Lake road changed its name to the Duluth, Winnipeg, and Rainy Lake Railway in 1905, in keeping with its enlarged goal of connecting Winnipeg with Chicago, and later became the Duluth, Winnipeg, and Pacific. In anticipation that the line between those two towns would be double tracked, an 80-foot right-of-way was surveyed.

The decision to cross into Canada at the narrowest point, where Rainy Lake empties into Rainy River, was in part determined because Cook and Backus could not agree on a price for the road to enter the Falls. It is reputed that the real reason Backus objected to letting Cook and his railroad into the Falls was that they wanted to control the bridge over Koochiching Falls, which was not to Backus' liking.

In 1906 Cook and others formed the Rainy River Bridge Company, purchased land from Mr. Holler, and secured the right-of-way over the Rainy River, where Ranier was established, to Pither's Point. In 1907 construction started on a drawbridge, and plans were made to build a large sawmill closer to the Fort. Builders of the Duluth line were determined to beat the M & I into the area. The DW & P was so determined to beat the M & I that when its crew members hit large sink holes, instead of digging them out, they filled them with logs, covered them with dry dirt, and laid the track.

Most homesteaders willingly granted right-of-way for a modest payment because they expected drainage benefit from the railroad ditch and because rail service would end their isolation. The only exception was a woman homesteader who wanted $5,000 for right-of-way and lay down between the ties to stop construction. The sheriff arrested the woman, and the track was laid while she was in jail. The decision of damages was left to the court.

During the latter part of the winter of 1906–07, provisions were delivered along the right-of-way to supply the grade-building crew during the summer when roads were impassable. However, that summer provisions ran low, partly because so much food was consumed by quitters, stragglers, and visitors. An attempt was made to deliver more provisions by pack horses, but they could not make it through the muskeg and floating bogs, so Indians from Bois Fort (Nett Lake) were hired at $2.50 a day to carry goods 20 miles to the advance cook camp. Despite the gallant efforts of the Indians, for three days, when the grade was being built between Arbutus and Ray, the crew had only pancakes and prunes to eat. On the afternoon of the third day about a dozen men walked back to the end of the rail and acquired all the ham and eggs they could carry for breakfast the next day.

By September 1907, Ericsburg had passenger service, but the roadbed to Ranier was so soft that it was not until freezeup permitted ballasting that the line could support heavy trains. On April 28, 1908, the first passenger train crossed the bridge and entered the Fort. In 1910 the DW & P became a subsidiary of the CN, and in 1911, after the MD & W connected with the DW & P at Ranier, the Falls and the Fort had a railroad link with Duluth.

The DW & P opened the area to the southeast, but, more importantly, it linked the mills at Virginia with the forest of eastern Koochiching and western St. Louis counties. In 1911 the Rainy Lake Railway Company transferred its timber holdings, which consisted of much of the area between Vermilion and Rainy lakes, to the Virginia and Rainy Lake Railroad Company (VRLRR). During the next two decades the VRLRR built nearly 2,000 miles of branch forest railroads (100 miles a year) in addition to sleigh roads and lake terminals. The DW & P on the east was a counterpart of the M & I on the west. Most of the timber it hauled went to Virginia, but some from as far south as Ash Lake went to the Falls or the Fort. Because there were many large lakes in this area, timber was toted to the lake shores and floated to forest rail lines, where it was hoisted to flatcars and carried to Virginia. This represented a considerable savings where railroad building was particularly difficult.

It was company policy not to skid logs with horses more than one-fourth mile, which meant that rails were laid and moved as often as monthly. On one occasion ties and rails were laid over tamped-down snow to get the timber out before spring thaw.

In 1913, 17-year-old Alex Gerber was employed by the VRLRR as a mechanic's helper for $35 a month plus room and board. Railroad workers had separate accommodations to avoid disturbing the lumberjacks. His small room had an iron bed, a straw-filled tick, and several heavy woolen blankets. After a stint in World War I, Gerber was rehired and promoted to engineer at $125 a month, room and board, and overtime for time beyond the 10-hour day, 26 days a month.

The engines were Shay-geared locomotives capable of climbing 10 percent grades at a top speed of 12 miles per hour. Speed was not important, because spurs ranged from only one-fourth to three miles in length. On very hazardous sites, a Russell car was used to take timber out. It could haul only 3,000 board feet, about half as much as a normal flatcar, but using it was still cheaper than using horses. When Gerber's engine got off the track because of a broken rail, he remained in the cab all night to keep the tender from freezing. He walked 1½ miles to the camp for supper. When he returned to the locomotive, wolves followed him "too close," but he kept them away by swinging his lantern.

Scott Erickson's World War I naval experience qualified him as a tugboat operator on Kabetogama, Namakan, and Vermilion lakes. His job was to tow a 32- × 76-foot scow delivering provisions, supplies, machinery, sleighs, hay, oats, and horses to the various campsites. In the spring he pulled booms of logs to the loading hoist. Much of the time he worked out of Camp 75, on Hoist Bay, on Namakan Lake, which was the end of the VRLRR. On one trip from Hoist Bay to Lost Bay, on Lake Kabetogama, Erickson pulled a scow loaded with sacks of oats and 20 wild horses. One of the horses broke loose, dashed to the top of the pile of oats, and jumped into the lake. About six weeks later Erickson passed an Indian camp, where he saw Indian children riding the trained horse.[7]

Decline of the Railroad

When the CN opened the wilderness in 1901, the era of riverboat traffic from Koochiching Falls to Kenora was doomed. Like riverboats, railroads had a short-lived history, serving as the dominant form of transportation south of the border only from 1907 to 1937. At that time service was discontinued on the Loman Line, one of the biggest feeder lines to the M & I. Only World War II rationing of fuel and tires kept the Deer River Line in service until 1947.

In 1911 the CN approached the M & O for the privilege of crossing the international bridge it was building between the Falls and the Fort, but Backus was not interested. That did not affect the CN's business, which increased steadily into the 1920s, when a train an hour passed over the line through Baudette.

Throughout the period from 1911 through the late 1920s, the CN hinted at building a direct line to the Twin Cities. After the Canadian government purchased the railroad in 1917, the CN was as aggressive as ever with those plans. However, starting in 1925, it began to close smaller stations that could not generate $8,000 in profits per year and dropped all plans for expansion. Pitt was one of the first American stations to be closed by the CN even though local citizens argued that the figure should be $8,000 gross volume, not profit.

The pattern was similar on other railroads. Passenger traffic dropped rapidly in the late 1920s after roads improved and the automobile took over. When the last steam passenger train left Kelliher in February 1929, it was replaced by a combination baggage/passenger car powered by a gasoline engine, which remained in operation until 1932. At the same time, trucks took over the less-than-carload freight business. After the mill in the Falls closed temporarily in 1931, the logging trains never operated again, except for a brief period during World War II.

In 1925 there was discussion in communities from the Falls to Virginia along the DW & P about the Northland Transportation Company starting a bus line. The Railroad and Warehouse Commission warned that if buses began operating, rail passenger service would be discontinued because trains to Duluth were already losing money. In 1927, when the DW & P reduced to one passenger train each way daily from Ranier to Duluth, interest was renewed in starting bus service. Passenger and mail service soon was reduced to tri-weekly.

Because traffic dropped off so heavily in 1928, General Manager Gemmell threatened to close the M & I headquarters at Brainerd. By moving to Bemidji, where the freight and passenger business could be combined, the M & I office was saved until August 1, 1933, when the NP merged the M & I with its Lake Superior Division. In 1933 the round-trip Pullman rate from the Falls to Minneapolis was reduced from $7.50 to $5.65, but that did not help the cause, for the next two runs in and out of the Falls had no passengers either way. Business revived briefly when the CCC camps were established; sometimes there was standing room only in the coach. The revival of the economy with the advent of World War II did not stimulate passenger traffic, however, for the love affair with the automobile was too strong.

Like passenger traffic, freight business also sought its way to the highways. Correspondence about the consequences if people shipped by truck first appeared in 1928. The question was always whether or not the depot would be kept open. Shipping cream from nearly every community to centralizing stations was a sizeable business and one of the first areas where trucks were competitive. When a truck route was established, the time-consuming chore of delivering cans to the depot was eliminated, and the cream arrived at the processors in better condition. In an effort to retain the business for the railroad, some agents actually took cream to the depot for the farmers during their busy season.

Dry conditions in 1929 forced the sale of a larger than normal number of cattle, and for the first time marketing to South Saint Paul by truck took place. Most of those shipments were from the western part of Koochiching and all of Lake of the Woods counties because train connections in those areas were poor. The $0.80 per hundred freight rate compared favorably with rail rates, and livestock arrived at market in 15 to 20 hours instead of 2 days by rail. This resulted in less shrinkage. Smaller shippers had less difficulty getting their consignments handled by trucks rather than waiting for a full carload to be gathered.

In off-woods season, individuals who hauled timber to the railroad put livestock racks on their trucks. Farmers appreciated not having to drive their animals to the local railroad stockyards, where they were assembled for shipment. Railroad agents in every community campaigned against turning to trucks. They claimed that, unlike the railroads, the truckers had done nothing to build the country. One agent commented, "I cannot see how stock handled from here [Gemmell] to So. St. Paul by truck could be in good condition for market." The farmers saw just the opposite results and were more likely to get better prices for animals shipped by truck.

The forest railroads deteriorated rapidly when the camps were idled after the mill was closed by the Backus bankruptcy. A minimum maintenance program had been in effect for several years prior to the shutdown. New ties and ballast had to be added in many places at a cost that was exceedingly high compared to the original construction cost. This made everyone aware that trucking timber products, even with the equipment of the early 1930s, had merit.

After the last log drive on the Little Fork River, there was no need for the Loman Line. In 1940 the Interstate Commerce Commission granted permission to the MD & W to abandon it. On June 30, 1947, the Deer River Line was closed, and the last of M & O's woods railroads became history. Since its opening in 1914, the Deer River Line had hauled 2 million cords of timber, an average of 5,000 flatcars a year. The once glorious and romantic era had come to an end, overcome by a far more labor efficient, if less dramatic, method of operation using the latest technology.

All that was left of the woods empire railroad network was 35 miles of MD & W trackage within the Falls and 3 miles of its subsidiary, the IBT, that operated out of the Fort. About 50 employees operated 4 diesel locomotives to pull 200 flatcars, of which 95 were used to haul pulpwood from the landings to the mill at the Fort, and the remainder to haul timber from the storage yards to the mill at the Falls. The locomotives switched 700 leased boxcars, which supplied the mills with materials and transported the finished products throughout Canada and the United States.[8]

Early "Roads"

The inaccessibility of the wilderness was well known. Once people started to settle the area, travel had to be facilitated. In November 1909, the Koochiching County commissioners petitioned the state to supply cable for a lighter (a tow chair) over the Little Fork River. The request was honored, and on January 27, 1910, A. T. Scarlett was put in charge of the crossing. That lighter served until 1914, when it was replaced with a swinging/walking bridge, dubbed the Nett River Township Bridge, which sufficed for several years until a bridge capable of supporting wagons and automobiles was erected.

Many settlers were extremely isolated by the lack of adequate roads. In 1910 Annie Shelland Williams visited 83-year-old Mrs. McGilliwary, whose deserted-looking cabin was surrounded by grass up to the armpits. It could hardly be seen from the road and was at the end of a two-mile trail that would not have been taken by anyone who did not know a home was located there. Mrs. McGilliwary cut, trimmed, and split the trees closest to the cabin for firewood. The neighbors, who did not want to encourage her to stay for fear she would fall or become ill and lie sick without aid, refused to help. "She does not want to go . . . but admits she would like a small place on the main road."

Annie Shelland Williams commented on teachers who often walked 15 miles to a dance in the winter or paddled 30 miles in the summer. Many female teachers tied their shoes around their neck when they walked through the wet forest, put them on when they arrived, and carried them back home after the dance.

A popular story that circulated in rural areas was that whenever mail carriers realized that a family received more than one mail order catalog, the carriers used the additional copies to fill in holes in the road. This was jokingly known as "trail improvement."

Roads were scarce and poor. The 1912 map of Koochiching County indicates that 80 percent of the area was designated as swamp, and there were only 108 miles of roads. The longest stretch was 31 miles from Northome to Big Falls. There were another 24 miles from Northome east and another 20 miles along the Rainy River in the northwestern corner of the county. Only one road of seven miles is shown out of the Falls toward Jack Fish Bay. The Canadians had approved a road from Rainy River City to the Fort in 1912, but work did not start on it until the spring of 1913.

In 1912 school bus drivers were worried that the horses would break their legs when the water got high enough to cause the corduroy road (logs laid perpendicular to the line of travel) along the Rainy River to float. Plummer noted that his family had started out with ponies and a jumper to visit neighbors, but the roads were so soft that they could not make it. Joyce Kohlhase recalled a farmer who purchased oats for his horses in Mizpah and carried the feed to his farm because he could not travel with horses and wagon.

Roads were nothing more than 6-foot ungraded paths cut through the woods. In 1913 the 110 townships in Koochiching County had a total of 47 miles of township roads, most of which were corduroy and built by local farmers. When townships later became involved in building roads with aid from the Elwell road plan, the roads were 2 rods wide with all the trees cut flat to the ground, and stumps were removed from the center 10 feet. One of the Johnson brothers, in Dentaybow Township, received $195 a mile to prepare such a road, but gravel was not used. Roads were so bad that wagons and automobiles often traveled on the railroad tracks.

In August 1916, the first car driven in Dentaybow Township traveled out of Littlefork on the railroad for 2 miles, then followed ditch grades, traversing 41 miles to get to a location 18 miles from the starting point. Typical townships in well-settled rural regions had a potential 72 miles of roads, but Dentaybow never had more than 20 miles, most of them passable only in good weather. Many other townships had less. More settled areas, such as Rat Root Township around Ericsburg, had only a few miles of corduroy road prior to 1909, when the first two bridges were built.

An excellent example of the impact of rural isolation is found in a letter from J. D. Lowe, who taught school in Indus 1913 through 1915 and then became an attorney. He wrote to Annie Shelland Williams in 1961 that there was no common religion or other activity and that many people apparently just came to get something for nothing. There was a struggle to have a community club, but the people were "slow, lethargic, indifferent, and cynical . . . not cheerful people to work with or for." They came to meetings and listened and "would always eat. . . . We had a little fun but it was slow."

Williams described some of the problems of rural isolation:

> In visiting schools I stayed at homes of the people over-night, and heard all their troubles in regard to roads, unequal taxes, no train cars for crops, the fact that thousand of bushels of potatoes were dumped into the river each year because they could not get them to market. I found many of the people planning to leave the country because they did not have a sale for their products. . . . This, with the fact that the schools could not be maintained properly on account of lack of taxes [delinquent taxes] and poor roads. . . . I finally got up enough courage to call this to the attention of the state legislature, a committee came up, 300 men turned out to meet with them, only 5 of whom could drive their teams to town in summer.

She became the leading campaigner for good roads and was backed by the Northern Minnesota Development Association. She argued that without roads there could be no markets, no way to get to school or to obtain medical help.

In a speech before the Minnesota Conservation Congress in Minneapolis, in November 1912, she said:

> Give us good roads or appropriations equal to the taxes the state should pay on its land . . . and in ten years time we'll show you the best schools. . . . It is hard to realize . . .

what it means to live 25 miles from a railroad without even a dirt road running through the swamps and forest. I have had to wade up to my knees in swamps and literally cut my way through a wilderness in trying to get from one house to another. . . . There are women . . . that for 10 years have never been more than 10 miles away from their homes. No one who has not seen it, can realize what the desolation of that country is, where no news from the outer world is ever heard within three weeks of its occurrence. With no trains, no boats, and no roads the situation is desperate.

Communities were often no more than six or eight families scattered along the railroad and separated from other settlements by swamps. The only way these families could get out during the summer was by "walking the great sponge which continually sinks beneath the foot." If someone became sick and did not recover rapidly or died, he or she had to be carried 10 to 20 miles by stretcher to the nearest railroad, river, or town. Later, Annie Shelland Williams wrote in the *American Magazine* that there was no point in calling people to the wilderness unless they had roads, schools, churches, and markets. If they came without them, they would leave as soon as the timber was floated down the river. This fact was verified by the Minnesota Immigration Agency, which reported that settlers were coming to the state at the rate of 200 a day, but were reluctant to go to the northern counties because they lacked adequate roads.

The northern counties slowly improved their road network, but the task of building both township roads and major highways was more than they could finance. In March 1911, the commissioners appropriated $1,000 for use on State Road No. 7, in Watrous Township. In 1912 they approved 36 road projects ranging from $100 to $500 each. People were so anxious for roads that they willingly accepted the offer of county officials to use county equipment and do the work themselves. The county set $4 a day for an assistant engineer to supervise their work. Volunteer clubs also helped keep roads in repair once they were built and later purchased equipment and contracted to do the work.

Settlers used their teams and wagons to haul gravel. The standard rig was a wagon with a 2 × 4 bottom and 6-inch sides that held 1 yard. The gravel was hand loaded, but it was unloaded by lifting up the individual 2 × 4s and letting the gravel drop through. In many areas there was no gravel, and no funds were available to have it shipped in. In that case, corduroying was done, and the county paid for material and labor at the rate of $2 per rod. This practice continued through 1918, after which castoff road building equipment was available from the military.[9]

Road Legislation

To minimize the cost of building roads, counties attempted to have highways designated state roads so the cost would be shared. However, in the early 1900s the state had little experience with road work, and it had to use care to build roads where they provided maximum service. The road from Northome to the Falls was the first to profit from state funds.

In 1911 Minnesota passed the Elwell Law, which initially provided for aid in cities of the first class and was later enlarged to aid rural highways outside of cities and villages. The first road approved under that law, in November 1911, was from the western Koochiching County boundary along the Rainy River to where Pelland Junction was later located, joining with U.S. Highway No. 71. As soon as that road was approved, the commissioners petitioned for aid for a road from the Falls southeast to the county line near Ray (now U.S. No. 53). By April 1912, that road was approved, and the county was notified that it would receive $3,000 out of a total $340,000 allocated for the year, covering projects totaling $6,700,000. The state would provide half of the funds, the counties one-fourth, the benefited property owners one-fourth. Elwell road meetings were held in every community to urge people to petition for roads and to cooperate with the Good Roads Association. Plummer was made secretary in his area for both the Elwell and Good Roads groups.

Northern Minnesota had about one-fourth of the total Elwell system allocated to it, and work started as soon as conditions made surveying and stumping possible. Everyone was excited about having road connections to Duluth, the Twin Cities, and Winnipeg, because all three roads were approved. An election was held in October 1913 to approve the sale of $300,000 in bonds for road construction. Highway No. 4 (now No. 71) was built in 1914, but not graveled. On August 12, 1915, a local farmer using team and wagon traveled over the road with state highway engineers on an inspection tour.

In 1919 C. M. Babcock, state highway commissioner, proposed an even more extensive system of state highways. In 1920 service clubs in every community urged voters to support Amendment No. 1, the Babcock Road plan. As car numbers increased, a campaign for hard-surfaced roads started. To pay for such roads, an average license fee of $18 was assessed on each car. The promoters encouraged everyone to vote for hard surfacing, which would reduce car expenses. The license cost on 370 cars in the county would only be a fraction of the $5.4 million cost of hard surfacing the 180 miles. Koochiching County still had 470 miles of gravel roads.

By 1922 local papers boasted that Koochiching County car owners had paid $15,236 in automobile taxes and that the county had received $91,792 from the state—more than any other county. After 1923, Lake of the Woods County received similar benefits and campaigned for a highway south to link with Bemidji and then the Twin Cities.[10]

Road Improvement

When the streets of Koochiching village were first improved, gravel was not available, so crushed rock from the gold mines at Rainy Lake City was barged in. Having streets "paved with gold" made good headlines, but it was costly to ship material about 15 miles down the lake.

In April 1913, the Falls council advertised for bids to pave Third Street between Second and Fifth Avenues. When Baudette decided to improve its mud streets in 1914, it contracted with the CN to ship in 75 carloads of gravel, since none was available locally. Three years later the Baudette editor expressed his feelings about the streets: "The 'canal' by the church has been deepened so that boats of seven feet draft can pass through."

When the wagon road was surveyed from Warroad to the Falls in 1914, only a few deposits of gravel were located, so surfacing was delayed until 1917. Drainage-ditch banks were used as roads, but most of them never became all-weather roads. The greatest advantage that the ditch-bank roads had over the usual graded roads was that jill poles (stumps and tree limbs that extended from the road surface) were absent.

County Extension Agent Mark Abbott complained in 1919 that it was difficult to visit farms because, other than the three main highways, there was only one mile of graveled road in the county, outside of the Falls. Some farms were accessible in the summer only by boat. If Abbott caught the logging train, he could get to Craig in four hours at a cost of $0.53. If he went to the same area by public transportation, he had to take the train 35 miles to Big Falls, then hire a livery for 14 miles, and walk the last

25 miles. During 1919 he traveled by automobile, passenger, freight, and logging trains, gascar, gas speeder, pump speeder, handcar, ox team, livery team, horseback, motorcycle, bicycle, launch, rowboat, canoe, and on foot, for a total of 8,106 miles by rail, 202 miles by team, 1,441 miles by automobile, 64 miles by boat, and 200 miles on foot. When he drove, he preferred a car with spoke wheels, because it was easier to put the prying pole into them to lift the car out of mud holes.

In 1927 the three state highways out of the Falls were impassable from March 15 to June 15. The full Farm Bureau board never met that year because it was impossible for many of the members to get to the Falls. Nearly all the livestock shown at the fairs at Littlefork and Northome as late as 1928 was walked in. One boy led his calf 24 miles in two days to get to Northome; his calf placed sixth.

One of the chief problems with ungraded roads was that the snow was not removed during the winter and was packed solid by the traffic. This made a smoother surface, but when it thawed in the spring, the roads were muddy for a longer period. It was not until after World War I when large 4 × 4 trucks, track-type tractors, road graders, and snowplows were released by the military, for a nominal cost, that any sizeable road equipment was used. By 1922 the three major highways—to Duluth, to Bemidji, and to Baudette—were graded and graveled, and Baudette also had a road running straight south. Koochiching County had 165 miles of state trunk highway, a portion far beyond its ability to pay.

After losing heavy equipment in the muskeg, where even horses and scrapers could not work, it became standard to work late in the fall and early in the winter to complete some of the worst grading and much of the graveling. Hand loading the gravel wagons and hauling on cold winter days was uncomfortable work, but was carried on with little complaint because settlers desired a better road system and they desperately needed the cash. Plummer worked in a nearby gravel pit dynamiting the gravel loose and loading wagons, while son Jim hauled with a team. Carl Dahlberg earned $6 a day in 1925 for himself and his team, pulling a slusher with gravel to the hopper that loaded the trucks. The trucks were the first Dahlberg had ever seen for graveling roads. The gravel was not screened, but the larger rocks were quickly buried in the soft soil.

Roads often were referred to as being bottomless. The road

from Ray to the Falls was one of the worst stretches. For several years the DW & P provided flatcar service between Ray and Ranier, for $8 one way, to enable motorists to avoid disaster. To combat muddy conditions, planks or culverts, cut in half to provide troughs for the car wheels to run in, were laid in the worst spots. Mark Abbott's comment that one did not travel over the roads but through them was most fitting.

In October 1926, Commissioner Babcock announced that for the first time state trunk roads would be kept open during the winter, if possible. The state had erected 1.5 million feet of snow fence. In addition, it had 800 farmer team patrols and a large amount of heavy equipment to combat the snow, but the men and the equipment went out only after 6 inches of snow had fallen. Initially, the state permitted farmers to work out their road taxes by clearing roads and cutting roadside weeds, but later it contracted that work out.

By the mid-1920s, agitation began for better than gravel roads. Studies proved that regardless of the amount of traffic, the paved surface was cheaper to maintain than gravel. The greater the volume of traffic, the more expensive gravel surfacing became. It was virtually impossible to keep gravel roads in good condition.

The first tarvia in the area was applied between the Falls and Ranier in the late 1930s, but most of the main roads were not hard surfaced until the 1940s. In spring, the best way to get to the Falls from Baudette was via the road from Rainy River City to the Fort. As late as 1936 there was a gap of 10 miles between Gemmell and Northome, which was "pretty much as God Almighty left it when He finished the world."

During the 1930s, the federal government, as part of the emergency federal works projects, provided funds to build farm-to-market roads, which improved the rural secondary system. At this time the road from the Falls to Island View was built. It opened a large area for lake-shore living to Falls residents and encouraged tourism on some of the best pike fishing grounds in Rainy Lake. Before that road was built, lake cabins were reached by hiking or by boat.

Bridges were a costly part of road building. Each spring ice flows and log drives washed out many first-generation bridges. Some were not rebuilt, because the traffic did not justify the expense, which virtually halted development in some townships. In 1927 there was talk that, because the river still was classed as navigable, any bridge over the Big Fork River where it entered the Rainy had to be a draw bridge. After the bridge over Koochiching Falls was completed between the Falls and the Fort in 1912, the other significant border crossing was between Baudette and Rainy River, Ontario. The CN spanned the river in 1901, but the public had to use ferries. Negotiations commenced in 1926, when Congress authorized a cost share project with Canada. Legislation was revised, but it was not until 1932 that the first work was done as part of the project.[11]

Car Fever

As soon as cars became available, area residents joined the national rush to purchase one. It appears that Henry T. Hetting, on September 4, 1910, had the "first automobile that ever whipped its cushioned tires on the streets of International Falls." G. W. Gonyeais was hired as chauffeur to carry passengers from the Falls to Ranier as soon as the road was graveled. Because there were no snow plows, plans called for packing the snow to keep the road open. The city council granted Hetting a license to run an automobile to carry passengers, freight, and baggage for hire. The August 3, 1911, *Journal* reported that George Holler was sporting a new automobile, which had arrived by train earlier in the day and "was the center of attraction for a few hours." On August 17, Ray Holler and Hetting purchased a seven-seated automobile for public hire because their business was "too much for one machine." Gina Erickson claimed that she saw her first car in Superior about 1904, so when she saw Dr. Burn's car on the logging road between Buyck and Crane Lake in 1911, she was not surprised. He had it barged across Lake Vermilion and then followed the logging trails north.

The Falls Automobile Company, owned by banker Nels Olson, et al., was established in 1912. Only one car was sold during its first year. The first buyer of the Ford Model T was Captain H. I. Bedell, who claimed it was the "finest thing of its kind in town," equipped with electric lights and "every latest device for the comfort and convenience of its owner." The first local newspaper ads promoting Model Ts appeared in 1913, with prices ranging from $525 to $625, including all equipment. During 1913 Olson sold 16 cars, but the Ford Company field man visited the Falls to determine why he had not done better. When Olson proved to him that the only roads were in the Falls and across the bridge to the Fort and one to Ranier, the representative was surprised that he had sold so many. Although Nels Olson had the first Ford agency and was also involved with the Buick dealership, he did not own the first personal car in the Falls. A saloon keeper in Ranier reputedly had the first car, and the taxi operator the second.

In September 1914, Plummer paid $0.25 for his first auto ride at a celebration in Boucherville, Ontario, after which he walked over eight miles to return home. The banker in Littlefork had a Velie in 1914. Within a year there was a Stutz and four Model Ts, even though there were no roads out of town, only paths useable in dry weather. The lack of roads did not bother Ross Slack, who reputedly owned the first car in Big Falls, for he used it only on the river during the winter.

Falls general merchant E. E. Peterson purchased a Buick in 1915, which was reputed to be the "acme of perfection." Cars were so numerous in Baudette in 1916 that editor Noonan wrote, "The average Baudette citizen now seems to have the idea that it's impossible to pursue happiness without an automobile." Mizpah had several cars by the time Joyce Kohlhase's father bought his Saxon in 1917, but his was the first one with a self-starter.

In 1917 M. E. Murray had the Maxwell agency, and the Baudette Machine and Welding Company had the Chevrolet agency in that community. Murray sold three cars the first week after he received a carload on consignment from the company. Within a few months, Murray was compelled to build a 50- × 105-foot building to take care of the "growing number of cars in town and the ever increasing number of outside autoists visiting Baudette."

There was only one road in the Buyck area in 1920 when the Finstad family purchased their first car. Gina Finstad Erickson, her sister Minnie, and their father each contributed toward buying a new Model T. Gina added, "We were really somebody." The Finstad family was impressed with Henry Ford's announcement about the $5 per day for 10 hours of work.

By 1920 the road census indicated that an average of 70 cars, trucks, and wagons used the road southwest out of the Falls during one week in August. The streets of the Falls had an average of 435 cars, trucks, wagons, and buggies daily during 1920. The following year daily average traffic increased 26 percent. In 1922 Koochiching County had 1,023 autos and trucks, which was less than any other county in the state.

George Hnatuik was seven in 1922 when his father purchased

a big red seven-passenger touring Oldsmobile off the show floor at the state fair. He remembered how people flocked around to look at it when his family first arrived in the Falls.

Vic Mannila worked hard to save the $608 he paid for his 1924 Chevrolet touring car and was always broke thereafter. He had never driven a car before buying one, but after the dealer gave him a few lessons in a field, he drove it home.

Cars were so plentiful in the Falls by 1927 that the street commissioner deemed it necessary to paint bright yellow no parking lines along some streets. Plummer, who was 50 when he learned to drive in 1925, recorded that in January 1934, he paid $0.35 for his first driver's license. His daughter, Grace, and son, Jim, said that he was a terrible driver—very hard on cars.

In the first five months of 1924, the Littlefork automobile dealers had sold 60 new cars and "almost as many used ones." The editor speculated that "$50,000 had been spent for gas wagons in just a few weeks." Fords were the best sellers, followed by Chevrolets.

By October 1920, Standard Oil had a bulk warehouse in Northome for gasoline. However, due to a lack of good roads, there were few service stations outside of the larger communities. Hardware stores had gas stored in 50-gallon drums, from which it was dispensed in 5-gallon cans. Motorists were warned that no stations were open between Northome and Big Falls on Sundays. Al Arney was granted permission to install a gasoline tank under the sidewalk in Lot 11, Block 10 for the first filling station in the Falls, c.a. 1922. By 1924 Arney (who later became a partner of P. Cusick), ILC, and Home Oil Company were the first to receive permits for locally owned "filling stations" at the Falls. In 1936 the Falls had 36 licensed gasoline pumps, which increased to 39 pumps at 14 stations in 1940.[12]

"Joy" Rides

It is often said, "They don't make tires and cars like they used to." Those who understand the shallowness of the statement retort, "Thank God they don't." The American public paid dearly for its rush to own a car. A few illustrations of the inconveniences and problems experienced should help us appreciate the bargain we enjoy today in roads, tires, and cars.

Someone who hated automobiles scattered tacks on the road from the Falls to Ranier during the summer of 1914, and "more than 24 automobile tires" were punctured. The victims pooled funds and offered a $100 reward for information leading to the "discovery and conviction of the person who did this dastardly deed."

Tire trouble was expected, as those who remembered early automobile trips testified. Ruby Olson Erickson remarked that her father, Nels, always said that every time he wanted to· use the car it had a flat tire. Emma Watson remembered that it seemed as if there was a flat every time her husband got stuck, and he had to fix the tire before he could get the car out of the mud hole.

Plummer made the 30-mile trip from his farm to the Falls many times delivering produce. If records had been kept, he surely would have been the "tire blowout title holder." As proof of that, his diary recorded: July 4, 1923, to the Falls, three blowouts; July 18, hauled hay with truck, "had some blowouts"; August 11, returning from the Falls, "punctured new Fisk tire, patched it six times, then ruined tube" and ran home on the rim; October 23, took "cabbage and carrots to the Falls, had two blowouts." He stored his truck for the winter, and no other tire problem was mentioned until he started hauling the next fall. On September 6, 1924, he hauled a load of produce to the Falls and had two blowouts. On the 24th he had "four blowouts and bought a new Fisk cord tire for $17.00."

Most early motorists carried a saw, a spade, and a chain or rope to clear trees that had blown over the road or had been downed by beaver. A tire-patching kit and a tire pump were standard accessories, for tires were patched on the spot. A special canvas bag filled with water was another necessity, because the engines boiled over after straining through the mud. Tire chains were carried in a running board tool box or over the spare tire. Even in the 1930s it was not uncommon to get stuck on Highway No. 71 after a rain.

Plummer lived along present Highway No. 11 and experienced his share of fighting mud. In September 1925, he left the farm in the afternoon with a 3,230-pound load of produce. He got into the ditch, and it was not until 8:00 P.M. that four teams were able to pull him out. Within a few miles he became stuck again. After unloading at the Falls, it took him until after midnight to get home. In October 1927, with a better truck, he got into a bad hole and had to sleep in the truck. He finally arrived home the next morning at 9:00 A.M. A few days later he used chains on the entire 60-mile round trip, and it took four hours to get home. He noted that many cars were stuck.

If the road paralleled the railroad line, and the driver was familiar with the train schedule, it was not uncommon to drive on the railroad tracks. Ruby Olson Erickson recalled that her father often checked with the depot agent at Littlefork before taking the M & I track to the Falls.

For those living in rural areas, a trip to the Falls was not a matter of a few minutes, as it is today. Even though Plummer made regular trips to the Falls on business, it was several years before the family made the journey purely for pleasure. When neighbors rode with Plummer, they expected to pay for the ride, and when Plummer rode with someone else, he expected to do likewise.

The Henricksons, who lived near Birchdale, made one trip to the Falls each summer in their "big Star car." They packed a lunch and left at 4:00 A.M., did their shopping, took in the sights, and returned home at dusk.

The Ettestads owned the first car in Wildwood Township— a 1918 four-cylinder Chevrolet. They went the 14 miles to Northome only once a month, but after the roads improved, they went to town every Saturday night. Other than that, the car was used only for important business.

The Nels Olson family had come from the Pelican Rapids area, and it was their custom to take a two-week vacation there each year. After they purchased their 1913 Model T, they loaded it on an M & I flatcar, and the family rode the passenger train as far as Bemidji, where they stayed over night. Early the next morning they began the final leg of their journey by road, arriving at Pelican Rapids late at night. After the road to Bemidji was finished, they drove that far the first day. They always carried a lunch from home, because there was no restaurant where Mrs. Olson cared to stop, and the family was not accustomed to "eating out." The children had vivid recollections of kicking dirt into the tracks so they could get through. Sometimes they pushed the mud out between the spokes, because the front wheels slipped instead of turned. The roads were of clay and muskeg, but no gravel.

The first trip that the Kohlhases, of Mizpah, took to Bemidji, 60 miles away, lasted from 5:00 A.M. to about 5:00 P.M. Joyce recalled that his father was "almost a wreck" when they finally got there. His mother and his aunt did lots of pushing. After a night's rest, they continued to Bertha, another 90 miles, but roads were better, so they made that distance in one day with less trouble.

The Watsons, of Ericsburg, visited relatives in Fosston once a year. The first day they traveled as far as Big Falls. If the roads were not too bad, and they got up early the next morning, they could get to Fosston by late that evening. But Mrs. Watson recalled, "The mud, mosquitoes, and flies made travel nearly impossible."

Going places by car became the thing to do. Fifty Baudette residents traveled to Warroad in June 1917 to see the local ball team play. The roads were good, except for one three-mile stretch "which was very poor," but there were enough people to help the cars through. The following week there was no trouble with the roads, except for dust, when 75 cars transported farmers to a picnic at the Rulien farm at Williams, because the summer was nearly as dry as in 1910. In July members of the Thief River Falls Commercial Club formed a procession of 100 cars and about 300 people on a two-day tour to Lake of the Woods.

The two longest motor trips of 1917 by residents of Baudette were undertaken by the Robertson and the Arnold families. The William Robertsons went to Yellowstone National Park, leaving on June 7 and returning July 26. Mr. and Mrs. George Arnold and four children took a two-month 4,000-mile trip east, with a trailer. *The Baudette Region,* reported: "The trailer is hitched to the rear of the car, and it can be made into a house at night, with beds, lighting system, etc." When the Arnold's returned to Baudette, they reported that their best mileage was made the first day out of Baudette and the last day coming home.

The thrill of speeding in automobiles became fashionable, and papers were quick to report the progress made. A. W. Atwater drove his Model T 24 miles to Williams in 32 minutes. All the editor of *The Baudette Region* could say in amazement was, "That Ford must have been bounding right along." In 1916 tourists from Minneapolis made the 249-mile trip to Northome in 9½ hours. The following year Joe Krohn, of the Falls, drove his father's new car 164 miles home from Park Rapids in 12 hours. In 1920 a neighbor gave Plummer a ride on his motorcycle. They traveled 7 miles to Indus in 30 minutes. By 1921 the road from Bemidji had improved sufficiently that Paul Winklusky traveled the 111 miles to the Falls in 7¼ hours. Both cars and roads were improved enough by 1925 so that C. J. Lenander, a Minneapolis race-car driver, drove his Pierce Arrow 289 miles to Ranier in 7½ hours. He reported that he attained a speed of 65 miles an hour.

Cars were simpler in the early days, but it was necessary to be a good "baling wire mechanic" to keep them going, since garages were not plentiful. Many of the first garages were blacksmith shops, but repairs were not readily available. A typical example occurred on December 19, 1923, when Plummer broke a spindle on his Buick pickup on his way home from the Falls. He stayed overnight at the nearest home, and the next day he pulled the truck with his horses to the Indus garage which wired to Duluth for the part. The $7.98 spindle arrived at Indus on December 28, but the local garage did not fix the truck until January 11. It was 20 degrees below zero when Plummer left the Indus garage for his home, about six miles away. He ran out of gas and walked home to get some. A neighbor gave him a ride back to his pickup to discover that the radiator was frozen, so he had to be towed home. He did not use the vehicle again until spring, when, on one of the first trips, he broke down about six miles from home. A man with a Holt tractor (track type) pulled him 15 miles to the Falls for $2.

The early cars did not have gas gauges, which sometimes caused a problem. A Northome car owner checked to see if there was any gasoline in the tank of his car by lighting a match. There was, and his car burned.[13]

Traffic Regulations

As traffic increased, it became necessary to enact regulatory legislation. For example, in 1914 the Baudette council voted to arrest any persons driving over eight miles per hour or in a reckless manner within the city limits. Persons speeding across the bridge between Baudette and Spooner when women or children might be endangered would be arrested. By 1917 traffic had become such a problem that the council placed a quarter-page ad in *The Baudette Region* serving notice that the speed limit was increased to 10 miles per hour in the "congested area" and 15 in the residential district. All cars were to be equipped with a suitable bell or other signaling device. No search light or other dazzling or confusing lights could be used in the city limits.

The Falls council required the use of a muffler in the city limits, and cars were not to be left on the streets unattended with the motor running. All motorists were expected to slow down at all crossroads outside the village limits and to blow their horns. In passing a vehicle driven by a woman, child, or aged person, the overtaking driver was expected to slow down to four miles per hour. The top speed permitted in the village was 10 miles per hour; at crossings or when turning, the top speed was 6 miles per hour.

By 1921 a campaign was started to employ motorcycle police, who were effective and collected enough fines to pay for their cost. In 1923 the first speeder in the Falls drew a 15-day jail sentence rather than a fine. However, it was suspended on condition that he refrain from driving or riding in a car for 30 days. In one weekend in September 1923, there were six automobile accidents caused by drunken driving and speeding. The following week 9 of the 11 cases in the municipal court were for speeding while drunk; the other 2 cases were for assault. Initially, traffic fines were $10, but by 1927 the charge was increased to $25.

"Business" Ventures

With the advent of motor vehicles and improved roads, truck and bus transportation became a part of daily life. In 1915 J. W. Collins, owner of the Red Boat Line, started a trucking service between Loman, the end of the MD & W line, and Baudette. He hauled passengers, mail, and freight at 15 miles per hour. In 1920 a second firm offered three trips a week between Frontier and Baudette with a new Ford truck. The rate for farm products and machinery was $0.45 a hundred, and for cream it was $0.50 per can. The firm advertised that, after roads improved, they would travel as far as the Falls. By 1926 petitions were filed to extend truck service from Ranier to Baudette. Gus Carlson, of Baudette, was arrested by the foreman of the maintenance crew for hauling a 3½ ton load on Highway No. 11, which was posted for 2 tons. It was the first arrest for such an offense, which bore a $25 fine, plus costs.

Trucks started to have an impact in the late 1920s and increased rapidly after 1933, when local roads improved. That year Vic Mannila purchased a used truck for $330 and got a contract hauling gravel to the worst spots along the highway between Northome and the Falls. The next year he paid $1,000 for a used semi-trailer rig. When not hauling gravel, he hauled fence posts to the Dakotas. Getting stuck on main roads throughout the Dakotas was his greatest problem. Mannila was not bothered by the rough dirt or graveled roads, because the trucks did not have enough power to drive fast.

Bus lines entered the picture in 1917, when the Lindholm

brothers, of Baudette, commenced one round trip a day to Roosevelt. Another line between Littlefork and the Falls made two trips per day. A bus line that started in 1921 made the circular route from the Falls to Baudette to Rainy River to the Fort with an 18-passenger White Motor bus; the fare was $0.06 a mile. Passengers were picked up at any point along the route. By 1924 service of two round trips daily was established between the Falls and Virginia. The initial announcement stated, "when the condition of the roads makes such a thing possible." A bus line also was started between Deer River, Craig, and Bigfork, and another between Bemidji and the Falls, to operate when the roads were in proper condition. The *Journal* editor commented, "It is not likely we will see any buses up this way for some time." Once hard-surfaced roads became a reality with the paving of Highway No. 53, the Falls finally achieved daily year-round bus service. Ironically, that put an end to railroad passenger service.

From 1907 into the late 1920s, railroads provided the public with an avenue of escape from the isolated wilderness. Unfortunately, there never was sufficient population and freight business, other than timber, to make the railroads profitable. With the advent of the automobile, people were willing to pay handsomely to gain the independence and freedom the horseless carriage provided. Fortunately for the residents of the northern border country, the major cost of their road system was financed by taxes paid by citizens of more populated areas.[14]

ENDNOTES FOR CHAPTER VI

1. Proceedings of the Minnesota and International Railway Company, on file at the Minnesota Historical Society, hereafter M & I RR file, MHS; *Fort Frances Times*, November 13, 1903; Walter E. Paul, "Memories of the Minnesota and International Railway," a typed manuscript dated April 1966, KCHS, hereafter Paul, "Memories"; *The Press*, March 22, June 28, 1905, October 2, December 4, 1907, February 5, 1908; *The Minneapolis Journal*, September 26, 1907; Proceedings of the Big Fork and International Falls Railway Company, on file at the Minnesota Historical Society, hereafter BF & IF file, MHS; Mark Abbott, "Fifty Years in Koochiching County," manuscript of a speech delivered to the KCHS February 10, 1969, hereafter Abbott, 1969.

2. Paul, "Memories"; George C. Kerr, "A Brief History of Northern Minnesota Railroads," a typed manuscript, 1961, in the Beltrami County Historical Society, hereafter Kerr, "Railroads"; *The Press*, April 19, 1905, September 29, 1910; H. Johnson interview; *Bemidji Daily Pioneer*, November 9, 1908.

3. Kerr, "Railroads"; M & I RR file, MHS; *The Journal*, March 22, 1930; Paul, "Memories."

4. *Historical Resources Inventory: Koochiching County, Minnesota*, prepared

for the Koochiching County Advisory Commission by Aguar, Jyring, Whitman, and Moser, Duluth, Minn., August 1967, p. 15, hereafter *Hist. Res. Inv.*; Elmer Braaten, "History Service and Scope of MD & W Railway Co.," manuscript, November 1984, KCHS, hereafter Braaten, "MD & W"; *The Press*, September 22, November 3, 1910; *Hist. Kooch. Co.*, pp. 10, 12, 290; ILC file on the history of railroad construction, 1921–22; Loman Line file, KCHS; *The Baudette Region*, October 17, 1913, January 23, July 17, August 7, 1925, April 9, 1926; *Fort Frances Times*, February 22, 1912; *The Journal*, November 28, 1912, March 1, 1930; Dahlberg interview; H. Johnson interview; Bussman file; Minnesota, Dakota and Western Railroad file, KCHS, hereafter MD & W file; Schneider interview; *The Mandonian*, Vol. I, No. 8 (July–August 1947); Lester Pollard, "Logging Railroad Development and Camp Organization and Operation," manuscript, January 26, 1979, KCHS, hereafter Pollard, "Logging Railroad."

5. Camp Account Books, ILC; Ettestad interview; Henrickson interview; Pollard, "Logging Railroad"; *The Mandonian*, Vol. I, No. 8 (July–August 1947); Ryan, I, p. 10; *The Journal*, April 24, 1924, December 8, 1927; interview of Fred Hilden, by Arnold Johnson, for KCHS, January 13, 1966, hereafter Hilden interview. Hilden was a buyer and a scaler for M & O from 1915 to 1958. Paul, "Memories."

6. Tive interview; *The Journal*, October 21, 1915; Bussman file; ILC file, table of wages for MD & W; Schneider interview; interview of Alfred J. Johnson, International Falls, July 26, August 11, 17, 1976, hereafter Alfred Johnson interview; Twomey correspondence, ILC file.

7. *The Press*, December 20, 1905, March 14, April 18, May 16, September 26, 1906, May 29, September 4, 1907, April 29, 1908, August 31, September 14, 1911; *Fort Frances Times*, March 8, 1906; Williams file; Nute, p. 93; Oehler, pp. 5–6; Gerber interview; Scott Erickson interview.

8. *The Press*, April 27, 1911; *The Baudette Region*, June 25, 1914, March 29, June 7, August 2, 1917, May 1, 22, November 6, 1925, May 6, September 9, November 18, 1927, April 13, 1928; Kerr, "Railroads"; Braaten, "MD & W"; Paul, "Memories"; Proceedings of the City Council of International Falls, Minn., hereafter City Council, April 18, 1932; *The Journal*, September 10, October 8, 1925, January 27, February 17, December 22, 1927, February 11, April 27, July 1, 1933, January 2, 6, 1934, January 12, 1940; M & I RR file, MHS; Kooch. Ext.; Pollard, "Logging Railroad"; *The Mandonian*, Vol. I, No. 8 (July–August 1947).

9. Kooch. Comm., November 19, 1909, January 24, 1911, August 8, 1912, July 14, 1913, June 6, 1916, June 6, 1918; H. Johnson interview; letter from J. D. Lowe to Annie Shelland Williams, November 22, 1961, Williams file; speech manuscript to Minnesota Conservation Congress, Minneapolis, November 1912, Williams file; M. Stanley, "Woman Tamer of the Wilderness," *American Magazine*, Vol. LXXII, December 1915, pp. 49–51, Williams file; *St. Paul Press*, February 4, 1913; Nancy Arleen Enzman, "Annie Shelland Williams: Pioneer Educator of Koochiching County, Minnesota," Research paper, University of Minnesota, 1976, KCHS, hereafter Enzman paper; *The Journal*, December, 21, 1911, January 16, February 20, May 8, 1913; *Fort Frances Times*, February 29, 1912; Plummer diary; Kohlhase interview; Rogers interview; *The Baudette Region*, February 19, 1914, March 29, 1917; Kucera interview; *The Northome Record*, August 9, 1918.

10. Kooch. Comm., October 27, 1910, November 9, 1911, April 4, 1912, August 26, November 18, 1913, April 6, 1920; *The Journal*, March 7, May 23, June 6, September 19, 1912, May 8, 1913, August 12, 1915, June 6, 1918, October 30, 1919, April 15, 29, 1920, March 2, 1922, January 14, 1926; Plummer diary; *Hist. of Kooch. Co.*, pp. 13, 99; *The Northome Record*, August 25, 1916,

October 8, 1920; Mannausau interview; *The Baudette Region*, July 12, September 27, 1917, April 6, 1923, February 13, 1925, March 19, 1926.

11. *The Baudette Region*, April 16, 23, June 18, 1914, September 13, October 18, 1917, January 22, October 22, November 12, 1926, September 30, 1927, September 9, 23, 1932, July 26, 1935; City Council, April 15, 1913; Ettestad interview; Henrickson interview; *The Journal*, October 17, 1912, July 23, 1914, August 4, September 29, 1921, August 31, 1922, October 15, 1925, September 16, October 21, 1926, February 10, May 5, July 7, October 20, 1927, January 31, February 8, 1930, May 26, 1933, November 7, 1935, May 7, 28, June 18, 1936, September 9, 1939; Kooch. Ext.; Plummer diary; Mark Abbott, C. A. Anderson, and Clarence Rogers, "Presentation to Rainy Lake Women's Club, 1969," KCHS, hereafter Abbott, 1969; *The Northome Record*, April 8, May 6, August 12, 1921; Dahlberg interview; H. Johnson interview.

12. *The Press*, September 8, 1910, August 3, 1911; *The Journal*, January 2, 9, 1913, July 30, 1914, January 15, August 12, 1915, June 18, July 14, September 30, 1917, March 29, September 9, 1920, October 20, 1921, July 12, 1923, March 6, 20, May 29, 1924, September 24, 1925, February 13, 1936; Gina Erickson interview; *The Baudette Region*, May 21, 1914, September 14, 1916, February 8, 22, April 12, May 17, July 12, August 16, 1917, March 27, 1925; Plummer diary; H. Johnson interview; Barber interview; Hnatuik interview; interview of Vic J. Mannila, International Falls, August 11, 1976, hereafter Mannila interview; Kohlhase interview; interview of Oliver Olson, International Falls, August 15, 1976, hereafter O. Olson interview; *The Northome Record*, December 14, 1917, August 6, October 15, 1920; City Council, May 15, 1911, April 29, 1940.

13. *The Journal*, August 13, 1914, October 4, 1917, June 16, September 8, 1921, August 13, 1925, March 31, 1927; Plummer diary; interview of Ruby Olson Erickson (Mrs. Rudolph), International Falls, June 8, 1976, hereafter Ruby Erickson interview; Henrickson interview; Ettestad interview; Kohlhase interview; Emma Watson interview; *The Baudette Region*, May 17, June 14, 28, July 5, 26, September 13, 1917; *The Northome Record*, September 8, 1916, September 16, 1921.

14. *The Baudette Region*, November 19, 1914, November 18, 1915, February 8, May 4, 11, 1917, August 14, 1925, February 26, 1926, May 4, 1928; *The Journal*, July 27, 1916, December 16, 1920, April 21, June 2, August 18, 1921, November 23, 1922, July 5, August 23, September 6, 13, 1923, May 8, July 17, 1924, November 18, 1926, April 28, July 21, December 8, 1927; *The Northome Record*, May 14, 1920; Plummer diary; Mannila interview.

CHAPTER VII

Refining the Wilderness

COLD WINTERS, muskeg, lack of roads, and the tyranny of distance were important factors in the settlement of the northern border country. Early settlers were discouraged by the lack of access to many of the refinements that were taken for granted in more developed areas. Community leaders and developers sought ways to improve conditions and make life more appealing to the newcomers.

Breaking the Isolation Barrier

In 1910 more than $268,500 was invested in new buildings in the Falls in addition to the millions in the paper, pulp, and sawmills. That encouraged boomers to move in. The population of Minnesota's newest county (Koochiching) increased from 6,431 in 1910 to 13,520 in 1920. Since not all county residents lived in the Falls, in 1911 the officials established eight other locations where citizens could pay their taxes. There were so few roads at that date that no road map of the county was available.

A few brief accounts show how isolated many of the early settlers were. Oliver Knox began living at Kettle Falls in 1904 and spent most of his time in lumber camps until he was married. When supplies were needed, he and his wife traveled down Rainy Lake to the Fort, usually three times each summer. On Mrs. Knox's yearly visit to her parents in Superior, they traveled by boat to Cusson, where she took the train.

The Knoxes were fortunate because Indians and travelers went through Kettle Falls, a main artery of travel along the northern border. Many isolated individuals in the woods did not see other people for months. When John Erickson, a fur dealer, called on Nels Olson, who lived in a shack on Johnson Lake, about 15 miles north of Buyck, he found a cat eating Olson's body. Apparently he had become ill and had shot himself.

171

Thomas Austin lived alone about a mile from Happyland. His shack was on the far side of a mile-wide muskeg swamp and was difficult to reach. His skeleton was found stretched on the floor clad only in underclothing. No foul play was suspected because there was money on the skeleton, so it was assumed that he had died from a heart condition.

In January 1922, the body of M. Haner, a 45-year-old sawmill worker, was found in the woods 200 feet from his cabin, 17 miles south of Williams. It was first thought that he had become lost and had frozen to death, because tracks in the snow indicated that he had been walking in circles. But he was very familiar with the woods, so it was doubtful that he could have been lost. A search of his shack revealed not a particle of food, so he apparently had become demented from a lack of nourishment and wandered in the woods until he was exhausted.

In 1933 Frank B. Whisinrand was found dead in his shack, about 5 miles south of Birchdale, where he had lived for 22 years. There were no signs of trouble. He had few friends in the area, and his only known relative was a brother in Nebraska. Those who lived in the woods generally did so by preference, and in isolated country the above events were to be expected.

Thanks to the demands of Backus, who needed to break the isolation to make his projects profitable, civilization came quickly in the Falls. In 1905 he established the International Telephone Company, and soon 60 telephones were in use. However, the first directory was not published until 1912. By 1918 there were 460 subscribers; a three-position switchboard was installed to handle the 800 numbers.

In early 1912 work commenced on connecting the villages along the M & I to Bemidji, where the International Telephone line was connected to the Northwestern Bell system, making long-distance telephone calls possible. By December the work was finished. A call to Minneapolis cost only $0.60; a telegram cost $4.00. Monthly rates increased to $1.50 for residences and $2.50 for businesses when this service became available.

The western end of the International Telephone line connected with the lines of the Border Cooperative Telephone at Loman in 1916, enabling settlers along the Rainy River to call the Falls. The biggest problem on the party lines, which had as many as 23 subscribers, was to "get the line."

By 1927 the telephone circuit to Virginia was rebuilt, and larger cables were installed in the Falls to accommodate expanding businesses. By 1930 there were 904 phones, 540 of which were residential, at $1.75 a month; 187 were $3.00-a-month business phones. The other 177 phones were on the 23 party lines with a monthly charge of $2 for the line, regardless of the number of subscribers. In 1930 Northwestern Bell extended several lines into the border area, including the Falls and Baudette.

M & O generated electrical power and provided the Falls with energy. In November 1911, it installed 30 arc lights in the Falls. This came none too soon, for in 1913 the city was notified that if it wanted free mail delivery, it would have to improve the sidewalks, put up street signs, and provide more street lights. The Commercial Club encouraged immediate action, but it was not until 1916 that two miles of cement sidewalk were laid. From that time on, lighting, paving, and sidewalk cementing were conducted at a regular pace until 1927, when the erection of 150 homes in South International Falls created a demand for a more rapid expansion of service.

On June 22, 1910, six months before the Falls was incorporated, the city fathers contracted with M & O to supply it with water. The M & O contract did not specify pure water, and in 1911 several cases of typhoid fever occurred. The citizens were advised to boil their drinking water, but many failed to do so, and as many as 30 cases were identified at one time. The city council ordered purifying equipment and took drastic measures to keep the city water clean. The school installed a boiler with a 30-gallon capacity to insure pure water there, but advised the public that unless parents provided only boiled water at home, the school's efforts would be useless.

The initial pumping contract provided that the Falls pay $0.07 per 1,000 gallons of water supplied by M & O. The city paid the bill through August 1, 1914, when a feud with M & O commenced. However, M & O continued to supply water and, in August 1920, sued the city for $58,596, including interest at 6 percent, for pumping 801,760,910 gallons of water since the last payment. The city countered that M & O had diverted water for use by the MD & W and that it had no right to do so. The city offered to buy land from M & O in 1914 to build a light and water plant, but the company refused to sell and instead agreed to provide pure water at $0.05 per 1,000 gallons at 70 pounds of pressure.

In 1919 the city installed water meters so it could more accurately charge its customers. The citizens complained because the city charged more per gallon than it paid M & O for pumping. Eventually, M & O and the city settled their differences. In the 1930s, federal project funds made it seem attractive to establish a city-owned water system. Those in opposition contested that it would cost much more to operate such a system than to continue purchasing water-pumping service from M & O. The deciding factor came when the city was challenged on floating a bond issue to cover the 55 percent of the cost not funded by the federal government.

The water problem was compounded by the fact that citizens habitually dumped their garbage into the Rainy River. City officials had first dealt with the problem in 1900, when the village of Koochiching was located at water's edge. After its relocation inland in 1905 to give M & O more waterfront space, the situation worsened, and each summer extra garbage teams were hired to remove the winter's accumulation. The muskeg soil did not lessen the problem, as illustrated in the following public notice:

> Notice—Clean Up!! Notice is hereby given that all citizens are required to have all their vaults and closets cleaned at once. Further that all Garbage, Ash piles, Manure heaps, and other refuse must be removed from premises. This work must be done at once before the roads get too heavy for hauling. G. F. Swinnerton, M. D. City Health Officer.

During 1913 G. A. Oveson started operation of an incinerator, which burned "everything from tin cans to dead horses" at a cost of $0.165 a ton. Tender labor was only $2 a day, but fuel cost $3 a cord, and several cords were burned daily. Even at that price incineration was imperative, for it was difficult to properly dispose of garbage in muskeg.

Many citizens living on the edge of town were in the habit of staking out their cows and horses to graze in vacant lots. Frequently the animals got loose and roved the streets. In 1913 the poundmaster was authorized to collect $1 for each cow or horse found running in the streets and held for 10 hours, plus $0.50 for each meal furnished after 10 hours. After lot costs exceeded $155, the stray cow and horse problem was reduced, but as late as 1930 citizens complained that too many dogs were running at large. "Packs of dogs . . . are seen on the streets at all times growling and fighting and getting in the way of pedestrians and cars alike. They flock into the post office, hotel lobbies, and stores."

Probably the most unique promotion scheme in the area commenced in 1909, when A. L. Jones, representing the American Suburbs Company, of Minneapolis, secured a franchise from the county commissioners to operate a streetcar line between the Falls and Ranier. In late 1910, *The Press* reported that the right-of-way had been obtained, the grading was finished, and the rails had arrived. The following year *The Press* reported good progress was made in laying track, the cars had arrived, and operations were expected to begin soon.

Nothing more was reported until July 1912, when local attorney L. H. Nord requested permission to build a streetcar line in competition with the American Suburbs Company. At first it appeared that the Falls council favored Nord, but in January 1913, it issued Ordinance No. 7 granting a 25-year franchise to the American Suburbs Company. The issue became involved in politics, and Nord also received a franchise. To clear the air, in March the citizens approved Nord's streetcar franchise by a vote of 360 to 55.

Soon after the election, the American Suburbs Company sold out to Nord, who formed the American Traction Company, which promised to finish construction in 1913. They failed to meet the deadline but were given extensions until finally, on July 3, 1917, a 30-passenger streetcar was put into operation. It made seven round trips daily carrying passengers and parcels between the two cities for $0.15.

The initial gas streetcar was a failure and was replaced by Edison Storage Battery cars. They functioned no better, partly because M & O was reluctant to supply power for recharging them. Old-timers all commented on the poor service, but that did not concern the owners of the streetcar company, for when they obtained the right-of-way, they also purchased adjoining land. This land was sold as lots at a handsome profit. One street was named Summit Avenue as a special appeal to St. Paulites desirous of having a summer lake home. Pioneer Mark Abbott said of the streetcar line, "It was a great lot seller."

In 1919 the county purchased the company's two bridges and moved them to the highway, which paralleled the streetcar line. The city and the county both brought action against the company in 1922 for the expense of removing the tracks and the ties and putting the streets back into condition.

In March 1926, the Koochiching Realty Company offered to sell Block 33, in front of the courthouse, which it suggested might be made into a playground. In November 1927 the city purchased that block for $17,595.66, and later Block 28. In 1937 the council voted to earmark funds from the municipal liquor store for the construction of a city hall. Federal funds of $83,565 were approved toward a municipal building and a civic center, whose combined cost, including fixtures, was $215,700. When the structures were completed in 1939, the 500 citizens who turned out for the dedication were pleased to learn from Mayor C. C. Craig that the total cost was $194,777.71. The city's share was $107,127.74, which was paid from accumulated funds. A new city hall was long overdue because the original city hall, which contained the fire hall and an auditorium, had been condemned as unsafe in the 1920s. It had long been a complaint of people attending dances, bake sales, and other socials that they could smell the fire department horses on the ground floor.

The first settlers along the northern border found it advantageous to get their mail at Ontario post offices, because the early mail came via the CN to the Fort and then was ferried to the Falls, from which it was distributed, mostly on foot or by boat, to the outlying post offices. At first, mail service was generally less than three times a week, but as population increased, the service improved. By 1909 there were 27 post offices in the county, and within the next decade the number rose to 41. In rural areas, settlers volunteered to carry mail, without pay, from the closest established post office. Sometimes the volunteer or contracted service was slower than normal train service, but it was better than no mail. At times it took a week for the newspaper to travel from Kelliher to Northome, or two days for a letter to get to the Falls from Northome, when the train made the same trip in two and one-half hours.

One of the first contracted mail routes was from Baudette to Birchdale, which included 7 post offices in a distance of 55 miles. The mail carrier's vehicle frequently broke down, especially on the early roads. He continued his route on foot, taking only the first-class mail.

A typical example of a rural route was contracted in 1926 out of Littlefork. It was 36 miles long and had 110 patrons—a much more densely settled route than in most of the north woods. The carrier was paid $1,440 annually plus $0.04 a mile to deliver mail Tuesdays, Thursdays, and Saturdays. The early carriers were respected for their efforts to deliver the mail under the most impossible conditions, but if the mail did not get through, they were quickly condemned.

Probably the most unusual mail delivery was performed by Maurice Miller, who piloted a mail plane from Baudette to the Northwest Angle and scattered settlements in February 1930. Miller's heavily loaded plane arrived at his destination and left Oak Island about 3:40 P.M. Saturday to return to Baudette. Soon after takeoff, winds of "hurricane proportions filled the air with snow, reducing visibility to a few hundred feet and hiding the ice below." Miller lost control of his plane and crashed; fortunately, he was not injured. He walked eight miles to Hay Island, where he received food and shelter. He borrowed a horse and a sleigh, returned to the plane to get the mail, and went to Baudette, arriving there by 11:00 A.M. Monday.[1]

The Northern Minnesota Hospital Association

One of the few enterprises that Backus did not invest in was the providing of medical services. In 1907 he contracted with three medical doctors—Robert H. Monahan, his wife, Elizabeth Monahan, and B. F. Osburn—to provide those services under the name M & O Hospital, which stood for Monahan and Osburn. This was not part of Backus' M & O ventures, as was popularly assumed. The original three doctors were joined in 1909 by another husband-and-wife team, Frederick and Mary Ghostley. M & O Hospital had its first offices at Blackduck and Kelliher, but in June 1909, the doctors also began practicing in the Falls in preparation for the mill opening. Until then, M. E. Withrow, who came to the Falls in 1905, and G. F. Swinnerton, who came ca. 1907, were the only doctors.

On February 26, 1910, the organization meeting of the Northern Minnesota Hospital Association took place at Blackduck. The minutes, written on M & O Hospital stationery, listed Robert H. Monahan, president; Elizabeth Monahan, vice president; Bert F. Osburn, secretary; and Mary C. Ghostley, treasurer. Directors were R. Monahan, B. Osburn, Frederick J. Ghostley, Clair C. Craig, and James Reid. The above were all listed as residents of the Falls, except Osburn, of Blackduck, and Reid, of Funkley. The purpose of the organization was to operate a general hospital business, build hospitals, and buy and sell real estate and timber products. Capital was $50,000, at $1 per share, of which $16,277 was paid at the time of the organization meeting. The business was to begin March 1, 1910, and to continue for 30 years.

Prior to the organizational meeting, the Monahans and Osburn showed an inventory in equipment valued at $1,126.50 at Blackduck and the Falls. This included $51 in two operating tables, $100 in a medical library, $154 in files, chairs, rugs, bookcases, and a couch, and $125 in surgical instruments. The new organization listed a lot at the Falls for $1,400.00, and a new hospital, $10,598.82, which included $7,598.82 for the equipment, plus $770.00 at Blackduck. It was agreed that physicians were to receive $150 per month as hospital heads and lady members were to be paid $75. In no case was any physician to be paid more than $5,000 a year until the capital stock paid 10 percent, at which time he or she could draw up to $3,000 additional. When the stock paid 15 percent, the members could draw whatever was available. In no case was stock to be sold to anyone but the spouse of a stockholder.

By December 1910, the new organization had added W. R. Beardsley, who was in charge of the hospital at Crosby. The Blackduck and Crosby hospitals each had 10 beds, while the one at the Falls had 25. Business was booming, and the association planned to build a larger facility in Crosby and another in Tower, but "buildings were so expensive." Elizabeth Monahan went to Crosby to start that facility, even though sewer and water were not connected. In addition to her medical duties, she had to assume the work of the hired girl and the cook, who had both quit. Besides cooking for five staff members, she also cooked for three adult patients and a baby. She later specialized in optometry and traveled to the various facilities giving eye examinations.

H. W. Froehich joined the organization as a replacement for Frederick Ghostley, who died shortly after arriving in the Falls. Mary Ghostley continued in the corporation until 1930, when she left to take charge of the Lake Julia Tuberculosis Sanitarium, at Puposky, where she remained until it closed. Baudette was added to the communities served by the organization, and B. F. Osburn practiced there until he was replaced by J. H. Drake, who remained until Mary Ghostley left the Falls. When Drake left Baudette after his office was destroyed by fire, that community was without a doctor.

Typical of many small rural hospitals, the Northern Minnesota Hospital conducted a nurses' training program to aid in recruiting nurses. Its first class graduated June 4, 1913.

The first Koochiching County building was the poor house, sometimes referred to as the pest house, and later as the poor farm. Its residents always represented a block of patients for the staff of the Northern Minnesota Hospital Association. In 1911 the county commission established the following fees: calls in the village, $1.50; calls to the poor farm, $3.00; ward and hospital charges, $12 a week; and private room charge, $18 a week. The fee set for doctors' trips to Ericsburg was $10; Ray, $15; Littlefork, $15; Big Falls, $20; and Mizpah and Northome, $25. Trips into the country from the Falls or any of those points were an additional $1 per mile. That fee included treatment of fractures and dressing of wounds in accident cases, transportation of patients, all medicines, surgical dressings, board, and nursing care.

By 1920 the contract for care of sick county paupers requiring hospital care was $60 per month. The county physician received $125 a month to care for non-hospital patients. The county paid the Red Cross county nurse $500 per year to give care and treatment to county poor. As county finances deteriorated, the fee schedule was reduced to $50.00 a month and $0.05 a mile for the county physician, and $1.75 a day for complete hospital care.

In 1938 there was a movement to establish a 40-bed municipal hospital at the Falls at an estimated cost of $105,000. In the first two votes the citizens rejected a bond issue for the project, and the Northern Minnesota Hospital Association continued to serve the community. A 1935 study of the northern region indicated that Northern Minnesota Hospital had provided relatively good service for Koochiching County. It had 370 people per hospital bed, in contrast to 4,194 for Lake of the Woods County, 500 average for the northern 14 counties, and a state average of 241. But the county had 1,564 people per doctor, compared to a state average of 869.

Except for the members of the Northern Minnesota Hospital Association, there were few medical people in the area. To fill a need, optometrists, dentists, and medical doctors had regular circuits, usually stopping at local hotels to see patients. Because of the difficulty of making their rounds, they often came to villages on Saturdays and Sundays. Once there was a sufficient demand, they established offices in one or two communities as the population justified.

The medical doctors frequently built extra large houses, which served as local hospitals. A typical example was J. E. Dufort, who came to Northome about 1913, when the lumber camps opened. He established a hospital and took care of the lumberjacks on a contractual basis. In 1920 Dufort contracted to operate the telephone switchboard in his office from 6:30 A.M. to 9:30 P.M. six days a week and three hours on Sunday. In the evenings he handled emergency phone service from his residence on an auxiliary switchboard.

When Dufort eventually lost his license because of alcohol problems, Northome was left with one physician, Dr. Skaro. He was judged to be only a "fair" practitioner, but had a considerable number of patients because he was willing to accept his fees in the form of vegetables and other produce.

In 1916 Dr. Pearson established a practice in Ericsburg, reducing the need for local residents to rely on doctors from the Falls. William F. Cantwell was influenced by M. E. Withrow to come to Littlefork in 1921. Cantwell married Margaret Jenson, a teacher, in March 1922. After the school year ended, she became her husband's nurse. They left to attend graduate school and returned in 1924 to practice in the Falls. The Cantwells were replaced by George Higgins, who stayed until 1933, when he decided to do graduate work. Not wishing to leave the town without a doctor, he advertised at the university medical fraternity.

Ralph Hanover and his new bride, Effie, a graduate nurse, decided that, despite advice to the contrary, they would like to work together in a small town. They came to Littlefork early in 1933, bought the practice and equipment from Dr. Higgins, and rented an office for $25 a month. They also rented a vacant building in Big Falls, and each Friday they spent the day there. Later, they rented a four-bedroom house in which they placed hospital beds and had one room for operating. Because Hanover was just out of medical school, he had an arrangement with a friend in Minneapolis who took the night train to Littlefork and performed operations the following morning. Room rates were $3.50 a day and $0.50 extra for nursing. Hanover continued to make house calls until the late 1960s.

By 1936 Ralph and Effie Hanover had everything paid for and decided it was time to build a new hospital or leave town. The bank could lend only $1,800, but the banker said that Abe and Minnie Olson had money to lend. The Hanovers hired Felix Kraft, a local garage man who was also a carpenter and could read blueprints, to take charge of the project for $1.50 an hour. Hjalmer Marklund was second in command at $1.00 per hour, and the regular crew was paid $0.40 an hour. One man walked 5 miles to work for 10 hours, 6 days a week. The eight-bed hospital with operating room, nursery, and delivery room, finished on the main floor only, cost $14,000. Hanover kept his office downtown until the second floor was finished, at which time eight more beds were installed.

Effie was head nurse and in charge of all purchases, including equipment. After the elevator, the largest purchase was an autoclave. Before that purchase she sterilized the sheets, wrapped in heavy double linen, in a large pressure cooker and dried them in the oven of a regular wood stove. The sheets quickly became brownish in color and did not last long, but they were sterile. The hospital opened in October 1936. When it was dedicated in May 1937, Dr. Chesley, of the Minnesota Department of Health, said that it was a model hospital and just what rural areas needed. But soon hospitals owned by doctors were no longer the vogue, and a community not-for-profit, board-run institution was established.

In those days mothers were hospitalized for 10 days after they gave birth. Patients were given a bath every day. One woman left after five days because she could not stand "all those baths." The Hanovers were swamped with work during World War II, but it was even more difficult after the war because young doctors did not want to live in small communities and put in the long hours. The hospital eventually was expanded to 22 beds. In 1951 the Hanovers gave it to Littlefork.[2]

Epidemics and Illness

The frontier tended to attract younger people and experienced a high ratio of births to deaths. Generally, births outnumbered deaths about two to one each year, but a high percentage of the deaths was among the very young because medical and sanitary conditions left much to be desired. The first report (covering six months) from G. F. Swinnerton, the Falls health officer, listed accidents, chronic alcoholism, acute intestinal diseases in children, suicide, and blood poisoning as the causes of death.

In 1912, the first full year of record keeping, there were 110 deaths in the Falls, of which accidents caused 25; tuberculosis, 11; pneumonia, 8; diarrhea in children, 5; and cancer, 4. Three women died in childbirth, and the remaining deaths were from other causes. Apoplexy, typhoid, food poisoning, scarlet fever, smallpox, and influenza were other causes high on the list throughout the early years.

Harry E. Pierce, principal and one of three teachers at Birchdale in 1913, wrote of an experience that resulted from a visit by the county nurse. She recommended that 19 students with bad tonsils and adenoids be taken to the Falls to be operated on at county expense. The next day Pierce and Maude Underwood, another teacher, crossed the frozen Rainy River and took the 19 children to the Falls via the CN, arriving at 9:30 P.M. It was the first trip there for several of them. The next day the students all were operated on, and the following day they returned to Stratton, Ontario, on the CN. Some of the smaller children were carried by the teachers and older students as they recrossed the Rainy on the ice.

In 1916 the public health nurse, sponsored by the Red Cross, examined 115 students in the Northome school. She found that only 14 had been vaccinated against any childhood disease, 96 had defective teeth, 19 had good teeth, and only 19 did not have any major defects. When the nurse returned to Northome in 1920 and examined 124 children, she found that malnutrition was the greatest single problem.

In her 97 visits to county schools from October 1919 to October 1920, she found students with the following problems: defective vision, 385; conjunctivitis, 3; defective hearing, 33; nasal obstruction, 196; abnormal tonsils, 441; enlarged neck glands, 862; defective teeth, 878; ringworm, 2; scabies, 16; eczema, 6; pediculosis, 76; malnutrition, 206; mental defects, 3; and suspicious symptoms, 41. Obviously, the $2,500 paid by the Red Cross that year for the nurse's expenses was well worthwhile.

Lack of proper dental hygiene was a major factor in the abundance of defective teeth. When Ed Pelland was interviewed at age 84, he said that he had never owned a toothbrush. Gina Erickson gave her 30 students toothbrushes for Christmas gifts and wrote to the Colgate Company for free toothpaste samples. One child ate his sample because he thought that it tasted good. In another family the father forbade the use of toothbrushes. Some families used soda or salt and rubbed their teeth with a cloth, because they did not have toothbrushes. Gina's family used toothpaste that came in solid form in a metal box. They rubbed their brushes on it to get lather. Gina's father was the only one in the family who did not brush his teeth, but he still had them all when he died in his late 80s.

In late 1910 Elizabeth Monahan took her children to Minneapolis when smallpox broke out in the Falls and in Littlefork. In the summer of 1911 the citizens of Birchdale "enjoyed an old fashioned siege of cholera morbus," while the Falls experienced a wave of typhoid.

Because so few people were vaccinated, when an epidemic hit a community the school system was closed for as long as three weeks, or until the epidemic abated. This was true of scarlet fever, chicken pox, smallpox, measles, influenza, whooping cough, typhoid fever, diphtheria, mumps, and even the common cold, when as many as 50 percent of the students were reported sick at one time. An outbreak of any one of several preventable diseases was good cause for enforced vaccination. Doctors went to the schools and vaccinated all the students and teachers at the expense of the county or the Red Cross.

The worst epidemic was influenza in the winter of 1918–19. Elizabeth Monahan wrote on October 25, 1918, that the Falls had 200 cases and that she was at the hospital daily. By December she informed her parents that she, their household help, and all three children had recovered from the disease. Many deaths occurred throughout the area.

The local papers appealed to the populace to notify authorities as soon as they needed help against the Spanish Flu. By November 1918, Littlefork had experienced several deaths, including three pregnant women. The papers advised people to burn sulphur on the stove and "watch the flu germs hustle to the doors and windows."

No groups of more than 10 people were allowed to congregate in private or public buildings. Pool halls and soft drink establishments were closed, and anyone ill with the flu had to be reported to John Berg, the assistant health officer. Influenza masks were dispensed free to persons living in homes where anyone was ill with the flu. M & O maintained a 40-bed emergency hospital for its employees and families.

In mid-November 1918, there were 177 cases of influenza in the Falls, in addition to those at the hospital. By January 1919, the Kelliher area had experienced 150 cases, but no deaths. Most of the deaths reported in Baudette for 1918 came from the influenza epidemic. By February 1919, the worst was over.[3]

House Calls

In the days before emergency vehicles, society expected doctors to make house calls. Today some of these calls would appear to be fantastic feats. *The Press* reported that B. F. Osburn spent three days making a professional call to the W. C. Hawn home, near Indus, where he found a number of severe cases of scarlet fever. Two persons had died by the time he arrived, and nine others were afflicted, two very seriously. His partner, Robert Monahan, wrote from the Falls in 1911 that he had been "seeing patients on long drives down the Black River and drove 90 miles one day, and went to Ericsburg and back another." The next two days he made trips into the country, including one to Laurel, from which he arrived home at 11:30 P.M., at a time when automobiles were not equipped with electric lights.

By 1911 Emma Watson had lost two baby boys in childbirth, which she blamed in part on a lack of concern by the doctors. When another child was due in 1912, the doctor was called from the Falls. He said that he was reluctant to come because his wife was out of town and he was having a "big beer party" at his house. He was drunk when he arrived and had forgotten the chloroform. Mrs. Watson recorded, "Grandma Pedersen made him drink strong black coffee." Mrs. Watson fainted when son G. Rowland was born, and the doctor failed to tend to her after the birth. It was only with the help of neighbor ladies that she finally "cleaned on the third day."

Two years later when Mrs. Watson was overdue with another child, she decided to get some exercise. She "put back" a load of hay (she did not say where, so we can only assume it was on a stack), and shortly after that Iris was born. When Malcolm was born in April 1927, Mary Ghostley was called from the Falls. She arrived at Ericsburg via a speeder on the DW & P. Four midwives were present, in case Ghostley did not arrive.

Frank Alexander worked for the Burnnett livery stable and came to know Mary Ghostley when she employed him to drive as she made house calls. On one call, using a team and buckboard, they went about a mile west of the Falls. It was 11:00 P.M. on a rainy late fall night. Where the road was not corduroyed, the mud was knee deep. The woman was expecting her twelfth child, and Dr. Ghostley anticipated no problems. Since the house was crowded, Alexander preferred to wait in the rain. But complications set in, and it was 7:00 A.M. before Ghostley came out of the house. By then the rain had washed much of the dirt from the corduroy, making the return ride very bumpy, but both were too exhausted to care.

Probably Dr. Ghostley's longest trip to make a house call was to attend Mary Knox, who lived with her parents at Kettle Falls. It was at a time of year when it was not safe to travel on Rainy Lake, so she took the train from the Falls to Cusson and then rode the logging train to Hoist Bay, from where she was taken the last eight miles to Kettle Falls by boat. She traveled over 80 miles to get to a point 40 miles from the Falls, where she diagnosed that Mary had infected tonsils.

Plummer recorded many instances of house calls in his diary from 1912 through 1939. On May 22, 1915, M. E. Withrow took the train to Loman and was brought to the Plummer home by Jesse Kennedy to help deliver Grace. The charge was $10. Dr. Young was called in 1919 to treat Jim's sprained knee; the charge was $11. He came again in 1921 when Marion had bronchitis; the charge was $7. Ten days later he returned to vaccinate the family of six, for which his fee was $5. In November 1923, Plummer met Dr. Young and his nurse at the river and took them to his home, where Young removed Marion's tonsils and adenoids and Grace's tonsils for $40. Plummer paid $25 and charged the rest until he sold some timber. After Grace had been ill for four days, Plummer decided to call Young. He diagnosed that Grace had a severe case of measles; the charge was $6. Three days later he was back, this time to treat Grace for a "very bad earache." Young was still practicing in 1939.

Doctors spent much of their time making house calls. They were never paid for many of those calls, due to the destitution of the patients.[4]

Medical Hardships

While some women living in rural areas, like Emma Watson, had the luxury of having doctors in attendance when their children were born, more of them had to be satisfied with a midwife or a family member. A few fortunate ones, like Nellie Plummer, could afford to return to friends or relatives who lived where doctors were readily available. Nellie went back to her parents in Wisconsin in January 1911, when she was expecting Marion, the Plummers' third child. He was born May 1, but she did not return to Loman until June 13. After departing the MD & W, she walked the four miles home.

A doctor was present only once for the 13 children born to Ellen Carlson's family, who lived east of Northome. The Hafdahls had 12 children, all born under the watchful eye of a grandmother. Sylvia, one of the 12, said that when twins were born, her father helped with the birth. He delivered one baby and gave it to Marion, an older daughter, and Gladys started to cry, because she thought it was her turn to take care of a baby. Her father said, "Wait a minute and I'll get another one." That was the first anyone knew that twins were coming. The two older girls each took care of the younger ones every day.

Marian Crabtree Peterson was too young to remember when her sister Lillian was born on the homestead with the grandmother in attendance. Everything went fine, but a few days later a porcupine quill was found in Lillian's side. Apparently it had come from a blanket.

Jennie Rasmussen's mother died when Jennie was in the eighth grade. Jennie had to quit school to help at home and then was called upon to help at homes where there were newborns. After gaining experience, she became a midwife and helped 12 babies into the world. She stayed at those homes from 7 to 18 days, earning a dollar a day for her services.

Appendicitis was one of the most severe threats to individuals living alone in the wilderness. A homesteader near Pitt suffered an attack for two days before someone came by his cabin and brought him into Baudette. Andrew Forsell, who lived 20 miles from Baudette, did not have such good fortune when he suffered an attack. Four companions attempted to carry him to town but could not manage. They searched for a team, but the delay was so great that by the time he arrived at the Northern Minnesota Hospital he was too weak to be operated on, and he died a few days later.

When Mrs. Fred Ham, who lived west of Fairland, about 40 miles from the Falls, became seriously ill, Dr. C. C. Craig received the call for help. It was early spring, but the temperature was 22 below zero. Craig rode with the mailman as far as Loman and walked the final 18 miles. Craig diagnosed Mrs. Ham's problem as acute appendicitis and suggested that 12 men be called to carry her out on a stretcher. Gertrude Broeffle, the Fairland teacher, located 10 men while Craig built a stretcher. The journey started on foot at 12:30 P.M. going directly through the woods to Birchdale and then across the river to Stratton, Ontario, from where the CN was taken to the Fort and the Falls, arriving at 11:30 P.M. The operation was successful, and several weeks later Mrs. Ham walked back to her homestead.

Oliver Knox lived at Kettle Falls and Crane Lake from 1904 to 1932. At age 48 he became ill with an attack of appendicitis, which gave him intense pain for several days. He and his wife drove to Cusson, where they caught the train for the Falls. After they were on the train, the appendix apparently burst. He felt better and wanted to return home, but his wife insisted that they continue to the hospital, where he was operated on. The bill for the operation and 11 days in the hospital was $80.

Frank White, who fortunately lived near the MD & W line to Loman, was dynamiting stumps when a charge went off early. He received 125 cuts on his body. Mrs. White had taken a home nursing course and was able to perform some emergency first aid while a sister ran to the section crew, who took White to the Falls on their speeder. Doctors Elizabeth Monahan and Mary Ghostley worked on him for a few hours, and on the fourth day they removed his right hand. White was in the hospital five weeks.

William Harrigan owned the only team of horses and the only sleigh in his area along the Little Fork River. His neighbors all had much slower oxen and depended upon him to deliver groceries, supplies, and mail from Gheen. As he was returning from Gheen just before Christmas, loaded with packages, one of the horses broke a trace on its harness. When Harrigan got down to fix it, a moose crossed the trail and frightened the horses. He was knocked down, and a sleigh runner passed over his legs, breaking them both. It was very cold, and he realized he would soon freeze to death. As he thought of his three-year-old daughter at Christmas time, he was determined to live. He managed to pull himself up over the back of one of the horses and rode a mile to Eph Ablemein's cabin. Ablemein set the legs, and 36 hours later the doctor arrived to put them in casts. He ordered Harrigan to stay in bed for three months, but he was out of the casts in six weeks because, he said, "God gave me a second chance . . . and I didn't want to lose any time."

Simon Hafdahl was injured while working in the woods and could not raise himself from the ground. It was cold, and he, too, knew that he would freeze to death quickly. He called his horse, Paddy, and fastened himself to the singletree on the harness. In that manner Paddy pulled him several miles along the trail to his home.

Many hardships experienced by the pioneers were caused by a lack of knowledge and were compounded by fear of the cost of medical attention, so they delayed seeking help. Often the extreme difficulty of getting to a hospital made it tempting to hope that the pain would go away.[5]

The Schoolhouse

Harold Barber, whose entire career was spent teaching in the north woods, stated that many families had little or no interest in education. School often was held in any structure available—a vacant house, an abandoned two-room log building with an attached woodshed (the smaller room served as a teacherage), a newly constructed log building with no frills, a store, or a deserted cabin.

Annie Shelland Williams, assistant state school commissioner, was quoted in 1917: "The Little Red School House is in need of soap, water, and paint. . . . Most of our schools are strangers to soap and water and some have not had paint for 10 years . . . it is customary to scrub the floors three times a year . . . conditions are far from sanitary and a general state of disrepair prevails."

Barber, who started his career at the Rossing school in 1922, recalled that the school was an abandoned cabin, and when he arrived in Craig, no one knew where the school was. He asked at Camp 29, but it was not until he met a lumberjack who had married a Rossing girl that he learned the building was only six miles away. He walked from the camp to the school carrying a suitcase and soon realized why everyone who walked in the woods carried a backpack. Once he got to the locality of the school he detected that most of the people were not very interested in education. He spent "a couple days cleaning the building before calling school to session. There was dust all over, very few fixtures, and almost no books." The first-year teacher was dismayed that no one offered any help to get the school started.

He had difficulty finding a place to stay because the previous teacher was very hard to satisfy. He finally stayed with the Rossings, who let him sleep in a bunkhouse, which was attached to their house but had no connecting door. The bunk had hay in it, and Mrs. Rossing gave him some horse blankets. The food was not good, and he had to eat fast before the flies ate it. He paid $25 a month for those accommodations.

Barber felt that he was a poor teacher because he had completed only one summer session of college after graduation from high school, but the children were good and most seemed happy to be away from home. No one in his school had ever seen a train or been in Craig, the only village in the area. The students liked him. They walked to school with him and helped start the fires each morning. He felt good when he was with the students, because they wanted to learn. They visited with him even when eating their lunch, which they carried in syrup pails. Regardless of weather conditions, parents never came to get their children.

Barber went to summer sessions each year. By 1932 he had a contract paying $1,125 for being elementary principal, teaching six classes, and coaching basketball. In 1934, when he was hired to head three schools, including the Mizpah consolidated school, the first thing he did was to scrub the walls of the cafeteria to remove the spots caused by vegetables having been thrown against them. His chief instructions were to enforce discipline, but he was unable to hire principals who were willing to cooperate. It was not until he got students involved via student council that he was able to achieve discipline and keep the maintenance problem under control.

Edith Watson, who taught at the Loman consolidated school for three years starting in 1934, shared a house with Mary Ellen Ettestad, another teacher. They enjoyed their stay because they did not have to live with a family and were freer to leave on weekends without having to account for their activities. They were 1½ miles from the school and always walked, unless it was exceptionally cold. They did not have to start the fires, because that was the responsibility of the principal.[6]

Getting to School

The absence of roads in many rural districts made school attendance sporadic, depending upon the ability of the children to get through the woods, the mud, or the snow. Travel was easier in winter season when snow was the only factor that impeded walking. Most teachers provided tables and blankets for the youngest children to rest after they arrived, because they were so tired from walking in the deep snow or in the mud and water. Mrs. George Vagts taught at the Paul school, at Border, in 1914. She had only 23 students until the ground froze; then 10 pupils who lived farther in the woods were able to get to school with less difficulty.

Gina Erickson's father bought an Indian pony and a light sleigh to pull 3 children, ages 8, 10, and 12, the 5 miles to school. He built a small structure where the pony could stay while school was in session and provided some hay. The children were expected to go to school in any weather. On the coldest days they used flatirons to help keep their feet warm. After two years the school district provided funds to pay for their room and board at Buyck while attending school. The home where they stayed had seven children from outlying families.

To meet enrollment requirements at the Hackett school, Ethel Laughlin, the 15-year-old teacher, carried Melvin Johnson to school on her back, because he was too young to walk. She was not paid her $30 monthly salary until the district found an abandoned cabin, which was approved as a school. With the onset of winter, 11 Indian children and 5 adults enrolled. The chief interest of the adults was to learn English.

The Hafdahls had 10 children in their 16- × 20-foot cabin, but that did not stop them from having Gerald Wheelock live with them while he attended Fairland school. On Sunday afternoons he walked 4½ miles from his home to the Hafdahls, and on Friday after school he returned home. Sometimes one of the Hafdahl children walked with him to spend the weekend. After the Fairland school closed, Gladys and Sylvia Hafdahl attended the Loman school, 18 miles away and stayed at the home of Mr. and Mrs. Ole Scheie. Some weekends they caught a ride home with the mailman, and when they did so they stayed overnight at the Parmeters, who had the Bannock post office. If they walked, they went the full distance.

During the 1913–14 school year, a few rural schools started serving hot lunches, which meant that one item was served hot daily—soup, cocoa, mashed potatoes, stew, or a meat casserole. Usually an older girl was assigned to help the teacher and warm the one item on the school space heater. Either the parents contributed the food, or they provided funds and the teacher secured it. At first some of the teachers were not given much direction, and they served pies, cakes, fried food, store-bought canned goods, and even coffee. A few parents became upset and involved the county extension agent and the county nurse. Even though a large percentage of the children were underweight, the county agent commented, "It seems difficult to interest people in an entirely education proposition, and especially anything related to health." By 1921 the county school board made hot lunches compulsory. As things became better organized, women's clubs and the Farm Bureau held socials to raise money to buy the food. Some clubs, encouraged by the county nurse, advocated oatmeal mixed with raisins, vegetables, milk, meat, and eggs. Under a government program during the 1930s, the variety and amount of hot food served was increased.

After the rural school in Gowdy Township was consolidated with the Big Falls school, the children who lived across the Big Fork River had to cross it and walk a half mile to where they met a motorized school bus. The bus was equipped with wooden benches and traveled on the grade of a logging railroad. The students who came in from the country felt that they were looked down on by those who lived in Big Falls.[7]

Too Many Schools

Great distances and nearly impossible travel conditions made the educational process difficult. The problem was compounded by misguided optimism that once the forest was cut, there would be the normal concentration of farmers. Such thinking caused too many schools to be built. When Koochiching County was organized in 1907, it had 801 students in 25 schools taught by 30 teachers. Only the Falls district had more than one teacher. By 1910 there were 52 schools with 65 teachers, of which 39 schools ran the full 9 months. By 1915 there were 2,174 students in 69 schools conducted by 122 teachers.

Annie Shelland Williams, Koochiching County's first superintendent of schools, campaigned for schools and the necessary roads to make them accessible. She was an extremely popular person in the area, and her name was mentioned in the Falls paper more than any other individual, including Backus. Williams walked to every area that called for a school, including settlements around lumber camps, and was known for her ability to outwalk nearly anyone who accompanied her on her travels, including the chairman of the county commissioners.

A large area of the county was never formally organized into townships and was known as unorganized territory. It was governed by the county school board, which consisted of the superintendent of schools, who was the clerk; the county treasurer, who served as treasurer; and the chair of the county commissioners, who was the chair. This board had great power, including the ability to borrow funds with the vote of the people. Under them 69 schools were formed in the unorganized area. In keeping with state law, school consolidation began in 1912. Northome, Big Falls, Loman, and Birchdale were the first four such schools planned in the county, even though the people were not ready for consolidation and transportation still was nearly impossible.

Williams was desperate, because money was not available to support the schools. It was by chance that a salesman for Rand-

McNally persuaded her to appeal to the state legislature for help to purchase books and supplies. She failed in her first attempt, but in 1911 she received $100,000 for all northern counties based on $0.03 an acre for each acre of state-owned land in the specified area. Each year thereafter, Koochiching County also received $25,000 to provide fire breaks, which, in practice, were rural roads. Williams became known statewide because she was successful but also because the women had found a champion. Her popularity was a benefit to the Northern Minnesota Development group, which used her to promote ditches and road building.

Starting in 1909, board aid was provided at the rate of $1.50 to $2.00 a week for students who lived more than two miles from school. They were expected to work for their room. By 1919 that amount was increased to $3.50 a week for elementary students and $2.50 for high school students. Notices were placed in local papers asking individuals to accept students into their homes. By 1923 about 45 students were taking advantage of board aid. Some high school students went to relatives living elsewhere in the state and were often gone for the entire school year. Others, like Harold Barber, walked home weekends "because I was only 14 miles from home." He was the only "board student" at Big Falls when he started school there in 1917.

In 1922 the Big Falls system built a dormitory, which was merely a building with beds and toilet facilities. All else was furnished by the residents. Rules required that parents were responsible for getting the clothes and bedding laundered "at proper intervals."

School consolidation caused a few schools to grow while many disappeared. In 1920 Northome was still growing and had 135 students, 30 of whom met in the Methodist Church. In July the district passed a $30,000 bond issue to finance a new school. With the exception of the Falls, the number of schools dropped steadily until 1931, when only 39 remained in Koochiching County. At that time Border, Birchdale, Loman, Indus, Big Falls, Littlefork, Gemmell, Mizpah, and the Falls all had high school departments. In 1931 the first four were all consolidated into Indus, and Mizpah and Gemmell became part of the Northome district.

During the 1931–32 school year, the county made drastic cuts amounting to 33 percent of the public school districts' operating budget. Warrants had been issued since 1926 and were initially discounted by buyers at 5 or 6 percent for labor warrants and

10 percent for supplies, fuel, and textbooks. When total outstanding warrants reached about $600,000, there were few interested buyers, so something had to be done. The unorganized districts' credit was exhausted, and the banks refused to cash any warrants unless the budget was balanced.

Koochiching County Superintendent Roy Larson announced that 18 of the 39 schools would be closed. The remaining teachers were given a 14 percent reduction in salary; janitors, 30 percent; bus drivers, 35 percent; and the superintendent, 35 percent. Harold Barber said that his first child was born in 1932, and his salary was cut from $100 to $35 a month. He took an examination to sell insurance, but after calling on a few prospects and realizing how cash poor they were, he could not bring himself to seek any more prospects. He realized that teachers were better off than most people in the community.

Larson said of the school closings: "This has been done without impairing the efficiency of the schools or denying any child an opportunity to secure a good schooling." Even though 63 more students were added in the county, a total of $74,500 was saved by dropping 20 teachers, closing 18 buildings, letting the busing contracts out on bids, and consolidating bus routes. Despite the reorganization, no bus ride was longer than one hour, and only 2½ days of school were lost because of blizzards and bad roads.

This massive change in the school system was made possible through improved transportation. The first school bus in the area was at Big Falls, which in 1908 let a bid for $45 a month to transport students. In 1911 rigs were purchased by the districts that were consolidating. Mounted on wagons or sleighs, according to the season, they were canvas covered, had wooden benches along each side, footwarmers, and blankets. Often the older students walked behind the "bus" to keep warm. In 1917 a Studebaker wagon school bus with glass sides was purchased by the Northome district for $279.50. By 1920 the first motor vehicles were put in use, and in 1931 three factory-built Ford buses, with hot-water heaters, were purchased.

Ernest Carlson, who drove a school bus for 16 years, furnished his own vehicle and gas for $50 a month. He knew it did not pay, but it was the only way his children could get to school, and no one else on the route was willing to take a turn with the job.

The economies introduced in 1931 paid off, for the district indebtedness was reduced steadily and the cost per pupil was reduced from $246 in 1931 to $154 in 1935. Even though the number of pupils increased from 1,518 to 1,575, total expenditures decreased by $95,000. A total of 960 students were transported by 48 buses at an average cost of $0.18 per day. The average length of the routes was 10 miles, because most of the people from the more isolated areas had already abandoned their homesteads, leaving blocks of settlements along the main arteries of travel. At the latter date, there were only a dozen boarding students from remote places.[8]

City Schools

The Falls school was established in 1896, but it was not until September 1909 that the first students were accepted into a high school program. That year the total enrollment was about 110. With the opening of the mill, the population swelled; 180 students enrolled for the fall of 1910. George Aiton, the state high school inspector, visited the Falls in February 1911. He declared that the school could not become state-accepted until it had a better building and added two more teachers to the high school faculty.

In the fall of 1911, enrollment in the system increased to nearly 300, including 32 in the high school. The seven-room building was overcrowded, so some classes were held in the Baptist, Lutheran, and Methodist churches. In February 1912, the citizens passed a bond issue for $125,000 by a vote of 123 to 14 for a new high school. The editor announced that children could now remain at home to go to school until they were ready for college. In 1912 the enrollment jumped to 379, with 13 teachers.

The big change for the 1913–14 school year came with the consolidation of the South International Falls school into the Falls system. The two schools were only two miles apart. In addition to the savings that resulted from a consolidated, larger school was the benefit gained from an approved agricultural program. The second innovation that year was the introduction of a night school for adults, in which 50 participated. Most of the night schoolers were recent immigrants interested in learning English, but they registered in courses from primary through high school.

The new combined grade and high school was dedicated May 28, 1914. The $150,000 92- × 182-foot school building, with three stories and a basement, was acclaimed "one of the best in the state." When school opened in September, every room but one was used, and it was predicted that the old building might be needed before the year was over. There were 26 teachers on the faculty. Seventy students were enrolled in the high school, of whom 15 would graduate in 1919. The Falls was still growing; by 1917 the high school had 75 students and the grade school 533. The city council granted the high school boys free use of the second floor of the city hall for basketball on nights that it was not rented for other purposes.

The public library was operated and funded by a volunteer group, The International Falls Public Library Association, until September 1913, when it gave its books and equipment to the city. A library board was created by the council to maintain a public library and reading room. The Falls applied for funds from the Carnegie Foundation for a library but was unsuccessful, and little progress was made until 1918, when the public library and School District No. 4 library were united. The school district paid $500 toward the salary of Carolyn Williams, the first trained librarian to be employed. At that time the library was moved to a rear room in the Koochiching Hotel.

By 1919 the Falls District No. 4, covering 10 townships, with 737 students in the two buildings, was one of the largest school districts in territory in the state. Only one motor bus and two wagons were needed to transport students.

In 1921 the school district purchased Block 29, directly east of the courthouse, from the Koochiching Realty Company for $12,000. A $300,000 high school was completed on the site in 1924. There were 335 students in the high school and 805 grade students in the Alexander Baker Building. The new high school had a state-supported training department, which offered a one-year teaching course for rural and semi-graded school teachers.

Ruby Olson Erickson was hired as the superintendent's secretary in 1924 at a salary of $75 a month, 12 months a year. Her hours were 8:30 A.M. to 5:00 P.M. six days a week, and every evening when events that required the handling of money were scheduled. When she left that job in 1934, her monthly salary was $110.

Blocks 44 and 97 were purchased in 1921 for $5,500 for future playgrounds, but in 1936 a $320,417 contract was awarded for the building of the E. W. Backus Junior High School on that land. Federal Project Works Administration (PWA) funds were provided to help the district finance its construction.

Each year the Falls High School continued to graduate more students. Starting with 2 in 1910, the number rose to 84 by

1933. That year the four other county high schools—Big Falls, Indus, Littlefork, and Northome—graduated 49.

After the Baudette fire, that district had virtually no taxable property, but plans were made to go ahead with a new school building in anticipation of an in-migration of farmers to settle on the burned-over land. School was held in temporary buildings until the new $35,000 building was completed in 1915. By 1917 there were 376 students in the Baudette school system, who spent much of their free time collecting and baling paper for recycling to earn funds for a gramophone, decorations, and medical and dental service for those in need.

Because the town showed little growth during the next decades, the school population remained relatively stable until 1936, when 33 students from Wabanica were bused in. The following year, in an effort to reduce costs, students from Spooner attended school in Baudette. The Spooner district paid $60 for each grade school pupil, and the state paid the high school tuition. Baudette gained 51 students that year for a total of 413. The following year, with the aid of Works Projects Administration (WPA) funds, a new high school was built. The resettlement program had taken its toll on the rural area, and most of the rural schools were closed by then.[9]

Leisure Activities

Residents of the area participated in many diverse activities when not engaged in making a living, once the area became more industrialized. In 1910 the steamer *Itasca* was still used as an excursion boat on the Rainy River, but the Corps of Engineers notified local residents that they would not make any improvements on the river for the purposes of navigation, and riverboat days were soon at an end. The *Keenora* and the *Agwinda*, however, were kept in use between Baudette and Kenora on the Lake of the Woods for a few more years. In 1917 the *Keenora* was dismantled and taken to Winnipeg, where it was enlarged and was used as a Red River cruise ship and dance hall. Launches, such as the *Florence*, continued on Lake of the Woods, providing all-day cruises for $1, and the *Koochiching* was used on Rainy Lake, giving excursions to special groups.

Mound Park, the Indian burial grounds at Laurel, has long served as a gathering spot for area residents. The Old Settlers' Association, organized about 1913, held annual picnics there until 1941. Initially, to be eligible to attend these picnics, one had to have lived in the area prior to 1907, when Koochiching County was created.

In 1924 "Grandma" Stillar, who had lived along the Rainy River for 35 years, was recognized as the oldest of the 400 settlers in attendance. In 1939 Dick Metcalf, who was born in Loman in 1892, was recognized as the resident of longest standing.

Speakers were the focal point of the program that consisted of a wide variety of activities. In 1933 Dr. A. L. Wilford, of the University of Minnesota, spoke to the 800 people in attendance of the work that Dr. A. E. Jenks, also of the university and a nationally known anthropologist, was planning to do on Grand Mound, 1 of 21 mounds located along Rainy River. Activity in the mounds stimulated interest among old-timers. A committee, consisting of C. S. Jameson, G. R. Scarlette, and John Berg, was appointed in 1933 to form a county historical society. However, it was not until much later that a formal society was organized.

For those not interested in rigorous activities, card playing filled the hours. In 1910 the IOOF lodge held a series of 10 weekly card sessions at a cost of $0.15 for each session. The Elite Club and the Royal Neighbors of America, at Baudette, had regular weekly meetings where "500" was played. For many years the Rebekah Lodge hosted up to 18 tables of bridge and 15 tables of whist at couples' card parties during the long winter nights.

Jess Rose, Ole Wold, J. J. Hadler, and Neil Watson were founders of the Ole Wold Whist Club, which grew to 17 members. Meetings were held on a member's birthday, when the group got together for a social hour followed by a "big feed" and played whist until 11:30 P.M., when they adjourned for midnight lunch.

For the more active, there was skating, bowling, dancing, and sports. In December 1911, the grand opening was held for a skating rink and dance floor that accommodated 500 skaters or dancers and 300 spectators in the balcony—a large structure for a community the size of the Falls. Nearly every fraternal organization held dances for its members in addition to dances held in homes. The Minneonto Pavilion east of the Falls was a popular spot for dancing, as was the old hockey arena at the Fort and the Rogers' and the Earlys' barns.

The hall above the Gorden hardware store was the center of nearly all community activity in Big Falls—dances, popcorn stringing, taffy pulls, silent movies, and basket socials. Edith Gorden Watson played the piano during most of the late 1920s and the 1930s. Social life was plentiful, and much of it was free.

Local baseball, frequently referred to as "cow pasture pool," was a popular sport. Nearly every community had a team that played neighboring towns as far as 50 miles distant. The eight saloons in Baudette sponsored a hired pitcher and a catcher, who were usually college athletes working on "summer jobs," and the rest of the team was made up of locals. Generally, the team played one or two games a week. Jess Rose managed the Baudette team for three years and said the biggest challenge was to keep the players out of the saloons before the games. Ticket sales helped defray the expense of keeping the park in condition.

During most of the 1920s and the 1930s, the American Legion sponsored the Royal American Shows at the Falls for four or five days each summer. They set up in the block in front of the courthouse, where the city hall and library eventually were built. On July 4, 1929, the Christy Brothers Circus came to the Falls. Plummer and his daughter, Grace, attended. He reported that they saw seven elephants, eight camels, and eight bears, in addition to lions, tigers, leopards, jaguars, wild boars, cheetahs, and other animals. His final comment was, "Very Good."

Probably the most unusual of all picnics was the one held in 1930 by the employees of the MD & W. The company provided them with a locomotive and two flatcars equipped with railings, and they secured two passenger cars from the NP. The 200 picnickers carried ample food for the trip to Thistle Dew Lake and were gone from early morning to late at night. In some respects that trip marked the end of an era, for the forest railroad network had already passed its peak year of business. Other signs of changing society were already around.

In September 1917, Mayor Frank Keyes, the Falls' largest private property owner other than M & O, purchased a flying machine. It was shipped dismantled and was stored until a company representative came later to help assemble it.

In March 1921, an "aeroplane" landed at Northome just at recess time, and the students all headed for the landing field. Repeated ringing of the school bell failed to entice many of them back to the classroom. Not until Lt. J. Earl Fladeland, of Fargo, made several passes over town were the children satisfied to return to their studies. He was promoting the boxing show that the American Legion sponsored at Bemidji. His efforts were a success, for 40 people from Northome purchased tickets to take the special train organized at the Falls to attend that event.

In September 1923, a "Daring British Ace" provided a flying

show at the Northern District Fair, at Littlefork. After the show was over, he agreed to spend a few days at the Falls giving rides. On the next to last ride before he was scheduled to leave, his plane developed engine trouble. One passenger panicked and pushed against the rudder bar, taking control away from the pilot, who was trying to land. That passenger was killed, but a seven-year-old boy and the pilot escaped with minor injuries.

The airplane gave tourists a new opportunity to enter the difficult-to-reach fishing spots, and they willingly paid the price. It also provided bootleggers with an easy means of crossing the border from Canada during Prohibition. It was not until the late 1930s, however, that the Falls area had an airport useable for more than a light, single-engine plane.

In February 1930, Northwest Airway, of Green Bay, Wisconsin, stated that they were considering establishing service and that the Falls would be connected to Tower, Virginia, Duluth-Superior, Wisconsin towns, and finally Detroit. Flight time to Detroit varied from 10 to 16 hours, depending on the route; the proposed fare was $58. Twelve-passenger Levin Wasp–Sikorsky amphibians would be used.

The council immediately named a committee to locate a site for the airport. In 1933 the county poor farm property was purchased with a federal grant; construction commenced in 1935. In 1940 an airport manager was appointed to serve without pay, but he had the exclusive right to sell fuel and provide services.

The theater played an important part in leisure time activities in the early years. In 1910, when the completion of the mill assured a solid population base, the Unique Theater opened. Business must have been good, for in 1911, 250 opera chairs were installed, and an electric-lighted marquee was added. In May the Idle Hour Theatre opened in the Stanton Building, on Third Street, with the latest moving picture machines and with Garwood's orchestra to furnish music. In 1912 the Savoy opened in a building without proper exits, in violation of city code. The Empress Theater, with a seating capacity of 350, was filled every night during its first week. It featured vaudeville, moving pictures, ragtime, sketch artists, and other traveling acts. To reduce competition, the Theater Company was formed, uniting the Unique and the Empress under one management.

In 1918 the city council granted licenses for the Grand, the Loyalty, and the Viking theaters. At the Orpheum's opening in October 1921, the film "Visions of 1970" was shown. It was described as being exceedingly funny. The Grand and the Unique were the most innovative and managed to survive by bringing in such acts as the "Frisco Frolics" featuring 4 male comedians and 10 chorus girls. They showed the Dempsey-Tunney fight continuously from 2:00 P.M. to 11:00 P.M. on their Tuesday special. Each week an amateur vaudeville night was held, and the acts were reported to be "a scream." When attendance declined in the early 1930s, bank night became the Tuesday attraction, usually drawing standing-room-only crowds.

In July 1936, the Grand was destroyed by fire. The following August the Quality Bakery, Keyes furniture store, the St. Charles Hotel, and the Black and White "hamburger shack" burned. Only the fireproof building which housed Rexall Drugs saved the city from further destruction. Within a week of the second fire, Frank Keyes announced that he would build a new modern Grand Theater seating 850. The new brick structure included a cry room for mothers with children, a circular stage large enough for 30 performers, an elaborate lounge, temperature and humidity control, and the latest in "talkie" equipment. By 1940 the number of theaters had decreased to three—the Border, the Falls, and the Grand.

A number of other organizations were active in the Falls. By 1912 the Eastern Star had 22 members, and the Moose Lodge boasted 120 members by 1913, including individuals from the Fort and Ranier. That year the Commercial Club was formed to promote social and literary culture. By 1926 it had 301 members and had the largest annual dinner meeting of any organization in town.

The Women's Civic League, first organized in 1911, federated with the Minnesota League in 1912 and with the national group in 1920. The women also organized the WCTU. In 1920 the League of Women Voters was formed. The Girl Scouts organized in 1921, the Kiwanis in 1924, and the Izaak Walton League in 1925. In 1927, the International Falls Country Club was incorporated and capitalized at $20,000. The shareholders agreed to lease the 90-acre P. H. Fogarty farm west of town for three years with option to buy. Membership was $25 for the season, and dues to play remained at $0.25 per round as late as 1933.

While the above activity was taking place in the Falls, outlying communities sought to keep up with the changing times. By 1916 F. V. Peterson, of the Falls, traveled to Northome each Thursday, where he had installed a projector and screen to show movies in the Town Hall. By 1921 the town had the Lux and the Scenic theaters, both of which seemed to have a difficult time staying open, even though they charged only $0.15 for juniors and $0.25 for adults on Saturdays and $0.10 more for both on Sundays.

The citizens of Baudette walked over the CN bridge to Rainy River, where the Empire Theater charged $0.25 for matinees or $0.35 for evening shows. The Grand Theater in Baudette could show films only three nights a week in February 1917, because the train service was "demoralized" by severe winter storms in the southern part of the state. A Magnavox was installed in the Grand, which "reproduced music and could fling it forth in almost limitless volume."

The entire Plummer family attended shows given by a traveling movie person at Loman on March 23 and 24, 1917, for $0.85 each evening. The movie the first night was good, but the one the second evening "not so good," although long—they did not get home until 1:30 A.M.

Movie theaters continued to abound. By 1920 even the Margie Theater boasted of a full house every night during its first week. The following year Mizpah had a theater. However, attendance dropped rapidly when the forest industry changed its method of operation, and all forms of the entertainment business quickly disappeared. But Eric Tive, of the Falls, jokingly said that if there was nothing else to do, one could always go fishing during the winter, because the fish liked to stay in the warm water from the mill.[10]

"Room and Board"

This area differed from the typical agricultural frontier, where families were essential to establish farms, because it was not until after the mill was built that families came in large numbers. Boarding house owners and hotel keepers moved in rapidly to offer their services to the workers.

Alice Peterson Tive's father was a buttermaker at Albin, Minnesota, but was told to go north for his eczema. He homesteaded near Loman but soon left to open a boarding house at "Slab Town," on the road to Ranier. The Petersons generally had about 20 boarders and roomers, but at times provided meals for as many as 50.

Andrew Koski stayed at a boarding house with 12 to 16 boarders, most of whom were immigrants, including the girls who worked there. He paid $15 a month for board, room, and laundry. Joe Miller paid $3.50 a week for board, room, and laundry. Of the 15 who stayed at Frida's house, he was the only one who could speak English.

For those not fortunate enough to stay at a good boarding house, there were always hotels. The J. J. Stones had one of the first in town and made it a point to cater to the attorneys, doctors, teachers, and traveling businessmen. They had 14 rooms initially and added more as the business increased. Mrs. Stone ran the hotel with the help of a cook and two girls. Their menu specials were beef and pork, but fish was served twice a week. In 1913 Eric Franson opened the Victoria Hotel on Third Street with steam heat, electric lights, hot and cold running water, and a telephone in every room. In November 1914, the Rex, the Falls' leading hotel, opened. Frank Keyes built the Riverside and the Commercial hotels and also owned a large number of apartment houses. M & O owned the Forest Inn, which consisted of two structures that catered only to mill workers. The Frederic, a downtown hotel, rented rooms by the month in later years.

Like boarding houses and hotels, the restaurant business was very competitive, but one restaurant kept the others on their toes. James Serdaris, a Greek immigrant, operated the Klondike Lunch Room in Grand Forks and invited his brother, Christ, to come from Greece to join him. James heard stories of the Falls from his patrons, who were lumberjacks in the winter and farm hands in the summer. When he visited the Falls in 1914 he liked what he saw and sold his Grand Forks business to Christ.

Serdaris started the Klondike Lunch Room, with 12 stools, in the Falls late in 1914, across the street from the newly opened Rex Hotel. When he came, the sidewalks were concrete, but the streets were still dirt. Rent was $30 a month. He served a half chicken, French fries, chicken soup, coffee or milk, lots of bread, but no vegetables or dessert, for $0.25 a meal. At that time chickens cost him $0.08 to $0.10 a pound. Soon he served meals to up to 400 people daily and grossed $125.

Serdaris said that he cooked out in front so everyone would be impressed by the cleanliness. To his surprise, he attracted a large number of business and professional people, which had not been his experience in Grand Forks.

In 1916 he moved to Third Street and started the 48-seat Chicago Cafe, so named because of the good experience he had in Chicago before he went to Grand Forks. Christ came to work with him, and he invited an uncle in Greece to join them. Now his rent was $75 a month, but in addition to a larger restaurant, he also had eight rooms upstairs for his employees.

The cafe was open 24 hours a day 7 days a week to accommodate the shifts at the mill. After James married in 1918, his wife, Helga, also worked in the business. Soon the Chicago had 12 to 14 employees, who worked 10-hour shifts 7 days a week. Waitresses were paid $8 a week, and cooks $25 to $30. Room and board was provided for all employees. The standard meal was two pork chops, three hot cakes, and coffee for $0.25. Pork chops cost Serdaris $0.07 a pound. About 125 meals were served each noon, mostly to the office staff of M & O.

Serdaris hired an excellent Norwegian pastry baker at the Chicago, so pie, a cream puff, or another pastry were added to the menu. The pastries were in such demand that Serdaris opened the White Bakery and served lunches there to take pressure off the Chicago. The bakery concentrated on sandwiches and pastry items, especially French pastries and cream puffs. The trademark of the bakery was a spotlessly white shop. Later, Serdaris increased the menu at the Chicago and specialized in prime rib of beef, which was a standard with the tourist crowd and earned repeat customers from the Twin Cities and Chicago. Turkey dinners were served during the holiday season for $0.35.

In 1933 the couple took a three-month vacation to Greece, leaving Christ in charge. The restaurant netted $1,500 while they were gone—enough to pay for most of the trip. The clientele changed in the early 1930s. By the end of the decade, very few lumberjacks were left, so the Serdarises catered to professional, business, trade, and tourist personnel. They continued to prepare most of their food on site. When they closed their restaurant and bakery in 1946, they were selling T-bone steak dinners for $1.25, pike dinners for $0.75, and baked ham and roast prime rib dinners for $0.60. Serdaris made money every month that he was in business in the Falls, which he attributed to the fact that he, his wife, and his brother put in long hours, they had exceptional help because they paid better than most of the other eating places, and they worked with their employees. There were 15 other restaurants in town at the time. His closing comments were, "The competition was great, and you had to be on your toes."

In many respects, the Falls was still a frontier town in the late 1930s, but the wooden shacks were disappearing, and it was taking on the appearance of a modern industrial community.

Unfortunately, the small outlying communities were not so lucky.[11]

ENDNOTES FOR CHAPTER VII

1. *The Press*, June 9, July 29, 1909, December 1, 1910, March 16, June 15, 29, July 6, October 19, 26, 1911; *The Journal*, November 9, 1911, February 8, 29, July 4, August 1, 8, September 5, 26, October 2, 24, 1912, January 9, April 17, May 8, 15, 22, July 3, August 7, 14, 1913, February 5, July 16, October 22, 1914, September 21, 1916, July 12, 1917, March 27, August 28, 1919, August 5, September 2, 23, 1920, April 7, June 23, October 12, 27, 1921, March 11, 18, April 6, June 29, 1926, February 3, July 7, October 20, November 17, 1927, January 21, 25, February 10, 1930, March 1, 1933, October 10, 1935, July 23, 1936, May 20, 1937, August 6, 1938, November 13, December 13, 1939; City Council, July 23, November 11, 1912, January 27, March 31, August 11, October 13, 1913, August 17, 1914, September 18, 1916, July 1, 1919, July 25, 1921, August 28, 1922; Alexander interview; Charlie Williams interviews; Abbott, 1967; Kohlhase, *Spruce*, p. 14; Kooch. Comm., January 3, 1911, December 19, 1912, January 6, 1914, April 8, May 6, 1919; Knox interview; Gina Erickson interview; *The Baudette Region*, January 6, 13, 1922; International Telephone Company, Bussman file, KCHS; May Smart file; *The Northome Record*, April 2, 1920; Ruby Erickson interview.

2. Minutes of the Northern Minnesota Hospital Association, MHS; James Christie letters, MHS, hereafter Christie letters, MHS; *Hist. of Kooch. Co.*, pp. 98, 205; *The Press*, January 13, 1909; *The Journal*, June 5, 1913, February 12, 1925, January 8, 20, 24, 1930, January 18, 27, 1934, March 7, 11, 1938, July 11, 1951; Kooch. Comm., January 23, 1911, January 7, 1920, January 5, 1921; *The Northome Record*, November 5, 1915, January 23, 1920, January 7, 1921; Jesness, p. 102; Rogers interview; Ellen Carlson interview; interview of Effie Hanover (Mrs. Ralph), International Falls, July 22, 1989, hereafter Hanover interview.

3. *The Press*, December 22, 1910, July 6, 13, September 14, 1911; *The Journal*, June 26, 1913, September 2, October 5, 1916, November 14, 1918, October 12, 1922, December 4, 1924; *The Baudette Region*, January 14, 1915, February 7, 1919, February 6, 1925; letter from Harry E. Pierce to Annie Shelland Williams, November 15, 1961, Williams file; *The Northome Record*, March 31, October 6, 1916, January 3, 1919, February 27, June 4, November 19, 1920, February 25, 1921; Ed Pelland interview; Gina Erickson interview; Christie letters, MHS; I. W. Hinckley, "Way Back When," published as a supplement to "Rainy Lake Legends," privately published, 1949, p. 92, KCHS, hereafter Hinckley, "Way Back"; H. Johnson interview.

4. Robert Monahan letter, March 14, 1911, Christie letters, MHS; *The Press*, December 15, 1910; Emma Watson (Mrs. George), Ericsburg, Minn., eight cassette tapes, made in 1965, in possession of the family, hereafter Watson tapes; Alexander interview; Knox interview; Schneider interview; Plummer diary.

5. Plummer diary; Ellen Carlson interview; Kohlhase, *Spruce*, pp. 26, 31; Marian Peterson interview; Rasmussen interview; *The Journal*, June 26, 1913; *The Baudette Region*, April 16, 1914; I. W. Hinckley, "Rainy Lake Legends: Recollections of Pioneer Days in Koochiching County," privately published, 1942, KCHS, hereafter Hinckley, "Legends"; Knox interview; Williams file; *The Chronicle*, April 6, 1975.

6. Interview of T. Neil Watson, International Falls, July 28, 1989, hereafter Neil Watson interview; Kohlhase, *Spruce*, p. 36; Harold Erickson interview; news article dated January 24, 1917, dateline St. Paul, Williams file; LOW Co. Hist.;

Barber interview; interview of Edith Gorden Watson (Mrs. T. Neil), International Falls, July 28, 1989, hereafter Edith Watson interview.

7. Kohlhase, *Spruce*, pp. 20, 36, 42; *Hist. of Kooch. Co.*, p. 28; Gina Erickson interview; LOW Co. Hist.; McLinn interview; Harold Erickson interview; Williams file; Kooch. Ext.; Marian Peterson interview.

8. *The Press*, September 1, 1910; Williams file; Kohlhase interview; *The Northome Record*, October 4, 1918, June 25, October 1, 1920; Enzman paper; *The Journal*, November 4, 1915, August 3, 1916, August 30, 1917, August 17, 1922, January 9, June 18, 1936; Kohlhase, *Spruce*, p. 41; Gina Erickson interview; Ellen Carlson interview; Barber interview; Lorraine Albrecht and Dolly Thomas, compilers, *Northome, Mizpah, Gemmell, Minnesota History 1903–1977*, Northome, Minn.: Northome Bicentennial Committee, 1977, pp. 125, 128, hereafter Albrecht and Thomas; "How One County Cut School Costs: Koochiching Is Operating This Year at a 33 Percent Saving," *The Farmer*, L, No. 6 (March 19, 1932), p. 7.

9. *The Press*, February 9, September 28, 1911; *The Journal*, December 21, 1911, February 15, 29, September 12, 1912, April 24, 1913, January 22, May 28, June 4, September 10, 1914, September 6, 1917, May 22, 29, 1919, September 22, 1921, July 13, 1922, October 17, 1923, April 10, November 6, 1924, May 23, 31, 1933, February 13, 1936, March 14, 1951; City Council, September 8, 1913, October 29, 1917, July 29, 1918; Ruby Erickson interview; LOW Co. Hist.; *The Baudette Region*, March 26, 1914, January 25, March 1, 1917, August 14, 1936, April 9, September 10, 1937.

10. *The Press*, June 16, October 20, November 24, 1910, May 18, July 13, October 19, 1911; *The Baudette Region*, October 15, 1914, January 4, 11, 18, February 8, May 17, July 5, 12, 1917, December 17, 1920, July 13, 1928; *The Chronicle*, May 26, 1974; *The Journal*, November 2, December 21, 1911, April 4, June 6, 13, November 21, 1912, February 13, April 17, 1913, September 20, 1917, April 1, June 17, September 30, 1920, October 13, 20, 1921, July 7, 1922, September 13, 27, 1923, July 24, October 9, 1924, May 21, August 6, 1925, October 7, November 11, 1926, March 17, June 30, October 13, 1927, January 30, February 25, March 28, 1930, February 7, April 20, July 7, August 4, 1933, July 30, August 20, 27, December 17, 1936, August 5, 1938, July 20, September 27, 1939, April 29, 1940; Plummer diary; Kooch. Ext.; typed manuscript of the Old Settlers' Picnic in files of KCHS; Rose interview; Hnatuik interview; Schneider interview; Neil and Edith Watson interviews; *The Northome Record*, July 28, 1916, June 25, 1920, March 11, April 29, June 3, 1921; City Council, May 6, 1912, July 22, 1918, May 4, 1931, December 4, 26, 1933, June 3, 1940; Tive interview.

11. Tive interview; Koski interview; Miller interview; Fraser interview; *The Journal*, April 3, 1913, November 19, 1914, January 4, 1930, June 20, 1940; *Hist. of Kooch. Co.*, p. 176; interview of James and Helga Serdaris, International Falls, June 12, 1976, hereafter Serdaris interview. Mr. Serdaris was born in Greece in 1885, and Helga Browmand Serdaris in Wisconsin in 1900.

CHAPTER VIII

The Wild Side of
the Wilderness

A 1913 NEWSPAPER AD boasted: "International Falls is the liveliest town in Minnesota. . . . Saloons run day and night. Gambling is wide open with no restrictions. This makes a good town and a good place to buy property and double your money." The town did not change much over the next three decades, and as late as the 1940s it still had a sense of the frontier about it.

The Legal Saloons

Saloons were often the first business establishments in most communities. A member of the construction crew of M & I wrote that when he arrived at Big Falls, "It was full of all the rough stuff common to the frontier town of those days. Saloons knew no closing time, gambling joints the same." When Andrew Koski first arrived in the Falls, the town was rapidly expanding, and there were so many saloons that "it seemed like there was one almost every other door and plenty of prostitutes to go with them." He did not understand how they all succeeded.

The annual liquor license was $500, half of which went to the local units of government for roads. By December 1910, when F. E. Patterson received his license, the Falls had 27 saloons, which set the tone for what was ahead. Townships and villages taxed saloons because they were an easy source of revenue. The license fee increased to $750 with a restriction on the number of establishments, many of which were no more than back rooms in other business places or mere shanties. Mizpah, which peaked between 1911 and 1924, had 14 saloons, even though its permanent population never exceeded 150. Ranier, with only four saloons, had the reputation of being the "tough place" because many of the ruffians came from the Falls for their poker, sex, and liquor. Early inhabitants claim this was a carry-over from the gold mining days of Rainy Lake City.

The county commissioners and all the saloon keepers south of the Big Fork River got the scare of their lives late in 1910 when the federal government declared that part of northern Minnesota as "Indian country." *The Press* stated that the Falls would be like "an oasis in a desert of powder dryness," for only Grand Falls, north of the Big Fork, the Falls, Littlefork, and Ranier would be able to legally serve liquor in the area north of Bemidji. Local liquor interests were relieved when, in January 1911, President Taft "raised the lid" on northern Minnesota, and all licensed saloons were allowed to reopen.

However, in the Falls, Mrs. Fred Kelly sensed the need for a "dry" hotel and in 1911 built the "first high grade hotel in the county without a bar" across from the depot and catered to the traveling public. The mood was changing, and some communities raised their liquor license fees to $2,000 in an effort to limit the number. An attempt was made by the Falls council to raise the liquor license fee to $5,000, but it failed for lack of support by the electorate.

In 1913, when the residents of Margie voted dry, the local news reporter to *The Press* wrote:

> Good times are coming to our town no doubt
> Because saloons have all been voted out,
> And folks are able now to purchase more
> The things they need, but went without before . . .
> Merchants and businessmen now all agree
> That times are better than they used to be
> Because the money that was spent for booze
> Is spent for food and clothing, boots and shoes . . .
> And somehow people seem to be well pleased
> I think because their consciences are eased.
> And since so many feel it is a sin,
> I don't believe they'll ever vote them in.

Letters to the editor condemned the commissioners for granting additional licenses. After the communities of Pelland and Indus voted dry, the commissioners granted licenses in both places. Their defense was that blind pigs (speakeasies) and houses of ill repute operated anyway, so the commissioners rationalized that they might just as well collect the $1,000. In reply, one protester wrote that such an amount would pay for "a whole mile of road in Koochiching County and fifty towards hell."

By early 1914, 14 cities and 215 villages had voted dry; only Lake Bronson, in Kittson County, voted wet. In an effort to protect the village, the council raised the fee to $10,000 and hoped that no one would apply for the license. By then the Falls was down to 13 licensed saloons. The Baudette council reduced the number of licensed establishments from 12 to 8 and increased the fee to $1,200. At the same time, the Minnesota legislature prohibited counties from granting liquor licenses outside of city limits. This forced 10 saloons in Koochiching County to close. By late 1917 the battle was over when prohibition became the law in Minnesota, but not before many cellars were well stocked in anticipation of a long dry period.

In 1932 Franklin Roosevelt campaigned for the presidency promising to fight for repeal of Prohibition. In response to his election, the Falls council acted "in conformity with the repeal of Prohibition" by issuing 12 off-sale and 8 on-sale liquor permits. In the following four sessions they increased the number to 35 off-sale and 33 on-sale establishments. The town's 5,000 inhabitants did not have to stand in line to quench their thirst. Eventually, there were 66 on-sale, off-sale, or a combination of both licensed liquor dispensers. By 1940 the total was reduced to a combination of 48 on- or off-sale establishments.

A bartender in Littlefork informed *The Journal* correspondent that he saw people "he had not seen for 14 years and it was like the return of Rip Van Winkle." Every community had its share of establishments: Littlefork had three; Big Falls, two; Craigville, at least six; Ray, three; and even Ericsburg had a tavern and a grocery store with a barroom.

Soon individuals in the various communities sought to divert some of the profits from the liquor stores to the public treasury. Baudette was ahead of the pack when it opened a municipal liquor store in the Rex Hotel in February 1934. As manager, Peter Lldved agreed to furnish all the needs of the store for one-half the profits. In March 1934, the Falls residents voted 1,359 to 656 for a municipal liquor store, which was located in the Rex Hotel. In its first year of operation it grossed $69,611.57 and yielded a net of 24.77 percent. The profits financed a new city hall and other real estate. Profits continued to grow until 1939, when they declined because of "growing competition—both legal and illegal."[1]

Caterpillar, with three sleighs of 25 tons each from Henry Keyes camp, pulling load over Black Bay from Island View to Lowma Spur on Rat Root River, Winter 1924-25. (KCHS)

C. G. Lindholm and probably the first timber being hauled directly from the woods to the mill, Baudette, 1925. (LOWCHS)

Four-wheel-drive truck towing sleighs of pulpwood from woods to rail siding, central Koochiching County, early 1920s. (KCHS)

Alfred Hanson operation, Camp 188, 1934-35 season. Caterpillar "75" pulling 16 sleighs of 12 cords of pulpwood each to rail landing. (KCHS)

Jammer loading from sleighs to rail cars, Parker's Landing, Cedar Spur on the CN, ca. 1912. (Elizabeth Rippey Clark)

Caterpillar with Hyster winch loading pulpwood by using a swing boom jammer, Alfred Johnson operation, Big Falls. Could load 10 cords in 15 minutes. (Alfred Johnson)

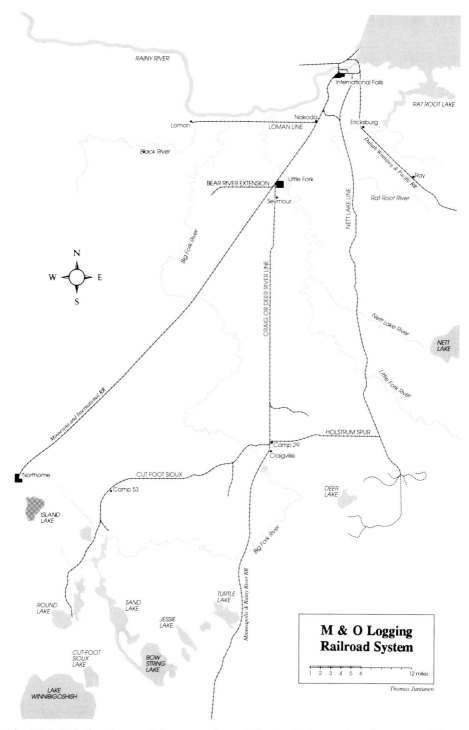

The MD & W Railroad network that covered over 150 miles in the woods and was extended at various times to nearly all of the 200 lumber camps operated by M & O from 1912 through 1937. (KCHS)

Scaling logs to determine a piece-maker's pay or logger's sale. Note writing pad on left arm. (KCHS)

Galvin branch of the MD & W showing switches into the woods where logging was being done from 1912 to 1938, when trucks took over. (KCHS)

Cody steam-powered jammer on hoist mounted on legs straddling the railroad tracks. Jammer could be moved. Empty cars traveled under the jammer for loading. (Alfred Johnson)

Rail-mounted steam-powered jammer, Camp 29, Craigville, 1920. Rail cars passed over the jammer car for continuous loading. (KCHS)

Fairmont gasoline-powered rail car used to carry lumberjacks from camp to cutting site and also to carry noon meals and supplies, Camp 29, Summer 1937. (KCHS)

VRL-converted Model T used as a railroad inspection car, 1922. (Scott Erickson)

Rapid River Lumber Company employees placing logs on the landing of Rapid River, Spring 1911. (NWMHC)

Logs banked along the West Fork River, near Loman, ca. 1920s. (KCHS)

Winter Road River west of Baudette, Spring 1910. (NWMHC)

Pulpwood on landing of Little Fork River, Spring 1937. (KCHS)

Log jam, Little Fork River, probably Spring 1935. (KCHS)

Log jam of 1916 that destroyed this bridge on the Little Fork River, which was built in 1908 for $7,500. (KCHS)

Putting logs back into the Little Fork River after the drive had banked them in the spring of 1935. (KCHS)

Completing the job of putting banked logs into the Little Fork River, 1935. This added greatly to the cost of the log drives. (KCHS)

Wanigans on Big Fork River, near Big Falls, spring 1914. First wanigan used for cooking and eating; second for sleeping. Man marked "X" is Ross Slack. (KCHS)

Wanigans on Little Fork River, which operated from 1910 to 1937. L-R: sleeping quarters, dining room, and cooking quarters. (KCHS)

Cribbing pulpwood by species with pike poles for hoisting to MD & W cars, Camp 6 on Black and Rainy rivers, July 1937. (KCHS)

Hoist at Camp 6, where logs were separated by species and loaded for the mill. Last drive, July 1937. (KCHS)

MD & W train at Camp 6 in 1915 leaving hoist, which caught all the timber from the Big Fork, Black, Little Fork, and Rainy rivers. (KCHS)

Boom of 3,000 cords towed down Rainy Lake by the *Hallett*. A tug could pull up to 6,000 cords, but the narrow channels of the lake limited the booms to 3,000. Towed booms used until 1937 on the U.S. side and 1979 on the Ontario side. (KCHS)

Pulpwood boom being sluiced under Ranier rail lift bridge. Looking west on Rainy River to the Falls and the Fort on right. (KCHS)

Alligator used to tow booms by anchoring to a tree and using a winch, piloted by Scott Erickson for VRL, 1922. (Scott Erickson)

Barge of baled hay for horses at a lumber hoist camp of VRL, 1922, on Namakan Lake. (Scott Erickson)

Edward J. Hines, Jr. house boat, 24 × 48 feet. Up to 40 could be accommodated. Used by VRL management on Namakan, Sand Point, and Kabetogema lakes. (Scott Erickson)

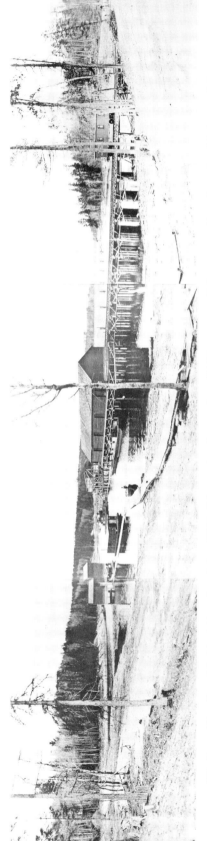

VRL Camp 75 railroad hoist at Namakan Lake, 1922. This was head camp for all VRL camps on Kabetogema, Namakan, Sand Point, and Crane lakes. (Scott Erickson)

Hauling baled hay to lumber camp near Cook, 1911. (NWMHC)

Road over Flint Creek near Cook, 1910. (NWMHC)

William Harrigan driving his dray, which operated between Gheen and Greaney delivering mail and goods from the railroad, ca. 1911. (Agnes Harrigan Mueller)

Corduroy road from Ericsburg to the Falls, 1910, built at a cost of $5 per rod. L-R: Joe Rogers, George Anthony, Knute Hagen, Joe Kucera. (KCHS)

On road from Loman to Littlefork, 1918. (Plummer)

Photography crew on CCC-built road near Camp 187, Nett Lake, April 1937, on way to photograph the final log drive. (KCHS)

Loading supplies to farmer's wagon, Littlefork, August 1937. (Chester Fritz Library)

V. E. Crabtree's (second from right) survey crew in northern Beltrami and Koochiching counties, ca. 1919. (Marian Peterson)

Survey crew, probably in the Waskish area, ca. 1915. (Beltrami County Historical Society, hereafter BCHS)

Dredge digging in 10 inches of frozen ground on judicial ditch No. 17 near Baudette, November 1917. Note tracks that had to be laid for movement of the dredge. (BCHS)

Rear view of Bay City dredge showing how it straddled the ditch as it dug. Probably Waskish area, 1914. (BCHS)

A floating dredge, which dug from the water source and used the water to travel. Cookhouse located behind the dredge operation cabin. North of Red Lake, west of Waskish, 1914. (BCHS)

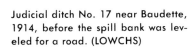

Judicial ditch No. 17 near Baudette, 1914, before the spill bank was leveled for a road. (LOWCHS)

Judicial ditch and wagon road after completion, between Pitt and Wabanica, northwest of Baudette, ca. 1916. (LOWCHS)

Cabins and boat of N. H. Sheldrup, prior to 1928. (N. H. Sheldrup)

Originally Dunsmoor Island, now Sheldrup Island. Tower was built in 1928 and then purchased by N. H. Sheldrup. (Illtis)

Ernest Oberholtzer cabin, 1930s. Gilbert and Katie Carlson delivering goods with sled. Sewell Tung wrote *Campaign of the Marne* here. (Katie Carlson)

Elizabeth B., houseboat of E. W. Backus, built by son-in-law Paul H. Kinports, June 1910. Used on Rainy Lake. (KCHS)

Hotel and store at Kettle Falls, 1910. (KCHS)

Kettle Falls Hotel, built in 1913 by Ed Rose. Owned and operated by the Williams family 1918-1978. On National Register of Historic Places, January 1976. (Robert Dodds)

Island View Lodge, on Rainy Lake, under construction, 1908. Until 1912 transportation was provided by the *Koochiching* at the dock. (KCHS)

Bartenders Local 310 picnic to Kettle Falls, 1915, on launch *Koochiching*. (KCHS)

Crystal Beach Resort, on Rainy Lake, 1916, owned by Burnie Lundgren. (KCHS)

L-R: Haakon Bjornaas, Stanley and Otto Leitch, on hunting trip, Rapid River area, ca. 1912. (NWMHC)

Hunting in the north woods by Fergus Falls citizens, 1914. (Oxley postcard)

Man on the right is 6 feet 2 inches tall holding a 200-pound sturgeon caught at Kettle Falls, 1912. (Oliver Knox)

Ole Wold children out for a ride, Ray, 1917. (KCHS)

L-R: Grace and Ellen Plummer; Henry Peterson (Bible school teacher); Marion, Nellie, and Sam Plummer; Rexford Smart (neighbor); with 1925 GMC truck. (Plummer)

Ernest Oberholzer, environmentalist, holding Robert Hilke, ca. 1937. (KCHS)

Bramble Russian Orthodox Church of St. Peter and St. Paul, established 1918, about 50 miles south of the Falls. (Cindy Williams)

Catholic Church of the Holy Apostles, the Falls. First services held February 4, 1906. (KCHS)

Birchdale Congregational Church members in front of the school they used for services, 1908. Rev. Thomas W. Howard, with beard, standing left of the door. (KCHS)

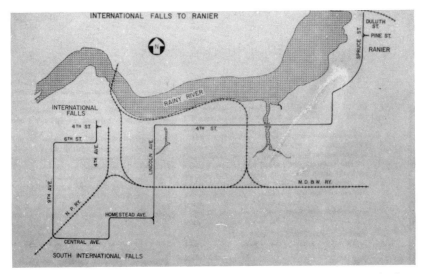

American Traction Company street car line from the Falls to Ranier, 1916. Chiefly a land promotion scheme. (KCHS)

L-R: Thomas, Susan, Elizabeth, and John Howard, ca. 1918, Birchdale. (Robert Howard)

Eighth-grade graduation, the Falls, 1911. Miss Scribner, teacher. (KCHS)

Dentaybow school, ca. 1910. Jay Bowman, teacher. Children were from the Moran and Cullen families. The building was erected by the settlers without labor cost to the district. (KCHS)

Loman consolidated school with buses, 1911-12. (KCHS)

Pelland school, 1915. (Laura Pelland)

Loman school bus, ca. 1925. Einer Johnson, driver. (KCHS)

Lester Pollard, 1940, examining trees planted in the early reforestation program. (KCHS)

Bronislaw "Bronko" Nagurski at East-West game, January 1, probably 1930. He played both tackle and fullback. (KCHS)

Edward W. Backus, 1860-1934, rural school teacher to industrialist, whose vision opened the wilderness. (KCHS)

Annie Shelland (later Williams), pioneer teacher, good roads advocate, and superintendent of schools for Koochiching County, December 1906 to 1915. Photo was prior to her appearance before the state legislature. (KCHS)

Harold Reich, union organizer in 1930s and 1940s. Born 1906; 1930s photo. (KCHS)

Engler sawmill on Rainy River, Baudette, 1911. (NWMHC)

Ranier main street. L-R: bank, beer wagon, Erickson store (background L), which operated 1907-1978, Ranier Hotel (center R). Note street car tracks, ca. 1916. (Marie Westermeyer Teufer)

Spooner Hospital and nurses training center, ca. 1914. (LOWCHS)

Indus waterfront, dock, warehouse, and fish-buying building, looking across Rainy River to Emo, Ontario, 1920. (KCHS)

V. E. Crabtree store, post office, and home. The only building in Faunce, 1932. (Marian Peterson)

Scenic Hotel with Neary's Restaurant, Northome, 1928. Built in 1920, it was one of seven hotels in the town. (KCHS)

Postmaster, store operator, depot agent, by his homemade stove, Funkley, Minn., August 1937. (Chester Fritz Library)

Craigville, September 1937. First building on right, Big Charlie's; two-story building in extreme background, North Star Hotel and Saloon. Photo shows five saloons, one gasoline pump, and several houses of ill fame. (Chester Fritz Library)

North Star Hotel, Craigville, 1978. Last owned by John Sivonen. (Cindy Williams)

Customs officers smashing 79 barrels of Canadian whiskey seized from a train carload of cedar shingles, Ranier, 1930. (Marie Westermeyer Teufer)

Sleeping quarters, Company 724, CCC Camp S-81, Davenport-Ray, 1934. (Walter Zatochill)

Recreation room, Company 724, CCC Camp S-81, east of Ray and south of Gappas Landing, 1934. (Walter Zatochill)

Post exchange, Company 724, CCC Camp S-81, Davenport-Ray, 1934. (Walter Zatochill)

Building the entrance to CCC Camp S-81, Ray, 1934. (Walter Zatochill)

CCC Camp 723, Faunce, 1935-1937. (Marian Peterson)

The first M & O control forest planted in 1936; photo taken in 1953. A program to provide forest products for centuries. (KCHS)

Bootleggers, the Law, and Stills

Billy Noonan, editor of *The Baudette Region*, had a few choice comments about Prohibition throughout the years in his weekly "Observations." In July 1919, he wrote, "Dark thought. Ninety in the shade and prohibition." The week after the nation went dry: "How did your dandelion wine turn out?" He expressed his opinion about the taste of moonshine: "Gasoline is $0.19 a gallon, hair tonic is $1.50 a bottle, and bootleg liquor $5.00 a quart, and it makes no difference which you drink. They all taste alike." About the effectiveness of Prohibition and economic conditions he wrote: "There is a lot of unemployment, . . . but it isn't in the bootleg industry." Eric Tive bought his moonshine from the dairy that also delivered milk to his home. "Farmers and townspeople alike made booze; everybody wanted to make money from it."

According to Jess Rose, a career customs employee in the area, probably the largest moonshine operator, or "ringleader," as he was referred to, was Bob Williams, of Ranier. Williams hired all of his work done and was never caught, even though the customs officials knew he was the man behind the scene. His front was a soft drink bar and restaurant at Ranier. Some of Rose's neighbors worked for Williams as smugglers.

Williams owned the *Mayflower* and employed Cap Thompson, the "most famous" Rainy Lake captain, to pilot it. In 1918 Williams purchased the Kettle Falls Hotel for $1,000 and four barrels of whiskey. His son Charlie noted: "Whiskey was expensive then." Later, Williams also purchased the steamer *Elizabeth Backus*, which he renamed *Mayflower II*, to help in the smuggling of liquor. Charlie said, "Dad had a string of six or more stills, so he had the whiskey to trade. Dad also had a farm, which fronted for one still that had underground tunnels to the chicken coop. Dad's stills were all movable; they had to be."

Stills were so numerous in the north woods that any number of revenuers could not have hoped to stamp them out. Soon after Prohibition commenced, the makers of "kill 'em quick whiskey" were found and charged. One of the earliest was a Rainy River, Ontario, farmer, who was fined $200. He paid the fine, even though he protested that he was only manufacturing pig feed. The magistrate thought that pigs should not be fed such luxuries as prunes, apples, and raisins. In 1922 the sheriff discovered a still on the farm of prominent citizen Ira Hinckley, an area pioneer who later wrote a local history.

A homesteader in the area near Craigville was unable to sell his potato crop one year. To support his large family, he turned his potatoes into moonshine. When he came to town with clear glass jugs, everyone knew what they contained.

When the sheriff raided the Axel Lindstrom farm near Crystal Beach, he found 20 barrels of 50 gallons each of moonshine, 2 giant stills, and enough extra equipment to double the output. The sheriff believed that the farm was the main supplier for the Ranier-Falls area. The local editor determined that the farm had enough liquor on hand to provide every man, woman, and child in the Falls with 25 drinks.

In a raid on a "chicken shack" along Highway No. 11, near the poor farm at the edge of the Falls, the sheriff found 5 gallons of moonshine and 150 bottles of beer. "When the officers entered the room, there was a scattering of the 'chickens' and their male escorts, but none of them got away without being given the once over." The manager's bail was set at $200.

Not all stills were hidden in the woods. When the Hilde's drugstore in Ray burned, 150 kegs of moonshine were discovered in the basement. Ed Reese and Andy Lien, repeat offenders in Spooner, had a 30-gallon still, 100 gallons of mash, and a supply of moonshine that the sheriff determined to be "a nuisance." Eight stills were found within the limits of the Falls, including five with a daily capacity of 75 gallons in a building owned by August Kline. The price of moonshine temporarily increased from $5 a gallon to $10 after Kline's building was raided.

The city police raided Jack Pennington's place at 806 Ninth Street and discovered a 75-gallon still, all the mash, kegs, corn, sugar, and equipment "rarin' to go." H. H. Foster's still at 720 Seventh Street had 800 gallons of mash, 45 gallons of moonshine, and 2,000 bottles of beer on hand when raided. Soon after Prohibition commenced, 20 gallons of whiskey and 2 barrels of port wine were found at the drugstore of pioneer R. F. C. Iltis. Two months later the three-story building burned.

As youths, George Hnatuik and his friends earned their spending money collecting whiskey bottles at $0.05 for half pints and $0.025 for pints. They knew where to find the bottles and who needed them. Hnatuik said that the people with whom he dealt got most of their moonshine made from potatoes grown in the Red River Valley. The cost delivered to the Falls was $4 to $5 a gallon. The "retailers" diluted it with two parts of water to one part of alcohol with a little tincture of bourbon or burnt sugar. This retailed for $1 a pint.[2]

Bootleggers and the Law—Transportation

The international border added to the excitement of Prohibition, because Canadian regulations regarding liquor were different from those in the United States. In March 1918, Canada stopped the manufacture and movement of liquor into provinces or states where it was illegal. After the war, manufacture was permitted, but importation was controlled by the provinces. However, in 1923 Manitoba voted wet, followed by Ontario in 1927. Then the customs service increased the number of patrolling officers in hopes of reducing the amount smuggled from Canada. The Canadian and U.S. officers had good communications and could trace goods across the border, but then they frequently lost the trail because the Canadian smugglers hid their shipments in the United States and returned to Canada without ever making contact with their unknown U.S. accomplices.

The Rainy River presented an obstacle for bootleggers, but it also marked the end of the trail for the customs people. For example, it was a well-known fact that a woman from Indus smuggled regularly, but she was so clever that there were not enough officers in the United States or Canada to keep track of her.

When Frank Alexander and his wife were picking blueberries in the fall of 1919, they came across a caved-in root cellar. Alexander followed a path into it and discovered 26 cases of "good Canadian Scotch," but did not tell his wife until after they returned to the Falls. He rented a truck, hauled the loot to their basement, and peddled it to Rube Grimoldby for $50 a case. He proudly stated, 56 years later, that he bought their first car with the money. The CN section crew found 23 cases of liquor valued at $2,000 in a ditch about a half mile from Baudette in August 1920, which verifies that Alexander's find was not an isolated one.

A close tab was kept on CN trains that crossed the border at Baudette and Ranier. Passengers attempted to carry liquor as they returned to the States, or it was mixed in with legal freight. George Arnold, of Baudette, had a carload of posts that he was sending south seized, because customs agents found seven cases of liquor in it. Because Baudette and Ranier were watched so closely, some smugglers attempted to transport liquor across at Kettle Falls and then to Orr, where it was loaded into railroad cars. Jess Rose, who was responsible for the border from Kettle Falls to the Falls, seized a full carload at Orr just prior to its departure.

Camiel DeCaigney was one of the largest successful bootleggers in the Crane Lake–Orr connection. He sunk cases of Canadian whiskey in the Vermilion River after each border crossing and waited until he felt free to make his next move. DeCaigney had one advantage that probably helped him from ever getting caught—he was not a drinker.

Most of the freight shipped on the CN was in bond, but that did not prevent smugglers from getting liquor into the States. Probably the best-known seizure occurred December 20, 1932, when customs agents under Rose became suspicious of a freight car which was invoiced as shingles. The car was not from a location or a shipper where shingles normally originated. After weighing the car, they determined that it was heavier than a car of shingles should be, so they had it unloaded. After they had removed several bundles of shingles, kegs and barrels of whiskey, which had originated from west of Winnipeg, were uncovered. A total of 79 barrels of Canadian whiskey, with a wholesale value of $32,864 and a Chicago retail value of $63,200, were taken—the "largest seizure of contraband whiskey" made in the district.

The confiscated shingles were auctioned at Ranier, and the liquor was stored in the Ranier bank building until it was hauled to the river, where the barrels were broken open. Citizens of Ranier came with pails to catch the flowing liquor, but when Rose and the other agents refused to let them do so, many knelt on the ice and drank what they could.

On another occasion Canadian officials warned Rose that a boatload of liquor had arrived at the Fort and was not being unloaded. It was late April, and the ice was just breaking up. Customs boats trolled the area and waited. Rose had all of his agents on hand when the smugglers arrived, but the smugglers spotted the agents when they were about 30 yards from shore and dumped the barrels into the water. They threatened to shoot it out, but, unbeknown to them, they were being followed by Canadian officers. The next day, barrels of liquor, including one of straight alcohol, were picked up from between the floating cakes of ice.

In Canada, liquor could be dispensed for medicinal purposes throughout Prohibition, but Dr. Murdock, mayor of Rainy River, was carried away by his privileges when he sold six quarts to one person. He was immediately jailed for 10 days and fined $2,000. Murdock appealed to the high court, for if the verdict was upheld, he stood to lose his position as mayor as well as his license to practice medicine.

After Manitoba voted wet, Americans preferred to buy the legally manufactured beer, wine, and liquor from Canada rather than the U.S.-made moonshine. Manitobans were eager to help Americans get liquor across the border, and Americans preferred smuggling, because it was less risky than operating a still. After Ontario voted wet, the entire wilderness border had to be patrolled, which presented a nearly impossible situation.

One father-son team, in Baudette, linked up with a gang in Minneapolis, who worked out of a garage, doing as much as $60,000 business each month. In October 1930, federal agents raided both Baudette and Minneapolis on the same day and put an end to the ring.

Carl Dahlberg transported lumberjacks and their packs by car from Effie to Northome for $7 a trip. When Harry Meyers requested that he be at the junction of Highways No. 6 and No. 1 at 6:00 A.M. and offered $10 for a trip to Bovey, Dahlberg was suspicious, because he knew that Meyers was a moonshiner. The next morning Meyers loaded two 10-gallon kegs into the car, covered them with blankets, and rode with Dahlberg to Whitmer's Hotel. Dahlberg knew that it was risky, but thought the pay was good, so he took a chance once. He added, "Never again."

Aviation also played a part in transporting liquor across the border. In 1921 Plummer recorded that an airplane flew over Indus, implying it probably was bootleggers. Bob Williams had a "beautiful Curtis Oriole" airplane, piloted by Dutch Rose, for delivering Canadian liquor or moonshine as far as St. Louis, where it sold for up to $300 a case.

Probably the most unique story about running booze involved two planes, one from Minnesota and the other from Canada, that circled over Lake Osakis in February 1930. When ice fishermen realized that the drops falling on them were liquor, they spotted a hose connecting the two planes. The loaded plane was later captured.[3]

The Law vs. the Lawless

An ad in *The Northome Record* offered a $50 reward for information leading to the arrest and conviction of anyone making for sale or selling intoxicating liquors in Grattan Township. The

sheriff raided Northome and improved the county finances by
$50, and the following day raided Gemmell, capturing the "biggest
distillers of moonshine whiskey" in the area. A short time later
deputies raided and fined the Northome "soft drink places." The
same day they located a still in the home of John Anderson,
which brought the treasury another $100 and costs. The Lake
of the Woods county sheriff was equally active. In one year he
made 31 raids that netted 24 convictions, which yielded $1,700
in fines. The following year the same places were raided and
paid fines in lieu of licenses, almost as if they expected to get
caught.

At the same time, others fought the law and its enforcement
officers. A horse owned by Herman Miller, prohibition agent at
Baudette, was shot in Miller's yard by a person Miller had
arrested in a recent raid. Jess Rose was threatened several times,
and Dr. Frank Lee Roberts resigned as a federal prohibition
agent because of threats. Roberts also felt that there was too
much "laxity in law enforcement."

Some citizens disagreed with Roberts and felt that often prohibition officers were too diligent. In June 1929, citizens of the
Falls held meetings and produced a long resolution protesting
the "United States patrolmen uniformed and plain clothesmen
who are heavily armed who make a practice of stopping cars day
and night, who freely use firearms. . . ." The protest was a result
of the death of Henry Virkkula, a known bootlegger, on June 8,
1929, via a riot gun or sawed-off shotgun used by customs officer
Emmett White. It appears that Virkkula ignored the officer, was
frightened, or had brake trouble when he was requested to stop.
A second protest was lodged against Henry J. Sullivan, of the
Immigration Service, who was cited for being "highly . . . obnox-
ious and officious beyond the degree to which his office entitles
him. . . ." The people felt that Sullivan brought shame to the
community already suffering from the unwarranted death of
Virkkula. A formal appeal was sent to the Secretary of Labor in
charge of immigration to remove Sullivan as the "official greeter"
in the community.

Dennis Baker, a Falls barber, who had served time in Leavenworth, was charged by federal prohibition agent E. C. Dike, for
serving two drinks of "colored moonshine" for which Dike paid
$1. This was done in Joy Gordon's "boarding house," where Baker
lived. Both Baker and Gordon insisted that Baker was merely
having a social visit because he was almost like a member of

the family. John Brown, the local U.S. Commissioner, wrote to L. L. Drill, U.S. Attorney, that he felt Baker had "gone straight" and lived a clean life for several years, and nothing could be gained from convicting him on such weak evidence. The case was dropped, but until Prohibition was repealed, there was no end of people who were willing to have a run-in with the law just to have a "snort" or make a buck.[4]

Blind Pigs

The term "blind pig" was so common in the area that children often stopped at business places and homes and asked where the blind pigs were. Most people laughed but never admitted knowing where one was, even though there was no shortage of them. The Falls usually had 30 to 40, with a peak of 46. Smaller communities also had their share. The blind pigs generally operated independent of any other business, but it was not unusual for a man to run the blind pig and his wife the "girl house."

Billy Noonan's "Observations" gave some idea of the contemporary view when he wrote: "An International Falls policeman dropped dead recently. He found a soft drink establishment with nothing but soft drinks on sale." On another occasion he noted: "There came near being a fight in a Baudette soft drink place the other night. A customer was served with a soft drink by mistake." The editor of *The Northome Record* wrote: "In spite of the fact that the country is bone dry, a great many of the men from the camps enjoyed an unlimited supply of 'bottled cheer' on Christmas day."

The Falls council was plagued with the fact that many establishments served liquor without purchasing a license. Frequently these were brothels, gaming places, or other entertainment sites where dispensing liquor was an added attraction to draw customers. Even the respected John Masters' bowling alley and pool hall had its "gaming room" and blind pig. Fines for no license were $50 and up, plus costs. The owners expected to be raided on a regular basis and generally paid the fine and returned to business. There was little effort to stamp them out.

An editorial of July 1, 1915, during the county option campaign, reveals the apparent indifference of the authorities toward blind pigs:

> A blind pig doesn't insist on a city council holding its star chamber sessions in its parlor. A blind pig doesn't frame up

with a county commissioner so as to get proprietors of its
joints on the grand jury. . . . Many of the businessmen of
this city who signed the mayor's wet petition did so because
they were afraid of a boycott, but they will vote "dry" all the
same. . . . Think of it, His Worshipful, the Mayor . . . has
so degraded himself and his office as to personally circulate
a petition among the local merchants in favor of retention
of the iniquitous saloon.

Frank Keyes, the mayor referred to, was well known for his
preference for a wide-open city. It was an accepted fact that "the
business was crooked and the law and lawless were connected,
the weekly raids were for show." A citizens-labor ticket was
formed in an effort to change the council and secure stronger
law enforcement. A good example of how the system worked was
told by deputy sheriff Vic Lindsten to Annie Shelland Williams.
A man arrested for drunkenness said that he had obtained the
liquor from Big Ole in Ranier. The sheriff asked Big Ole if he
had any liquor, and Ole pointed under the counter. The sheriff
told Ole he would need money for the fine. Ole dug up over $100.
Then the sheriff and Ole took a cab to the Falls. Ole paid the
cab driver, plus a generous tip, because he felt that what the
sheriff offered was not sufficient. Within a few days, Ole was
back in business.

When Koochiching County went dry in February 1916, the
licensed saloons closed at once, but within weeks prosecution of
blind pigs started. In April two Minneapolis detectives were hired
to clean up the county. In the first week they arrested 20 blind
pig operators in Littlefork, the Falls, Ranier, and Ray. *The Press*
stated: "Had . . . the presence of the detectives in this city not
leaked out every blind pig operator in this city would have been
nabbed. . . ." However, within another week 15 more were arrested,
most of whom pleaded guilty and were fined $75 and costs.

In an effort to improve the village's reputation, the city council
of Ranier raided eight blind pigs and arrested the operators.
Because the operators were repeat offenders, the fixtures from
their businesses, valued at $8,000, were confiscated along with
the illegal booze. The following week Sheriff White arrested 18
"piggers" in the Falls. In one month there were 31 indictments
and a large number of cases under consideration by the grand
jury.

The sheriff knew that the 12 blind piggers at Ray watched the
trains for his arrival, so he surprised them and walked the 12

miles from the Falls. Two men and two women were arrested; one paid $300 bail but failed to show up for trial.

No matter how often Ranier was raided, a new place opened for each one closed. Lookouts were posted to watch the cars, trains, and even foot traffic into that community, so Sheriff McIntosh hired a boat from the Fort and sneaked into town via Rainy Lake. After five women were arrested for disorderly conduct and fined only $5 each, they "returned to their joint rejoicing." The bartender was arrested and paid $75 and costs.

Big Falls had at least 10 blind pigs in addition to a large number of homesteaders who stepped up their home brewing during Prohibition to meet the demand. The best known team in that village was Pearl and Frank Rockstad. She ran the brothel and he the blind pig. "Both had business around the clock."

An association of blind pig operators tried to keep things under control. In July 1919, they agreed to increase the price of a drink from $0.25 to $0.35. The following day one pigger gave a lumberjack $0.25 and told him to go to another pigger's place to see if he was still selling drinks for the old price. The man got a drink for $0.25 but was told that the next time it would be $0.35. The local editor concluded, "It's funny those fellows can't stay by their agreements. They are such good sports, you know."

Probably one of the most serious aspects of Prohibition was the willingness of individuals to produce and consume drinks that often caused serious side effects. Hiram Frankel, who was with the Minnesota National Guard when it was called to the area during an MD & W strike in 1919, investigated activities of the IWW and learned what the blind piggers were doing. The Goslines, storekeepers at Big Falls, sold Hoffman drops, which were mixed with cider, or sometimes just water, and made the men intoxicated. Edna Peterson, who reportedly ran a disorderly house in Gemmell, used them to get her customers intoxicated. Mrs. Gosline also sold ginger and horse liniment, which were mixed and caused the men "to go crazy and walk around all night singing and hollering." Ginger, ginger root, or Jamaica ginger mixed with cider or wood alcohol provided "kick" for those who used it. Painkiller and essence of pepperment were often consumed because of their high alcohol content. In Mizpah, four men who consumed a mixture containing wood alcohol died within a few days of their orgy.

In 1923 the Falls council granted 18 soft drink licenses even though it was aware that the real business of the establishments was not the selling of soft drinks. The county commissioners protested this lax attitude of the town toward liquor, gambling, and prostitution, which created contempt for the law, even among juveniles. The commissioners were angry because so many of the destitute who burdened the county were the direct result of the existence of blind pigs and other dives and the county was compelled to care for them. As early as 1912 the commissioners had suggested that the saloon keepers be made liable for county expenses in caring for those who became wards of the public because of "overindulgence."

After the commissioners' request, a few raids were conducted, and the Falls became "as dry as the Sahara Desert." Within a few months all was back to normal, but then federal agents arrested the piggers and put them under $1,000 bond.

When federal agents entered the area, Billy Noonan noted: "Life is getting tough for owners of soft drink places who forgot what they were supposed to sell." In one series of raids federal agents gathered 30 men and women for a trip to federal court at Duluth, where they were fined up to $2,000 or given terms of up to three years at Leavenworth. Then they padlocked 12 soft drink parlors in the Falls.

The Falls was wide open from 1910 on, but probably no community gained as much notoriety as "that peculiar little city," Craigville. Although the number ranged from 9 to 26 at various times, Craigville normally had 20 saloons, each with a few women available. Blind pigs, gambling, and prostitution were rampant, with every day like the Fourth of July in the community's short heyday from 1913 to 1928. Hardly a week passed in the 1920s that did not have someone from Craigville appear in court. Pollard was afraid to go there, but his job forced him to "dig out men" and bring them back to work. The villagers took great comfort in the fact that it took at least a day before law enforcement officials could arrive if there was a problem, which did not help matters.

With about 400 permanent residents, the community's buildings were never more than rough-lumber shacks, so constructed because it originally was believed that their life span would be only a year or two. But the abundant timber supply in the southern part of Koochiching and northern Itasca counties provided harvest for two decades. Camp 29, the railroad camp for the MD & W, was only 1½ miles to the north, and the terminus of the M & RR was south of the Big Fork River. Reputedly up to 20,000 men passed through Craigville's limits in a single season.

The saloon names were quite descriptive—Johnny Welch's Steambath, Jim Reid's Big Ship, Big Charlie's (Warnstadt), the North Star Hotel, the Riverside, Broken-Ass Ole's, Island Rock Lodge, and Peggies. The same was true of the women's names— Box Car Annie, Mable, Rose, Mattie, Scarface Jean, Dutch Mary, Old Mille, Peggy, and Big Charlie's wife. Most of the women made the circuit of other northern towns, and some were in the Chicago-Minneapolis ring. The most attractive women seldom came to the area, but that did not bother the intoxicated lumberjacks.

Suicides, murders, and bodies floating in the river were a part of life in Craigville. The most publicized murder took place in April 1926. It resulted from a gunfight between Cunningham and McGinty, two saloon keepers, who hated each other. McGinty shot first and hit Cunningham in the abdomen; his other shots went wild. Then Cunningham fired; his first shot struck McGinty in the chest, and the others went wild, leaving the Gem Hotel with one dead man, one wounded man, and the walls peppered with bullet holes. The next morning a doctor arrived to examine Cunningham but left because he felt there was no hope. A clerk at the Norcross store, who had trained as a "male nurse," stopped in later in the day and felt that, since Cunningham was not hit in any vital organ, if he could get to a hospital, he could be saved. A gas railway car was hired to take him to a Grand Rapids hospital, where he recovered.

School teachers were not bothered by the citizens of the "joints" as long as they did not try to "clean up the town." Harold Barber enjoyed his stay there, even though he had to live at a home that made home-brew for the saloons, which made his clothes reek from the liquor. The only missionary ever to attempt working in the town soon left, because every time he sat down a prostitute tried sitting on his lap. No one wanted it any different, and an entire season's earnings were lost in a few days by people who apparently had no concern for tomorrow. Each drink, after the first few, contained more water, and the cost increased. If a lumberjack felt that the crowd was too quiet, all he had to do was yell "Timber!" and other lumberjacks swarmed up to the bar for free drinks.[5]

Rough and Tumble Life

Many residents of the Falls went to the Fort for entertainment because they could attend dances, the theater, and restaurants without being disturbed by the "tough element." When Harold

Barber's mother attended her first dance at Harsh's, in Big Falls, she noted that her husband was the only man wearing shoes; the others all wore spiked boots. She had been very active where they lived previously, but now isolated herself and seldom left the house unless the family went out of town.

J. C. Ryan, a strong defender of the lumberjack, wrote: "The lumberjack was a happy, clean living individual in camp. This was not true when he went to town to blow his stake. He then slept in 'dump hotels' or boarding houses and lived under pretty tough conditions until his stake was gone." When he was ready to return to camp, he was retrieved by a company man and taken back to dry out. Ryan added, "I have seen these men stay in camp up to two weeks before they were able to go back to work after blowing a big stake."

Fights and the wrecking of saloons caused the Falls Liquor Dealers Association to hold weekly meetings, starting in 1911, in an effort to eliminate those problems. Unfortunately, a certain element of the trade was not as concerned. When it became clear that municipal authorities often looked the other way, the town "loosened up." A juror failed to show for district court because he was drunk. After he sobered up, he resumed his duties with the understanding from the judge that he would be tried later.

Franz Jevne, who later became county attorney, arrived in the Falls on a Sunday morning in 1912 and was surprised to find the saloons all open. He asked the person next to him at the bar who was mayor, and the reply was, "I am." It was Dr. Morril E. Withrow. After he became county attorney, Jevne received support from church groups to close the bars on Sundays from 10:00 A.M. to noon. "That was as long as they could be closed without a lot of people getting the bends."

Lumberjacks often gave their earnings to bartenders for safe-keeping while they went on their orgies. The men enjoyed drinks, food, room, and girls until the bartender said the money was used up. The lumberjacks reasoned that this protected them from being robbed or rolled for their money, but the bartenders were not always good record keepers. Big Charlie was reputed to kick out lumberjacks once they signed releases for their paychecks. Such action, plus shortchanging the customer on drinks, resulted in frequent fights and even murder. However, other bartenders watched over the entrusted funds very carefully and at times helped the men sober up before they were completely broke. George Hnatuik's father often had as many as 40 men in his basement when they ran out of money and had no place to stay. "They just wanted a warm place to stay until they got work." The Hnatuiks fed them bread and soup. Hnatuik said that his father felt that these little deeds of kindness paid well.

A new 28- × 39-foot jail, with three men's and two women's cages, plus "a bull pen for the convenience of members of the tramp fraternity who stay over night in the city," was inaugurated in February 1912 "by the jugging of a bunch of Finlanders for disorderly conduct in a peaceful city." The Falls police report for 1912, when the city had about 3,000 residents, shows that 459 persons were arrested during the year, including 216 for drunkenness, 69 for drunk and disorderly conduct, 43 for assault, and 65 for vagrancy. Of those who were sentenced for more than short terms, 85 went to the county jail and 19 to a state prison. Ranier, which had only about 200 citizens, experienced 99 arrests in the first six months of 1913, of which 63 were for drunk and disorderly conduct and 21 for vagrancy. From January 2, 1911, to December 31, 1915, the Falls had 640 arrests for drunkenness, 142 for disorderly conduct, 98 for assault and battery, 84 for larceny, 72 for prostitution, and 164 for vagrancy. During that period the county jail averaged 12 to 30 prisoners a day. It was empty in early March 1916 for the first time since July 25, 1910. It appears that it was not until January 1934 that the jail was empty again, this time for eight days. The Falls editor wrote: "This is some record and well worth noting."

Deaths from suicide and murder caused by drinking took place regularly. Records for 1912 indicate six suicides and seven drownings associated with liquor, followed by seven deaths from alcohol in 31 days during February and March 1913. George Cox was run over by a train in the "dry" town of Big Falls after a three-day drunk. In Crimson Gulch, on the VRLRR near Orr, 31 murders took place in a two-year period, and there was speculation that many unidentified bodies were buried in Dead Man's Bog. In one year 17 men were run over by trains on a curve between Orr and Cusson; 15 of them had been murdered and 2 were drunks who were resting on the tracks.

Violence caused from drinking contributed to assorted news stories coming from the area. A blind pig in Loman was the scene of a drunken July 4 brawl in which a 27-year-old homesteader was kicked to death. On November 20, 1919, the county coroner reported two sudden deaths from drinking home-brewed booze. On the following day five cedar cutters, living near

Gemmell in a cabin that had been used as a still, came across what they thought was liquor and drank it. It was a poisonous liquid used in the manufacture of whiskey. Two were dead before the doctor arrived. The results were the same when moonshine was consumed from a Northome still at which formaldehyde was used to denature alcohol. Northome also experienced two suicides in one week by a farmer and a lumberjack, who had gone crazy from drinking moonshine. When "near whiskey with decided kick in it" got into a camp east of Northome, two of the lumberjacks used a grub hoe and pitch fork to settle their argument, which resulted in a visit to the doctor.

A "Russian" was buried at county expense after he died from alcoholic poisoning. He was found in a blueberry patch clutching a pint of moonshine in each hand. Odd Tone, who grew up on a farm near Northome, recalled hearing lumberjacks yell as they returned to camp after they had been in town for drinks during the "dry" 1920s. He also saw a dead drunk lying on the road by his place and the frozen corpse of another drunk in R. H. Collar's blind pig. Tone was 14 at the time and said that sight made a deep impression on him. John Ettestad was about the same age when he saw Otto Wilke dead on the road after he had visited Craigville. Between April 5 and 14, 1925, five moonshine victims were buried at county expense in the Falls.

In addition to dealing with the illicit trade in booze, law enforcement officials also were challenged with the smuggling of drugs across the border. Starting in 1914, the Fort became a jumping-off place to enter the United States. Equipment to make cocaine was seized from a man who authorities believed was furnishing Falls prostitutes with cocaine during the summer and fall of 1919. In 1923 Dennis Baker was one of three men sentenced to Leavenworth for four years for selling cocaine and morphine through the mail. Narcotic agents in the Falls watched for several women suspected of receiving dope from Canada and "passing it on to the poor souls who have the habit," not only in the Falls but also in the Twin Cities. The nearness to an international border and the attitude of the authorities served to make the Falls a wide-open city. That probably was part of the reason it held its frontier reputation for so long.

It was not unusual for the wilderness to serve as a refuge for members of the criminal element of larger cities. Ruth Monson said that her father, a minister at Mizpah, commented about a member of his congregation who was looking at a "wanted" poster in the post office in the 1930s. The parishioner observed that the person standing next to him looked just like the man pictured on the poster, except for a scar. When the man turned his head, the scar was visible, and he left immediately. It was "Baby Face" Nelson, one of many criminals who spent time in the area when "the heat was on" in the city.[6]

Wets vs. Drys

During the last decades of the 1800s, the temperance movement increased in strength. By 1910 federal regulations forced the closing of saloons adjacent to Indian reservations, but a court decision in early 1911 reversed part of the ruling, and several hundred saloons were reopened. Pressures mounted nationally for control of the manufacture and consumption of intoxicating liquors.

In 1914 citizens of the Falls voted 539 wet and 242 dry in the largest voter turnout in history. The drys claimed that they were satisfied with the number of votes they had received and made it clear that they were not through with their campaign. Beltrami County voted dry, and only Baudette and Spooner were allowed to remain wet. Plummer noted in his diary that he circulated a county option petition and was pleased that Indus township voted dry 27 to 2. In Watrous (Loman), the drys won by only 5 votes, 29 to 24. All of the communities in Koochiching voted dry in 1915 except Craigville, Koochiching Township, and the Falls.

The Journal, which carried a hard-hitting campaign, including editorials, for a dry vote, warned that "floaters" were the biggest threat in the upcoming election. The most dramatic ad covered a full page and was printed upside down in headline-size print, but the March 1915 election still favored the wets 411 to 280. The editor blamed the dry loss to a large number of hoboes, non-taxpayers, and non-residents. However, in August the county voted dry by 13 votes, overcoming a 403 wet plurality in the Falls and Koochiching Township.

This set the stage for the city council, which was referred to as "the saloon gang majority," to defy higher authority and keep the town open. Collusion between the saloon keepers and the council became conspicuous. The local editor asked, "Which Alderman did you say was playing cards and drinking in a saloon in the city at 1:30 o'clock Sunday morning with the proprietor and another old resident while four others were drinking at the bar?"

The Minnesota attorney general served an injunction against

the council for granting liquor licenses in violation of the county option vote. The saloon keepers appealed to the state supreme court, which ruled against them, and they were forced to close. Peace reigned for only a couple of weeks. In March, as predicted, the bawdy element drifted back into town. Gamblers and at least 50 undesirables, who had "no visible means of a livelihood," were back.

Enforcement of the liquor law was a joke, unless the county authorities did the job. At the April 17, 1916, council meeting, Alderman Frank S. Lang moved that the city attorney enforce the law against the unlicensed drinking places, but the motion failed for lack of a second. The Falls editor persisted in asking in which bootlegging joint the council met after each council meeting. When a strike occurred in the Falls in September, Mayor Keyes closed all but four selected "soft drink parlors" with ease. This was an obvious effort on the part of the saloon keepers and the council to keep peace in town when idle men roamed the streets.

The Minnesota Public Safety Commission took action against the city council forcing the body to require that the "soft drink parlors" be closed at 10:00 P.M.—the same time that the saloons in wet counties had to be closed. Proceedings were brought against 14 communities in the county at that time. At the request of county authorities, the M & I declared an embargo against all liquor shipments into the county, and similar action was expected of the CN.

In March 1917, Frank Keyes was re-elected mayor by a 387 to 293 vote. *The Journal* editor wrote that the Falls was "the only city in the state which would deliberately re-elect . . . to office a bunch of men whose former term had been one of favor to lawlessness and whose avowed intention was to continue the kind of law breaking regime." On October 8, at the request of the Public Safety Commission, Governor Burnquist suspended Keyes, Sheriff Thomas White, and Ranier mayor Peter Gibbons from office for failure to enforce the law. The only objection from the local citizens was that none of the replacement officers came from the county, but they did enforce the laws. In March 1918, the three men were reinstated on condition that the laws be enforced. Litigation about their removal was still pending.

In Beltrami County the big argument was over the right of the Red Lake Indians to vote in the county option campaign. Because the county voted wet by 21 votes, the drys brought suit on the grounds that individuals living on federal lands were not part of the county. The district court ruled that the vote of the

Indians, which was 79 wet and 13 dry, was legal. That ruling was appealed to the State Supreme Court, which declared that the Indian vote was not valid, and the county was dry. The saloons of Baudette and Spooner closed, which was a financial bombshell to the two villages, for the eight saloons in Baudette each paid $1,200 in licenses and the six in Spooner each paid $1,000. To see that the two villages remained dry, a branch of the Minnesota Safety Committee was formed in Baudette.

On January 16, 1920, when national Prohibition became effective, federal agents started working in the area. Many complaints were made that levying fines only served as a license for blind pigs to continue, and jail terms for the violators were requested. Billy Noonan was more philosophical: "Prohibition along the border has been a great success aside from the fact that there is more drinking than ever before." J. J. Hadler, attorney for the Falls, provided a list of names and addresses of 37 blind piggers who were arrested in 1924. A motion was made to institute abatement proceedings against the property where a conviction was obtained; however, the motion lost by a vote of four to two. The council still refused to cope with the problem.

This was contrary to what happened in the communities of Cusson, Gheen, and Orr, when a mass meeting was held at Orr on April 9, 1928, to formulate a protest petition to the governor. The resolution acknowledged that there were more than 75 dealers in illegal liquor, drugs, and prostitution that had operated in the past three years "almost without interruption." In two years, more than 20 deaths were attributed to the activities of the lawless element, including 2 murders and 1 death from alcoholism in one week. One of the murders was of an aged woman, who operated a store south of Orr. The 115 people who signed the petition stated that the lawless gang "has operated in this locality practically without limits." Copies were delivered to the St. Louis County attorney, the sheriff, and Governor Theodore Christianson by a committee of citizens from Cusson and Orr. After Prohibition was repealed, the 200 citizens of Orr incorporated and established a municipal liquor store to capitalize on the tourist trade. The moral issue of wets vs. drys was not settled, but at least the citizens knew where the liquor was being dispensed.[7]

Gambling

The timber frontier, like the cattle and the mining frontiers, with large numbers of single men and little to occupy their leisure time, was a magnet to gamblers and provided a natural setting in which to practice their trade. They were a problem in every community as soon as a shack was available. The Falls city council passed Ordinance XIV in March 1912, which prohibited gaming and gambling houses, but, as in the case of blind pigs, laws were only as good as the enforcement. The court records are filled with entries of individuals charged with conducting gambling or keeping a gambling device in their place of business. A 1914 ordinance limited the number of pool and billiard halls to five, but they had 28 tables. There were also shooting galleries, interior ball games, and bowling alleys. At first, fines for establishments having unlicensed devices of any kind were $50 and costs, but by 1915 fines of $100 and costs were not uncommon, especially for professional gamblers. However, as in the case of blind pigs, as soon as the fines were paid, it was business as usual.

Hiram Barber, an ex-school teacher, was one of the first professional gamblers in the Big Falls area. He came to town in 1910 to organize a fraternal insurance lodge and used his spare time to run the poker game for "the house" at Robinson's. His pay was 50 percent of the winnings, and games went on 24 hours a day. Barber always made good money when he played for the house, but in his free time he could not resist gambling, and often he had to tend bar to support his family. When his son, Harold, had time off from his teaching or summer school, he concentrated on penny ante poker and worked in the game room adjacent to the Fargo Cafe. He stopped playing at 5:00 A.M. each day and made more in the summer at that than he did during the rest of the year at teaching.

By 1915 several professional gamblers might be nabbed in a single raid, because individual establishments had as many as five working on a shift. Like the blind piggers, their names appeared frequently in the court records. In one raid in 1916, at Hasselbarth's and Bancroft's, "the two worst gambling joints," the authorities arrested 49 men playing blackjack and stud poker, of whom 10 were professionals. The other patrons all were freed, but the professionals paid fines. In most cases when a place was raided, all of the occupants were fined, and the money on the table went to the school fund.

During their short heydays, Gemmell, Mizpah, and Northome were virtually overrun by gamblers, who worked 24 hours a day in the busy season. If there was a raid in one village, the gamblers moved to the other two until it was safe to return. Pady the Pig was the best known of the gamblers who shifted between the three communities as the raids dictated. An outside observer at Northome in 1919 said, "It seems most of them who are card sharks find it easier to make a living playing poker than to work, and they are here to entice the unsuspecting into a game and rob them." Northome officials tried to stop the gambling because it brought "crooks and other lawless into town," but to no avail.

Gambling took place in nearly all pool halls and saloons (during Prohibition, "the soft drink parlors"). Money was exchanged through playing the punchboard; tossing California dice with their special slanted side table; playing simple craps, hearts, fan tan, smear, stud poker, blackjack, lowball, 21 or bust, or roulette; or tossing silver dollars on the sidewalks. In the last game, the winner was the one whose coin fell closest to the crack in the sidewalk. Several people recalled that Jess Rose was the local "expert" at that game.

Joe Miller, who admitted that he spent a great deal of time in brothels and gambling dens as a bouncer, a house player, or a patron, pointed out that there were different places and games depending on the financial status of the player. Games varied from the $0.05 punchboard, which gave away Valentine candy, fishing or hunting equipment, or trips, a dice game for a $0.10 beer, or $1.00 to $10.00 a game for the lumberjacks, to $100.00 a game for business and professional people, and up to $300.00 a game for a few Canadians and big-city visitors who came to the area for gambling. The number of players varied from 8 to 10 in a $1-per-person game to 2 players in the high-stakes games. Anyone who walked in could play the low-stakes games. Occasionally, games lasted for days and nights, stopping only for toilet breaks or lunch, but not for sleep. In such cases the room was filled with onlookers. Sometimes these were "domestic games," with only two players—one player from the house and an outsider. Other times these were "international games," which often were played by resort owners from both sides of the border for stakes as high as $10,000.

Another high-stakes hobby among those who liked to gamble was horse racing on the ice on Rainy Lake. Bob Williams owned Hamlin "J," who could run the mile in 2 minutes 12 seconds. The Burnette brothers, Frank Keyes, and several of the resort saloon owners also had at least partial interest in horses. Horse racing provided another means of gambling and drawing tourists.

Bert Johnson, who spent much of his working life distributing gaming machines, observed that many lumberjacks appeared almost obsessed with the idea of spending their paychecks. They often were determined not to quit until the money was gone. One man, who was not on good terms with his immediate family, deliberately spent his money on gambling, booze, and prostitutes whenever he had a certain amount saved to make sure none of them would inherit any of it when he died.

Probably no person was more involved with gambling in the Falls than Frank Keyes. The Keyes Arcade, which was the largest building in town after the mill, had gaming in the entire basement, the Keyes Motor Company on the ground floor, and rooms and dancing on the second floor. Keyes purchased and stored a large quantity of bar and gambling equipment when businesses were raided or closed, which he later sold piecemeal at a good profit.

As methods of harvesting timber changed, fewer men were required. This produced a change in area gambling operations. In 1936 all slot machines, race-horse machines, pinball machines, and similar devices were outlawed. At that time the Falls had more than 200 slot machines. In an article about the removal of such devices, the editor closed, "Now perhaps we will have an occasional nickel for the collection plate on Sunday."

However, new devices to get that coin—such as the Wurlitzer music machines and skill machines that did not have a payout—came on the scene. The pinball machines—"electric marvels"—managed to re-enter the pool halls and bars. They paid out less than 75 percent, but appealed to the instinct for gambling. A franchised distributor recalled, "I have seen lumberjacks play machines and not even wait until the play started to see if there was going to be a payoff. Some even put money in ahead of time to stop the payoff. It didn't make sense."

Edward LaPage and Nick Hnatuik had 64 pinball machines in the Falls in 36 different establishments, and each required a license fee of $37.50 in 1939. Twenty of the locations were on Third Street, and the others were within a block, indicating that the location of the gambling haunts had not changed. A petition signed by 500 citizens protested the availability of "games of skill" in the city, but the council unanimously voted to legalize them and to set aside the funds derived for recreation purposes only.

Within a few months the management of the Avalon Lounge, on Third Avenue, decided to test the limit of the law by "re-introducing" the slot machine. A raid in December 1939 indicated that the "one-armed bandit" had been "devouring coins at a lively rate . . . and was well filled." Two miniature slot machines were seized from Carroll's Bar. At Al Hausmann's cigar stand, the police found "cleverly disguised green box-like instruments" that, when closed, could be taken for harmless vending devices.

When a fire swept the "Bowery district" in December 1939, three Third Street buildings were destroyed, leaving 125 persons, mostly single men, homeless. The Svea Hotel, the Victoria Hotel, The Valhalla, People's, Scotty's, and the Victoria bars, plus the People's Cafe, all burned "like tinder boxes." It was an omen marking the end of an era.[8]

Prostitution

Prostitution was a natural companion to liquor and gambling and played a major role in the leisure life of lumberjacks and mill workers. The Falls was on a gambling and prostitution circuit that included the pimps who traveled to East Grand Forks, Minnesota, the twin ports of Duluth-Superior, and to Hurley, Wisconsin—all wild towns. The smaller towns in the area had a circuit among themselves, but it appears that the women in it were not tied in with an organized ring. The Ranier, Ericsburg, Ray, and Orr communities were favored by some, and Northome, Mizpah, Gemmell, Big Falls, and Craig by others.

A long-time Falls municipal employee indicated that the original ordinances protected prostitution, because the medical people convinced the authorities that that was the only way to keep disease under control. Elected officials attempted to eliminate prostitution late in 1910, but they did not succeed. Ordinance 31, passed July 3, 1912, made prostitution illegal within the city limits and set fines of from $5 to $50 and costs, or 60 days in jail. As was true with gambling houses and blind pigs, the women often were informed when raids were planned, so they knew when to refrain from business or to move to a neighboring town for a short time.

The women were arrested on a periodic basis, examined, fined, and, if not infected, allowed to return to their trade. This cycle is evident from a study of the court records in which the same names appear on a regular basis for many years. Probably no name appeared more the first of each month than that of Joy Gordon, a madam, who ran a "boarding house" and was active for at least 32 years.

Except for a few who worked independently, the women always had funds to pay the fine, and rarely was there any record of protest. A major exception occurred in 1927 when Lillian Miller, who conducted her business at 400½ Third Street, proceeded to tell the court a few things about running the city. Judge John Brown called her to the clerk's desk, ordered that her check for $100 be returned, and sentenced her to 30 days in jail.

The greatest offense appeared to be soliciting on the street near the saloons, which sometimes drew a sentence to leave town or be jailed. Medical doctors spent a considerable amount of time examining girls and treating lumberjacks. The madams were strict about having their girls examined and kept their health records. If one became diseased, she was forced to quit her trade or leave town.

Surprise raids, such as the one that took place on the Koochiching Hotel in November 1915, often produced comical results:

> Although only five women and two men were arrested, there was a general scamper through doors and down fire escapes of other well known persons. . . . Some men were found hiding among the dress goods in clothes closets. It must have been a lovely sight to see those gentlemen, who are so faultlessly dressed and so pompous when in the public street, in such places minus their finery.

Baudette and Spooner were just as wide open as the Falls regarding prostitution. Everyone knew where the houses were, but they continued to operate. One house had from 10 to 12 women. Complaints from local citizens forced a surprise raid in March 1915, resulting in closure of three resorts.

After a complaint from a clergyman, a raid in Old Spooner netted Mr. and Mrs. F. F. Anderson, "proprietors of the joint," and nine women. The Andersons were one of several husband-and-wife teams who ran brothels and blind pigs. Billy Noonan, in his usual descriptive style, wrote that the deputies had "stormed a maison de joie . . . which was not to be frequented by members of the Y.M.C.A. nor Ancient Order of Rainbow Chasers. . . . When the deputies and their prisoners arrived in Baudette it looked like a burlesque troupe about to hit the road." The nine women were named and each was fined $50, and the Andersons were each fined $100. The Andersons paid all the fines.

Noonan continued:

The aggregation presented a motley array in the court room. There wasn't a "good looker" in the outfit. They resembled a bunch of remnants on a bargain counter at the close of the season. Much sympathy is expressed for Hazel Wood. She is a young girl and looked decidedly out of place amongst the rest of the "junk." She appeared to be . . . unsophisticated in the ways of the world. . . . She was the first to be fined and as she sat she turned her head and tears filled her eyes. Near her sat a couple of "veterans" and they would at times turn toward her and with meaning looks shake their heads.

One ex-lumberjack, who had worked in many camps from Kettle Falls to Craigville to Loman, very matter of factly commented, "Every little place had its girls. They needed the business and the men on free time needed a place to sleep."

Rainer was reputed to have had a higher portion of houses and blind pigs than the Falls. They were probably the main sources of revenue in the town. One of the oddities of Ranier was the "Beef Trust" at Bob Williams' nightclub—four women who together weighed 1,000 pounds. By the late 1920s, tavern operators in the Falls no longer allowed prostitutes to operate within their establishments, but in Ranier they continued to do so well into the 1930s.

When Williams moved to the Kettle Falls Hotel, there were usually eight girls who rented rooms and "operated" strictly on their own. Jen Rose, Lumberjack Karey, and Big Belle were three of the regulars. Williams often moved his young son from one room to another to provide a place for the girls. Oliver Knox said that in all the years he lived at Kettle Falls girls always were available, and more than once he saw a lumberjack, who had been knocked out and rolled, lying outside.

Big Falls had a large house covered with red tin where 8 to 10 women were in business at all times. Harold Barber accompanied the paperboy one morning, but all he saw was a long bar and a few chairs before Frank Rockstad yelled at them to get out. The Cusson-Orr area had between 30 and 40 prostitutes, who used pimps but also worked with the bartenders. At least two dwellings in Ray housed prostitutes, with Daper's Hotel the most popular. Activity in Ray, Cusson, and Orr died down considerably after the VRL shut down in 1929. Northome, Mizpah, Gemmell, and Margie all had houses of prostitution during their heyday and were periodically raided by law officers.

Probably no community had a more open attitude toward

prostitution than Craigville. Women were available in every saloon. The community's heyday was reached in 1928 and declined slowly as logging activities continued in the old mode until the 1940s, when the MD & W was discontinued. But because of its reputation, Craigville persisted. In 1940 Anne Mattice, better known as Peggy, the most renowned of the community's entrepreneurs, came to town. For 30 years she ran a tavern called Peggies. She denied being a madam, but admitted to hiring girls, because the competition did. However, she claimed that she never took a cut from any of them. Whatever the prostitutes charged or stole was theirs. One could not buy a loaf of bread in Craigville, but there was ample liquor, gambling, and prostitution. However, in later years the clientele was far different from that of lumberjack days.

Just how many prostitutes the Falls had at its height is still a mystery, but everyone knew that Second Street and the second floor of Third Street housed women, even as late as the mid-1930s. Jim Serdaris' Chicago Cafe "got lots of orders from the 300 girls who were in business in town." Serdaris said that most of the time he carried the orders up "to keep the help out of trouble. Frank Keyes often came in and took out big orders. The girls kept themselves out of circulation and only came in during the night hours by themselves."

Serdaris continued that the town was wide open and that "Keyes had the town in his hand, the police chief, and the rest of the city officers under his control." It was common knowledge that Keyes brought girls to town, sold them furniture, clothes, jewelry, and cars, and set them up in business. They always paid their rent and made the payments on their purchases, or they were kicked out. The prostitutes had money, but "the madams always had to give permission and approve of charge accounts." One madam wanted to purchase "only the best mattresses for her hard working girls."

Nearly all people doing business with the brothels were happy to do so, because it was cash on delivery plus a generous tip. This was true for newspaper boys; vegetable peddlers; furniture, grocery, and coal deliverers; wood splitters; and even those soliciting for charities. In one charity drive to sell lyceum tickets, a prostitute bought more tickets than any other person in town. The girls often provided the largest gifts to church groups preparing boxes for the needy.

Prostitutes' fees ranged from \$0.50 to \$3.00 throughout the period from 1910 to the late 1930s. "Rolling" customers was a common practice, and many prostitutes managed to steal more from their clients than they were paid. Persons who were friendly to prostitutes often had an opportunity to buy watches and other valuables that had been taken from their clients. In most cases the fee was shared with the madam, who paid all expenses. However, some girls had their own rooms or houses. The number of customers a prostitute saw each day was unpredictable, but, except for those who had another job, the girls were available around the clock. During a busy period they hoped to have at least 15 to 20 customers a night.

These women came from all backgrounds. Some got into the business by free choice, some through adverse family circumstances, and others were virtually trapped by professional recruiters. Although many were very attractive, those best remembered fit Billy Noonan's description: "May Rice, who has not been in court for four years, was back again today looking terrible. She had a black eye and was otherwise disfigured and looked for all the world like the dove that she thinks she is." She was sentenced to 30 days or to leave town at once. Gertie Hilton also was ordered to leave town. Instead, she married a local man and then refused to leave, hoping that she would be forgiven since she was married. Judge J. J. Halder did not excuse her and sentenced her to the "county bastille" to face felony charges.

Many prostitutes became quite well known. Some became relatively well-to-do; others married local men at various levels of affluence. Many disappeared in a short period of time, either because they were on a circuit or, hopefully, because they wanted to start a better life elsewhere. Stories are prevalent about those who became despondent and climbed the "high dive" that reached 60 feet into the sky to put an end to it all. A few lumberjacks met the same fate. The number of persons buried by the county without having any reference to next of kin is a reflection of the kind of life that many lived on this wild frontier.

It is easy to generalize, but probably life was no more sinful and carefree here than on other frontiers. Masses of men, many of them virtually homeless, came to work in the woods, where few skills were needed to earn their keep. They were unconcerned about saving for a rainy day, even at a time when care for the destitute was far less generous than it is today. Others were more serious and saved nearly all that they earned working in lumber camps in the winter, toiling on bonanza farms, or doing construction or road work the rest of the year for a "grubstake" to establish a farm or a business of their own. The prostitutes, gamblers, and liquor dispensers were all part of the natural progression of events. The fact that much of this activity took place as late as the eve of World War II reminds us that we are not far removed from the frontier.[9]

ENDNOTES FOR CHAPTER VIII

1. Interview of Fred Hendee, International Falls, August 12, 1976, hereafter Hendee interview; Paul, "Memories"; Koski interview; Kooch. Comm., October 29, 1909, September 12, 1911; Albrecht and Thomas, pp. 43, 44; Kohlhase interview; City Council, December 12, 1910, March 12, 1912, March 24, 1913, January 9, April 11, September 26, 1933, April 6, 10, June 15, 1936, May 17, June 7, December 13, 1937, April 29, 1940; *The Press*, November 17, 1910, January 12, March 30, 1911; Rose interview; *The Journal*, April 17, October 30, 1913, March 5, 19, 1914, April 22, 1915, February 17, 1916, April 6, May 2, 1933, April 30, 1936, April 18, 1939, April 17, 1940; *The Baudette Region*, January 11, June 7, November 29, 1917, April 7, 1933, February 16, 1934; interview of Bert W. Johnson, Island View Route, International Falls, June 10, 1979, hereafter Bert Johnson interview.

2. *The Baudette Region*, July 4, November 7, 1919, January 12, 1923, January 30, 1925, February 12, April 2, September 3, 1926, April 13, 1928; Tive interview; interview of Charlie R. Williams, International Falls, August 15, 1976, hereafter Charlie Williams interview; Plummer diary; Ettestad interview; Henrickson interview; *The Journal*, November 8, 1917, January 3, 1918, May 31, 1923, February 18, 1926, March 17, 1927, February 22, 1930, March 10, 1933; Pearson interview; Hnatuik interview.

3. *The Canadian Encyclopedia* (Edmonton: Hurtige Publishers, 1985), Vol. III, p. 1491; Alexander interview; *The Journal*, July 31, August 14, 1924, February 10, 13, 20, 1930, January 11, 1933; *The Baudette Region*, February 27, May 21, June 18, August 13, 20, 1920, August 20, 1926, October 10, 1930; Rose interview; *The Chronicle*, February 17, 1974; Henrickson interview; Ettestad interview; *Crane Lake Portage*, a manuscript in KCHS, p. 4, hereafter *Crane Lake*; Dahlberg interview; Plummer diary; Charlie Williams interview.

4. *The Northome Record*, June 25, November 26, 1920, January 14, 1921; *The Baudette Region*, October 1, 1920, January 22, March 26, 1926; Rose interview; City Council, June 10, 17, 1929; *The Journal*, February 13, 1930; transcript of testimony in the *United States Government* v. *Dennis Baker*, March 30, 1931, in KCHS; letter from John H. Brown, U.S. Commissioner, the Falls, to L. L. Drill, U.S. Attorney, St. Paul, April 7, 1931, KCHS; letter from L. L. Drill, to John H. Brown, April 18, 1931, KCHS.

5. Malerich interview; Hnatuik interview; *The Journal*, July 1, 1915, February 10, March 23, April 6, 13, September 21, October 26, 1916, April 19, November 22, December 13, 1917, March 28, July 11, 1918, July 18, August 21, 1919, April 29, 1920, April 30, December 10, 1925, February 11, 1926, July 14, 1927, February 12, 18, March 1, 1930, December 12, 13, 14, 1977; *The Baudette Region*, March 8, July 26, November 29, 1917, February 3, 1922, September 14, 1928; City Council, March 18, 1911, February 18, 1915, April 16, 1923, May 11, 1925; Kooch. Comm., March 12, 1912; Alexander interview; Miller interview; Williams file; *The Northome Record*, February 11, 1916, January 19, 1917, December 31, 1920; Neil Watson interview; Gorden interview; Ettestad interview;

Henrickson interview; Hiram D. Frankel, Adjutant to General Rhinow, of the Minnesota National Guard, "Report on Labor Disturbances in Northern Minnesota, December 1919, January 6, 1920," pp. 38, 59, 64, MHS, hereafter Frankel; Pollard interview; John Fritzen, "The Cunningham-McGinty Gun Fight," a typed manuscript in KCHS. Fritzen was a forest ranger, who was in Craigville the night of the fight. Barber interview.

6. Fraser interview; Barber interview; Ryan, I, p. 3; *The Press*, November 19, 1910, May 18, 1911; *The Journal*, February 15, 1912, January 23, March 27, July 3, 1913, March 19, 1914, July 1, 22, November 11, 1915, January 27, March 23, 1916, July 12, 1917, November 20, 27, 1919, July 8, 1920, July 19, 26, 1923, April 16, 1925, February 18, 1926, January 11, 13, 1930, January 6, 1934; Hnatuik interview; Records of the Municipal Court, International Falls, May 22, 1907, through December 31, 1915, hereafter Municipal Court; Kooch. Comm., August 8, 20, 1912, April 15, May 13, 1913, January 6, February 26, 1914, January 5, March 2, 1915; *The Chronicle*, March 3, 1974; Scott Erickson interview; *The Baudette Region*, July 12, 1917; *The Northome Record*, November 21, 1919, March 19, 1920, September 9, 1921; Tone interview; McLinn interview; Ettestad interview; conversation with Ruth Monson, December 20, 1990.

7. *The Press*, January 12, 1911; Gerber interview; *The Journal*, April 9, 1914, March 11, 25, April 1, 8, August 5, 12, November 18, December 12, 16, 1915, February 10, March 2, June 8, September 21, December 7, 1916, April 5, October 11, 1917, March 7, 1918, January 30, 1919, October 27, 1921, June 19, 1924, May 28, 1925; *The Baudette Region*, October 22, 1914, August 5, 1915, March 1, July 26, August 2, 17, 24, November 22, 1917; Plummer diary; City Council, April 17, 1916; *The Northome Record*, August 10, 1917, March 25, 1921; copy of petition dated April 9, 1928, written at a meeting in the Orr Town Hall, in the possession of Scott Erickson; Scott Erickson interview.

8. *The Journal*, March 21, July 25, 1912, February 10, 1916, March 2, 1922, May 8, 1924, March 5, 1936, July 18, December 4, 28, 1939, March 7, 1940; Municipal Court, February 24, December 30, 1911, January 2, March 23, 24, 1915; City Council, November 23, 1914, July 24, 31, August 7, 1939; Barber interview; Alexander interview; *The Baudette Region*, May 17, 1917; Frankel, pp. 29, 37, 45, 49, 52; *The Northome Record*, April 30, 1920; Hnatuik interview; Rose interview; Miller interview; Bert Johnson interview; Charlie Williams interview; interview of Monte F. Keyes, International Falls, August 19, 1976, hereafter Keyes interview. Keyes is the son of Frank Keyes and was born February 8, 1907.

9. Malerich interview; *The Press*, November 24, 1910; Municipal Court, November 18, 1911, January 2, 15, February 21, September 3, 6, 1912, July 7, August 14, 1914, February 19, 24, April 13, July 17, 1915; *The Journal*, July 4, 1912, September 11, 1913, July 15, August 12, November 11, 18, December 2, 1915, June 8, 1916, September 5, 1918, June 7, 14, 1923, July 17, 1924, October 6, 1927, February 24, March 7, June 2, 1933; Hnatuik interview; Rose interview; *The Baudette Region*, March 11, November 25, 1915, March 29, 1917; Arvid Peterson interview; Bert Johnson interview; Charlie Williams interview; Knox interview; Barber interview; Scott Erickson interview; Pearson interview; Neil Watson interview; Jim Kimball, *The Minneapolis Tribune*, January 30, 1972, 1F; Paul Anderson interview; Serdaris interview; Schneider interview; Alexander interview; Rasmussen interview; O. Olson interview; Keyes interview; Miller interview.

CHAPTER IX

The Unyielding Wilderness

MUCH OF THE NORTHERN BORDER COUNTRY was not attractive to settlers who were interested in farming. Except for those who cut the trees and left, the homesteaders soon realized the futility of their efforts. The tree-covered muskeg virtually prohibited farming and travel in the area. To overcome the obstacles and provide the proper environment for agriculture, it was necessary to drain the land and to provide roads.

Ditching Fever

One of the most popular, but least understood, topics of discussion about the "old days" is ditching. Many people envisioned prosperity and relief from isolation if the proposed ditching and associated road schemes succeeded. What was not realized was that the flat muskeg-covered land did not permit sufficient drainage to aid farming. At the same time, the land was drained just enough to create an additional fire hazard and to make the area less desirable for wildlife and trees. Those factors, combined with blind optimism and corruption, made the ditching projects responsible for crippling the involved counties financially for decades to come.

In late 1903 *The Laurel Press* stated that muskeg drainage and road building were the two most important issues of the area. The editor suggested combining the two tasks—dig ditches and use the dirt to make roads. Lyman Ayer, Backus' chief scout, noted in his diary that the growth of the "almost continuous body of spruce" in northern Beltrami and Koochiching counties "will be greatly accelerated by the great drainage ditches which the State of Minnesota is just starting in this territory."

That was good news to developers of the paper mills, but there is little evidence to indicate that they were involved with either ditching or associated road building. Did the paper manufacturers feel, as did most of the local citizens, that the days of forestry were numbered and that farming would be the ultimate industry? In any case, the powerful Backus was never visible in the ditching affair other than to complain about taxes.

State leaders encouraged ditching throughout the state, because many of them felt that the state would profit greatly, especially in the north, where it owned most of the 11 million acres of forest land. The loosely organized state drainage commission focused on draining state lands, until a state drainage convention was held in Bemidji in 1905, and many of the 300 delegates felt that privately owned land should also be served. The theme of Governor John Johnson's speech to that group was that drainage was the best investment the state could make. The Minnesota Drainage League was formed to spread information about drainage, enact favorable drainage laws, and educate the populace about drainage.

Prior to the convention, the legislature had appropriated $15,000 to determine where the state wetlands were located and which could be drained to make them valuable for farming. The federal agencies involved were reluctant to commit themselves for or against drainage of Minnesota swampland, even though they admitted that it might be good for the Indians and would attract settlers. But everyone was amazed when they announced that such a project would cost $12 million. League officers quickly countered that the 11 million drained acres would be some of the "very best farming land, as the soil is of the richest kind."

In 1906 Congressman Halvor Steenerson, of Crookston, introduced a bill which provided that proceeds from the sale of public land in Minnesota should be set aside in a special "drainage reclamation fund" to be used for future surveying and drainage. The campaign intensified as members of the commercial clubs and as industrial and political groups throughout the state, including the Twin Cities, toured the area. Drainage programs in the southern part of the state and the Red River Valley were successful and made the local citizens more determined than ever.

Legislation was enacted that permitted county boards and district judges to proceed with a drainage project when six affected landowners filed a petition. If the ditch was solely in one county, the commissioners could approve; if more than one county was involved, the district judge had to act.

After the wetlands survey was completed, the state drainage

commission issued the following statement: "We are convinced that the time has arrived when it is imperatively necessary for the State to pursue a vigorous policy in dealing with [the wetlands]. . . . We respectively [*sic*] recommend that the reclamation of the State swamplands be continued on a more extensive scale. . . ."

Koochiching County profited from the first project when two ditches were dug—one between the Falls and the Little Fork River, and the other from Littlefork to Big Falls. George A. Ralph, engineer for the drainage commission, got the work started. The northern project to the Falls would extend 18 miles and reclaim 25,000 to 30,000 acres at a cost of $25,000. The $12,000 Big Falls project would reclaim 12,000 acres of land. It was suggested that highways be built on the ditch banks. A smaller project was also provided for in the Northome area, making Koochiching County the scene of the greatest drainage activity in the state in 1908. A campaign was started to get the state to divest itself of the 900,000 acres of land it was being accused of holding for speculation, which was unfair to Koochiching and other counties where the state owned large blocks of land.

Fuel was poured on the fire with the passage of a drainage act designed specifically for northern Minnesota by Congressman Steenerson and Senator Andrew Volstad, which permitted an individual to qualify for a 160-acre homestead without living on or improving the land. The federal government was entitled to $1.25 an acre or could grant the land under homestead provision, and Minnesota could charge up to $2.75 an acre to cover drainage cost. Volstad likened the act to the Desert Land Acts and expressed that as many as 100,000 people would move onto those drained lands. The Indians were reimbursed $1.25 an acre for any land drained on the Red Lake Indian Reservation and granted to homesteaders.

In 1909 the drainage acts were relaxed so a single affected landowner could request a ditch, which had to be granted if the authorities felt the request was a valid one. The counties were authorized to issue bonds to cover the cost of the ditches. But the state was still reluctant to sell any of its land, for it was concerned about forest protection and about greater income potential from timber after the drainage projects were completed. Local citizens protested that population in the rural areas was already decreasing, and they felt that they were bearing the cost of road building, drainage, and other community needs without help from the state, which did not pay taxes on its land. A state representative challenged the state to pay taxes and help the area "bloom instead of lying dormant, dotted with deserted log cabins, and second growth clearings." The county commissioners protested that the state was retarding progress and that the overflowed land created "unhealthy conditions for man and beast."

By 1911 the Northern Development Association, representing most northern counties, actively promoted immigration to the area. Governor Adolph Eberhart strongly promoted drainage, roads, and consolidated schools as part of a campaign to attract settlers. *The Farmer*, Minnesota's leading farm publication, ran a series of articles that were extremely positive about the results of the drainage program. It was claimed that using a walking ditcher cost from $0.05 to $2.00 an acre and that the landowner had 20 years to pay. A lead article stated, "Wherever such lands have been opened to cultivation, in almost all instances the results have been so far beyond proving expectations as to astonish and delight the owner of the land."

After the Elwell Road Law was passed, ditches, roads, and firebreaks were intertwined into a single project in which the county paid half the cost, the state one-fourth, and the benefited property owner one-fourth. This made the urge to ditch irresistible. Koochiching County built two roads—from the Falls to Northome and to the Itasca County line, and from the Falls west through Clementson to the former Beltrami County line. Those roads were through some of the best soil and greatest areas of settlement. Ditches 13 and 20, in Beltrami County, were the key to a Baudette to Bemidji highway.

The legislation and ditching projects created an interest in land. In 1912 nearly 25,000 acres were sold to 173 buyers for an average price of $5.35 an acre. This was twice as much land as had been sold in 1911. The very respected county superintendent of schools, Annie Shelland, took an active part, because she knew that without roads there could be no effective school system and that the easiest way to get roads was to promote ditches. A private colonization company, of which L. H. Nord, a Falls attorney and later state senator, was a partner, purchased 4,500 acres for settlement. Nord and L. L. Enger, another partner, also headed one of the major ditching companies.

The 1913 report of the state drainage commission indicated that 6 million acres of land had been reclaimed and that 4 million were left to be reclaimed. It continued, "Every dollar invested in reclamation . . . brings a return of from $5 to $8. The outlook for increased activity in drainage work throughout the state was never more favorable." It is true that many projects in the state were effective, but generally that was not the case in 14 northern counties.

Stuart Robertson, a Loman resident since 1904 who worked on a ditching machine for Nord's company, recalled that initially everyone thought ditching was a good idea, but it did not take long to realize that the ditches would not work and that the cost was excessive in relation to the benefits. However, the roads built from the spoil bank were so welcomed by those still living in the remote areas that they overlooked the cost.

Others learned that they could personally profit from the ditching and road-building programs. Robertson knew an attorney in the Falls who was not doing well. The attorney made up a petition, presented it at the Indus Township meeting, got the signers, and had a ditch approved and surveyed. He received $1,200 for his services and left for California, but the ditch was never dug.

Attorney J. J. Hadler, later county attorney, pointed out that as ditching gained momentum, it created a false sense of prosperity and provided jobs as well as some hope for improvement in conditions. The process continued, because even though people realized that it was neither practical nor financially sound, they hesitated to speak against it. Twenty-four major projects in Koochiching County and a larger number of smaller projects in Beltrami County were initiated. As long as there were no safeguards and financing was done through bonding the county, the temptations were great.

In addition to attorneys and the project workers, others who profited from ditching were contractors, district judges, clerks of court, county auditors, engineers, and local newspapers, who all received fees for work done. Salespersons for bonding companies and financial brokerage houses became active promoters once they saw how much money was involved.

Unscrupulous land agents enticed outsiders, who believed that drainage would work, to buy acres and acres of land, sight unseen. Most did so purely to speculate on the rising land values. Realtors used newspapers and direct-mail advertising to promote the "last frontier." "Chance of a lifetime," "garden of Eden," and other well-worn phrases were used to catch those looking for a chance to make easy money. World War I accelerated the price of even the submarginal swampland. People flocked to buy, though many of the original homesteaders had already abandoned the area. Most buyers qualified for the low price of $1.25 an acre under the Volstad Land Law, with no resident requirements. Trusting buyers learned that they owed the unpaid taxes, including the assessment for ditching. Some paid those costs, but most realized that the land was worthless and let it revert to the state.

Most ditches were built between 1913 and 1917, but in Governor John Burnquist's 1917 inaugural address, he pledged that Minnesota would follow through on the 1909 legislation and said he hoped to gain more federal help in the extension of projects in the planning stages. County Attorney Middleton, of Baudette, an outspoken advocate of ditching, stressed that ditch 25 was essential to put thousands of acres of worthless land into condition for farming. He noted that the 200-mile ditch would employ 5 machines plus 200 men but would obligate the county for $550,000. He did not say that that was $120,000 more than the original projections.[1]

Trouble on the Horizon

Legislation provided sufficient cost sharing to bait many people to favor ditching and allowed counties to finance via bond sales. In fact, the counties had no alternative under the law. Koochiching County's two state-funded ditching projects in 1908 totaled $60,000—the largest appropriation in the state. Koochiching paid $7,500, and even that small amount was financed by 10-year bonds; the remainder was charged against state land.

The county debt at that time totaled $69,393.76, much of which was incurred in the construction of the courthouse and jail. In late 1909, after the passage of the new state ditching law, the commissioners were faced with the request for three ditches totaling about 44 miles. Only one commissioner voted no.

In 1910 the Koochiching County commissioners, already concerned about financing the ditches, sought to determine the constitutionality of a proposed law to levy 1 percent against state land, which was not to be assessed at less than $5 an acre. It was obvious to them that, if the ditches worked, the state would gain at a ratio of about 3 to 1 over private landowners but that the counties would be saddled with much of the cost. This was particularly dangerous in Koochiching County, where only about 850,000 of the over 2 million acres of land were in private hands. The rest was government or unproved homestead land and, therefore, was not taxable.

At their July 15, 1912, meeting, the commissioners voted to issue $150,000 in bonds as per provisions of the law to provide funds for four ditches. At the same meeting they raised personal property taxes 50 percent. Within a few months the commissioners were faced with financing another six ditches at a cost of $225,000. They had difficulty selling the bonds and agreed to pay G. A. Elder, a broker from Duluth, 4½ percent of face value to sell them. By the end of 1913, more ditch and road requests increased the total bonded indebtedness to over $700,000. In 1914 ditch projects, ordered by the district judge, increased the burden another $280,000, but *The Journal* noted that one would provide a 44-mile road.

When the commissioners met on May 4, 1915, they were faced with an additional four ditch projects; their cost brought ditch bond debts to $765,000. That did not seem to concern them, for at the same meeting they agreed to build four major roads in the county—an increase of 85 percent over 1914.

At their meeting on September 5, 1916, the commissioners postponed a bond issue "owing to the present financial conditions of the County and the uncertain money market." Auditor L. H. Slocum presented his resignation, but after "considerable debate, no action was taken in the matter." This was the first indication that something was amiss in county government.

Before ditch fever subsided, $1,645,628.75 in judicial ditch bonds were issued, most bearing 5 and 5½ percent interest. The county also became embroiled in a series of lawsuits, which stemmed from the improper activity of many insiders. However, for practical purposes, World War I brought an end to ditching, except for a few projects that were delayed until 1920 and 1921.

In the meantime, the identical activity was taking place in northern Beltrami County. By 1914 six ditch projects at a cost of $224,000 and six roads totaling $300,000 had put that county well in debt. Ditch 42, which was postponed in 1918, was ordered completed by Judge C. W. Stanton. *The Baudette Region* boasted that the ditch would not only drain a large acreage, but would provide 91 miles of road.[2]

Ditching

The nature of the terrain caused digging the ditches to be costly, time-consuming, and tedious work. Digging ditches in a floating bog, where the muskeg kept sliding back into the ditch behind the dredge, also was dangerous work. Stumps and large roots added to the problem, and work with a large dragline (ditcher) proceeded at only about 200 feet per day on the first ditch dug east of Littlefork. George Ralph, chief drainage engineer, soon realized that if the projects were to be completed, ditchers had to operate 24 hours a day 7 days a week. In July 1908, the first electric generator was installed so crews could work at night.

Early bids were let at $0.2233 per cubic yard under some conditions. Others bid $0.20 a yard, $30.00 a mile for clearing the proper width ahead of the ditcher, $50.00 a mile for grubbing, and $125.00 to $200.00 a mile for making a road out of the ditch bank—"turnpiking." The cost per mile varied from $1,000 to $2,500.

The Nord and Snyder Construction Company, owned by State Senator L. H. Nord and by former county treasurer George Snyder, had five draglines—four track machines and a floating dredge. Each track machine had four stationary feet, each of which was a 14- × 14-foot platform upon which the machine sat, and two feet that lifted the machine and pulled it forward on skids placed ahead of it by the ground men. Because the ditch was dug behind the machine, if too long a move was made and the undug area could not be reached, the ground men made the ditch with dynamite. The machines originally were built for use in the Wisconsin cranberry bogs.

Each machine weighed about 55 tons but could carry itself on muskeg. It used about 50 gallons of fuel in each 12-hour shift and dug 400 to 600 feet of ditch, depending on the size of the ditch. The track machines dug in the opposite direction of the flow of water, in contrast to the floating dredge, which dug from the high end, or water source. The floating dredge was about 12 feet wide and floated in the ditch that it dug. It had "spuds" on each side which rested on the spoil bank and stabilized it.

The survey and right-of-way crew cleared a path ahead of the draglines and set the depth stakes along the route of the proposed ditch so the crew knew how deep to dig. Barrels of gasoline were strung along the proposed ditch route during the winter. In some cases when the machine reached the barrels, the crew found them empty, because the gasoline had been stolen or it had leaked out of bullet holes.

The machine could dig up to 1 foot of frozen ground; then dynamite had to be used. A forge was set up between the two operators in the dragline and was used to heat a steel rod

1½ inches × 3 feet, which was rammed into the ground to make a hole for the dynamite. The holes were placed two or three abreast, depending on the width of the ditch, and about every 6 feet along the route to blast the frozen ground. Sometimes the platforms on which the machines sat froze into the ground and had to be jarred loose with dynamite.

Each crew consisted of two ground men, who laid the tracks and placed the dynamite in the cold season, and two men in the machine—a bucket operator, who loaded, hoisted, and dumped the bucket, and a crane operator, who swung the boom and the bucket. The night shift also had an engineer. If either the bucket operator or the crane operator was a good engine man, an engineer was not needed. If ground conditions were extremely bad, an extra ground man was added. Other members of the crew were a cook, a bull cook, and a tote team operator, who brought fuel, food, repairs, and mail.

These 8-man crews, who worked 12-hour shifts 7 days a week, earned from $40 to $125 per month, depending on the position. Each crew had two double-walled tents, with side walls 6 feet high—one for sleeping and the other for eating. Bridge plank needed to move the machines served as flooring for the tents. High-quality food similar to that served in the lumber camps—"a lot of it and good"—was provided.

Because draglines could travel only about a mile in 12 hours, they frequently were moved by rail. It took about three days to dismantle them for loading onto rail cars and about a week to reassemble them. Only one machine of the Nord and Snyder firm ever became so stuck that it could not get out on its own power; it settled in quicksand near Frontier. A long cable was anchored to large trees and 8- × 8-inch timbers were dug into the ground under the two lifting feet so the machine could climb and pull itself onto them.[3]

The Tide Turns

Criticism of the ditch projects started with the construction of the first ditch, but because the forces favorable were so enthusiastic and outspoken, the opponents did not speak up. Those involved in building ditches and roads were often careless about doing a proper job. Because travel was so difficult, contractors assumed that much of their work would never be inspected. By 1911 the legislature demanded stricter supervision of the work. Even George Ralph, the state's chief engineer, was accused of carelessness. The editor of *The Press* assured his readers that such criticism was premature and suggested that after the initial ditch was dug and the water had drained off, giving the earth a chance to settle, the contractors would go over their work again and put the ditch in "proper form."

It soon became evident, especially to the farmers and those working on the projects, that ditches effectively drained only about one rod for each foot of depth. This meant that the original concept of having a ditch every two miles was totally insufficient. The ditch banks provided roads but were nearly useless for agriculture, except west of Birchdale, near Lindford and Erics-burg, and gave very marginal help from Dentaybow to Grand Falls. The biggest success for Lake of the Woods County was the 60-mile road (now State Highway No. 72) from Baudette to Shooks. Some of the ditch banks gave loggers access roads to areas that previously had been inaccessible. As one who spent much time in the woods joked, "They marked the section lines." In 1910 State Representative Charles Warner expressed what many northern Minnesotans already knew: "The work of the drainage commission, with all its seeming virtues, is a farce."

Plummer initially favored the ditching program and in 1913 advocated bonding the county for roads and ditches. He circulated petitions to secure signers and in September 1914 spent three weeks away from his farm working for the program. He received $5 a day for getting signers and for posting notices of petition meetings. Even though he had 10 days of his time deducted by Judge C. W. Stanton, he still collected $238.25 for his efforts. But within the next two years Plummer changed his attitude about the ditches and began to oppose them vigorously. He saw the fallacy of assessments of $800 to $1,000 on 160 acres of land that had a market value of $600 to $800. He knew from digging ditches on his farm that they provided poor drainage but had hoped that the larger commercially dug ditches would work. His son, Jim, recalled that his father often remarked, "They did not drain land more than 10 feet away."

The tide turned in 1916, and Plummer was just one of many who switched sides. His friend and neighbor, respected community leader Simon Hafdahl, working with Rev. Thomas Howard, got the people in Birchdale to protest, which climaxed in an appear-ance at a ditch hearing. Because Howard led a delegation of 12 local farmers, the attorney pleading for the ditch reputedly com-mented something to the effect that the preacher had come with his 12 disciples. That reputed remark received wide publicity in the area and was still repeated 60 years later.

At the December 12, 1916, Koochiching commissioners meeting, Commissioner C. P. Ellingson moved twice that "no further ditches be authorized" and seven ditches in process be delayed "because the county cannot finance more." In both cases his motion lost for want of a second. By then the county had begun an investigation of some of the ditching activity.

The attempt to get ditch 24 constructed from Fairland into Beltrami County (later Lake of the Woods) proved to be the final straw. That ditch would have brought an assessment of $10 an acre against the land when better state land was selling for $5. Ole Scheie, Carl Murray, and Simon Hafdahl hired an attorney and appeared before Judge Stanton at the petition hearing in Bemidji. After their testimony, the judge disallowed the petition, and in his decision stated that continuance of the projects would bankrupt the counties involved. Many other projects were in process, but they never were completed.

Persons who did not own land affected by the ditches were denied the floor at hearings, and it appeared as though the feasibility of most ditches was not considered. As one study on the ditch projects read: "Up to 1917 . . . the district judges, before whom the petitions were laid, appeared to take the view that they were warranted in granting any petition upon suspicion that water would run in a ditch." A county official was ousted from office because he owned land that would benefit from ditching. But it was not until the bond market came under pressure with the nation's involvement in World War I that the ditch projects were suspended. Attempts were made after the war to revive the program, but protests against it were effective. The damage was already done, however, and the counties had to pay for their eagerness to change the wilderness.[4]

Paying Penance

There is little doubt that many homesteaders never intended staying any longer than was necessary to harvest the trees. Homesteading and then selling or abandoning the property took place on all frontiers under the Homestead Act, but the wilderness frontier had marketable timber. In some respects, this made it more attractive than farm land, which required breaking to get cash. Once the trees were gone, the homesteaders sold their rights to the property or abandoned the nearly worthless land, thereby diminishing the tax base.

Even though the idea of harvesting the trees and moving on might sound appealing, homesteaders did not rush to the area, for they knew the difficulties and hardships involved in living in the forested wilderness. This created a problem because the counties were unable to tax the state and federal lands within their boundaries.

When road building and ditching activity commenced, the counties realized the hardship that public land imposed on the local tax base. In January 1913, the Koochiching County Commission passed a resolution that the state should contribute $0.25 an acre to the treasurer of each of the counties where it owned land. The state did not agree, but countered with cost-sharing legislation, which initially was very appealing to the counties but which, in fact, compounded the problem. First came the cost-sharing ditching program, which proved very ineffective and expensive. Second was the Elwell Road Law, which was declared unconstitutional after many miles of roads were built. Roads were desperately needed and were approved by overwhelming votes of 10 to 1, but the per-capita cost was overwhelming in the sparsely populated marsh country.

These problems were compounded as land was abandoned once the timber was gone and were intensified by corruption among those involved in ditching, road construction, and financing on the local level. Illegal activity in 1916 involving as much as $200,000 in public funds caused Governor J. A. A. Burnquist to suspend County Auditor L. H. Slocum and three county commissioners—R. S. McDonald, William Harrigan, and Harold Royem. N. B. Arnold, an attorney from Duluth, was hired by the new board of commissioners to represent the county as special prosecutor for the next three years.

The Rev. Thomas Howard headed a group of over 100 citizens who held a mass meeting before the commissioners, asking them to explain what they had done to bring about the suspension of county officials. The group approved the governor's action and passed a resolution condemning the actions of Northwestern Construction Company, which had received funds improperly for work on State Highways No. 5, 9, 20, and 24 and had abandoned the jobs prior to completion. Accusations were made against brokers and financial firms for taking excessive commissions, not paying accrued interest on bonds, illegally discounting county bonds, and in one case actually failing to produce $175,000 received from a bond sale.

Shortly after the investigation commenced, commissioners John Bursack and M. A. Ulvedahl also were suspended, but they were reinstated a few months later. Auditor L. H. Slocum resigned as soon as he was charged with accepting a $1,500 bribe, making improper payments on construction contracts, and auditing and allowing fraudulent claims. Commissioners McDonald, Harrigan, and Royem stood trial for knowingly letting county bonds be sold at a 5 percent discount.

The investigation produced 13 indictments against Slocum; 5 against G. A. Elder, a broker; and 2 against R. S. McDonald. The case against Slocum was dismissed for lack of evidence. This undermined the county's chance of a major recovery, because it was believed that this was the strongest case it had against any of the accused. The verdicts totaled $64,744.22, of which slightly over $15,000.00 eventually was paid. There was little hope of collecting any additional amounts, because most of the individuals being sued were not financially "responsible." By then the total investigation and court costs of $26,210.84 had been paid, with another $8,662.72 of expenses pending. Attorney Arnold insisted that the county continue the cases, but the commissioners decided otherwise and released him.

Of the 707,496 acres in Koochiching County involved in the drainage enterprises, only 14,146 were improved by the ditches at a cost, as of December 31, 1919, of $1,281,238. The ditching expense, disregarding any future interest payments, was about 40 percent of the value of all the land involved. For the improved acres, the cost was nearly 20 times the market price.

The preliminary costs for eight ditching projects stopped by World War I finally were paid via additional bonding, but the ditches were never dug. Some of those projects were the largest yet planned. Even though the tax rate increased over 220 percent in seven years, when the state first proposed putting 600,000 acres into a forest preserve to relieve Koochiching and other impacted counties of some of their financial problems, the Koochiching County Commission protested because it felt that such a move "would prevent future development." Koochiching County had $1,981,084 in bonds and outstanding warrants. Its tax base continued to erode with a larger ratio of uncollected taxes annually, because most settlers could not pay the taxes or because others cut the timber, pocketed the cash, and left. Many of those who remained were indifferent to the growing financial problem of the counties.

The financial situation of 14 northern counties was so bad due to ditching and road-building debts that the state became involved to save its credibility. Both Koochiching and Lake of the Woods counties had bond offerings on which they did not initially receive any bids. By 1927 Lake of the Woods County had a bonded indebtedness of about $300 for every man, woman, and child in the county. At this point a delegation of citizens urged their county board not to levy taxes to cover the delinquent ditch bonds, because the ditches did not benefit public health or serve as a public convenience as their promoters had claimed they would.

In 1929 the Red Lake Game Refuge was created specifically to help Beltrami, Koochiching, and Lake of the Woods counties. Chapter 258 of the Laws of 1929 was "more in the nature of assistance to counties overburdened with bonded indebtedness arising out of ill-advised drainage projects than a conservation measure." Under that law, about 1,500,000 acres of land in the three counties were set aside in the preserve, for which the state initially assumed $2,500,000 of their bonds. In Koochiching County the area covered comprised 14 northwestern townships, containing roughly 330,000 acres, in what became Pine Island State Forest. In Lake of the Woods County, 444,912 acres, about 53 percent of its land, were put into the Beltrami Island State Forest. The remaining acres in Beltrami County were placed in the Red Lake Wild Life Management Area.

This temporarily improved the financial situation of those three counties. However, when some of the first Koochiching County bonds started to mature in 1931, they sold for as low as $0.42 on the dollar. The state stepped in and offered to lend money to any county that was delinquent on its bonds if the county used the money to reduce debt, had an assessed valuation of under $5 million, and had a tax delinquency of more than 40 percent. With the state loan, Koochiching County offered $0.55 on a dollar for maturing bonds or new bonds at par but at a lower interest rate. Enough people took cash, so the county reduced its debt by $100,000 and its annual interest obligation by about $5,000.

In 1933 the state again allowed 11 impacted counties to dissolve any township that met one of the following criteria: an assessed valuation of less than $50,000; a tax delinquency of 50 percent of its assessed valuation; state ownership of 50 percent of the real estate; or tax delinquency that exceeded 70 percent in any one year. Lake of the Woods County dissolved all of its townships, because 24 had over 70 percent delinquency and the other 14 had less than $50,000 assessed evaluation.

At the same time, those 11 counties were put on a cash basis, which required that they could not issue refund bonds without a vote of four-fifths of the county board to bring the issue before the people in a special or a regular election. The 1933 law also allowed any county with more than 40 percent tax delinquency to apply 50 percent of its share of the gasoline tax to retire road bonds.

By 1935 Beltrami, Koochiching, and Lake of the Woods counties again were in trouble because the appropriation of $2.5 million in 1929 was not adequate to make them solvent. Under Chapter 242 of the Laws of 1935, $1,451,207 was appropriated to save those counties. The Pine Island area was increased to 441,784 acres, including nearly 19 townships in Koochiching County alone.

Chapter 278, also of the 1935 laws, provided a more simple, less expensive way for the state to divest delinquent owners of title to their land. Most of these individuals had no intention of ever paying their back taxes, yet it was costly under the old law for the state to obtain title. Bill Zauche, of Baudette, was selected to lobby for the 1935 bills for the three counties, but it was J. J. Hadler, self-proclaimed savior of Koochiching County, who claimed to have originated the idea of easier title acquisition.

Under Chapter 278, the Koochiching County commissioners resolved that they would no longer give real estate tax abatements, because many who were in a position to pay were using the old law to shirk their tax liability. They declared that all property on which taxes had not been paid for 1929 and prior years would revert back to the state. The state then assumed the tax liability via bond assumption.

Unfortunately, in 1938 Chapter 278 of the 1935 law was declared unconstitutional. This time 23 counties in which tax delinquencies were greatest united to fight the case. J. J. Hadler was made chairman of the group and took the case to the Minnesota Supreme Court—Case 31980 entitled *State of Minnesota v. Aitkin County Farm Land Company, a Corporation.* The purpose of the counties was to prove to the state that the settlers did not want to hold the land after it had been logged.

The counties proved that, under Chapter 39 of the Laws of 1937, delinquent landowners could redeem their land upon payment of 60 percent of the original taxes, with no penalty or interest, but they did not do so. They were interested only in retaining the fruits or holding the land for speculative purposes "without discharging their duty to the government which ownership of the property entails." It was pointed out that tax delinquencies first appeared in 1915, by 1924 had reached 47.3 percent, and in 1933 were 89.9 percent. In all, 72,036 parcels of land, consisting of 3,294,594 acres, reverted to the state, of which 21,759 parcels were in Beltrami, 20,462 in Koochiching, and 12,200 in Lake of the Woods counties, in contrast to only a very small amount of land reverting in other Minnesota counties. Even when the state passed laws increasing the period of redemption, people made no effort to redeem the land, and the delinquencies continued.

By 1937 *The Baudette Region* boasted that Lake of the Woods County had reduced its indebtedness by $923,028.35. What it did not say was that the state had assumed $958,544 of the ditch and road bonds. By 1939, forfeited land that was not taken over by the state was sold for the amount of the unpaid taxes, plus 4 percent. The counties had learned their lessons and by the late 1930s were clearly on their way to solvency. This would not have been the case if the state had not taken drastic steps and also assumed much of their financial burden.[5]

The Taxpayers League

The ditching projects were effectively put to an end in 1917, but, except for the mass meeting in 1916 led by Rev. Howard, there had been no organized protest regarding management of county finances. Thousands of abandoned parcels of land with subsequent tax delinquencies, plus the granting of tax abatements in the ensuing years, resulted in major problems for the counties. The remaining residents realized that they were being saddled with a tremendous tax burden and decided that it was time to express their discontent.

On December 8, 1925, a taxpayers' meeting was held at the Falls to consider what should be done about the delinquent ditch bonds. Plummer attended that meeting, which drew a large crowd, but only he and 57 others were willing to pay the $1 membership fee to become involved. The intent of the organization was to have every taxpayer join, to gather facts about the finances, and to combat rising taxes. Similar groups were formed in Beltrami, Lake of the Woods, and Roseau counties. Those from the Loman area besides Plummer who attended the Falls meeting attempted to reorganize the Loman Farmers' Club to support the anti-tax movement.

In an effort to recoup back taxes, the state had increased the redemption period from 3 to 5 to 7 and finally to 10 years. Many residents of the respective counties took advantage of the generous state laws that lengthened the period of redemption for delinquent taxes. Instead of getting funds from those who abandoned the land, a new problem arose from those who decided to let their taxes become delinquent because that was an inexpensive way of financing. This angered those who paid their taxes, because it was clear that the lenient delinquency law was being misused. Therefore, the tax league in each county headed drives to secure relief from the ditch bond tax problem.

On March 29, 1930, supposedly at the request of Koochiching County taxpayers, the Taxpayers League of Koochiching was formally organized. With the exception of *The Northome Record*, the local newspapers generally declined to give any favorable publicity to the League. All the directors and the attorney served without pay and assumed their own expenses. Farmers made up 90 percent of the membership, but Falls attorney Frank Palmer, Falls realtor Frank Keyes, and Falls publisher Moyle Edwards were also involved. Keyes owned a massive amount of real estate in the Falls and used the generous tax redemption laws to his advantage. He frequently protested to the commissioners and to the city council by withholding his taxes.

The stated purpose of the League was "to study the economic and financial conditions of the county . . . and do such works as will lead to a more efficient and economical administration of the affairs of the county." In a brief history, the League pointed out that the tax problem had started in 1910 when the county board, without notice to anyone, had reduced the assessed valuation of M & O from $1 million to $490,000. However, a special state-appointed assessor later raised the figure to $690,000. The League emphasized that, in spite of testimony by Backus that he had invested $10 million in the Falls and in the Fort by 1911, he was assessed on only $841,000 in 1930.

The League took the standard populist approach that industry received unfair tax advantages, while others defended M & O, because without it, the demand for the one product the area had to sell would be reduced, resulting in almost no employment other than servicing a limited agriculture. The company's defenders argued that without M & O, taxes for the other residents would be much higher. The local authorities generally took that position when levying taxes and generally were able to defend themselves. After the fall of Backus, M & O took a less aggressive stance and worked to become a good citizen.

At a second organization meeting in 1930, the agenda of the League was broadened to include closer supervision of expenditures—especially the County Poor, Revenue, Road, and Bridge Funds. The League wanted to limit county salaries and expected department heads to do "their share of the office work." It also recommended the elimination of the county extension office, which was contrary to the wishes of the Farm Bureau, the largest local farm organization. It wanted all railroads to perform as common carriers or be assessed for local tax purposes. This was aimed at the forest railroad network.

The League condemned the state system of fire control, because the membership felt that the Forestry Department should aid the landowner in clearing land by fire as the cheapest method of preparing it for agriculture. The following argument was used to defend its position: "After 25 years of logging, the large scale production of timber products is a thing of the past. The era of the 'Big Woods' in Koochiching County has gone." It was noted that, with the exception of the Falls, the county had lost population in the previous decade:

> We are in a period of transition from lumbering to farming—always a dangerous period in a timbered country. The future prosperity of this county is largely dependent upon the development of the farming industry. One good crop of clover, under favorable conditions, is of more value to the owner of the land and the country in general than all the timber that was ever produced on the same land, but under the present conditions this cannot be done.

The League requested that any person clearing at least 80 acres of land for farming be given a special reduced real estate tax. It again protested that large-propertied interests had been given special tax considerations, forcing the small property owner to pay taxes on valuations that were greater than market price. Nothing should be done to hinder the important industrial interests, "but they are no longer infant industries that are in need of coddling."

Its final statement of purpose was to keep check on public affairs and "public men" and to keep the voters informed; but the leaders were "hampered in getting information about the affairs of the county." To get "reliable information before the taxpayers," a brochure was published. Plummer mailed 438 copies from his home, with help from the Hafdahl twins.

Several examples of tax comparisons were given in an attempt to prove that the northern counties had far too high a rate. The League wanted the price of state land kept lower so more farmers would consider coming to the area. It was suggested that the state was "reaping an unearned increment" when homesteaders cleared land.

The League took a strong position against the education system, pointing out what it considered wasteful procedures and "extravagant" expenses for teachers, janitors, busing, and the board of the unorganized territory, which contained 49 schools. It wanted to shift the system of caring for the poor from the county to the townships, because "there will be more scrutiny given to the eligibility of persons seeking relief. . . . At the present time there is no one whose business it is to check up on the enormous amount of money that is paid out to 'paupers.'" The poor farm could be closed, and the poor boarded more reasonably at hotels. "There was a time when 'Over the hills to the Poor House' had a spirit of sadness. Now it seems that to become a county charge has a spirit of gladness."

Business leaders were not strong advocates of the League, even though many of them felt obligated to belong, because a large portion of their customers were farmers. Ernest Oberholtzer wrote in 1931: "If Koochiching County expects to really improve its tax situation, I think it will have to rely on itself rather than state aid." Clearly that was the thinking of the members of the League, except that they were not reluctant to shed their tax burden to the state when the opportunity came to do so. The League had a clever motto: "There is one person wiser than Anybody, and that is Everybody," which it used on circulars sent to its members advocating a favorable vote on the issuance of bonds to refinance the original ditch bonds.

Plummer's last reference to the League came after the annual meeting in 1936, when he penned, "fair crowd." If the League had any impact, it probably was that the citizens overwhelmingly voted to cut costs and reduce county spending. For several years Koochiching County's general spending was limited to $70,000 annually, as mandated by the state when it agreed to help Koochiching and other northern counties out of their financial dilemma. The only thing unique about Koochiching County in this respect was that, on a per-capita basis, it and Lake of the Woods were the two counties most severely impacted by the ditching fiasco. Their financial survival came about because of acts of the state legislature and not because of any single local leader.[6]

Resettlement

Probably no single event of the 1930s so changed the direction of the northern counties, especially Koochiching and Lake of the Woods, as did the resettlement program. The Resettlement Administration, established April 1, 1934, was part of the Federal Emergency Relief Administration, designed specifically for rural rehabilitation. The national goal of the program was to remove 525,000 farm families from relief, with each state given a quota.

These surplus farm families resulted from the success of the Homestead Act. Changing technology mandated that they could serve society better in other occupations. One of the chronically most depressed pockets of poverty in the nation was the cut-over forest region of the lake states of Michigan, Wisconsin, and Minnesota. Original projections indicated that if 5,000 farms could be eliminated in the 14 northern counties of Minnesota, $100 annually per farm family could be saved in welfare costs. Individuals under age 45, in particular, would be resettled in areas where it was possible to make a living without being on welfare.

Recognizing the problem was easier than developing a remedy. It was hoped that people would leave farming and move to areas of greater opportunity. Unfortunately, the economic downturn in the early 1930s complicated the solution. Luckily for the people in the wilderness, the groundwork was carried out by persons knowledgeable about agriculture, the area, and the settlers. John T. Howard, son of pioneer missionary Thomas Howard, provided the basic field work for the program that covered both the Beltrami and Pine Island projects. Howard had excellent knowledge of the country and used extreme care and thoroughness in performing his research, which made the local program not only the first to start removal of its settlers, but also one of the most successful nationwide. Only 29 communities started with the program nationwide, and more than half of them got no farther than the purchase of land.

The social and economic problems of the people living in the area can best be understood from the income figures which revealed that in 1930 gross annual per farm income was $757 in Lake of the Woods County and $820 in Koochiching County— the lowest and third lowest of all counties in Minnesota—in contrast to a statewide average of $2,267. Besides the substandard living conditions of the farm families, the area suffered because tax income was less than the cost of public services. From 1912 to 1920, 14 schools were established—5 were closed by 1926, and 5 more by 1930. From 1929 through 1934, in the Beltrami Island area, $93,587 was levied for school purposes, of which only $19,519 had been paid by March 1, 1936. If mail delivery, roads, fire protection, and other service costs were included, the county was far better off by abandoning the area. The projected figure of $100 annual savings per farm proved true in all 14 counties.

In addition to inadequate schools, most of the impacted communities had scant medical facilities, few markets for their farm produce, and probably only a general store/post office as a business and social center. Only one congregation in Beltrami Island was able to survive any length of time, and that was because it had the services of a non-resident pastor. Travel conditions were so terrible that even communities within the area were separated from each other, except for foot trails through the muskeg. Horses could travel only in the winter when the ground was frozen. It became evident that "contrary to popular impression, living off the country supplied the minimum physical needs of people for food, clothing, and shelter." It did not provide cash to pay for public services, and "children were practically denied education beyond the grade school level."

There was a sigh of relief when the news came in early 1934 that $270,000 was allocated to Koochiching, Lake of the Woods, and Roseau counties for relocating 306 farm families. Lake of the Woods County was the first in the nation to get the movement underway. By December, 266 families had agreed to move, based on an average appraised buy-out of $5.75 an acre, less back taxes and mortgages.

Part of the reason for the success of the Beltrami Island and Pine Island projects has to be attributed not only to the excellent research provided by John Howard, but also to the able leadership of project manager A. D. Wilson. Until 1921 Wilson was Director of Agricultural Extension for Minnesota. From that date until assuming control of the project, he had farmed in Hubbard County and knew first hand the problems that the farmers faced. Wilson picked an excellent staff, who were drilled on the fact that a primary concern was not to upset the people. Every case was to be treated individually, according to the needs and talents of the person involved. The long-range goal was that the project should pay for itself in future savings to the local government.

A second goal of the government specified that as much local employment as possible had to be provided. In this respect, 250 to 800 people worked on the project at various times—appraising the land and the buildings, testing the soil for future use, counseling individuals to learn their potential for future occupational choices, and restoring the land for conservation purposes. This included building overnight cabins for rangers, patrolmen, and game wardens, installing over 200 miles of telephone lines, and constructing lookout towers, fire breaks, and dams on the drainage ditches. The dams were needed because fire protection costs were greatly reduced if the land was resaturated.

There were almost no settlers in the Beltrami Island or Pine Island districts prior to 1900, but when other frontiers in other areas of the nation were closed, homesteaders drifted into the region, which had the added potential of cashing in on the timber. Some individuals were attracted by "the freedom of a wilderness life." The population of Beltrami Island rose from 0 in 1900 to 62 by 1910, increased to 796 by 1920, and declined to 568 by 1930. Over 200 homesteading tracts can be attributed to one settler, in Bankton, who became an active locator.

Of the settlers still remaining in 1934 who were studied for resettlement purposes, only 2 came prior to 1904, 11 more by 1909, 43 during 1910 to 1914, 63 during 1915 to 1919, 37 between 1920 and 1924, 25 by 1929, and 47 more by 1934. Most of them admitted that the opportunity to market timber and the ability to establish a farm without much capital outlay were the major reasons for coming. The lumbering industry had tapered off sharply in the mid-1920s and was nearly extinct by 1930, because the remaining timber was too remote for economic harvesting. A significant number of settlers were lumberjacks, who realized that their jobs were over and wanted to retire where they had once worked. Many of them lived in shacks without any effort to "prove up"—a common practice in the area. In 1933 the ILC placed former timber land on the market, which enticed a few new farmers. Others, who came between 1930 and 1934, were Dakota farmers who had dried out and were attracted by an area that always appeared to have ample moisture.

The 13-township area included in Beltrami Island contained an average of 10.6 farms per township, in contrast to about 30 for the better farm areas in Lake of the Woods County and a potential of 144, based on the 160-acre homestead, for a standard township. Telephones were available only because the forest service installed lines after 1930 for fire prevention purposes. Under that system, one community of 26 families had one telephone. About half of the homes had radios powered by batteries kept charged by wind generators. They were tuned to stations in Fargo and Winnipeg. The other homes relied on the weekly newspaper for contact with the outside world.

The initial project contact people found that they had to overcome the defeatism of the settlers, which came from lack of opportunity. Poor diets, substandard living conditions, and lack of medical attention contributed to poor health, which proved to be the second greatest negative factor. Long winters and isolation constituted the third major problem faced by the settlers. The more isolated they were, the more they were removed from the economic realities of the world, and the more stable the community was, despite its impoverishment. Those most accessible to the outside left earlier than those in the more remote areas.

The project workers learned that these settlers had the following characteristics: most of them lived a relatively free wilderness life; they had a varied, but generally limited, ability and desire to farm; they were nearly all farming on too small a scale to support themselves; most were financially insolvent; a large portion of them received relief between 1932 and 1935; and they were debt-wary and were uncooperative with any venture that involved debt. "The few who would accept any heavy government advances offered the least promise for rehabilitation." Of those families that moved from Beltrami Island between May 1935 and the end of 1936, all but 10 percent were "deemed to be responsible and capable of improving their life style under new conditions." The remainder were either too old or too incapacitated to attain complete self-support.

By March 1936, the 1,156-square-mile Beltrami Island project, involving 309 families, proved so effective that Washington gave its approval for the same program in the 1,277-square-mile Pine Island area, from which 298 families were relocated. At that point the nationwide drought brought reduced rainfall to the area, enabling excellent cropping conditions. Combined with higher prices for specialty seed crops, the drier weather gave agricultural producers some of the best years they had experienced, but this was not enough to stem the tide. The per-acre productivity of Koochiching and Lake of the Woods counties averaged only 25 to 30 percent of statewide yields. Most residents felt that they did not suffer as much as other parts of the nation during the 1930s, because they never had much in the first place. In fact, many proudly stated that they never took relief when it was available.

Except for settlers who had a few hundred dollars in savings and no debts, most were quite eager to sell and to move. In the early 1930s, the average yearly income per household in the Beltrami Island area was $282; the average farm had only 27 cultivated acres. Thirty-seven farms in the area produced less than $100 income, and only six yielded more than $500. Where the forest had once produced a substantial part of the family income, in 1933 it averaged only $20 per household.

The original appraisal determined that the land had no private value, but cruisers were employed to determine a public value, which they placed at $2 an acre. Improvements were appraised, and the maximum price of $13 an acre was arrived at for the standard 160-acre homestead. This figure sounded great to the settlers, until they learned that they would get only what remained after unpaid taxes and mortgages. In many cases the value was less than the encumbrances. For example, a 160-acre farm with an appraised value of $480.00 had back taxes of $1,346.42 and a mortgage of $300.00. The government placed an artificially high value on the property so that the settlers received something. This figure was determined by the amount the government would save by getting the settlers out of the area, a conservation value, and the reduced fire-fighting costs. The justification given was that the government should never have let the settlers move there in the first place. Those who moved could take any usable property. Any buildings that remained were destroyed to prevent squatters from moving in.

Marian Crabtree Peterson's parents sold their farm, which had never been plowed after the timber was removed, and moved to Baudette. The person who purchased the Crabtree store at Faunce sold it to the government and moved to Loman. Mrs. Crabtree's parents, the Gustafsons, sold their farm and moved to Spooner. The family was happy when the grandparents moved because there was no way out of their farm in case of fire. All the people that Marian knew moved to nearby small towns or went to the western part of the country. This was true of most of those who moved, except for 67 families who agreed to go to the Matanuska settlement near Palmer, Alaska.

The communities of Bankton, Clear River, Elkwood, Famerer, Faunce, Hillwood, Norris, Oak Camp, Southridge, and neighboring areas to the south and west in Lake of the Woods County were abandoned. In Koochiching County the major areas deserted were Rapid River, Fairland, Kline, White Birch, Waukanka, Henry, Big Falls, and Gowdy townships. Sylvia Kohlhase later wrote that not one person remained in the area. But the counties got out of debt, and nearly all of those who stayed with the program improved their life style. About the only ones who spoke against the program were small-town merchants, who lost customers but were not fortunate enough to have the government buy them out. Only about two dozen families remained in the areas as of April 1937, but they had no services normally provided by government.

The project workers were careful to match the people with their new situation. Those who wanted to farm were moved to areas of better soils and were required to have enough acres under cultivation to provide a living. Loans for 33 years, bearing 3 percent interest, were provided, but not more than 20 percent of the gross income potential of any farm could be planned for debt service. If the relocators were averse to debt, they could purchase land under the "grubstake plan" devised by A. D. Wilson. This enabled the use of family labor to build capital by clearing land. A recheck of those who decided to farm indicated that all had improved their financial position. The government had invested less than $2,000 per family, of which nearly 75 percent was secured by real estate under the Farm Security Administration.

The federal government specified that if the abandoned land remained in conservation, the state had title and could take the income from it. If the land was sold to private sources, the title reverted to the federal government.

A unique part of the conservation program was an attempt to rebuild the herd of 17 caribou—which were the only ones remaining in the United States. In 1937 a herd of 12 caribou was transported from northern Saskatchewan to the Waskish area. In 1935 a herd of 27 elk was introduced to the Red Lake Game Reserve and weathered the first winter nicely. By that date, at least 50 varieties of game animals, fowl, and fish were inventoried in the abandoned area.

In 1920 some townships in Koochiching County already had become unorganized. By 1933 the county extension service started a land utilization committee to prevent individuals from settling on land that could not sustain them. Land use programs became a part of the extension work. Melvin Johnson, a Littlefork farmer who had come to Koochiching in 1934, was chosen to spearhead the program for both counties. By 1940 Koochiching and Carleton became the first two counties to establish zoning so that another resettlement program would not be required at some future date. By then, all of the 14 northern counties were well on their way to recovery from the excessive burden of ditching and road building, and most of them again relied on forestry instead of agriculture for a major source of income. This was as nature intended.[7]

ENDNOTES FOR CHAPTER IX

1. *The Laurel Press*, November 13, 1903; Lyman Warren Ayer, Cruiser Book covering his exploits in the north woods after 1902, KCHS, hereafter Ayer; *The Press*, December 21, 1904, May 3, June 14, August 9, October 25, December 6, 1905, January 10, October 31, November 14, 1906, May 29, August 14, October 2, 1907, March 17, October 21, 1908, November 4, 1909, May 12, December 8, 1910; *The Journal*, November 16, December 21, 1911, November 14, 1912, February 6, 1913; Alton A. R. Anderson, "A Study of the Beltrami Island Resettlement Project," Master's Thesis, University of Minnesota, St. Paul, July 1937, pp. 23, 24, 25, 26, 27, hereafter Anderson, "Beltrami Island"; H. R. 19541, "An Act to Authorize the Drainage of Certain Lands in the State of Minnesota," 60th Congress, 1st Session, March 20, 1908, hereafter H. R. 19541; J. J. Hadler, speech to the Rainy Lake Women's Club, November 9, 1967, KCHS, hereafter Hadler RLWC; Hadler file; *Hist. of Kooch. Co.*, p. 15; Kooch. Comm., June 9, 1910; "Northern Development Association Meeting," *The Farmer*, XXIX, No. 24 (June 17, 1911), pp. 781, 785; "County Drainage Work in Northern Minnesota," *The Farmer*, XXIX, No. 28 (July 15, 1911), pp. 861–862; *The Baudette Region*, April 2, May 7, 1914, January 18, July 12, October 21, November 8, 1917; LOW Co. Hist.; interview of Stuart Robertson, International Falls, July 10, 1980, hereafter Robertson interview; interview of Stuart Robertson by Mary Hilke, International Falls, October 13, 1977, in KCHS, hereafter Robertson-Hilke interview; Bull. 334, pp. 11, 12, 14.

2. *The Press*, February 2, 12, March 11, 1908, December 8, 15, 1910; Kooch. Comm., April 29, June 2, 1908, May 7, October 12, 1909, May 11, 1910, July 15, 1912, May 24, November 18, 1913, October 27, 1914, May 4, 1915, September 5, 1916, March 2, 1920, May 19, 1921; *The Journal*, August 1, 1912, June 11, 1914; the Koochiching County Auditor's book; *The Baudette Region*, May 7, 1914, February 27, 1920.

3. *The Press*, July 15, 1908, February 2, 1911; Kooch. Comm., April 4, 1912, April 2, 1914; Robertson interview; Robertson-Hilke interview.

4. *The Press*, December 8, 1910, January 19, February 2, April 20, 1911; H. Johnson interview; *Hist. of Kooch. Co.*, p. 15; Pollard interview; LOW Co. Hist.; Plummer diary; Plummer interview; Robertson interview; Hadler, RLWC;

Kooch. Comm., December 12, 1916; Anderson, "Beltrami Island," pp. 23–27; Bull. 334, pp. 12–13; *The Baudette Region*, March 1, 1917.

5. Kooch. Comm., January 7, 1913, September 16, November 8, December 12, 1916, January 24, February 6, September, 11, 1917, April 4, June 6, September 5, 1918, January 7, 8, February 4, 1919, October 5, 1920, May 19, 1921; *The Journal*, October 9, 1913, September 7, 28, December 7, 1916, December 27, 1917, June 13, August 1, 1918, March 31, 1921, February 28, 1924, August 6, 1925, January 6, 1927, January 23, February 18, March 11, 1930, March 8, April 18, 1933, August 27, 1936, July 24, 1939; *The Northome Record*, January 19, 1917; transcript of testimony on Case 21492, January 19, 1917, *County of Koochiching v. George A. Elder, et al.*, KCHS; Frank B. Green, County Commissioner, "Results of Koochiching County Investigation, 1917, 1918," KCHS; *The Baudette Region*, June 21, 1917, February 13, 27, 1925, August 5, October 21, 1927, March 26, 1937; City Council, March 12, 1923; letter from Ernest Oberholtzer to Louis Lemieux, January 27, 1931, KCHS; Jesness, p. 124; Hadler, RLWC; LOW Co. Hist.; J. J. Hadler, "Sketches of Koochiching County Finances from January 1931 to October 1945," April 9, 1973, KCHS, hereafter Hadler, "Kooch. Finances"; Anderson, "Beltrami Island," pp. 28–32; Hadler file; Bull. 334, p. 15; transcript of Case No. 31980, *The State of Minnesota v. Aitkin County Farm Land Company, a Corporation*, Hadler file; Alex Enzman, "Pulling Koochiching County Out of the Financial Mud," a typed manuscript prepared by the then county treasurer, June 15, 1942, KCHS.

6. *The Journal*, November 26, December 10, 17, 1925, December 9, 1926; Plummer diary; *The Baudette Region*, December 10, 1926; "Taxpayers League of Koochiching County," a 31-page brochure with no date or name on file in KCHS, pp. 2, 3, 4, 5, 6, 7, 11, 15, 19, 22, 24, 25, 27, 31; Paul Anderson interview; Kooch. Ext.; letter from Ernest Oberholtzer to Louis Lemieux, January 27, 1931.

7. *The Northome Record*, March 4, 1921; Anderson, "Beltrami Island," pp. 13, 15, 16, 19, 20, 22, 33, 34, 36, 37, 39, 44, 46–50, 66, 73–76, 92; Bull. 334, pp. 4, 5, 7–11, 15, 16, 19, 22–27, 31–35; W. W. Alexander, "Overcrowded Farms," *Farmers in a Changing World: The Yearbook of Agriculture 1940*, ed. Gove Hambidge (Washington: U.S.G., 1940), pp. 883–884; "Synopsis of Events Leading to the Creation of the Beltrami Island and Pine Island Resettlement Areas," Minnesota Department of Conservation, an undated manuscript in the files of MHS, pp. 3–5; Jesness, pp. 85, 256–257, 265–267; *The Baudette Region*, October 13, 1933, April 20, November 9, December 28, 1934, February 14, 1936, December 10, 1937; R. W. Murchie, "Minnesota Rural Rehabilitation Corporation," *Minnesota Municipalities*, July 1935, pp. 286–288, hereafter Murchie, "Rehab."; R. W. Murchie, "Beltrami Island Minnesota: Resettlement Project," University of Minnesota Research Bulletin No. 334 (St. Paul: December 1937), pp. 19, 23, hereafter Murchie, Bull. 334; LOW Co. Hist.; correspondence between Simon O. Hafdahl, A. D. Wilson, and Mrs. Nels Larson, Wayland, Minn., various dates, Resettlement file, KCHS; letters from Gust Palm, Baudette, Minn. to Annie Shelland Williams, February 24, March 4, April 11, 1954, Williams file; Marian Peterson interview; Bill Beck file of important events in the history of Lake of the Woods County, in possession of the author, hereafter Beck file. Beck was a publisher of *The Baudette Region* for several years. Interview of Raymond Johnson, Littlefork, Minn., August 3, 1989, hereafter Raymond Johnson interview. Mr. Johnson was a district forester. Kohlhase, *Spruce*, p. 49; Gorden interview; Big Falls Community file, KCHS; McLinn interview; Arnold Johnson, manuscript on land surveying, June 1966, Miscellaneous file, KCHS, hereafter Arnold Johnson, surveying; *The Journal*, January 16, May 21, 1936, January 26, 1940; Kooch. Ext. including the 1940 Rural Zoning Ordinance Adopted by Koochiching County; Kooch. Comm., March 2, 1920; Melvin Johnson interview.

CHAPTER X

Enjoying the Wilderness

A FEW RUGGED CANOEISTS had penetrated the northern wilderness prior to any activity at the Falls. However, it was not until railroads were built that others were enticed to see the sights of this great wooded area. Once the area became more accessible, retreats owned by wealthy city dwellers lost much of their glamour.

Rainy Lake Aristocracy

Backus and associates were eager to promote the area, either for their own glorification or to impress those who might be of assistance in their various enterprises. In June 1908, a group of 30 Minneapolis "elitists," including at least four medical doctors, journeyed to the Falls to search for summer vacation home sites and to enjoy fishing at the Nemenkeno Resort, at Kettle Falls. When the paper mill commenced operation, Backus arranged for the first visit by a Minnesota governor when Adolph Eberhart toured the mill and took a boat trip on the steamer *Moose*.

In 1910 Backus built a houseboat and hosted a houseboat party that traveled up the river to Sand Point. The following year Mrs. Backus and their daughter spent the summer on the houseboat. The Backuses began construction of an elite summer home on Red Sucker Island in Rainy Lake, directly north of Island View, about 10 miles from the dam and just off Jackfish Island. Red Sucker was also known as Huckleberry Island and was later called Curtice Island.

In 1918 Mr. and Mrs. S. W. Backus had a party for their friends, among whom were Mr. and Mrs. Coler Cambell, "perhaps the fastest couple of the fast set of the famous Minnetonka lake region"; Miss Mary Cambell, "the famous long distance swimmer and noted singer"; Miss Beulah Todd, "renown for her beauty and athletic qualities"; John Ware, attorney, "noted for his sporty clothes both in the city and in camp"; Albert Vanfevere, "grocery broker, who has set several yards of records as a world wide sailor"; Harry Doer, "who manufactures everything from cigars to drugs [and] is, of course, extremely popular with the ladies"; L. J. Burg, "the furniture manufacturer"; C. F. Dahlberg, "famous in St. Louis sporting circles"; and T. E. Dahlberg, cartoonist.

Other summer homes were established about 1918. This small group of between 6 and 10 families was known locally as the Rainy Lake aristocracy. This phrase was not used at the time the little group was in existence, but was coined much later by Ted Hall, who published *The Rainy Lake Chronicle* for years and wrote several articles about these wealthy families. Their activity was at its height between the late 1930s and the mid-1950s.

Robert Monahan, who had practiced medicine in the Falls prior to World War I and relocated in Minneapolis, built a cabin on Birch Point in 1921 that was used by his family for over 40 years. Monahan later renewed practice in the Falls, which accounts for the family's long tenure on the lake.

N. H. Sheldrup, a medical doctor from Minneapolis, built Dunsmoor (named for his wife's family) on the Canadian side of the border about 1922. The Sheldrups patronized Falls businesses infrequently and hired only one local employee, Ed Johnson, who served as caretaker and boatman.

Major Horace G. Roberts, who owned a sash and door factory in Davenport, Iowa, built Atsokan, a one-story, all-log structure. The Robertses were known for their big birthday parties, which drew friends to the lake from distant cities. The title "major" apparently came from large government contracts that Roberts held in World War I. Locally, he was known as a great storyteller. Roberts acquired Rainy Lake property through his friendship with Ernest Oberholtzer, also a Davenport native, who spent much time with the aristocracy, even though he did not have the means to be one of them.

One of the later aristocracy to build was Henry (or Harry) L. French, owner of a firm that manufactured wheels for wheelbarrows and farm machinery. French, also of Davenport, married Virginia Roberts, the Major's daughter, and built Green Mansion in 1935. He was an alcoholic and spent most of his summers at the lake until 1950, when his daughter, Audrey, drowned; the Frenches stopped coming in 1953.

The best-known summer place was Redcrest, built during the 1920s by Bror and Mary Dahlberg. Dahlberg initially came to the area as an employee of Backus but split with him and founded the Celotex Corporation. Dahlberg and Backus became bitter enemies and continued their rivalry on the lake.

It is reputed that the Dahlbergs paid a premium for a high, windy promontory—not the most desirable location—on Jackfish Island so Mary Dahlberg could look down on Mrs. Backus, just across the channel. A popular local story relates that as soon as the Dahlbergs had purchased their land, Mary Dahlberg cut the anchor ropes to set the Backus two-story houseboat adrift.

The Dahlberg summer estate consisted of the main house (called Redcrest because of its bright-painted shingle roof), a guest house, a caretaker's cottage, Dahlberg's office cottage, an ice house, a power plant, and a 40-foot-high birch bark tepee for guests. The main house contained six bedrooms, a huge living room, a dining room, a sun porch with a large eating area, a large kitchen, a butler's pantry, a large tiled veranda, and two baths. The guest house had four bedrooms and a bath for guests as well as three rooms and a bath for servants. The caretaker's cottage contained two bedrooms and other spacious rooms. Telephones connected the caretaker's cottage with the main house and the guest house. A boathouse, set on concrete pilings with four slips, rounded off the buildings.

Mary Dahlberg wanted an Indian tepee and got Oberholtzer to design it and Emil Johnson to build it. The tepee was furnished with a Chinese throne and with eight red satin cushions 4 feet square and 1 foot thick that were filled with silk and reputedly cost $200 each. The pillows were placed in a ring around the circular white quartz fireplace located in the center of the structure. A red piano with golden dragons completed the furnishings in the tepee, which was large enough for a party of 20. There also was a bronze statue of Alma Lee, Dahlberg's adopted daughter, which had been made on the Isle of Capri.

In 1924 Mary bought Bror a 26-foot Chris Craft speedboat, the *Bee Gee*, powered with a Liberty airplane engine. In 1928 they purchased an airplane so they could commute directly from the lake to Chicago.

After a financial setback in 1929, Dahlberg divorced Mary and married Gilda, a New York chorus girl, who was not "a high powered socializer." He added a 42-foot cruiser called the *Gilda* to the "fleet," which, along with the *Bee Gee*, consisted of several smaller boats.

Redcrest was known for the many distinguished guests who spent time there, in addition to the 8 to 10 members of Gilda's family, who were there for two months each summer. In 1926 Princess Maria, cousin of King Alfonso, of Spain, made a well-publicized visit. Dahlberg constructed a miniature castle in her honor. The following year Sinclair Lewis wrote part of *Elmer Gantry* in the tepee. Several debutantes received considerable attention from the local media when they visited Redcrest.

Mr. and Mrs. N. Carlson were caretakers of Redcrest from the mid-1920s until 1936, when they were replaced by Mr. and Mrs. Don Johnson, who served in that capacity until 1944. The Johnsons received $90 a month for 12 months, plus living expenses for the entire family in the summer months. When they quit in 1944 they were earning $125 a month. In addition to the local caretakers, the staff consisted of an Austrian butler and his Jewish wife. He was a perfect butler but could not stand Gilda. Dahlberg and his first wife treated all the help well, but "Gilda did not know how to treat anyone well." Bertha, a Jamaican, was the cook; she was assisted by either Mrs. Carlson or Mrs. Johnson. Two local girls were maids, and two local men were handymen, along with either the Carlson or the Johnson families. Sometimes the Dahlbergs brought a masseur from Chicago. Dahlberg worked several hours each day and always had a full-time secretary, either male or female. It was common for him to alternate secretaries during the summer so each had an opportunity to be at the lake.

Two pages of explicit instructions for the Redcrest butler were given outlining his duties. For details, see the Appendix.

Redcrest had a generator, but it was operated only during the two months that the Dahlbergs were in residence. Ice was always used for cooling. Three fireplaces provided heat, but bottled gas was used for cooking. Each summer a cow was rented from a nearby farmer. The caretakers raised about 100 chickens, had a garden, and also butchered. The Johnsons lived in their own log cabin on Deer Island during the winter and watched over Redcrest. The three Johnson children boarded in Ranier when school was in session, because it was too difficult for them to travel back and forth.

The Rainy Lake aristocracy had a cycle of cocktail parties when they were not entertaining relatives and friends from their home areas, but they seldom socialized with local people, other than Oberholtzer. They shipped in much of their needs; when they purchased goods locally, they expected and generally received discounts.

Probably the last couple to be considered part of the Rainy Lake aristocracy were Dr. and Mrs. Hvoslef, who built on their island in 1942. Bryne Johnson did chores for them and operated their boat. The Hvoslefs, like the others in the group, had a car stationed near the city docks and generally had their employees make all necessary purchases at the Falls, rather than go to town themselves.

The first break in the group came in 1931 with the bankruptcy of E. W. Backus, but most of the others continued coming to Rainy Lake until the late 1940s. The Dahlbergs' last full summer was 1944. After Bror Dahlberg died in 1954, the property, including Gold Shores, was sold to John Barkowski for $50,000 and then became the Musket Inn.

By the time the aristocracy stopped coming to Rainy Lake, resorting became popular as society prospered in the post–World War II era. Better roads and improved automobiles and airplanes made the area more accessible.[1]

Tourism—East

Soon after the area was settled, it became apparent that Rainy Lake and Lake of the Woods could become popular summer resort and tourist attractions. H. I. Bedell, who owned a homestead east of the Falls, was the first to plot and to improve his property with that in mind. He had two cottages finished on the south shore of Rainy Lake by June 1905, at which time he promoted a party for 50 people, who traveled to his "attractive summer resort" via the *Seagull*. After the railroads arrived in 1907, he plotted 16 one-acre lots along the lake and named the area Crystal Beach.

In 1908 George Graham, president of the Rainy River Navigation Company, approached officials of the NP in an attempt to establish a through rate for tourists who wanted to stop at places between the Falls and Kenora. Tourism was helped when William Loeb, Jr., secretary to Theodore Roosevelt, and George Thompson, editor of the *St. Paul Dispatch*, visited at Camp Kobikana, near the Falls. In 1908 R. H. Bennett, proprietor of the Hotel International, built Island View Lodge, the first of its kind on the lake. The main two-story structure was 24 × 40 feet. The lodge was leased to A. Lassard, who operated it from 1910 until Bennett sold it to Bob Cole in 1930.

In 1909 the Falls Commercial Club, with the help of the Koochiching Development Company, published an attractive brochure that described the natural advantages of the area as a tourist resort. When several groups of prominent Twin City and Chicago residents visited the Falls, they nearly always were accompanied by Backus or Brooks as they toured Rainy Lake. It was claimed that 400 "men of wealth" purchased islands for summer homes because of that promotion and that Ranier was "fast becoming known as a summer resort."

The 1910 season started with the announcement that Bedell had sold 15 lots in his Forest Point division along the lake and Jackfish Bay. By April, Bedell reported that all of the Crystal Beach lots and most of the Forest Point lots were sold. He started developing the Lake Park addition with 23 half-acre lots with 100-foot lake frontage. Fred Coxon opened a supper club and dance hall on Crystal Beach and engaged the launch *Koochiching* to transport patrons from the Falls. The launch, dancing, and dinner were available at a cost of $1 for the formal opening on June 14.

In 1912 motorboat owners formed an association and contributed funds for a proposed new dock for commercial and pleasure purposes between First and Second streets along the river. The city council approved, contingent to permission from the Corps of Engineers.

In 1915 Andrew Koski was employed full time to build cabins on Pelican Lake, near Orr, for $0.50 an hour and room and board. In the next 30 years he built either frame or log cabins for 31 different resorts, which included 27 at Max Herseth's Tomahawk Resort on Kabetogama.

After spending 26 years in Kettle Falls, Oliver Knox moved to Crane Lake in 1930 to offer his services as a guide. At first he charged $1 a day, but increased his rate each year without any loss of business. Later he purchased a 14- × 42-foot houseboat which held six plus the crew. His wife served as cook and he as the pilot and guide. In his best year he spent 108 days guiding fishing and hunting parties.

John Nelson started as a telegrapher on the Great Northern at the Superior ore docks in 1909. In 1914 he married and took his bride on a honeymoon to visit his parents on a homestead near Buyck. She fell in love with the country, and each year they returned to canoe. When they discovered the remains of a homestead shack, they contested the claim and acquired the land. In 1930 they purchased a small resort with five cabins on Crane Lake, which had experienced four failures in eight years.

The Nelsons noted that tourism had increased steadily since about 1910, so they added two more cabins in 1932. In 1934 they built a lodge because they observed that, even though most people talked about roughing it, they preferred the luxury of eating in a lodge. Housekeeping cabins rented for $30 a week; boats were an additional $7. For those who stayed in the lodge, the charge was $3.50 per day for three meals and a room. When the Nelsons increased to 27 cabins and added on to the lodge, they lengthened their season from three months to nearly six months.

About 1916 Thomas Watson built Watson's Lakeview Resort, one of the first two resorts on Lake Kabetogama; the other was Gappas Landing, about eight miles from Ray, built by Robert Chute. Both resorts secured some of their fish, berries, and tourist items from the local Indians. John Wooden Frog had an outboard motor and towed five or six canoes filled with berries or birch items to trade for salt pork, tea, tennis shoes, and snuff. The Watson resort was about 20 miles from the hotel at Kettle Falls, which was being added on to by Ed Rose. By the mid-1920s, there were four other resorts within a few miles, but they all seemed to prosper.

Neil Watson was 11 years old when the Lakeview Resort was being built. At 4:00 P.M. each day he quit helping the carpenters to fish for walleyes for the construction crew's dinner. The first cars did not come to the resort until 1920. After the Watsons completed six two-bedroom cabins, with kitchens, they started a combination store and small cafe and added a bar in 1933. The weekly charge for the cabins was $25. After the first year they never advertised. About 1917 the Watsons purchased Evinrude outboard motors with external flywheels for cranking—popularly called "knuckle busters." Thomas Watson operated the resort until 1944, when other members of the family took over.

In 1920, after the highways were open from Virginia and Bemidji, as many as 29 automobile tourists were registered in one day at the Falls. About the same time, big-game hunters started arriving in sufficient numbers to prolong the tourist season. In 1923 the Falls city council provided funds to build a tourist park. During July over 700 people registered at the park. Additional money was allocated in 1924 for more land clearance and for sanitary toilets, hot and cold showers, two buildings for dining tables and a kitchen, and cook stoves. The editor lamented that only the poor condition of the "Babcock" roads forced many to turn back at Virginia.

In 1924, 1,354 cars brought over 5,000 visitors to the Falls, and the city council decided that a $0.50 per day charge had to be levied to cover the $125.00-per-month wages of the caretaker. In 1926 the Falls council records show that tourists paid parking fees on 1,483 cars, which had 5,963 passengers, and spent an estimated $15,000 in the town. The Moose Lodge had its second state convention in the Falls in 1927. The Kiwanis Club arranged for J. J. Hadler to speak on WCCO's 90-minute Booster Program, May 18, on the topic "Rainy Lake—The Future Playground of America."

Scott Erickson opened a retail lumber business at Orr in 1926 and got off to a good start because, for several years, he sold materials and built cabins priced at $300 and up. Most of his customers were from the Twin Cities, Chicago, Sioux Falls, southern Minnesota, and northern Iowa.

The Lloyds ran a general store at the Fort from 1905 until 1930, when they started Lloyd's Tourist Emporium, which specialized in outfitting canoeists and guiding campers into the wilderness. They advertised in Illinois and Iowa and received 80 percent of their business from those states. The Lloyds provided canoes, guides (most of whom were Indians), food, camping sites, and all necessary equipment. They traveled into the Pipestone, Manitou, and Trout Lake areas of Ontario, which were northeast of the Fort. The initial charge was $35 for 10 days.

The Lloyds owned 100 canoes but never took more than 12 canoes with 3 people each in any party. They preferred canvas canoes because the upkeep on them was much less than on aluminum canoes. The Indians made special baskets that remained right side up to carry cotton bags of bulk food. Rice, beans, canned butter, dry milk, raw potatoes, dried fruits, bacon, and salt pork were the basic foods carried on the junkets. Fish were eaten as they were caught, but none were taken home.

The Lloyds soon learned that their patrons loved to "rough it if everything was furnished and done for them." They capitalized on that with great success as long as they could get good Indian guides who could locate the fish and cook and who knew the woods and were patient. They were fortunate in this respect throughout the 1930s; after that, the Indians tended to prefer work in the sawmills. The greatest problem on the junkets came from mosquitoes and black flies. Traveling without a head net was impossible.

An added impetus came to tourism and lake living in 1933

when the state highway to Ranier, Crystal Beach, and Black Bay was constructed. *The Journal* deemed tourism to be important enough to the local economy by 1935 to warrant the publication of special tourist editions during the three-month season. Paul Anderson, who later became the editor, noted that the biggest challenge was keeping up with the fast changes in that industry. On July 4, 1936, more than 6,500 persons crossed the International Bridge, surpassing by 1,000 the previous record set in 1929. Tourism was really catching on. That day all the hotel rooms were taken and many out-of-town visitors "were compelled to seek beds in private homes."

In 1938 Bob Williams, owner of the Kettle Falls Hotel, gave tourists a chance to see both that hotel and Rainy Lake by using his boat, the *Mayflower*, for daily round trips for $3. The *Mayflower* left the Falls at 8:00 A.M., toured Rainy Lake, and arrived at Kettle Falls in time for the passengers to partake of refreshments and to exercise by walking around the falls and viewing the sights in the frontier-like hotel.

In January 1939, the Falls' first Winter Sports Day drew 4,000 spectators to the Black Bay area, where festivities took place. A seaplane loading dock was authorized by the state, because so many tourists wanted to continue their trek into the wilderness, which was most easily reached by seaplane.

Whether making beds in lodges, constructing up to 4,000 fish boxes per year from scrap lumber, selling gasoline, serving as guides or as camping trip outfitters, building cabins, or helping tourists in other ways, the local residents all admitted that tourism improved opportunities for those living in the wilderness.[2]

Tourism—West

Tourism in the Lake of the Woods area started slightly later than in the eastern region. The first significant happening occurred in 1914, when a group from Chicago showed interest in building a summer resort on Lake of the Woods. Over the next few years the number of launches giving tours on the lake increased. By the 1920s the *Gull*, the *Clipper*, the *Agwinde*, the *Ginger*, the *Gale*, and the *Tramp* were in service. The *Agwinde* was the largest of the lake boats and also was used as a 30-room summer hotel.

Tourism started when several local people became experienced as guides and took groups to fishing and hunting spots. William Coutts, owner of the *Gale*, was one of the first well-known guides.

Another was E. D. Calvert, who spent much of his time on Rainy River.

About 1920, local individuals became involved in building cabins on the lake. By 1925 the recreational fishing interests were strong enough to petition that certain bays and islands be closed to commercial fishing to maintain a fish supply for tourists. Summer camps for church groups and fraternal organizations also were being built. The local chamber of commerce conducted an advertising campaign proclaiming "Baudette, Gateway to the Lake of the Woods." Another ad read, "The seven wonders of the world are seven days of the week in the lake country of Minnesota in summer."

A. E. Hoover, one of the first large-scale resort owners on Lake of the Woods, built Lakeside Resort, near Lude, in 1925. It contained a lodge with a dining hall and a series of summer cabins. Ed Russell was already in business on Four Mile Bay. In addition to providing food and lodging, he owned the *Tramp*, which he used for excursions on the lake and for fishing parties.

Dr. and Mrs. Klimek, owners of the Rex Hotel in Baudette, purchased the Four Mile Bay Resort from Russell in 1926. They had enough business to justify the installation of a generator to produce electricity for the entire resort, including the cabins. This proved a bonus in attracting tourists from the larger cities, who considered electricity a necessity. Like tourists in the Rainy Lake area, people enjoyed being in the wilderness more if luxuries were available. Billy Noonan said, "Judging by the appearance of the shore at Four Mile Bay, many a tourist's wife can cook anything if you give her a good can opener."

Dr. H. M. Waldron, of Drayton, North Dakota, became interested in commercial activity on the lake after a few visits. In 1925 he purchased the *Ginger*, later renamed *Lake of the Isles*. He employed local people to operate the excursion and group fishing business. At the same time, the Waldrons purchased Passage Island, on the Canadian side of the border, where he built a summer home.

Lake of the Woods had at least two dozen resorts built on it from 1925 to 1932—with good reason. Muskies weighing 44 pounds and measuring 54 inches in length were caught. For five of seven years starting in 1920, the biggest trout in the country were caught in the lake. As a bonus, the best prize was an 8-foot-long sturgeon, weighing 256 pounds and estimated to be 350 years old. The world's fourteenth largest fresh water lake was established as an excellent fishing spot.

Reports of such impressive catches reached major companies in midwestern cities, who responded by holding summer meetings at the lake for their officers and boards, including those of Sears-Roebuck, who came in special rail cars attached to the CN trains. Others who came in those years were Field Marshal and Mrs. Earl Haig, of England, accompanied by the Honorable Robert Rogers, formerly Minister of Public Works and later a member of the Canadian Parliament, and Mrs. Rogers; governors of Minnesota and North Dakota; former British Prime Minister Ramsey MacDonald, who spent the entire summer with his family on the lake; and at various times Chicago gangsters, including Al Capone.

In 1925 Congressman Harold Knutson introduced a bill to secure $50,000 for a federally funded fish hatchery. A rider was attached suggesting that President Coolidge's summer home be built on the lake. Billy Noonan stated his views: "To anybody east of the Mississippi River it sounds like treason, but anyway it was a good advertising stunt." Changing economic conditions delayed the funds, but a hatchery eventually became a reality. In the meantime, the game and fish department planted 20 million pike for future fishing enthusiasts.[3]

Commercial Fishing

Commercial fishing began in the area prior to 1895, when the Arion Fish Company set nets in Namakan Lake. The following year the Booth Packing Company purchased the Connable Fish Company, which operated on Rainy and Crane lakes. The Baltimore Fish Company, operating at the Reid fishing station at the mouth of the Rainy River, employed as many as 80 men prior to the turn of the century.

As population in the area increased, control of commercial fishing became more complicated due to the tremendous area of water that had to be patrolled and because two governments were involved. Commercial fishing was restricted in Rainy River as early as 1909 because of complications in the international waterways. Commercial fishing on the lakes was important, but it was in constant conflict with those who wanted to promote tourism for sport fishing. Every time the conflict surfaced, the commercial fishermen noted the economic benefits and insisted that commercial fishing improved rather than harmed game fishing. However, illegal commercial fishing activity hurt their cause.

In either case, fishing was desirable, and hatcheries were established at the Fort and at Ranier by 1920. In 1924 American commercial fishermen objected when the state game and fish commissioner attempted to close Rainy Lake, while the Canadians were allowed to continue commercial fishing. The fishermen of the Falls area cited their sales of over $400,000 worth of fish the past season.

Alfred Johnson, who began commercial fishing on Rainy Lake at a later date, said that by the time he started, there were only seven U.S. and three Canadian firms still active, supplying Dan McCarthy with fish to ship out. At the height of commercial fishing, there had been at least 50 firms on the lake. It was no longer attractive enough to be more than a sideline activity.

Lester Pollard, of Redby, was the breadwinner of his family after his father died, when Lester was 13. His first job was to help put up ice for the fishermen on Red Lake, but he could not continue after he was stricken with polio. He was assigned the job of nailing fish boxes at $0.04 a box and finished about 100 a day. Red Lake was overpopulated with fish and had to be fished down. Members of the Red Lake tribe used gill nets to harvest the fish and prepared them for shipping. By the early 1920s, about 750,000 pounds of walleyes and another 300,000 pounds of perch, white fish, goldeye, suckers, and sheepshead were shipped each year.

Commercial fishing started on Lake of the Woods when boats came down from Kenora. In 1893 the Sandusky Fish Company employed tugboats to tow little sailboats used to fish with nets. Reportedly 1,300,000 pounds of sturgeon were caught that year. The fish all went to Kenora, until the Great Northern Railroad was extended to Warroad in 1904, and then they were shipped south. By 1909 sturgeon had nearly disappeared and were off-limits. White fish, tullibee, and walleyes were the major catch until World War I, when Russian exports of caviar were halted and there was a resurgence of sturgeon fishing. The government requirement during the war for meatless days contributed to a heavier demand for all fish.

As tourism in the 1920s increased, the battle against commercial fishing intensified, but the commercial men persisted. Joe Rowell, Billy Zippel, and others formed the Lake of the Woods Fishermen's Association in 1926 to promote commercial fishing, protect fish, and assist law enforcement agencies. In 1929, 1,600,000 pounds of fish were caught—one-third pike, one-third tullibees, and the remainder rough fish. When Lake of the Woods caviar was $4 a pound, Billy Noonan quipped, "The situation is relieved somewhat by the fact that there isn't any." The supply of sturgeon was never replenished after heavy fishing during the war years.

One of the bright spots of the Baudette economy appeared as a result of commercial fishing on the lake when Joe and Ted Rowell contracted with local fishermen to deliver one ton of burbot livers to their factory each week. Burbot was a scourge to game fishermen and was used chiefly as mink food, but Ted Rowell, Sr., had learned to extract the oil, which was used as a source of vitamins. By October 1903, their plant could produce six gallons of fish oil per hour. Within two years Rowell Laboratories started commercial fishing on their own to assure a steady supply of fish. To meet the demand, they soon had to purchase all the burbot caught in Rainy and other lakes in the region.[4]

Kettle Falls

In January 1976, Kettle Falls, an early important passageway to the area, was placed on the National Register of Historic Places in recognition of its historical significance. Its location in a remote area that can be reached only by boat does not deter tourists, who flock to visit the setting of local folklore. Mary Lou Pearson, historian for the National Park Service, gave four reasons why people lived around Kettle Falls: "the two waterfalls required sluicing of logs destined for International Falls"; it was the site of dam construction (1910 to 1913) and logging camps; it appealed to tourists; and the portage around the falls was an assembly point for commercial fishermen.

Voyageurs were well acquainted with the site of the twin Kettle Falls, for it was on the trail of lone tree islands, which was the *voyageurs'* way of designating the route through the islands and lakes on their journey to the plains and the Rocky Mountains. Anne Stone Fraser was 16 when she accompanied her parents as they traveled from Duluth to Tower to Kettle Falls via rail, lumber wagon, and boat. Her mother received a black eye from being bounced around as they rode over the rapids, because the captain of the small steamer, which held 10 or 12 people, was drunk. The steamer, which was nothing more than a tugboat, then continued its journey to Koochiching Falls.

In 1909 Harry Berger, who had a trading post and stopping

place at Kettle Falls, announced that he intended to improve his hotel accommodations, because tourist trade was on the rise. He said at that time, "Kettle Falls, while it may never become a city, will certainly grow to be a popular summer resort."

Congress had first consented to a dam on May 4, 1898, and repeatedly gave extensions until July 1, 1911, when it gave its final approval to build at the outlet of Namakan Lake. In April 1912, the Rainy River Improvement Company, an M & O subsidiary, applied to the International Joint Commission for approval to build dams at Kettle Falls. The purpose of these dams was to hold water back for easier sluicing of logs in the spring, and to allow for the lowering of Sand Point and Namakan lakes an additional 5 feet to keep a greater flow of water over the Koochiching power dam in the dry season.

In 1912 Oliver and Anne Knox, who had lived in tents and in birch or log structures at Kettle Falls since 1904, prepared themselves for the construction boom by erecting a spacious 28- × 30-foot two-story log house, with six bedrooms upstairs. Later they added a 24- × 24-foot kitchen.

The following year Ed Rose built the 18-room Kettle Falls Hotel. During the dam construction period, the hotel and an additional bunkhouse were filled. The Knoxes had 10 guests, who paid $1.40 daily for room and board—a high price by boarding house standards, but the cost of getting all provisions from the Falls mandated such charges.

After the dams were finished in November 1914, two sets of rail tracks were laid by Fred Lassard to aid portaging between the lakes. One set of tracks circled the dam and was capable of transporting tugboats called "gators," while the other ran behind the hotel but connected the lakes. These tracks were particularly useful to the commercial fishermen, who transported as many as 5,000 boxes of fish over them each year and often contacted buyers at the hotel. The tracks were removed when commercial fishing declined after 1920. Prior to dam construction, 9 families were located there; in 1920 there were 120 residents in the immediate area.

In 1914 the Knoxes purchased a gasoline-powered boat that pulled a barge capable of hauling up to 15 tons. They operated on the upstream side of the dams from Kettle Falls to Sand Point, near Crane Lake, charging $2 a ton to haul freight and $1 for each passenger on the 30-mile trip. In 1916 they purchased a second boat, the *Rambler*, and each piloted a boat. Until she went away to school, their daughter, Mary, rode with her mother. Knox said that Anne knew Rainy Lake as well as he did. They supplied the camps of Shevlin and Clarke by boat in the summer and by horses and sleds in the winter.

The Knoxes had nine horses for their freight business, plus three head of cattle for milk and meat. Hay was cut on the lowlands, and grain came by barge from the Falls. A large garden, berries from the woods, and an occasional sturgeon enabled them to earn additional income by catering to summer tourists who did not want to stay at the hotel.

Robert S. Williams, a professional chef at the Palmer House in Chicago, came to the Falls in 1916 for health reasons. He purchased the Dutchroom, then Brennen's saloon in Ranier, and finally the Kettle Falls Hotel. At the height of commercial fishing, as many as 300 people passed through on peak days. Girls always were available at the hotel for the pleasure of commercial fishermen and lumberjacks in the area. In the summer, other girls "worked" from tents and small buildings.

During Prohibition, blind pigs were operated by John and Jazzbo Beaton, Chappy and Nellie Campman, and the hotel. Reportedly, the Campmans and Bert Upton (aka Catamaran), a hermit, never went to town in 25 years, but somehow Upton always had money. The community also had two trading posts, which relied on business from the Indians as well as the tourists. Chris Monson tended the dams for the first 40 years after their construction. Since then, members of the Williams family have handled that task for M & O and its successors.

The first travelers through Kettle Falls, after the *voyageurs*, were those seeking minerals. Then came commercial fishermen, followed by the lumberjacks, and by the late 1920s, tourist trade became important and remained so for the following decades. The dams still serve as a vital link in the water control system, monitored by the International Joint Commission.[5]

Summer Camps

The idea of summer camps associated with tourism never really caught on in the Rainy Lake area, probably because it is too removed from major centers of population. However, two were attempted.

In 1918 John Hungerford, a professor at Iowa State College, at Ames, came to Rainy Lake to locate a site for a summer camp for students majoring in civil engineering. He found that site on

Brown's Bay, near Emerald Isle. In 1922 he returned with his family, about 50 students, a faculty of 6 to 8, and 2 cooks. They built a cook shack with classrooms above it, another classroom building, a faculty house, and six cabins for students.

The camp ran every year from 1922 to World War II, when it was moved to a site between Wirt and Talmoon, in Itasca County, to reduce travel expense from Ames. In 1936 the Hungerfords platted Blueberry Island and built a home, because Mrs. Hungerford was afraid of forest fires on the mainland.

During the early 1920s, W. P. Hapgood, of Indianapolis, developed a sheep farm and resort on Deer (aka Grassy) Island with the help of Ernest Oberholtzer. Later, Jack Vance, a Northwestern University coach, and Max Winters, of the Falls, started an independent boys' camp there. The camp held 75 boys, each of whom paid $125 for 8 weeks. The staff totaled 22—1 counselor for every 5 boys, plus cooks, caretakers, and a carpenter. Emil Johnson was the carpenter and the blacksmith. Don and Layna Johnson were year-round caretakers from 1929 to 1936. Mrs. Johnson also served as camp barber. They received $75 a month and housing, which was a tent in the summer and a log cabin in the winter.

The program was chiefly oriented around teaching the boys how to live outdoors via 10-day canoe trips. A big boat hauled the boys and the counselors to the north shore of Rainy Lake, where they divided into parties of 10 boys and 2 counselors using four canoes. In between canoe trips, the boys enjoyed sailing, swimming, football, baseball, physical education, and target practice on the rifle range. A self-policing system kept discipline problems to a minimum.

Parents often visited their sons, which proved to be a boon to the tourist trade. Indians were encouraged to stop at the island, which was a novelty to people from the large city, and they also profited by the sale of their wares. When Jack Vance decided to take up other summer activities, the camp was discontinued.

The camps added to the folklore of the area, but they did not significantly boost the local economy because only a few people were involved. The area was too removed from centers of population to attract others interested in developing camps. Camping and tourism conflicted with forestry, the basic industry, for they both were dependent upon trees—the former for enjoyment and the latter for a livelihood. Too many campers and tourists were not always compatible with forestry, so, to safeguard the area's future, it would have to remain basically a wilderness.[6]

Bronko—the Gentle Giant

There are a few people in every community whose names become a household word, at least for a period of time. Sometimes they have a public building, park, or street named for them or have their portrait in a prominent place. Five such individuals filled the pages of the Falls papers in its first half century: Alexander Baker, the first settler; E. W. Backus, the founder of the basic industry; Annie Shelland Williams, the first superintendent of county schools and early promoter of roads and school consolidation; Ernest Oberholtzer, the environmentalist, who stopped Backus from developing his extended water power plans; and Bronislaw "Bronko" Nagurski, All-American football player at tackle and fullback in 1929, and in 1963 a charter member of the Football Hall of Fame.

Baker's reputation did not reach beyond the immediate area of a few square miles around his homestead, which was known chiefly because it was where Backus wanted to build his paper mill. Backus was known in his time in financial, industrial, and political circles, because he was the last of the timber barons of Minnesota and a leading industrialist nationally. Williams was known statewide, partly because she was a woman who was not afraid to speak up for what she believed, at a time when women were not given a great deal of attention. Oberholtzer's reputation came because early environmental leaders aided his cause and partly because he challenged Backus, whose very name provoked many. Nagurski was known by more people nationally in his day than all of the others, because he was a sports hero. He was a talented athlete, physically and intellectually, whose name was in the limelight for three decades. Unlike Backus, Williams, or Oberholtzer, he disliked attention. His ego did not demand that he be in the news, but he accepted it as part of his career.

Bronislaw Nagurski was born November 3, 1908, at Rainy River, Ontario, to parents of Ukrainian descent. Bronko's mother had married in her early teens in Russia, had a child, and then lost her husband. Because conditions in the Ukraine were so bad, she left her child with a sister and emigrated. Years later they were reunited at the Falls. Elsewhere in the Ukraine, Mike Nagurski also experienced difficulties and, like many others, was "caught up by the promotion" of steamship and railroad companies about the great opportunities in Canada and the United States.

Shortly after 1900, the two, unknown to each other, left the

Ukraine and worked their way across Canada. Eventually they met on a large grain farm in North Dakota, where they worked for about a year. The couple married "about 1906 or 1907" at Rainy River, Ontario, where Mike worked for the sawmills as a carpenter. The Nagurskis moved to the Falls, where Mike continued as a carpenter for the ILC sawmill. Within a few years they purchased a store at 708 Fourth Avenue and named it Nagurski's Grocery.

The Nagurskis were aggressive people. As the store prospered, they purchased a farm about four miles south of the Falls, about 1922. Mike built a portable sawmill and sawed and sold timber as he cleared the land. He did custom work with the mill, traveling as far west as Baudette, helping others clear their land. In the meantime, he broke and cultivated his land and also purchased and/or built small houses in the Falls. Mrs. Nagurski continued to run the store and to care for the four roomers who lived above it.

Bronko, the eldest of four children, used a hand-pulled wagon to deliver groceries while they lived in town. After they moved to the country, he farmed, worked in the woods, and delivered lumber and logs. All family members helped, either in the store or on the farm. Bronko was expected to do so much work at home that, according to his contemporaries, he had little time to be involved with school activities. His father had no schooling and was determined that his children should at least finish high school. His home influence tended to make Bronko a loner.

Bronko played basketball and football in high school. He played both tackle and fullback in his sophomore year, but as a junior played only in the backfield. Bronko was not negative about Ralph Baker, the first full-time coach in the Falls, whose primary interest was physical training, but he remarked of those years, "I really learned football on the sand lot."

Robert "Buck" Robbins, the Bemidji coach, noted Bronko's abilities when Robbins' team played against the Falls in Bronko's junior year, and Robbins solicited him to play for Bemidji. Bronko said of that experience, "I tell people I was kidnapped to play for Bemidji High School." But just before Bronko's senior year, H. R. Peterson, superintendent at the Falls, lodged a complaint with the Minnesota High School Athletic Association. Bronko could not play for Bemidji.

Robbins did not want Bronko to return to the Falls for his senior year, because Bemidji had to play them. Instead, Robbins let him scrimmage on the bomber squad against the varsity. Of that experience Bronko said, "I could run through Bemidji's line, and they were winning everything, so I knew I had potential." Bronko was 6 feet 2 inches tall and weighed 180 pounds. Robbins got Bronko a job as school janitor, and he slept in the furnace room, for his parents were unable to contribute anything toward his expenses.

Under Robbins' guidance, Bronko learned how to use his talent and was "practically guaranteed" four years of college at the University of North Dakota, where Robbins had attended. A high school friend, Bob Fritz, recalled that North Dakota Agricultural College, at Fargo, was also interested in Bronko, and he would have received aid by joining the ROTC program.

Bronko was eligible to play basketball the second half of the school year, which was another reason why the coaches kept him at Bemidji. They had a good team but needed a center to give them a chance to go to the state tournament. Bronko had an excellent vertical jump and was a good shot, so Bemidji had a great season until they were beaten 26-2 in the final game of the regional tournament.

Scouting and recruiting of high school players was very low key in those days, for colleges depended primarily upon alumni to attract athletes. Bronko was approached by Northwestern, but Dr. Dietrich, a Bemidji dentist, contacted the University of Minnesota, where they were noncommittal about scholarships or handouts but did promise a job. Bronko recalled, "They were slow in giving jobs, but I eventually was made a night watchman at a lumber company." He received board and room and lived in the basement of the company office.

Early during the first quarter, Bronko "was almost on the verge of leaving" and told the equipment man at the stadium. He passed the word to the coaches "who made sure that Bronko stayed" at the university. Freshmen were on the bomber squad only, and once Bronko settled down, he played at both tackle and fullback. He realized that the coaches noticed standouts on the squad, "but never Dr. Spears." As he gained confidence he decided to make the most of it, but he always remembered the encouragement of the Bemidji coach.

In his sophomore year, Bronko weighed 205 pounds and played tackle, because All-American Herb Joesting was in the backfield. Dr. Clarence Spears was head coach all four years that Bronko was at the University of Minnesota. Of him Bronko commented:

"He was tough and had great ability. I think he got too rough with some of the people. I did not really like him because of that. But he made me put out. Sometimes I played because I loved the sport, and sometimes I played hard because I was afraid of getting a good chewing."

Bronko did not feel that he was being used by the university. Rather, he looked at football as an opportunity. He was very aware of what the newspapers wrote, and that provided an incentive for him to set higher goals. After some deliberation he added, "After I played a while I learned the potential of success, which was possible if you really put out."

Minnesota had an All-American every year, and this hurt the underclassman's chances of getting any recognition, but in his junior year Bronko played fullback and received honorable mention. In 1929, as a senior, he divided his time between tackle on defense and fullback on offense and was named to one of the All-American teams in both positions. Ironically, he was named All-American tackle on three teams, even though he played that position for only 32 minutes in conference games.

Bronko's parents saw him play only once while at Minnesota—his final game. According to Bronko, they were not very interested in sports, and the only other time they saw him perform was in a wrestling match in the Falls. They never saw him play in a professional football game. "They didn't really understand; it was such a different life."

While Bronko was at the university, the assistant basketball coach helped him start a basketball team called the Bronks, later the Galloping Gophers. They were a good team and were strong competition for other professional teams, such as the Harlem Globetrotters and the Phillips Oilers, which were just becoming active at that time. Most of the players were from the football team, and their popularity helped to get an abundance of bookings. Bronko managed the group and insisted on a $75 minimum guarantee, plus a percentage. He paid $10.00 per game to the best players and $7.50 to average players. After expenses, he netted $22 to $25 a night for himself. The Bronks played throughout the Dakotas, Michigan, Minnesota, and Wisconsin.

Bronko continued his pursuit of a degree in physical education after his college football career was finished but ended a quarter short of getting his degree. He became so involved with the Bronks, professional football, and wrestling that he never took time to get his diploma.

Coach Spears said of Bronko:

> It was more than power, speed, and strength that made Nagurski a great star. . . . He was amazingly gifted on those points. . . . What set him apart was his fire and athletic intelligence. He had a knowledge of football that could not be taken from a book or from the words of a coach. He had it because he was perfectly in tune with the game and that, of course, will make him a successful coach.

In a major article by St. Paul sports columnist Dick Cullum, following Bronko's college football career, it was claimed that Bronko had listened to 500 offers during his senior year, which made it certain that he would be "a glamorous figure when all the stories had been written." Cullum wrote that Bronko received 42 "actual offers and propositions" in the two days before he left for the East-West football game at San Francisco, in January 1930. "He reported guarantees from $5,000 and upwards for a season in boxing, wrestling, or football."

However, in 1976 Bronko stated that he had no contact with anyone from professional football until after his senior year, with the exception of Minnesota football alumni who were in pro ball and visited the university. After Bronko played in the Shrine East-West game at Northwestern, George Halas, founder of the Chicago Bears, offered him $2,500 for the 1930 season. Bronko had at least three other firm offers, but he was pleased with Halas' proposal, because it was much better than what other players were getting for the 13- to 15-game season. But he was unsure as to what to do and recalled:

> I did not feel close enough to Dr. Spears . . . to ask his advice. . . . Dutch Bergland, the Minnesota backfield coach, was the biggest help I had at Minnesota. I got a good contract my first year [1930] because I got $5,000. A big share of the backfield in pro got $100 to $125 per game and line got $75 pretty standard. It was a man from Chicago who helped me get the contract and I never saw or heard from him after that.

Bronko was an admirer of George Halas, who had started the Bears at Decatur, Illinois, as Staley's Corn Oil team. Halas had a difficult time financially, and Bronko did not receive all of his pay on schedule for the first two years, but it arrived before the next season started. Fortunately for his immigrant parents, their son was doing well at a time when the banks foreclosed on the

Nagurskis, causing them to lose most of their houses in the Falls. His parents signed the farm over to Bronko, who then helped his sisters get their education, "because the folks were as good as broke." They closed their store, and his father returned to work in the mill.

Because Bronko was reared in a family with a strong work ethic, he had reservations about the "easy money" from professional football. "Sometimes I almost felt ashamed because I had the feeling that people thought it was not an honest sport." Under Halas, the players worked even harder than under Spears. The training rules were strict, and the coaches "didn't fool." In Bronko's first year the team practiced from 9:00 A.M. to 3:00 P.M., with only a half hour off for lunch, which was brought to the field. The team stayed at the Wellington Arms Hotel.

As soon as the football season with the Bears was over, Bronko activated his basketball team, which by now included not only ex-Minnesota players but also some top athletes from other schools. They were on the road virtually every night, and the Falls paper seldom missed reporting on every game, no matter how small a town they played. Their schedule included a week's engagement at the Minnesota Theatre, in Minneapolis, followed by a trip to the Falls, where Bronko received a five-minute ovation after he was introduced by J. J. Hadler. Tickets for the "biggest crowd ever" in the Falls high school were $0.25 and $0.50. Bronko's all-stars won 54 to 21.

After several years of nightly stands with the Bronks basketball team, Bronko "had had enough and was looking for something else." Tony Stecker, who had been a wrestler, wanted to become a manager and promote wrestling, but he needed a well-known local figure. He approached Bronko with the idea of becoming a professional wrestler. This was appealing, for it gave Bronko something to do in off-season from the Bears—especially since his salary had been reduced because of the Depression. It was not until 1937 that he again received $5,000. After three years of pro football followed by basketball, his weight had climbed to 235, and for the rest of his career it remained between that and 242.

Bronko did not like wrestling as well as football. "Traveling made it a rough life, on the road 5 days a week, 500 miles a day quite often. . . . Wrestling was a grind," but he made from $50 to $150 a night. He wrestled throughout the United States and Canada and later did some refereeing.

The money in wrestling pulled him away from pro football, and he was away from the Bears just as things started to improve for them. He lost much playing time in 1935 because of a sciatica problem, but the excellent medical attention he received enabled him to play the final game. His injury was well publicized, and it was then that Bronko sensed that other players respected him. The New York Giants were ahead of the Bears in the last game of the season, and every time Bronko carried the ball and was tackled, four Giants always helped him up.

During the early months of 1934, while at the Falls recuperating from a knee injury suffered during the 1933 season with the Bears, Bronko met Ileen Kane, a friend of his sister. The romance led to marriage in 1936, but Ileen never traveled with him while he played football and only rarely when he was wrestling.

The highlight of Bronko's wrestling career came in 1937, when he defeated Dean Detton at Minneapolis for the World's Heavyweight Wrestling Championship. By then he was performing before crowds in excess of 10,000 against wrestlers from other countries as well as the best in the United States. On July 8, 1937, soon after he won the wrestling title, Bronko agreed to return to the Falls in one of his very rare home-town appearances for the sole purpose of being honored.

Bronko decided to drop professional football in the fall of 1938, partly because he wanted $6,500 and Halas would pay only $6,000, and partly because he had an opportunity to make a world wrestling tour. At that time noted sports columnist Grantland Rice wrote, "If I were picking an all-time, all-star backfield, I would place Clarke at quarterback, Grange and Thorpe at the halves, and Nagurski at fullback."

Another watershed in Bronko's life was December 10, 1938, when he received his final citizenship papers. Sometime in 1912 his parents moved to the Falls, and finally, at age 30, the All-American became a citizen.

Bronko continued wrestling full time until the fall of 1943, when Halas persuaded him to return to the Bears and play tackle. During the season he was switched to fullback and received a bonus, ending his career making $6,500.

After the 1943 season, Bronko continued to wrestle and to referee until he was age 52 in 1960. In 1963 he became a charter member of the Football Hall of Fame, along with his Bear backfield teammate, Harold "Red" Grange.

Late in life Bronko was asked to comment on modern football. He replied, "I played nine years with the Chicago Bears. . . . But today, with two platoons, I'd be able to play 20 years." He regretted that he did not stay with pro football, for he thoroughly enjoyed George Halas and the Bears, in contrast to his days at Minnesota.

Looking back on his career, he said, "If I had to do things over again I would not have wrestled. It was too hard work and did not pay that well. I would have been better staying with pro ball."

He spent the last eight years of his working career operating a gasoline service station, which he said was a "good deal." Then his legs "started getting really bad," and a change in the business made it easy for him to retire. This unchanged, quiet person—an intense family man—spent a good portion of the final 20 years of his life very much in seclusion. In 1976 his son-in-law said it best: "Bronko was always close to his family; he preferred that to anything else. We never have to look for a baby sitter, because he waits for the opportunity." The arthritic-impacted gentle giant, whose size 19½ ring was the largest the class ring company had made to that time, was happiest when he was with his grandchildren. He was a person of great warmth and sincerity, who accepted the aches and pains caused by his career without complaint.

Bronko became the Falls most widely publicized figure. His name was familiar to more Americans, especially sports fans, than any in the history of the area. This modest sports hero was an ideal symbol for an area that was known to the outer world for its rugged life style, its hardy lumberjacks, and its good fishing.[7]

ENDNOTES FOR CHAPTER X

1. Interview of Welles Eastman, Wayzata, Minn., July 16, 1974, hereafter Eastman interview; *The Minneapolis Journal*, June, 7, 1908; *The Press*, June 10, September 1, 1910, June 29, 1911; *The Journal*, July 4, 1918, February 24, 1930, June 23, 1935; interview of Bryne L. and Don A. Johnson, Ranier, Minn., April 12, 1990, hereafter Bryne Johnson interview. Don Johnson was born in 1906 and came to the area in the 1920s. *Hist. of Kooch. Co.*, p. 205; Rainy Lake, Community files, KCHS; *The Chronicle*, August 4, 1974, June 1, 1975; *The Baudette Region*, August 6, 1926; Bryne Johnson, "Growing Up on Rainy Lake," speech given to the KCHS, January 27, 1986, on file at KCHS; instructions for the butler at Redcrest, on file at KCHS; telephone interview of Robert Hilke, International Falls, April 11, 1990. Hilke was acquainted with many of the individuals who lived on Rainy Lake and were part of the Rainy Lake aristocracy.

2. *The Press*, April 19, June 7, 1905, September 25, 1907, January 22,

August 21, 1908, January 13, February 10, July 8, 1909, March 24, 31, May 5, June 2, July 28, September 8, 1910, August 3, 1911; *The Minneapolis Tribune*, July 1, 1909; *Hist. of Kooch. Co.*, p. 285; *The Journal*, February 29, 1912, November 17, 1921, August 2, 1923, May 15, June 26, August 28, 1924, May 7, 1925, August 11, 1927, January 6, May 13, 1933, July 9, 1936, June 11, 1938, January 16, November 29, 1939; Koski interview; Neil Watson interview; Emma Watson interview; Emma Watson tapes; City Council, May 27, 1912, July 2, 1923, April 21, May 12, 1924, April 20, 1925, September 20, 1926; Scott Erickson interview; interview of William A. Lloyd, Fort Frances, Ontario, June 4, 1976, hereafter William Lloyd interview. Mr. Lloyd was born in Fort Frances in 1911 to a pioneer family which was involved in lake and riverboat business. Knox interview; interview of John H. Nelson, Crane Lake, Minn., July 26, 1976, hereafter John Nelson interview; Paul Anderson interview; Pearson interview.

3. *The Baudette Region*, August 6, 1914, August 16, 1917, May 21, 1920, January 9, 30, February 20, March 13, April 3, 17, May 22, June 5, 19, 26, July 3, 10, 17, August 21, October 16, November 6, December 11, 1925, January 1, April 2, 9, 16, 26, May 21, 28, June 11, August 6, 20, 1926, April 29, August 8, 1927, June 15, 1928, September 11, 1931; LOW Co. Hist.

4. *The Rainy Lake Journal*, June 20, 1895, November 5, 1896; Nute, p. 68; *The Press*, August 12, 1909, September 8, 1910; *The Journal*, March 8, 1917, November 6, 1919, July 22, 1920, February 14, May 29, August 21, 1924; Hinckley, "Way Back," p. 26; Alfred Johnson interview; Pollard interview; Beck file; Anderson, "Beltrami Island," p. 6; LOW Co. Hist.; *The Baudette Region*, January 22, 1915, December 21, 1917, July 9, December 17, 1926, November 4, 1927, December 20, 1929, October 20, 1933.

5. Fraser interview; Mary Lou Pearson, "The Kettle Falls Hotel and Dams," Kettle Falls file, KCHS; Knox interview; the *Press*, July 22, 1909; *International Joint Commission*, hearing, Fort Frances, Ontario, June 1941, published January 1942, hereafter IJC, 1942; the *Fort Frances Times*, April 18, 1912; *Report to the International Joint Commission: Relation to Official Reference Lake of the Woods Levels*, Adolph F. Meyer, Arthur V. White, consulting engineers, Washington, D.C., and Ottawa, Canada, 1916, p. 206, hereafter Meyer and White; Hnatuik interview; Charlie Williams interview.

6. Harry Anderson interview of Mary Dodds Slick, International Falls, July 22, 1987, KCHS; manuscript on the life of Ernest Oberholtzer, KCHS, hereafter Oberholtzer file; Bryne Johnson interview.

7. Interview of Bronislaw "Bronko" Nagurski, International Falls, August 16, 1976; interview of Robert F. Fritz, Fargo, N.D., January 30, 1991, hereafter Fritz interview. Fritz, a native of the Falls, was a boyhood pal of Bronko Nagurski and remained in contact with him. *The Journal*, November 3, 1927, January 15, 23, 25, February 8, March 7, 10, 1930, July 8, August 5, September 30, 1937, January 5, August 12, November 19, December 12, 1938, February 1, June 24, 1939, March 8, 1940; *The Baudette Region*, September 5, 1930; *The Forum* (Fargo), January 9, 15, 1990.

CHAPTER XI

Strife in the Wilderness

INTERNATIONAL FALLS has the reputation of being the "ice box of the nation," but outsiders who have attempted to understand it are not sure whether that title derives from the cold climate or the bitterness that exists between labor and capital. One is not in the community long before sensing the tension caused by that rivalry, and those who live there and are not directly involved in the ongoing dispute are uncomfortable with it and do not understand why it must be.

Speculation exists that this hostility may stem from the fact that the area "drew the disadvantaged types [whose attitude was] we have nothing so let's soak the rich. This was the old populist idea and it has stuck. . . ." Immigrants from Europe, who were blacklisted there for their union activities, continued that behavior once they settled here, while others with that experience became anti-union in their new home.

A second-generation resident, not involved with either faction, was dismayed because labor always "knocked the mill but they worked there anyway." Another of the second generation went away to college and refused to return to the Falls because of the factionalism. Others dislike the long-standing animosity but are at a loss as to how to reduce that ill feeling. A detailed labor history probably would reveal that few towns of its size, nation-wide, are more unionized than the Falls and have lost as many hours to strikes as it has.

M & O Unions and Early Strikes

To get his new state-of-the-art mill going, the hard-driving and ruthless Backus employed skilled paper makers and artisans from paper-mill towns of New York, Maine, Wisconsin, and other forestry states, who brought unions with them, causing the two combative elements to be on the scene from the start. [A biography

288

of Edward W. Backus, being prepared by Charles Skrief, will shed more light on labor relations.]

Papermakers Local 159 was organized July 1, 1910, with Fred Donley as president. One charter member was Matthew J. Burns, who went on to serve 8 years as secretary to the American Federation of Labor (AFL) International Papermakers Union and 16 years as its president. Describing the local's early days, he said that the union's ideal was to "keep improving the lot of the masses of the people—a social order where the strong protected the weak." From the beginning, "officials of M & O . . . recognized and conceded the right to organize and negotiate on wages and working conditions." The contract that was signed after two years continued basically the same for several decades.

Papermakers Local 159, the first labor organization to celebrate Labor Day in the Falls in 1910, took an excursion on Rainy Lake, played a ball game with the Falls team, and sponsored a public dance in the village hall that evening. This tradition continued, making the Fourth of July and Labor Day the two big celebrations of the year with button-wearing union members marching in every parade.

One of the first labor disturbances occurred in March 1911, with a riot at the pulp mill and a strike by machinists—a clash, which already was referred to as one "of long standing." Shortly after that, John D. Chubbuck, organizer for the AFL, spent several weeks in the Falls to form a trade and labor assembly. He helped to organize the following trade union locals: clerks, bartenders, electricians, carpenters, pulpwood makers, sulphite workers, and barbers. Those locals and the paper makers were united into the assembly, providing the Falls with a strong union base.

No major event in labor relations took place until 1916, when 500 mill employees at the Falls and the Fort struck for an 8-hour day and increased wages. By then the paper makers already had an 8-hour day with 10-hour pay and time and one-half for overtime. The strike was successful.

When World War I stimulated economic activity, the unions struck again, causing a local disturbance. The county commissioners protested, because the district judge had approved the hiring of deputies to preserve order and to protect property, causing $4,000 in additional police wages, which county finances could not bear. The unions took advantage of the labor shortage and staged a 96-day strike, in which they won time and wage concessions.

To make up for the shortage of men, M & O employed women, three of whom were Jennie Baker (later Rasmussen), Alice Marie Peterson (later Tive), and Mary Curran (later Malerich). They held jobs in the woodsroom, the Insulite mill, and the sawmill, respectively.

After the nation was involved in World War I, everyone toed the line, and it was not until the spring of 1919 when the economy slackened that disturbances again occurred. This time the strike was called by the national union leaders over a disagreement with the U.S. War Board as to when the war officially ended. The unions asked for an 8-hour day, time and one-half for overtime, and double time Sundays and holidays, extended shutdowns during certain holidays, 50 weeks guaranteed pay, and a 15 percent wage increase. The number of workers involved prompted the city and the county to add deputies to prevent disorder. Because of its national nature, this strike spread to the mills at Baudette and Spooner, but the overall results were somewhat minimized due to the availability of outside workers.

In December 1919, the 43 employees of MD & W struck, and Sheriff Hugh McIntosh secretly asked the governor for assistance from the National Guard. Captain Hiram Frankel, adjutant to the general in charge of troops from the Twin Cities and St. Cloud, wrote of the guard's arrival in the Falls on December 13:

> We met the sheriff, a weak sister who having called for help because citizens here would not allow themselves to be sworn in as deputies, felt later that he had made a mistake, because the workmen here are voters and he is afraid he is going to be kicked out at the next election. So the first thing the sheriff did was to ask the general not to let anybody know that he, the sheriff, had wired for help.

A mob of 300 strikers and others jeered and made disparaging remarks at the Guard members, but no violence took place. Local citizens attempted to convince the soldiers that the town was "lily white" and there was no problem, but by that time 1 of 10 or 12 strikebreakers quartered at the Forest Inn had been beaten up. The Guard maintained strict neutrality and soon realized that "both sides feared the other and did not want the public to know that there was disorder." It was clear to Frankel that "real rioting" would have broken out if the guard had not come, and he added, "If we leave before things are settled there will be merry hell here."

New strikebreakers arrived daily, but, fortunately, coal continued to be delivered to the mill via the M & I. Frankel speculated
on what would happen if coal shipments stopped, the mill shut
down, and 1,200 idle workers were "let loose in a town with few
amusements and reds running around working on the minds
none too favorable to the company even if employed by them."
Local merchants were caught between the two sides, and "No
Scab Trade Solicited cards were put up in windows of the com-
moner class of stores." General sympathy for the strikers prevailed, and local politicians maintained that the troops had been
needlessly called. Post office employees refused to cash money
orders for guardsmen, many city and county officers were "controlled by the unruly element," and many fistfights took place,
but no guardsmen encountered any significant problems.

The strikers were under the control of J. M. Laricey, first vice
president of the Order of Railway Conductors, from Cedar Rapids,
and Mr. Johnson, first vice president of the Brotherhood of
Locomotive Engineers, from St. Paul. This was an important
strike for the unions. Both sides kept calling for protection from
the Guard, but, upon investigation, it always was determined
that none was necessary, and the guard refused to be involved
in any way that would show partiality.

Strikers cut water pipes on locomotives, causing them to break
down after they left the railroad yards. One engine's brake wheels
were frozen by muriatic acid, and the oil cups were filled with
emery powder, which cut the bearings. It was determined later
that many of the breakdowns came from reckless handling by
the strikebreakers. The ILC sawmill shut down because the
switch engines for hauling logs directly to the paper mill were
unable to run.

On January 6, 1920, Laricey left town, but the strike was far
from over. Backus and the union leaders had a tug of war about
the cause of the strike, but it cooled down, and in early March
the governor recalled the National Guard. In April 1920, 70
MD & W employees were "taken back without prejudice."

The local press carried little information about the MD & W
strike, but, in the meantime, Bror Dahlberg, of M & O, petitioned
Governor J. A. A. Burnquist to remove Sheriff Hugh McIntosh
because of the "lawlessness and violence" that had grown out of
the strike. McIntosh had been missing since January 22, and
prior to that date he had transferred property and left town with
"a lot of cash and liberty bonds." Later, the governor formally

suspended McIntosh and replaced him with John Wall, of Minneapolis, who had served as sheriff temporarily in 1917. In mid-March, McIntosh told a friend in Minneapolis that he had resigned and said, "To ___ with International Falls." On April 15, 1921, *The Northome Record* reported that McIntosh had written from Alaska.

The next disturbance came in May 1920, when the national Timber Workers Union strike, which was in effect in other timber-producing camps of the lake states, finally reached Minnesota. Workers demanded an 8-hour day with 10-hour pay. ILC announced that it would close sawmills at the Falls and the Fort rather than submit. Several million feet of reserve stock were on hand, and supervisory personnel could fill orders.

At the same time, workers at the Spooner sawmill were unsuccessful in their demands for an increase from $4.25 to $5.25 per day, because many refused to join the walkout. This enabled ILC to fill orders at the Falls and the Fort with 60,000 feet of lumber daily from Spooner. When workers at the Falls and the Fort realized what was happening, they returned to work under their previous agreement.

When the union contract expired in May 1921, M & O asked for a 30 percent reduction in wages for both the Falls and the Fort. The workers struck and countered with an agreement to accept the reduction, but wanted a nine-hour day, no overtime, and a readjustment in May 1922. The strike failed, for 30,000 workers in the industry were out on strike in 19 other companies, which held fast because they had enough newsprint on hand to fill orders for 60 days.

MD & W had a prolonged strike from July through November 1922, during which the road kept operating by using outside workers, who were housed locally in Pullman cars. A strike against M & O in 1923 was settled by the national officers without a vote of the locals, due to the serious conditions in the industry. That was followed in 1924 by a strike against M & O, which failed to secure the desired pay increase, but the company was forced to recognize the union at the Kenora mill.

Relative calm prevailed on the labor scene in the late 1920s and during the period of the Backus bankruptcy and takeover by the receivership. The unions accepted a $0.05-per-hour reduction on June 15, 1931, a 10 percent reduction on May 13, 1932, and a cut from $0.27 to $0.25 an hour on June 15, 1932, with a reduction in hours from 10 to 8. But when a cut from $0.25

to $0.225 an hour was announced for April 1, 1933, they objected. The sawmill employees were not unionized, but they joined forces with the strikers at a mass meeting to protest and decided to form a local. Within a few days Harold Reich, the local AFL organizer, informed George Lawson, president of the Minnesota Federation: "At once after installation of [the sawmill local] officers the bubble burst and the strike is the condition which exists. I could not hold them, the iron was hot." On the same day, Reich sent $17 in initiation fees to William Green, national president of the AFL, for 17 employees of ILC. At the same time, shop employees of MD & W were organized as a separate local by someone who Reich suspected was motivated by "greediness for membership."

Sawmill Workers Local 18242 was organized April 5, 1933, and within two weeks had 97 members out of 147 sawmill employees. Reich stressed that the strike was completely out of his hands, but he hoped the AFL officers would accept the new local. The employees at the lumber yard, the pulp yard, and the planing mill, as well as the truck drivers, all struck because they would not accept the proposed wage reduction. This shut down the lumber and pulp yards and the planing mill. ILC made no attempt to reopen the facilities, and union members busied themselves by holding dances and other fund-raising events. In the meantime, workers in the steam plant also decided to oppose the wage reduction and organized Local 937, making the steam plant and the sawmill the last M & O departments to be unionized. The unions prospered by gaining members, but on May 1, 1933, when the mills reopened, the workers accepted a 10 percent reduction in wages.

Reich explained that settlement to AFL leaders by saying that the reorganized company had to reduce or they could not compete. President E. B. Hall, of the Minnesota Federation, replied that word of the settlement at the Falls "is some of the best news that has come to the office for some time. . . . The organizations . . . are to be congratulated in the settlement of what promised to be a very bad situation." He understood the condition of the industry better than the local people and added that news from the East was that wage reductions had about reached the bottom. President William Green simply wired congratulations on the agreement.

After work resumed, Reich was kept busy getting the president of Sulphite Local 49 reinstated to his job. The national president of the sulphite union was satisfied that "Brother Hale," local president, had used poor judgment because he was impulsive and lost his head, causing many members to leave their jobs in a violation of the union contract. A clipping from President Green recommended that strikes should be used only as a last resort. Hale apologized to management and was reinstated after being off the job for nearly six months. Reich wrote to the national president saying that R. W. Andrews, of M & O, had been "very tolerant and personally I think him a really big man in this particular case." This was after the national president had reminded Reich of the "vicious factions" within the local.

Governmental action in December 1933 forced M & O to raise the minimum wage back to $0.38 an hour—$0.02 less than the figure suggested by federal guidelines. In May 1934, agitation surfaced for an increase back to the 1929 levels, and Reich asked Green how to handle the local situation: "These men are now disregarding leadership and lay little importance on the conventional procedure of handling labor affairs." Sawmill Local 18242 voted 199 to 10 to strike. Green wired to the president of the local: "Do all you can to make a peaceful settlement. . . . Take no action until organizer Reich has had opportunity to make investigation and forward his report to this office." Local officers had not informed Reich that Green had requested his involvement in an attempted settlement.

The sawmill local disregarded an agreement between M & O and international officers of the Papermakers, Pulp, Sulphite, and Paper Mill Workers unions and struck at the Falls, the Fort, and Kenora. The international union, knowing the trends in the industry, ordered the men to return to work and refused to provide strike benefits. Within two weeks an agreement was reached, and 1,500 workers at the three locations were informed the mills would be reopened. The people of the Falls no longer complained about the sulphur smell; they were happy the mills were running. The industry started a slow upward trend, and as the economy improved, workers regained their old wage scale. Except for those working in the woods, relations were quiet for several years.[1]

Harold Reich—Union Organizer

Probably the most prominent individual in the local labor movement during the 1930s through the 1950s was Harold Reich. Born July 26, 1906, Reich was only 14 when he worked in an ILC camp for the 1920–21 season. The next year he helped with work on Koochiching Dam before he started in the paper machine room at the mill August 15, 1922. He joined Papermakers Local 159 in October 1922 and in 1923 became a delegate to the Federated Trades and Labor Assembly. He was elected secretary the following year. He served as a delegate to the assembly for 18 consecutive years, in addition to serving three terms as president of Local 159. Reich held every office in his local and in the assembly. From 1933 through 1936, he was organizer for the AFL in the Falls, and in 1937 he worked in Ohio and on the West Coast organizing locals for the AFL.

Reich was liked by people in and out of the labor movement, which is probably the reason for his success. He apparently was a good compromiser and avoided irritating the opposition. In a letter sent to all organizers, AFL President William Green warned: "You must understand that such work is not always of the most pleasant character, but on the contrary requires much sacrifice. To be an active worker in the Labor Movement . . . means that the ordinary pleasures of life must be often forgone. . . ."

Reich immediately focused on a union label campaign and worked with the clerks in an attempt to reorganize the dormant Retail Clerks Union Local 1281. Next, he concentrated on the Insulite mill employees, because they were not included in any mill unions. By June 1933 he had contacted employees in the sawmill, the planing mill, the green-lumber yards, the dry-lumber yards, and the horse barns; at the log landing; in maintenance; and at the Falls Lumber and Coal Company.

He gained further recognition in 1934, when the Trades and Labor Assembly suggested his name to the local compliance board of the National Recovery Administration. His first duty was to attend a conference in Washington, D.C., to learn the lumber worker codes. This position helped him become acquainted with others outside the labor movement, especially in the government, which later served him in good stead.

He was elated when M & O offered him a salaried position in the payroll department and was granted a 90-day leave of absence to prepare himself for the work. His chief concern was how it would affect his activity in the labor movement, which was his major interest. After three weeks of deliberation he resigned his new position to return to his job as backtender in the paper room.

During May and June 1934, he organized Sawmill Workers Union Local 19614 and Truck Drivers Union Local 230 in the

Fort. His work with the National Recovery Administration, especially dealing with restaurant workers, bartenders, teamsters, and taxicab drivers, intensified. He did not overlook what was taking place inside the union organization, for in July 1934 he informed both Green and Frank Morrison, secretary-treasurer of the AFL, of a salaried local vice president who also was receiving "a substantial salary" as chairman of the grievance committee. He continued: "The family of officers have developed a pork barrel potential machine within the organization and several members have requested me to help in cleaning up the mess."

Reich sought a position with the Minnesota Industrial Commission, because he felt that he could do more to foster improvement of working conditions. This was due in part to his being upset by what he considered slights from "grasping and unencouraging" state union officials, and he protested to national union headquarters in early 1937. He asked for a study of his contribution to the AFL, but he was denied even a trip to a convention, so he submitted his resignation as an organizer. The national leaders apparently realized his worth to them and gave him an assignment organizing for the AFL on the Pacific coast. He was granted a six-month leave of absence from M & O for this work.

In 1939 he sought the office of secretary-treasurer of the International Brotherhood of Paper Makers without success, but in 1946 he was again granted a six-month leave from M & O to help organize a Regional Brotherhood of Paper Makers in New York State. His long-term goals were vacations with pay, re-establishment of the craftsmanship card, a system of learning between industry and unions, and full pensions for aged employees. He felt very much a part of the labor movement and apparently was impressed with Green's statement of March 1934: "In a sense, the National Industrial Recovery Act is the constitution for a new industrial order."[2]

A Union Town

Reich's work paid off, and the Falls became one of the most unionized communities in Minnesota. The Retail Clerks Local 1281, first organized in 1911, was defunct in 1932 when he reactivated it and secured the employers' cooperation in the process, thereby making the Falls' F. W. Woolworth store the first of that national chain to have unionized clerks. The clerks in the Fort recognized Reich's ability and called upon him to organize a clerk's local. Eventually, he also organized the Fort's paper makers, hotel and restaurant employees, and bartenders.

Early in 1933 he laid the groundwork for a teachers' local, and by April 1934 he was in the process of forming Teachers Association Local 331. The painters, decorators, and paper hangers were the next targets of this tireless organizer, followed by local garage mechanics and mechanics working for the city.

His big challenge in 1934 came with the Waitresses and Maids Local 359, because the restaurant owners resisted the unions and formed an association for that purpose. However, prior to a planned strike, 20 restaurant owners submitted to union demands. Reich was assisted by officers of the state office of the National Recovery Administration in overcoming the restaurant owners. They empowered Reich to represent them and also used him as an informant in the Falls.

Because the restaurant owners association was relatively strong, the battle continued for several years, even after closed shop rules became effective January 1, 1935. Weekly wages were set at $10 for waitresses, who were limited to 48 hours and 6 days in any week but received board for 7 days. Dishwashers got $8.00; utility girls, $8.50; and barmaids, $12.00, with 7 days board in all cases. A three-day strike occurred because the Sugar Bowl Confectionery hired non-union help and was picketed, so the restaurant owners countered with a lockout. Before the month was over, the Falls waitresses and barmaids were 100 percent organized with what Reich called "a good group of girls with the right militant, aggressive, and progressive spirit. . . ." Jim Serdaris, one of the early holdouts against unionization, felt that the only change in relations was an occasional union "complainer who could really cause trouble."

Because union sentiment was strong among many of their customers, the proprietors of taverns expressed interest in joining a local. Reich left no stone unturned and signed them under the Hotel and Restaurant Employers and Beverage Dispensers International Alliance of the AFL.

When juke boxes appeared about 1930, the American Federation of Musicians advertised constantly to enroll people in the "Music Defense League as one who deplores the elimination of living music from the theatre program. . . . Mechanical music is fine at home but it hasn't the right kick for a dance." It was not long before Reich organized Musicians Local 156 under the American Federation of Musicians.

By 1935 Reich had led the formation of nine locals and had many more prospects. By 1937 there were 19 strong locals in the Falls and the Fort that looked to him for leadership.

At various times the unions exerted themselves in the community. In 1933 they sponsored an ad in the local paper and suspended a barber who refused to abide by union guidelines. In 1934 the Trades and Labor Assembly petitioned the city council to establish a city liquor dispensary for all liquors stronger than 3.2 percent. A delegation from several unions appeared before the city council to appeal for more employment at the mill. In 1936 the unions again appeared before the city council and asked them to go on record against the employment of married women until the labor market improved. In 1937 members of Government Employees Local 821 asked the council to approve their guidelines for terms, conditions, and wages. Labor officials protested to the council the firing of a union truck driver and the hiring of a person who was not in good standing with his union. They also objected to the hiring of a patrolman who had not been a resident of the city for 12 months. In nearly every case, the union was able to win its point.

A person fresh on the scene in the mid-1930s commented that the unions were well established when he arrived, and the Falls was one of the state's powerful Democratic-Farmer-Labor union towns. Reich requested input from higher authority regarding political activity and received this reply:

> This is a matter over which the Federation has no control nor can give any advice, except that you recognize . . . that every International Union provides . . . [that] members' civil and religious duties and obligations are not interfered with . . . and this freedom must not be interfered with by compulsion exercised in any way through local unions.

Soon Reich received a letter which posed a question and made a suggestion: "Have been wondering why the various crafts at International Falls have not affiliated with the Farmer Labor Association. . . . This would give them representation without having to join, or in other words, without a dual organization for the same purpose. . . ."

Many people in the Falls were caught in the middle and did not want to take sides. The opinion of one such individual was that the unions were a big force which had a stranglehold on the town and that the business people were either immune to them or so afraid that they would not resist. Another added, "One of the reasons I am leaving town is the stranglehold the unions have on everything. Most people, including union members, dislike it, but no one speaks about it except in private. . . ." The Falls was clearly a union town, and, ironically, the founder of the town's basic industry probably was as responsible as anyone for making it so.[3]

The IWW

One of the most vicious periods of labor activity, nationally and locally, fell between 1916 and 1923, when the Industrial Workers of the World (IWW) attempted to seize the lumber camps and take control of labor. Founded by Socialists in 1905, the IWW sought to organize unskilled workers, abolish the wage system, and destroy capitalism. The organization was effectively destroyed nationwide by 1920, but locally some of its followers continued to work in the camps until 1923. There were two distinct periods of major activity in the north woods, referred to as the "red" scare—the first between 1916 and 1917 and the second during the 1919–20 season.

Elizabeth Monahan, writing to her mother in January 1916, described some of the activity. About 450 IWW men were in the Falls, and more came at the rate of about 200 a day. They had closed down 10 camps and idled 1,000 men between Gemmell and Northome and agitated for the shutdown of the mill. "They won't let a man go to work on pain of death." The mayor closed the soft drink parlors, and the business community debated how to react to their presence.

The IWW demands included: $60 a month wages, free hospital and doctor of the workers' choosing, authority for the camp cook to "order all supplies without question," and a seven-hour work day, which included going to and coming from work in daylight. When the sheriff, along with 25 deputies, went to Gemmell, "The IWWs told him there would be no disorder but the first man who went to work would be dead in one minute and for the deputies to mind their own business and go home." There were about 450 IWWs at Gemmell, so the sheriff left, but returned the following day with more deputies. At the Falls, where there was talk of a riot, the IWWs were arrested on any pretext. Except for the fact that the IWWs had hit the camps of VRL, their activities surprised ILC leaders, and they were unprepared to cope with them.

IWW activity the following season was even worse, as armed agitators toured the big camps proclaiming a general strike and "driving lumberjacks away from work by the thousands." Again, the IWWs effectively shut down production at VRL camps and moved on to ILC camps. In two days in January 1917 they drove over 1,000 men from ILC camps, and then moved to Crookston Lumber Company camps. All through the north woods the IWWs met trains to turn lumberjacks away. They proclaimed that the workers would own the camps and mills if they struck, and sang, "It is outrageous to work for wages."

The price of pulpwood rose from $4 to $9 a cord in less than two years. How much of that was due to IWW activity and how much to inflation caused by wartime pressures is uncertain. Despite the IWW activity, 1917 was the year of largest production ever for the giant ILC sawmill in the Falls.

It was not until February 1917, after a large number of leaders were convicted and sentenced at Duluth and Virginia, that the tide turned against the IWW. The Minnesota legislature appropriated $50,000 a year for two years for deployment of deputies by the governor to put down labor disorders. Deputies were placed on trains and stationed at depots to meet workmen and escort them to camp.

By late March, the last IWWs left the camps, promising to return in the summer after the log drive and again in the fall to close "the blankety blank sawmills." The lumber companies armed their night watchmen with automatic weapons in an effort to guard against those threats. In Bemidji, bands of citizens drove IWWs out of town but not before Mill No. 1 of the Crookston Lumber Company, which had been having trouble with the IWW, was burned, throwing 300 men out of work. Shortly after the fire broke out, "a number of men were seen crawling around the west end of the yard," prompting 150 Bemidji citizens, armed with clubs, to visit the IWW headquarters. Thirty men and one woman were forced to leave town on the train. In reaction to the fire at Bemidji, the U.S. Attorney General called all Minnesota attorneys general together to "make plans to suppress the menace."

When the nation became more involved in World War I, it was apparent to IWW leaders that the populace would not tolerate any activity that hindered the war effort. This resulted in less disturbance in the area, until the fall of 1919. Billy Noonan wrote: "Some of those IWWs will fight for anything—except their country." The lumber companies were better prepared for the troublemakers and had assistance from another element unfriendly to the IWWs. The returned veterans were almost solidly opposed to their actions and were not afraid to confront them. By then the IWW had a Canadian branch, and leaders moved back and forth across the border to flee from the law as the occasion demanded. Correspondence between the IWW in the United States and the One Big Union (OBU), as it was referred to in Canada, was intercepted by Canadian Mounted Police.

Still another factor entered the local IWW activity. The IWW's efforts in the Centralia, Washington, area had so aroused the citizens there that many leaders left for the Dakota harvest fields and the Minnesota lumber camps. As an observer with the National Guard, that had been called to the Falls to cope with the MD & W strike, Frankel suggested that the lumberjacks were a "fertile mental field and wonderful soil in which to plant the seed of discontent. . . ." He commented that they were buried in the woods in the dead of winter "with no amusements, far away from all civilization, not educated, as a rule, sufficiently to even read or spend leisure hours in reading, . . . spending their leisure time listening to whoever will talk to them. Many have left families behind, are homesick, blue and out of humor."

All the lumberjack had to do to change his way of life was purchase a red card for $1.50 to $3.00. The IWW delegates worked on the camp cook first, because, next to the foreman, he was the most influential person in camp. If the cook did not freely join the IWW, bribing, coercing, and even threat of death were tried. If the cook signed, he was used to work on others. One story that circulated was that if the lumberjacks did not sign, "the cooks might put rats in their soup."

Fortunately for ILC, Sam Hazlitt, general foreman for six camps in the southern part of their territory, experienced some trouble in the 1918–19 season and succeeded in driving out most of the troublemakers. He avoided problems by hiring men from Chicago, St. Paul, and Duluth instead of men who drifted into camp. Hazlitt's good work greatly reduced problems for ILC in 1919–20. The delegates for IWW concentrated in the small towns near the camps rather than in the larger centers. They often allied themselves with prostitutes and blind piggers to gain their influence and persuaded them to deny admission to lumberjacks unless they presented a red card or purchased one.

Among the leaders of the IWW in the 1919–20 season were

one ex-convict and other "notorious leaders," who promised that they would seize all the properties of Backus in the Falls and the Fort and of Shevlin-Carpenter in Virginia, the Iron Range, and other eastern Minnesota logging firms. The only local person named as an IWW activist was Arthur Thorne, of Baudette; apparently the others all were outsiders.

National Guard agents worked undercover in an attempt to determine any IWW move, locate the major IWW centers of activity, and identify community leaders who aided the IWW. They reported to the Guard by their code number only.

IWW locals were formed in Gemmell and Mizpah. Hoyt's Hotel, the headquarters at Gemmell, was described as a rough place. Agent 41 planned to sleep there but found it "too cold and dirty." The men were charged $0.25 a night; most slept with their clothes on. The patrons were chiefly Finns and Russians, "who are all IWW." August Wilhelm, a barber and a German Socialist, also had a restaurant and rented rooms at Gemmell. Apparently he led activities at Gemmell and Northome. Lumberjacks could obtain IWW information at Gosline's store and blind pig, but in the process they often were made intoxicated and then separated from their money in poker games. The Joneses' Restaurant and Soft Drink Parlor, "a real dive," and the Merchants Hotel were the two chief IWW centers in Northome.

The IWW was aware of the National Guard agents but was never sure of their identity. Agent 29 was accepted as a member of IWW Local 500 in Gemmell, and agent 70 was given a handbook of the IWW by someone who suspected him. Agent 41 reported from Gemmell that Louis Hoover, the chief organizer there, seemed more interested in selling moonshine than in soliciting memberships, but he was heard to say, "What do we care what the men do as long as we get the money?" A Finn in Mizpah said, "One big union means more money, short hours or one big fire." The agents observed that generally those who had worked with ILC for 8 or 10 years did not accept the IWW line, nor did the returning veterans, but the younger lumberjacks seemed most susceptible. One veteran lumberjack posed the question to an IWW delegate attempting to get his membership:

> Why can't your delegates meet the government and con-
> gress like the delegates of the A. F. L. and other decent labor
> unions? What have you done for your members except making
> outlaws out of them? You say you want to better the working
> condition for the men working in the woods. It seems to me

you are kind of late. The woods are all gone in this state and so is the lumberjack. I intend to work here without paying you [IWW] anything for the privilege.

When trouble was suspected in one of the southern camps east of Northome, 5 guard officers and 13 expert riflemen were selected to tour the camps. There were two purposes for this tour: to check housing and food conditions in the camps to determine if there was cause for complaint, and to make the Guard's presence known to possibly squelch the chance of any outbreak. They observed places where IWW people had written "Join the IWW" in red on walls and learned that some members had made knives of discarded files and practiced throwing them. They also saw that large numbers of men were waiting to take the place of those who went on a strike, if the IWW managed to call one. They were welcomed in Northome, because the deputy sheriff had difficulty getting deputies. The pay was only $3.50 a day, and men did not want to take the risk for that pay.

Near the end of December 1919, the IWW delegates became more cautious as to whom they approached for membership. They stopped work in the camps during the week but went there only on Sunday, because that was the only day men were free to talk with them. Often they were seen leaving Monday morning with a few new recruits. More and more the lumberjacks concluded that the delegates were chiefly concerned about getting their money, but the peak of activity seemed to have passed.

The big "blow off," as the IWW's called their takeover, was first planned from December 23, 1919, then the 31st, and finally January 7. But after a meeting in Minneapolis, all plans for a takeover were canceled. That cancellation coincided with the nationwide demise of the IWW, but the movement still continued locally. The officer in charge of gathering information for the National Guard expressed the feeling that if the Guard had not been on hand, the "reds" would have taken over. One IWW delegate was overheard to say, "We are perfectly willing to buck the city and county authorities, but when it comes to them [*sic*] steel bayonets, me for Canada."

The lumber companies formed a Minnesota Loggers' Association aimed at maintaining uniform wage rates and passing information among members. In 1922 ILC had 2,500 men in the woods at $35 a month for general work, and about the middle of the season ran into difficulty securing new workers for less than $40. The pressure came from nearby eastern VRL camps, which paid $40. On December 26, 1922, Industrial Union Local 120 of the IWW called a strike in ILC camps. Posters listing demands read:

1. That all class war prisoners be released.

2. That we demand an eight-hour day from camp to camp. And the scale of wages be $50 low.

3. That we receive a payday twice a month in the form of a bank check or cash, according to state law.

4. In case of sickness or accident that the person or persons get medical attention at once.

5. That all camps be made sanitary including bath house, wash house and drying room.

6. That wholesome food be furnished.

Jim Sedore, an operative for ILC in the 1922–23 season who posed as a forest service man, wrote: [his writing]

i have looked things over and removed the caus of some of the trouble. . . . i hear they are framing up something in Bemidji for 91 [camp 91]. i am going down and see if i can get on to what it is and ship back up from there.

They know there is a man up here but dont know who it is. i am supposed to be a Forrest Service man looking after the burning of brush. it works until they spot me then there wil be no use in me staying as i wil get no more information and might have to shoot one or two of them they are sure to spot me. . . . here is a list of the men responsible for the trouble so far. all i. w. w.

He listed 40 names and designated who the agitators or leaders were. This list was quickly sent to all camp foremen, along with news that trouble was planned for February 10, 1923. Individuals on the scene in 1923 related their impressions of the IWW activity. It appears that most of the IWW agitators after 1920 came from other areas. The local men did not care for them and said that they "presented a nervous problem more than a real threat." Another former lumberjack recalled their motto, "Wooden heads for wooden beds," but was quick to add that the companies soon provided steel beds, improved facilities for bathing and laundry, and a greater variety of food.

The companies apparently realized that improved conditions were the best and least expensive way to minimize problems. In addition to the improved conditions, there was more freedom and less pressure in the work schedule. A career lumberjack felt that the "Wobblies" (IWW) helped the men unionize. "It was a just case of where they had to get organized."

Labor conditions stabilized for a period of time after the IWW disappeared. However, in the late 1930s, several events took place that drastically changed the method of harvesting the forest; consequently, the lumber camp era ended. The independent logger had far different relations with his workers than M & O.[4]

ENDNOTES FOR CHAPTER XI

1. Hendee interview; Arvid Peterson interview; Paul Anderson interview; Hnatuik interview; Arnold Johnson interview; Fritz interview; correspondence between Harold Reich and George Lawson, E. B. Hall, John Burke, and William Green, Reich file, KCHS, hereafter Reich file. Reich was an organizer for the American Federation of Labor and by far the most significant labor leader in the community for many years. Although its dates are from March 15, 1933, to March 21, 1935, the file contains many articles, clippings, and letters up to the 1960s. Address by Matthew J. Burns, May 1, 1960, Reich file; *The Press*, August 8, 1910, July 27, August 17, 1911; *The Minneapolis Journal*, March 10, 1911; Kooch. Comm., January 2, April 3, 1917; Tive interview; Malerich interview; Rasmussen interview; Alexander interview; *The Baudette Region*, September 30, 1917, May 28, 1919, May 7, 1920; Frankel, pp. 1, 2, 5, 7–10, 18, 20, 21, 25; *The Journal*, January 29, February 12, 26, March 18, 1920, May 10, 1923, March 5, 1930, January 31, February 24, April 17, 20, 21, 1933, May 1, 3, 14, 1934, May 6, 1937, January 15, 1938; *The Northome Record*, May 16, 1919, March 19, April 30, 1920, April 15, 1921; Schneider interview.

2. Correspondence between Reich and William Green, Frank Morrison, John Burke, George Lawson, Sawmill Local 18242, C. T. McMurray, E. J. Chilgren, and Endorsement Committee Local 159, Reich file; *The Journal*, January 2, 17, 1934.

3. Correspondence between Reich and C. C. Coulter, Florence Hanson, G. D. Hargrove, J. C. Allen, George Lawson, Lewis Dillion Peterson, E. A. Scallen, Anne Dickie Olesen, Robert B. Hesketh, William Green, and Frank Morrison, Reich file; *The Journal*, February 3, 17, 1930, March 9, July 14, 1933, April 22, 1937; Ruby Erickson interview; Serdaris interview; Bert Johnson interview; interview of Peter Hemstad, International Falls, July 20, 1979; interview of Neil Hardina, International Falls, June 19, 1979; City Council, December 3, 1934, May 11, 1936, June 21, 1937; Paul Anderson interview.

4. Letter from Elizabeth Monahan to her mother, January 2, 1916, Christie letters; *The Baudette Region*, January 4, 11, 18, February 1, March 1, 22, July 19, 26, August 2, 9, 16, 1917; *The Northome Record*, February 9, 1917, December 26, 1919, February 13, December 10, 1920; Frankel, pp. 3–6, 8, 10–14, 30, 32–33, 35, 37, 39, 42, 49, 52–53, 57, 60; ILC file; Northern Logging Congress correspondence, ILC file; correspondence between ILC and camp foremen, posters of IWW, ILC file; Jim Sedore file, KCHS, hereafter Sedore file; Scott Erickson interview; Gerber interview; Miller interview; Costley interview.

CHAPTER XII

Adjusting to the Wilderness

IN THE FIRST THREE DECADES of the 1900s, settlers generally fought a losing battle against the wilderness. They had expected to carry on traditional agriculture, which was still looked upon as a way of life and part of the American dream. In that respect, those who violated the Homestead Act by cutting the timber, pocketing the cash, and leaving their property were the gainers. At least they avoided any prolonged agony for their families. For others, it took three decades of suffering to learn that Nature would not yield and that they had to adjust to her.

Before the change in thinking was complete, a few events took place in the northern border country which helped to determine the ultimate purpose of the area. First, a conflict occurred between those who wanted to use the timber in the traditional sense and those who preferred to let it stand for recreation. Second, with the Depression of the 1930s, national funds supported a major conservation effort to deal with the forest and pointed the way to a more stable future. Third, also related to activities in coping with the Depression, a program of forest management was begun which blended with the previous two developments to strengthen the resource base.

The Developer vs. the Environmentalist

E. W. Backus upset people because he let no one stand in the path of his dreams. His thinking about the future of the area and how he could use it was far beyond the comprehension of most of his contemporaries. That alone would not have created a problem, except for his complete disregard of others. His plans for the area can be traced to 1895, when he first obtained permission to build Koochiching Dam, which was quickly followed by approval for a dam at Kettle Falls.

From October 25, 1905, when the coffer dam was finished,

Backus was able to control water levels to maximize its effectiveness. From March 1909 to 1930, the water level of Rainy Lake was artificially controlled at 1,101.61 to 1,108.61 feet above sea level. Basically, there was little argument with the practice, because nearly everyone appreciated that water control was essential to the mill's success. But as the mill grew, the demand for more water power—by far the cheapest energy—also increased. The mill eventually became so large that the dam provided only 25 percent of its total power requirements. To satisfy his wants, Backus visualized a series of 16 dams, beginning with North Lake along the border, nearly 500 feet higher than Koochiching Dam, to impound billions of feet of water to generate power for the mills at the Falls, the Fort, Kenora, and Keewatin.

At the same time, events were already taking place that would prevent his dreams from materializing. In 1909 the Ontario government set aside about 1 million acres as the Quetico Forest Reserve. President Theodore Roosevelt responded by setting aside 1.5 million acres as the Superior National Forest. During the following years, individuals living along Rainy Lake, Rainy River, and Lake of the Woods complained about the water level, because it affected their homes, farming, navigation, or fishing. Later studies would prove that there was less fluctuation of the water level under controlled conditions than there was in the natural state, but that is not what the residents perceived, and they wanted something done about it. This created an emotional conflict between two opposing points of view.

In 1910 the Minnesota Canal and Power Company received a permit to divert water from Birch Lake—one of many in the chain of lakes that make up the border—to develop a power system for Duluth. Such a plan would reduce the amount of power available for Backus, who immediately filed a protest with the federal government. No more was heard of the plan. The next move in Backus' plan came when Congressman Clarence Miller introduced a bill to authorize the United States to build a dam across the outlet of Namakan Lake at Kettle Falls. Such action had been authorized earlier, but because the time limit had expired, new legislation was required.

Next, Backus interfered with navigation along the Rainy River by building a boom at Loman and had suits brought against him to recover damages to state land caused by his actions. Fourteen years later those suits still had not reached the courts. Prior to

1920, the International Boundary Commission made an extended study of the border to determine what was best for water power, agriculture, fishing, lumbering, shipping, and recreation purposes. The conclusion was that the most people could benefit if the level of Lake of the Woods could be kept between 1,054 and 1,061 feet. Backus was free to control the water levels; the Commission would step in only if they were not kept between those figures.

The decision about the level of Lake of the Woods was not necessarily part of the conflict that developed between Backus and environmentalists relative to what happened from Koochiching Falls east, but feelings were aroused along the entire border. Much of the ill will was caused by the indifference of Backus to any complaints. When talk was heard in 1925 that some of his ideas could cause water levels to rise anywhere from 3 to 82 feet, the public became increasingly concerned. The battle heated up when Backus issued a 30-page report in which he stated he was "considerably entertained" to learn of the "dire calamity" his projects would create. He was convinced that they would be a "detriment to no one."

Ernest C. Oberholtzer, of Davenport, Iowa, came to Rainy Lake about 1909. He had an entirely different view than Backus had of the wilderness country. He envisioned it as a spot to be enjoyed by future generations, whose working life would be spent primarily in an urban setting. Oberholtzer, unlike Backus, did not have an abrasive personality. This factor helped those who sided with him win their battle. His ideas about preserving the wilderness were not shared by a large sector of society in the early 1900s, but the efforts of President Theodore Roosevelt got the nation thinking about conservation. Oberholtzer devoted his life to the cause, relying on income from articles and speeches, conducting canoe trips to the wilderness, and being subsidized by those who appreciated his efforts. His great reward came with the satisfaction of seeing the Quetico-Superior region preserved as a large national playground.

The controversy between Backus and Oberholtzer was fully developed by 1925, when the latter made his first presentation against the former at an International Joint Commission hearing. During the 1920s, a group led by Frank Hubachek, Welles Eastman, John Reynolds, William Dorr, Wilbur Tusler, and others, all of Minneapolis, worked very quietly to establish an organization to stop Backus. Oberholtzer was their front and the most visible opponent. By 1927 this group had the backing of the Minnesota Conservation Council, which included many conservationist groups, in addition to the Boy Scouts, the Girl Scouts, the League of Minnesota Municipalities, the Minnesota Forestry Association, the American Legion, the Legion Auxiliary, the Minnesota Federation of Women's Clubs, the Minnesota Farm Bureau Federation, the Minnesota Arrowhead Association, and others. Eventually, 80 civic clubs in Minneapolis supported the Izaak Walton League, one of the key groups in the Council. In November 1927, Oberholtzer was elected permanent chair of the Quetico-Superior Council and was obviously the point man for the organization against Backus. His two closest co-workers, Hubachek and Sigrid Olson, a wilderness writer, were backed by individuals with the inside connections and money-raising ability needed to conduct the campaign. Backus publicly stated that the campaign was more of an attempt to get at him than an effort to block water power. It was apparent that his Rainy Lake neighbor bothered him.

In 1929, when the Shipstead-Newton bill (later the Shipstead-Nolan Act) was first presented, the Falls city council opposed it because it favored no increase of water power and they feared it would hinder progress. The council's resolution claimed that the bill would "perpetuate a great injustice to the pioneers of said territory for the sole purpose of affording pleasure to a few adventurous scions of wealth and leisure to spend a few weeks in summer recreation. . . ." The vote was four favoring the resolution and two opposed.

The city council's vote was a result of a change in the position of the Minnesota Federation of Labor, which initially opposed the Backus plan for more dams and then in a convention in the Falls asked its delegates to oppose the Shipstead-Newton bill. This change in position was in response to testimony by members of the Falls Trades and Labor Assembly. Except for an occasional editorial from the M & O–owned *Journal*, that was about the only support, except for some Duluth power interests, that Backus appeared to have.

In the 1928 election campaign, Republican politicians avoided a direct connection with Backus, who was said to be as popular as a "nest of hornets at a picnic." Because Herbert Hoover was a conservationist, Backus supported Frank Lowden for the Republican presidential nomination. State newspapers declared that was a direct asset for Hoover. This came at a time when Backus was at the peak of his power, with estimated holdings of $100 million.

The turning point in the battle came when the Shipstead-Nolan Act was passed in July 1930. This measure set aside public land among the northern boundary waters for a national park and prohibited the development of water power in the Superior National Forest without the consent of Congress. The act was a cornerstone for future conservation activity.

The victory did not come without expenses, and funds were not easily raised after October 1929. Oberholtzer used his limited personal assets to carry on. By 1930 he was considering selling his property on Rainy Lake. In a letter to L. P. Lemieux, of the Koochiching County Abstract Company, he said:

> There is no telling when I shall ever be able to live again on Rainy Lake. I have never been interested in real estate transactions. I merely want a place where I can be sure that I will not be molested when Rainy Lake begins to be crowded with tourists. The little island out in the channel has always appealed to me as a possible refuge, if my present location begins to be too closely hemmed in by neighbors. Moreover, I have large debts which can be adjusted more easily by turning over whatever I have at Rainy Lake as part payment for my notes with the understanding that I shall always be able to go to the Lake and enjoy my old haunts and that some day, when I am able, I shall be permitted to buy back these small reminders of my long association with the Lake.

On March 1, 1931, Backus received a second blow when he could not raise money to pay certain financial obligations, and M & O was forced into bankruptcy. However, he continued his fight as if he were still in full control, even after 1933 when the International Joint Commission decided against his proposals. In March 1934, seven months before a fatal heart attack, he was still battling Oberholtzer in Washington, D.C. Oberholtzer wrote of Backus to Judge John Brown, in the Falls: "He is holding forth at the Cosmos Club, where all the scientists and government men congregate, and seems to be settled permanently with his staff—very much like a separate government of his own."

Backus fought to the end. As was written 17 years after his death by one who knew him, "He could be brutal, remorseless, ruthless, and not always (to say the least) ethical. . . . His personality was such that he could obtain a respectful hearing before distinguished political groups of men on both sides of the international border."

The water development battle continued for years after Backus' death. However, the bitterness of the campaign was over once he was no longer involved, because the issue was not as personal to the receivership officers and the restructured M & O. A far more complete story of this episode is found in *Saving Quetico-Superior: A Land Set Apart*, by R. Newell Searle. The story did not end in 1934; the battle continued for several decades.[1]

The Civilian Conservation Corps

On March 31, 1933, the Civilian Conservation Corps (CCC) Reforestation Relief Act was passed as an unemployment relief measure to provide work for 250,000 jobless men between the ages of 18 and 25. It was one of the more successful measures passed during the early years of the New Deal. Fortunately for the area of this study, the CCC provided some very practical solutions to immediate problems that were not being addressed because of indifference and/or lack of funds. It also helped to point a new direction in utilizing the forest. The act specifically listed reforestation, road construction, soil erosion prevention, flood control, and national park improvement. Most of the activity was classified as emergency conservation work. In northern Minnesota, recently abandoned lumber camp sites were used, because they already had wells and roads.

Army and forestry personnel directed planning for the camps and worked closely with local citizens, who were familiar with the area and had experience in the woods. The army was in charge of providing the men with food, clothing, housing, and health care. In a typical camp of 200 men, about 30 military personnel served as cooks, orderlies, hospital attendants, clerks, mail-truck drivers, and supply-truck drivers. The forestry department provided a camp superintendent, four general foremen, an engineer, one or two trained foresters, a game manager, a carpenter, and other specialists.

In April 1933, it was announced that Minnesota's initial quota was 5,250 men. On May 1, 1933, the forest supervisor at Cass Lake was informed that he would be getting a contingent of 800 men to serve in four camps. A few days later army officers and foresters arrived to pick the camp sites and make preparations for the men.

The first camp in northern Minnesota opened June 11, 1933, and it was the last one to close, late in November 1941. Before the Minnesota program was complete, there were 30 State Forest Camps, 30 Federal Forest Service Camps, and a few soil conservation camps. Nationally, there eventually were 4,000 camps that had 500,000 men at the peak. Before the program came to an end, over 2 million men had spent some time in the CCC. Individuals signed up for three-month hitches and then could quit or continue as they saw fit. Initially, the turnover was very low, because employment opportunities were not promising. That changed in the late 1930s as the economy improved prior to World War II, and only weeks before Pearl Harbor, the CCC was discontinued.

Tents were used to house the men until more permanent structures of Insulite were built. The military had used Insulite for its camps in World War I and found that it provided easy-to-build but relatively sturdy buildings not intended to last many years. Some camps where the buildings survived were used to house prisoners of war during World War II.

Originally, all Minnesota camps were directed out of St. Paul, but later the headquarters was transferred to Park Rapids. Then local headquarters were established to operate in either state or national park areas. In 1908 the Minnesota National Forest was created east of Bemidji. It included parts of Beltrami, Cass, and Itasca counties. In 1928 it was renamed Chippewa National Forest and was managed by the Forest Service until May 1933, when the CCC took over. The Forest Service had merely maintained fire control and timber sales in the three ranger districts, but new things were in store for the park under the CCC. Camps were initially erected at Cass Lake, Bena, Winnibigoshish Dam, and Cut Foot Sioux. Most of the forest was surrounded by cut-over and burned-out timber land. However, before the CCC was finished in the Chippewa National Forest, the original 4 camps were increased to 23, the area of the forest was doubled, and productivity was greatly enhanced.

Farther north, camps were established at the following locations: northwest of Big Falls in the Pine Island State Forest; east of Big Falls; east of Grand Falls station, along the Big Fork River; 16 miles southeast of Big Falls; southwest of Littlefork; at Nett Lake, exclusively for Indians; and at Effie. Lake of the Woods County had Camp 723, south of Faunce; Norris camp, with about 30 buildings, 15 miles southwest of Williams; and Hiwood—all in the Beltrami Island State Forest. To the east, in St. Louis County, camps were located at Cusson, at Side Lake, at Vermilion River, at Angor-Idington, east of Ray near Kabetogama, and in the Superior National Forest.

Scott Erickson's firm was contracted to furnish materials and direct the construction of several camps on the western edge of St. Louis County. Even though most of the men were young and inexperienced, they worked well and fast. Their motivation was that as soon as the buildings were finished, they could fold their tents and move into the structures.

Walter Zatochill's experience was very typical of that of many young men who went into the CCC. As sole support of a family of five, his mother earned about $50 a month by doing housework and laundry for others. Zatochill and his brother, Bill, worked on farms and gave their mother and younger siblings whatever funds they could spare. Zatochill made $20 a month, plus room and board, working at his farm job in southern Minnesota. As soon as the CCC was established, Bill joined and was in the first group to leave Fort Snelling for the north woods in June 1933. He drove a truck to Cusson, and his company spent their first winter living in tents, because they had to build a camp from scratch. He liked the CCC and remained with the organization for its entire history. When the CCC was terminated in 1941, he drove a truck to the various camps to pick up the usable equipment and records, which he hauled to Grand Rapids for storage and safekeeping.

When Zatochill received a letter from his brother stating that Bill got all his clothes, food, shelter, and medical attention, plus $5 spending money and $25, which was sent to his mother, Zatochill decided to join. He entered the CCC in April 1934. His company traveled by train from Fort Snelling to Ray. The snow was still waist deep in the woods, and some men from St. Paul refused to get off the train. They were taken by truck 10 miles northeast to a site a few miles south of Lake Kabetogama. Their camp of 400 men was S-81, Company 724, Davenport Barracks.

The camp had four barracks, each furnished with double-deck bunks and toilets. A separate building housed the shower facilities. The barracks were heated by large barrel stoves, which were kept going at night by the person who had fire-guard duty, but they were not warm on the coldest nights. The buildings were laid out in a star-shaped design under one roof so that it was possible to move from one to another without going outside. A five-bed hospital was staffed by a first-aid person and a doctor, who came on a fixed schedule or when called. The dining hall was a separate building adjacent to a recreation building, which included the camp exchange and postal facilities. Three other buildings, removed from each other and the cluster of living quarters, were the garage, a blacksmith shop, and a place for the electrical generator.

Zatochill's first observation was that the place was "spick and span." He was often hungry at home, "but the food in camp was good and *all you wanted.*" He said, "We lived like kings compared to home." The breakfast menu was pancakes, bacon, pork links, milk, and fruit. At noon there were vegetables, the very best grade of meat, pies, doughnuts, "and all the milk you wanted." He emphatically added, "Supper was more of the same. . . . The Cs were for hardship families."

When a new group arrived at camp, they were held apart from the others until they had their shots and basic training. "We were treated just like in the army—regular inspections . . . and we had to be in on working nights at 10:00 P.M." Anyone missing bed check was assigned latrine duty the next day. Zatochill liked his turns at K.P. because he always got extra food.

The average camp day started with bugle call at 6:00 A.M. and departure for the job site at 8:00, usually by truck. Hot lunch was delivered to the woods at noon, and the workers were returned to camp at 4:00 P.M. Zatochill, who had worked long, hard hours on a dairy farm, found the 8:00 A.M. to 4:00 P.M. schedule "a snap," but lots of city boys hated it. "They weren't hungry enough to put up with the CCC routine," he said with a bit of sarcasm. "They had never had an axe in their hand before." The men could spend from 4:00 P.M. until lights out as they wished. Every camp had a school room, where training courses were offered for mechanics, truck and tractor operation, office clerks, supply and tool clerks, fire fighting, road building, and firebreak construction. The men attended the classes if they chose.

Camp recreation consisted of movies at least once each week, boxing matches, swimming, table games, pool, letter writing, and calisthenics. On weekends there were organized activities, such as softball, baseball, and touchball. Once or twice a month, girls were brought in for dances. On other weekends the men were chaperoned to dances at neighboring communities. Most camps had nearby clergy, who took turns holding services. Peter Onstad, who served congregations around Littlefork, traveled to the Pine Island camp east of Big Falls and also to the camp at Effie on a regular basis. Unlike the lumberjacks, the CCC youth caused few disturbances because they were chaperoned and were under threat of discipline.

Most persons remembered the CCC personnel as well behaved and happy to get to small villages, such as Big Falls, Ray, or Baudette, just for the experience. It was news when a group of blacks from a camp near Warroad came to the Falls one weekend for shopping.

Marian Crabtree Peterson was 15 when a camp was built 1½ miles south of Faunce. Even though the only building in Faunce was a combination beer joint and store, with gas pumps, and the Crabtrees' living quarters, the CCC men often walked there just to "have a beer or pop" and visit. Marian recalled that most came because they were lonesome and wanted to visit with someone outside of camp.

The business places at Ray received some patronage from the CCC personnel, but since it was on a U.S. highway to the Falls, the men generally went there. Many who had never been out of the state crossed the bridge to the Fort so that they could say they had been in a foreign country. Trucks went to nearby towns each weekend, and all one had to do to get a ride was sign the roster. If the return truck was missed, the men took the train or hitchhiked back to Ray and then walked to camp.

Zatochill's camp was 28 miles from the Falls, and most of the men he knew went there only about once every two months. He visited his brother at Cusson, only 30 miles away, a couple times during the 18 months that he was in the CCC. Gappa's Landing, the nearest resort on Lake Kabetogama, was only three miles from Davenport Camp, and once in a while the men walked there for a beer or just to see the lake. Generally, most of the men were not used to much excitement and were sufficiently involved with activities at the camp (plus the food was so good) that they were content to stay there.

Most of the work performed by the CCC was directed toward forest improvement. The men built fire trails, fire towers, telephone lines, and dams and bridges, laid corduroy roads in the swamps, cleared underbrush, removed dead trees, burned brush in winter, planted thousands of trees, counted wild game, surveyed lakes, constructed contour and soils maps, determined oxygen and food content of lakes, recorded fish growth, planted fish, and thinned and pruned trees. They also fought fires set by campers, by lightning, or by farmers who wanted to clear land the least expensive way. They searched for people who became lost while hunting, berry picking, or hiking in the woods. The right-of-way for Highway No. 11 east of the Falls to the end of the trail was cleared by CCC personnel. They also spread poison bait along Rainy Lake when an army worm invasion occurred in 1936. The jobs varied, and no detail lasted long, so it was never tiring to those who appreciated the opportunity. In some camps there was so much activity planned that those who operated machinery, such as road equipment or tree planters, worked split shifts, from daylight to noon and from noon to dark. If the temperature was colder than 20 degrees below zero, they did not have to do woods work.

Zatochill had a unique opportunity to experience life in the wild when he was one of 16 men selected to spend 6 weeks on an island on the north side of the Kabetogama Reservoir in what was referred as a "side camp." There were 12 regular CCC enlistees, a forester, a cook, and 2 leaders. They used a scow to cross Kabetogama, with two horses, backpacks, tools, and enough food for one week at a time. Their job was to build fire trails around the island. Each week the supply scow met them at a pre-arranged point with another week's supplies. They slept in the open for the six weeks, except when they found buildings at old logging camps. They drank lake water the entire time.

When they first got to the island, it was so free of flies and mosquitoes that they wore only shorts and shoes as they worked. Once the deer flies and mosquitoes arrived, they had to be fully dressed, including face nets. The men took turns on a "side detail," which involved shooting a deer or catching fish to "spice up the already good meals." The only bad memory of those six weeks was some heavy rain and wind storms, but the workers were compensated by receiving a keg of beer every two weeks when the supply scow arrived. Zatochill commented with a grin, "It wasn't exactly permitted, but who was going to find out?"

The accomplishments of the CCC have remained for succeeding generations to enjoy. Most of the men who enlisted in the Corps have good memories of that time. This is especially true of those who were destitute and appreciated the opportunity the CCC provided. Walter Zatochill, at age 76, remained a strong booster of the CCC for what it meant to him, his brother, and his mother. Those who lived in the area of the camps generally enjoyed their association with what they considered good people. The business generated by the camps was especially appreciated by the entertainment establishments and by the farmers who sold vegetables. Not much milk or meat produced locally went to the camps, because government standards were too high for local farmers to meet.

The CCC opened the eyes of many people to the possibilities of a better future through improved forest management, and thereby had a profound impact on the attitudes of local settlers involved with the forest. Complaints from the local citizens when the camps were being discontinued is probably the best evidence about how much they were appreciated, not only for their business but for the work they did.

More than a half-century later, most of the camp sites have disappeared, but there are a few monuments to the work of the CCC, such as the fire tower that rises 168 feet above the water from a rock outcropping near Black Bay. Camp Robideau, east of Blackduck, has been preserved as a historic site. More importantly, there is an improved forest that can be enjoyed by generations to come.[2]

Coping with Hardship

Any area with resources based on a single industry which relies on many unskilled workers is destined to experience cycles that cause a hardship on the work force. The northern border country, relying on timber and having limited alternate opportunities (as was the case during the decades covered by this history), had its share of needy to care for. Except for a few brief periods, some of which were self-inflicted strikes, the mill workers were well-off by contrast with the woods workers, who often arrived broke and left broke. If they could not get work as soon as they arrived, they were destitute.

The minutes of the Koochiching County commissioners' meetings are filled with accounts of providing for the homeless, some of whom were not yet American citizens. Records from the "poor farm" (the county home) indicate that from 1909 to 1935, over 42 percent of all who registered there were foreign-born and often had no relatives in this country. In the first years the reason for enrollment was given. Consumptive, insane, aged, worn out, destitute, blind, frozen feet, shingles, lost legs, and rupture were common ailments listed, along with standard diseases of the time. In one year, 10 out of the 29 who entered the facility died there. Discounting a few children and women, most residents were single males, who ranged in age from 15 to 86. Many of the older ones were lumberjacks who could no longer get a job and had no place to turn. The peak year in that respect indicated that 52 out of the 60 admitted were over 60 years of age. The county records contain many notations of individuals who died in their hotels, in their rooming houses, or on the streets and were buried at county expense. For the three decades covered, the standard fee allowed for burial and a wooden casket was $20 to $30.

To cope with these problems, the Koochiching Relief Association was formed in 1925, and all communities in the county were invited to send two delegates to the Falls to determine how to raise money and how to investigate those who were reported to be in need. The idea was noble, but the task was too great to handle, so little came of the efforts. The counties going through financial restructuring under the watchful eye of the state were limited as to how they could spend their revenues, but funds had to be provided for welfare. Koochiching County's general fund was limited to $70,000 because of state refinancing.

In 1930, during a shutdown in the woods, the Falls police were instructed to use the city hall as a shelter for the unemployed. When the problem lingered, the city purchased stumpage on 160 acres of timber land for $262.50 and furnished the unemployed needy with saws and axes to clear the land. The number who applied to work varied from 30 to 80 each week. They received from $3.50 to $33.00 for the week, depending on the time spent. Most of their checks were assigned to the banks.

The Backus bankruptcy caused the mill to close in 1931, and again the Falls was faced with a problem. This time Rev. H. J. Graven was granted permission to renovate a vacant building on Fourth Street at Fourth Avenue for sleeping quarters for the unemployed. He also was granted a permit to install an outside toilet at the rear of the building. The county extension agent reported that the Farm Bureau Board and the Extension Committee met in an attempt to find ways to help with relief work. A program calling for farmers to donate potatoes, other vegetables, clothing, and wood was established. This resulted in several truckloads of produce, which was turned over to the American Legion, the city council, and the county commissioners for distribution.

In 1932 the Reconstruction Finance Corporation made funds available to communities to build camps and manage them for the benefit of the unemployed. Because the program came during the Hoover administration, these camps were called Hoovervilles, or Hoover Hotels. When the lumber camps reopened early in 1933, many of the unemployed refused to take work. Labor in a lumber camp did not appeal to them. When the police chief was notified, he collected the meal tickets from those at the Hoover camp who had refused to work. The chief commented that any who did not accept work at the next opportunity would be sent out of the city as soon as possible. After the first call for employment, the number at the camp was reduced from 200 to 140. Two days later 42 cases of flu at the camp were treated by Dr. B. F. Osburn.

A few days later, when two farmers came to the Hoover camp to look for workers, the men again refused to go. The local editor commented that they had been given warm clothing and perhaps had been fed too well. Restrictions had to be reinstated. For families living in their homes, it was announced that federal regulations required that further relief aid would be denied "unless they grew a suitable garden in 1933" and supervision for that activity was provided through the extension service. In April 60 men from the camp were employed five hours daily by the county to repair roads.

In November 1933, the Civil Works Administration (CWA) was created to put 4 million unemployed to work on government projects. Within a month, 73 were employed in Koochiching County, including 18 women and girls. The men were assigned to road work, woods work, airport construction, and school re-modeling, and the women to projects at local public and school libraries and cafeterias. Some were transient homeless, who were cared for in each county, but most were local residents.

A few complaints were registered that sometimes outsiders were hired and local residents were overlooked. Workers at the mill complained because they earned less than those under CWA, but the conditions in the paper industry did not warrant a higher pay scale. Shortly thereafter, a new national code reduced the pay scale and the number of hours worked for the 4 million under CWA. This limited those in the Falls to 24 hours a week and those in all communities under 2,500 people to 15 hours.

When a camp for 150 homeless men was established' at Pratt, nine miles southwest of Ray, the Hoover camp was dismantled. All of the equipment that had come from lumber camps was returned to M & O. At the Pratt camp, men were fed, housed, outfitted, and given a $0.90 weekly allowance for luxuries in return for working 33 hours each week. A second transient camp was established at Plum Creek, near the southern border of Koochiching County. An abandoned CCC camp southwest of Littlefork housed a third.

Conditions improved enough by 1936 so that the federal government informed the counties that they did not have to provide funds for work relief. Camp residents were informed that the change in the labor market meant that they were expected to look for jobs in private industry, even if the work was of a temporary nature. All persons on relief who owned their homes were ordered to cut wood from the public lot for their fuel needs.

The largest project in Lake of the Woods County was at the Norris camp, which was capable of handling 225 persons. By 1938 the number was down to 100, but there were still 250 persons in the county engaged in various government projects. Those at the camp at that time received $44 a month, of which $20 was withheld for room and board. At the Falls, about 370 were still employed on federal projects, which by then paid $0.55 an hour, but, again, there was protest, because some of the workers objected to wage-and-hour requirements. The welfare committee ordered that all who refused work would be cut from welfare.

Although the various federal projects did not prove quite as effective in the woods as the CCC, in many cases they were an extension of that organization's efforts. Most of the work in the woods and in the communities would not otherwise have been done. The airport, the city hall, and the municipal building in the Falls were results of those programs. By 1938 many of the programs and camps were closed, and nearly all were discontinued by 1939.[3]

Forest Management

In the early decades, little effort was made to conserve the forest for future harvesting. Even though wages appeared low by today's standard, the timber industry was labor intense, which meant that only the best timber could be harvested. Some persons are critical of the way the timber was taken in the early 1900s, but if it had not been removed, most of it would have died or blown down by the 1960s and would have presented a major fire hazard. Vic Mannila said it best: "I have climbed over enough dead timber to know that if it is not harvested when it is mature, it will go to waste." Backus knew this, and if he had remained solvent and lived, he would have been a leader in forest management because it was the only way to protect his investment.

By 1926 Minnesota showed concern about its timber supply and initiated legislation to encourage better forest management.

The first step necessary was to adjust the timber tax laws so as to make timber farming more profitable. M & O started a reforestation program in 1935, which was about the time it was becoming solvent after the bankruptcy.

The federal government initiated new reforestation legislation in 1935. The first M & O replanting was done by hand in 1936 on 36 acres at a cost of $20.97 per acre. Each year from then on, plots of similar size were planted with about a thousand or more trees per acre. Mechanization was essential to continue such a program so that the work could be economically justified. Programs such as the CCC had proven the workability of reforesting, but profit was not a concern. It was not until after World War II, however, that mechanization made reforesting economically feasible.

The 1930s marked a watershed, but it was clear to M & O and local farmers involved in logging that, unless school projects or major programs, like the CCC, were provided to reduce labor costs, reforestation was still in the future. In the half-century since the close of this study, reforestation has progressed and has assured a perpetual supply of timber into the foreseeable future.[4]

Cattle Country ??

One of the most unique experiments in 14 northern counties was the cattle pasturing program of the summer and fall of 1934. It was obvious in early 1934 that the drought, which had started in 1932, would continue, and farmers in southern Minnesota, Iowa, and the Dakotas began to clamor for some kind of relief for their cattle. The northern counties of Minnesota, which historically are waterlogged, had experienced a reduction in rainfall but still had an ample amount for good grass growth.

By June 1934, agricultural leaders, in response to pleas from farmers with livestock, decided that cattle should be taken to the northern counties. The state responded by thoroughly searching areas that might be feasible for pasturing cattle from the drought-stricken regions. Koochiching County was appraised as probably having the best supply of grass, although distance, lack of fencing and other facilities, plus unfavorable soil conditions, made it less than a prime prospect for supplementary grazing. However, it was concluded that 20 acres of wild pasture would be adequate for a cow in Koochiching County; only 10 acres was thought necessary in Lake of the Woods County.

On June 6, R. C. Shaw, Koochiching County Extension Agent, and area farmers met with other county agents, farmers, railroad officials, and foresters to determine the feasibility of grazing drought-impacted cattle. At that time it was determined that Koochiching County could support 25,000 cattle, and the prime areas in which to start the project were the valleys of the Big Fork and Rat Root rivers. Foresters agreed to help by identifying good water supplies and isolated pasture areas. The Agricultural Adjustment Administration (AAA) would purchase cattle from the farmer, and the state of Minnesota was in charge of caring for them. Farmers providing the pasture and care "for short periods of time" would receive $1 per head. Farmers were advised that pasturing cattle on grass in the forest would reduce the fire hazard.

Shaw soon was besieged by desperate farmers anxious to earn the $1 per head, because they thought it would be easy income. One farmer offered to care for 1,500 head but had only one water pump. Other over-anxious farmers offered to take cattle but did not have adequate pasture, water, backup feed, or fencing. But the drought-stricken farmers continued to pressure AAA officials, and near the end of July, the first cattle arrived. In the first shipment, 3 percent of the cattle were blind (probably from vitamin A deficiency because of poor feed, but that was not common knowledge at that date). There were three dead animals, but it was obvious that they were not starved-thin Minnesota dairy cattle. At least 80 percent of the animals were "wild beef stock"—white-faced Herefords, Shorthorns, or a beef cross; there were very few dairy cattle among them. It was apparent that the cattle were not from Minnesota and that "someone was working the system." Unlike dairy cattle, which are used to being handled, these animals had "never seen men and were dangerous." One group became mired in mud, and when men tried to extricate them, they charged. The farmers, not used to western range cattle, quickly realized that the $1 per head was not as attractive as they initially thought. Shaw went to St. Paul to protest the shipment of any more such cattle into the area and attempted to lay down guidelines, but instead he was informed that 31,000 cattle would soon be sent to Koochiching.

Cattle flowed into the county until the third week in August, after which shipments were diverted to Lake of the Woods County. The first 17 carloads of 436 cattle arrived in Baudette with a notice that 3,000 more animals were in transit. Farmers realized that they had a 24-hour-a-day job if they wanted the project to succeed. The restless animals wandered everywhere, and some began to calve. For protection of local herds, the imported cattle were taken to the Falls for TB and Bang's testing. Predatory animals, such as bears, bobcats, and wolves, became a problem and attacked the herds each night, especially in the Ericsburg and Ray areas.

To ease the situation, experienced western cattlemen with horses were brought in to work the cattle, but there were not enough of them to prevent cattle from getting into unfenced crops. Soon complaints came from the farmers who lost crops to the wandering cattle, and the farmer pasturing them was responsible for the damage. Hard feelings, antagonism, and unkind words between neighbors resulted. Arbitration committees were formed to determine the liability, and real trouble started when some farmers learned that the damage done exceeded the income from pasturing the cattle. Shaw heard one old-timer say, "Hard telling what we'll get out of this project, but we'll get acquainted."

Other unexpected surprises surfaced, for the imported western cattle brought ticks with them, and local herds were infested. Local citizens, who were short of cash and/or food, shot a few animals, but not many of those were in the 325 animals unaccounted for at the end of the grazing season. Another 73 were lost to natural and/or violent causes, and 108 were killed by trains. Some were sold to local farmers at the original government cost; others were found later roving in the area. Of the original 11,634 cattle shipped in, about 930 fewer were shipped out. Shaw felt proud of that figure, because Koochiching had the largest government herd but the lowest loss percentagewise experienced by any northern county in the project. The 14 northern counties involved pastured 66,464 cattle.

The average gain on the cattle was 59.2 pounds for the time they were on pasture. Shaw was surprised at that very satisfactory figure and felt that it might be an incentive for individuals in the county to enter the cattle business. He cautioned, however, that the cattle had come after the fly season; otherwise, gains would have been less. The cattle were supposed to remain in the area until October 15, but because of difficulty in locating them and rounding them up, the last ones did not depart until late December.

The 11,634 cattle were placed with 17 farmers in the county; the largest single herd was 1,990 head. Most of the cattle were in the eastern third of Koochiching County, but there were large herds near Northome, Birchdale, Big Falls, and Norden. Shaw's assessment of the situation was that the farmers should have received more for their contribution to the project and that they would not do it again for the same fee. They received $11,634 for their efforts, and the railroad got $21,680 for transportation, about half of which originated in the county. Federal funds totaling $10,000 were spent to employ 85 people on relief for about 5 months to help with the cattle. Shaw's conclusion was that the native grasses were not particularly good for grazing and farmers were not equipped to handle the cattle, but it was a good way to spend money for those on relief who needed the income. Shaw's final comment was, "I hope I never have to live through this project again." That appears to have been the consensus of most of those who remember anything about the project.[5]

☐ ☐ ☐ ☐ ☐

Slowly but surely, the wilderness experienced a transition during the three decades covered in this study. First, the environmentalists gained a place in the sun against the industrialists, who opened the region; the CCC and forest management projects proved the value of rehabilitating the wilderness for economic and recreational purposes; the transient camps were no better or no worse than elsewhere in the nation, but, in some respects, they were less conspicuous here, because many who lived in the woods never had much to begin with; finally, the cattle project proved that the wilderness was not a hospitable place for animal husbandry. Lessons, both good and bad, were learned. The good lessons were the most important, for they set the stage for a brighter future by showing how a rejuvenated forest could serve society for centuries ahead.

ENDNOTES FOR CHAPTER XII

1. Meyer and White, pp. 6, 11, 169, 190; P. C. Bullard and S. S. Scovil, *Preliminary Report to International Joint Boundary Commission Re: Levels of Rainy Lake and Other Upper Waters* (Ottawa, Canada, 1930), p. 33; interview of E. R. Gustafson, International Falls, June 10, 1976, hereafter Gustafson interview. Gustafson was a surveyor with the U.S. Corps of Engineers and later an engineer with M & O. *International Joint Commission on Rainy Lake Reference: Final Report* (Washington, D.C., and Ottawa, Canada, 1934), p. 74, hereafter IJC–1934; *The Press*, September 29, 1910, February 9, July 13, 1911; *The Journal*, May 28, August 20, October 1, 1925, February 13, 19, 1930, June 1, 1933, February 7, 1934, February 27, 1981; *The Baudette Region*, January 28,

1915, February 1, June 14, 1917; Hilke interview; letters from Ernest Oberholtzer to L. P. Lemieux, April 11, 1930, and Judge John H. Brown, March 21, 1934, Oberholtzer file; *The Duluth Herald*, September 30, November 30, 1927, January 19, February 28, 1928; *The Minneapolis Journal*, May 27, June 15, July 2, 1928; Eastman interview; Backus file; City Council, February 4, 1929; C. K. Blandin, "Edward W. Backus, The Last of the Lumber Barons," *Blandin Broke Pile*, Vol. IV, No. 8, August 1951, p. 7; *Hist. of Kooch. Co.*, p. 13; see R. Newell Searle, *Saving Quetico-Superior: A Land Set Apart*, Minnesota Historical Society, 1977, for an excellent account of this topic.

2. *The Journal*, April 21, July 8, 1933, January 25, February 1, 1934, June 4, July 23, 1936, January 14, 1937, August 5, 1938, September 20, 1939; Ryan, II, pp. 4–6; Charles Knoblauch, "The Impact of the CCC on a National Forest," a typed manuscript, 1983, KCHS, hereafter Knoblauch; Kooch. Comm., July 19, 1935; Kooch. Ext.; *The Baudette Region*, October 27, 1933, May 3, 1935, January 3, 1936, January 22, 1937; City Council, April 2, 1934, January 16, 1939; Onstad interview; Scott Erickson interview; interview of Walter L. Zatochill, Owatonna, Minn., June 20, 1989, hereafter Zatochill interview. Zatochill was born October 18, 1913. Marian Peterson interview; Neil Watson interview; Richards interview; Gerber interview; LOW Co. Hist.

3. The Register of the Poor Farm (County Home), Koochiching County, Minn., 1909–1952, in KCHS; *The Journal*, February 5, 1925, January 3, 4, February 4, 22, March 28, 1933, January 2, 3, 8, 11, 16, 18, 23, 31, February 1, 9, 1934, August 15, 1935, January 16, June 11, July 2, December 5, 1936, March 30, 1938, July 13, 1939; *The Baudette Region*, May 26, September 15, 1933, January 26, February 9, March 23, 1934, January 14, March 4, 1938; City Council, October 20, December 3, 1930, November 16, December 7, 1931, November 29, 1932, March 19, April 2, 1934; Kooch. Ext.; Ettestad interview; Henrickson interview; Pollard interview; Raymond Johnson interview; Richards interview.

4. Mannila interview; *The Baudette Region*, October 8, 1926; *The Journal*, May 27, 1940, May 24, 1951; Kooch. Ext.; interview of Arnold R. Johnson, International Falls, July 25, 1989, hereafter Arnold Johnson interview. Johnson was originally an Iron Range Resources Rehabilitation Commissioner.

5. *The Journal*, June 9, 1934; Kooch. Ext.; *The Baudette Region*, August 10, 1934; Plummer diary; Ettestad interview; Henrickson interview; Minn. Rural Rehab., p. 289.

CHAPTER XIII

The Changing Wilderness

MAJOR TECHNOLOGICAL IMPROVEMENTS occurred in all phases of forestry after World War I. Some of those changes were the result of technology introduced in the war; others were caused by the continuing push to reduce labor costs, which had accelerated rapidly during the conflict. Wartime labor shortages encouraged unionization, which increased the cost of labor and hastened the substitution of capital for labor wherever possible. Reduced immigration changed the makeup of labor, and a lumberjack's life was no longer appealing. In the meantime, massive social legislation caused labor expenses to skyrocket and intensified the need to economize in every way possible. Radical changes in outlook and social structure nationwide forced changes on the industry and on those who remained in the wilderness.

Early Tractors

The tractor was perfected by 1892 and in World War I had proven very adaptable. Early tractors were costly and clumsy by modern standards. They were met with resistance by traditionalists, especially farmers, who felt that they could never do the job as well as horses. The tractor, however, had an ally in the lumber camps—cost accounting. While the majority of farmers relied on unpaid family labor, that was not so in the lumber camps. Any means to reduce costs helped to combat competition.

Power needed to transport timber from the woods to the landing was provided first by oxen and then by horses. Horses were rented from bonanza farmers, road contractors, and others who needed them in the summer but not in the winter. Horse rent was $1.00 per day, plus maintenance, which was at least $0.65. After transportation, medication, and death losses were added, the cost per horse was at least $2.00 per day. This was in contrast to the total worker cost of about $1.50 to $1.75 per day. In extreme cases, the cost of keeping a horse per work day was four times that of a worker.

The Crookston Lumber Company, an ILC subsidiary, introduced the first mechanized power in the woods of the area via steam skidders. The skidders were used to haul logs and pulp from the woods to the landings in the Kelliher, Mizpah, Northome, and Blackduck areas between 1910 and 1920. The steersman often suffered from facing the cold (see picture), yet he had a warm back because he was near the boiler. To keep his legs warm, he might wear chaps similar to what cowboys wore when riding the range, but it was not long before some ingenious lumberjack tapped the boiler and ran hot water pipes under the steersman's feet. Then all he needed to keep warm was a robe to trap the heat around his legs.

The next step was the introduction of Holt caterpillars in November 1917 by the Engler mills, at Baudette, where they pulled tow sleds, each containing a carload of logs. By 1919 the Empire Coal and Lumber Company, operating in the Northome area, had a Waterloo Boy tractor which pulled two sleds that had required a four-horse team each. In 1920 Empire purchased a second tractor—a five-ton track-type Holt. Those 2 rigs with 2 men did the work of 4 men and 16 horses.

ILC used its first Holt tractor in November 1920 in the Northome area, where it had over 20 camps. The company added several Holt caterpillars in the 1921–22 season, but the lack of trained operators and the problems caused by extreme temperatures hindered their success.

ILC employed Dan Hiner, a "tractor expert," who wrote about the handicap of working nights holding a lantern with one hand and a tool with the other. There was no one who was trained to assist him. He also had difficulty getting parts, because they were not inventoried at the camps and it took several days to get them from the Falls. He requested a gasoline section car to travel to the Falls to get the parts himself so that he could repair the machines and have them back on the job in less time. He complained that the operators did not properly maintain their machines and were unable to detect when something was wrong. When a breakdown occurred, they wanted "to tear the whole machine apart" rather than first determining the problem.

Maintenance and fuel cost, not including capital cost, was $10.82 per working day. This seemed excessive, but in reality it was not, because it replaced the cost of eight horses and one extra worker. In addition, horses had to be rented and provided for every day, not just on work days. It also was getting more difficult to hire skilled teamsters than it had been prior to World War I. ILC successfully appealed to the Holt Company to reschedule their operators' school so woodsmen could attend.

Seymour Backus was not happy about the switch from horses to tractors and complained to J. D. Twomey that ILC could have purchased and maintained 50 horses for less money. He suggested that if skilled operators could not be found the tractors should be discarded. Seymour might have been able to stem the tide of change had it not been for the fact that large farmers and contractors adopted tractors, reducing the supply of rental horses and making them more expensive.

Holt continued to enlarge and to improve its caterpillars. More skilled operators were available, and soon they preferred driving machines to horses. Within a few years, small tractors were used to pull 5 sleighs, and RD-7 Caterpillars could pull 10 sleighs, replacing 2 to 4 horses and 1 driver for each sleigh. By the mid-1930s, one tractor could move as much timber in one day as a team could in several weeks, and the end was not yet in sight.[1]

Shackers and Independent Loggers

The forests needed to be cut by the time ILC arrived on the scene. If they had not been cut when they were, much of the timber would have gone to waste. Time was important as far as the timber was concerned, and that coincided with the demand of a rapidly expanding nation.

If there had been an adequate base of farmers in the area, the lumber camp phase might never have played such an important role. Backus knew that the cheapest method of obtaining timber was to buy it from the independent farmer/logger, who logged to clear his land and to supplement his inadequate farm income. He was willing to sell either timber or labor, which was cheaper for ILC than having to purchase stumpage and to pay labor.

Another early source of timber was homesteaders, who filed a claim only to harvest the timber and then left. A third source was shackers, who did not want to live in the lumber camps and were satisfied to eke out a subsistence living by logging. Their shacks were 10 × 12 feet for 1 man or 10 × 20 feet for 2 men, constructed of Insulite sheathing on the outside, and lined on the inside. They contained a bunk for each man, a table, a cupboard, and a specially-built stove for cooking and heating. The shackers often were long-time lumberjacks, who had no other place to go as the lumber camps started to shut down and who generally were not interested in becoming union members. They existed in the transition period between full-scale lumber camps and total contract logging.

ILC started the transition after the 1928–29 season, when it closed a large number of camps in the Northome area. That was the last big year for the camp system. Camp 149 east of Effie had a turnover of 1,700 men but at no time had more than 150 on the payroll. By 1933 the receivership still used eight camps but also had five independent contractors. Woods logging tapered off sharply, and when labor unrest renewed in 1935, M & O decided to discontinue the camps. The scattered stands of good timber were better handled by the more flexible trucking system, which made the woods railroad network obsolete.

The 1936–37 season was the last for the lumber camps. In the fall of 1937, M & O shifted entirely to relying on 25 independent contractors, who had been working with the company and were prepared for the change. Most of the time ILC harvested 50 to 70 percent of its needs from its own land, but after 1937 it shifted to securing only 30 percent from owned land using contractors. This marked the end of a need for a large mobile labor force.

ILC was willing to use independent contractors (or farmer/loggers) wherever possible, especially where there were small areas of timber to be harvested or where the timber was in places that were excessively difficult to reach. As time passed, the farmer/loggers realized that logging, not farming, was the way of the future.

In 1925 Carl Dahlberg purchased stumpage on 160 acres, about 11 miles north of Effie, for $400 payable in 4 monthly installments. The house on the acreage served as the center of his camp. He had 10 teams, 34 men, the minimum of equipment, and an open-sided mess house, where the flies were so bad that the soup looked like it was "raisin soup." Dahlberg was new at the business, and his 34-man crew was admittedly not the best, but they produced 34 cords a day.

Dahlberg did the bull cooking, which included making six trips a day to a well located about two city blocks from the kitchen and carrying two 20-quart pails of water each time. Eight of those pails were for kitchen use, and four for the men in the bunkhouse. He milked the cow twice daily, sawed and carried in wood for the kitchen and the bunkhouse, then did the book work. The average day for the lumberjacks was 9 to 10 hours, but his day was longer.

Dahlberg luckily was able to borrow $1,000 from his uncle on the strength of a contract with M & O to start his camp and used credit wherever he could until he was able to collect for his timber. At the end of the season he paid off all his creditors and still had $1,000 for his risk, management, and five months of labor, which he remembered 65 years later as being about equal to the work of four men. He continued contracting with M & O and its successor, Boise-Cascade, for the next 55 years. After a few years in business Dahlberg was joined by his brother-in-law. They rented stumpage from absentee landowners and gradually enlarged their output with little increase in labor force because of improving technology.

In 1928 the Mannausau brothers started contract logging by harvesting 110 acres of M & O land in the Birchdale area. They hauled the timber by truck to the Rainy River, where it was floated to Spooner-Baudette and loaded onto CN cars destined for the Falls and/or the Fort.

Alfred Johnson paid $15 for stumpage on 40 acres of tax-delinquent cut-over land on which the birch and the tamarack had been left standing. He harvested 40 to 50 cords per acre from that land. VRL built roads when it cut the original timber, so he had no problem getting his out. When Johnson first started logging, it took three man-hours to get a cord of wood from the forest to the Falls. He asked M & O for a logging contract in 1937. His timing was good, for he was able to purchase used equipment from M & O. In his first season he sold the company 600 cords of pulp and 200,000 feet of pine logs. His only problem was that he was unable to deliver timber while the lumberjacks were on strike, so he used his crew to improve the roads on newly leased stumpage south of Littlefork.

Johnson established a camp of 40 men; his wife, Margaret, did the cooking. They used New Castle china instead of the traditional metal tableware that was used in the lumber camps. The menu was much the same as in the past, except they were able to provide a greater variety because they had refrigeration. Like Dahlberg, Johnson not only managed his camp but filled in wherever he was needed. He observed that as the old-time lumberjacks became scarce, he had difficulty maintaining production. His records indicated that he was making only a small margin per cord, so if he wanted to remain competitive and profitable, he had to mechanize and increase his volume.

Johnson used tractors and trucks from the start. Next, he added jammers (mechanical loaders), which reduced the time to load a truck from 150 to 60 man-minutes with less effort. About the same time, he adopted fuel oil stoves, because using them was less expensive for heating and cooking than having a worker cut and supply wood for those purposes. It also saved the expense of a night watchman to keep the stoves stoked and to guard against fires.

Independent contractors, with 25 to 75 workers each, operated near where the laborers resided so they could be with their families. This stabilized the small logging communities, which had started a slow decline soon after the big lumber camps passed through their area. The greatest impact fell upon Big Falls, Littlefork, and the Falls, because the number of lumber-jacks in those communities dropped sharply, although a few were still seen around until after World War II.

Initially, the total number of woods workers did not decrease significantly. More importantly, the mills in the Falls and the Fort were assured of a steady flow of raw materials from more than one source of supply. As mill capacity increased, the con-tractors mechanized to expand output without adding forest workers. Social and legislative problems pertinent to employing workers were transferred to them, and in 1938 they formed a Timber Producers' Association to help them deal with what they could not handle as individuals.

M & O was pleased with the results of using independent contractors. In July 1938, F. L. Bussman noted that "most con-tractors completed their work in good manner, [but] a few had equipment, housing, labor, and breakup problems." The 23 U.S. contractors (another report indicated 25 contractors) received from $2,938.83 to $150,374.89, while the lone Canadian contractor received $285,012.30. The conclusion was that there was "con-siderable savings by using the independent contractors"—at least a 20 percent reduction in equipment and provisions and a 25 percent reduction in labor costs. The piece cutters averaged 1½ cords per day compared to only 1 cord per day the previous year under the camp system. By 1939, man-hours per cord were half of what they were in 1910.

The contractors employed 985 men, who were supplemented

with 230 horses, 10 tractors, and 125 trucks, all of which the contractors owned or which came from the community of operation, as did much of the supplies and produce. This was in contrast to the camp system, where everything was centrally purchased and run through the Falls. Only two camps experienced labor problems, which were caused by poor food. The contractors had established their operations with greater efficiency and economy and less waste than M & O could have done. Even with a much improved output of the one remaining M & O camp, the bottom line said it best—the company cost of producing a cord of pulpwood was $10.081 in contrast to $9.295 for the contractor cost. The contractor cost varied from $7.740 to $12.009 per cord, because some worked where no M & O camp could have considered operating. Clearly, a new and much improved way of harvesting the wilderness and a far better life for the woods worker was established.[2]

Trucks in the Woods

After tractors broke the tradition barrier against mechanization in the woods, it was inevitable that trucks soon followed. According to *The Baudette Region* of February 20, 1925, Clarence Lindholm successfully hauled $7,000 worth of timber each day to Baudette. The editor concluded that the truck would eliminate river drives forever. In 1927 the Tones, near Northome, started using a truck to haul timber 10 miles to the local mill. A man with a truck hauled two loads per day with twice as much per load as a team could pull. Therefore, a man with a truck could do four times as much per day as a man with a team.

Carl Dahlberg became sold on trucks in 1929 when he saw how quickly they could make a five-mile haul to Craig in contrast to what horses had done. He received a $0.13 bonus on ties that he had sold for $0.65 because he was able to make immediate delivery. The following year he paid $700 for a slightly used truck and hired five additional truckers for delivering cord spruce 48 miles to Grand Rapids at a premium. He paid $4.50 a cord for hauling, but that was far less than for the old method of hauling wood to the rail landing with a team and reloading for shipment. A truck enabled him to reach the more hilly and remote areas not accessible with horses. At the same time, he increased production with no additional men.

In the 1930s, ads by independent contractors appeared in local papers seeking trucks for hauling pulp. In the 1920s, trucks could haul only three cords of wood, but by 1933, when some of the first semi-trailer rigs were used, they could haul six cords. The truckers kept their rigs busy in the off-woods season delivering forest products to distant markets and hauling feed, livestock, and freight.

Farmer/loggers, like Plummer, made the switch to trucks in 1930, and the number of truckers increased each year. By 1935 Plummer used four truckers regularly to haul from his roadside to the mill. In the winter trucks ran day and night to provide a steady flow to the mill and also to stockpile for the season when roads were impassable. The truckers received $2.75 a cord to haul a 3½-cord load 30 miles to the Falls. The woodsmen got $1.50 to cut the cord and place it at the roadside. Some farmer/loggers, like the Bergstroms, realized that by integrating trucking with their logging they could increase their profit. They discontinued farming.

The natural sluggishness of the corporate structure prevented M & O from adopting innovations as rapidly as the contractors, but by the 1931–32 season, it used trucks to pull sleighs from the woods to the main rail line. Spur line construction was discontinued with that adoption, and by 1936 removal of some of the woods rail network was started. The Galvin Line, which stretched over 20 miles, was taken up, and the 60-ton Lima-geared locomotive was transported to the Logging Museum at the State Fairgrounds in St. Paul.

By 1938 the shift to trucks was nearly complete, with about 200 trucks hauling 3,000 cords a day to the Falls. Plummer wrote that about 500 cords passed his farm daily. By 1938–39, the cost per cord delivered in the Falls was $7.09 by truck and $8.24 by rail; as trucks improved, the margin became greater. That year nearly 28,000 cords were delivered by truck over distances of 7 to 87 miles, and nothing was hauled on the M & O railroad. In 1939 pulp was trucked from Thistle Dew Lake, a distance of 110 miles, but there was still doubt about taking up the remaining track. The idea of leaving the Deer River Line intact from Camp 29 to the Falls was discussed so that trucks from the south could deliver to Camp 29 for reloading. That year 80 percent of the total M & O production in the United States arrived by truck. Ironically, nearly 100 percent of the Canadian production still moved by water.

Bussman expressed the need for M & O to assure the truckers that they would be guaranteed sufficient business so they could buy good equipment to provide a steady flow of timber to the mill. He leaned heavily toward complete reliance on trucks and commented that he anticipated trouble from the unions in that respect. He wrote, "[B]ut this is only another chapter in the progress of revolutionizing methods of operation and transportation which will have to be adjusted as have similar problems in the past."

Another innovation that came to the forest in the 1930s was the airplane. Airplanes were first used by the government for surveying, but in the 1939–40 season, Vic Mannila, who had learned to fly in 1937, used his partnership-owned plane to spot timber and to locate roads and camp sites. The plane became increasingly valuable for cruising timber. One of Mannila's partners used the plane to travel to his beehives, which he had scattered throughout Koochiching County wherever clover seed was produced. The third partner, Dr. Hanover, used it for recreation.[3]

Unions in the Wilderness

After the IWW threat disappeared in 1920, and the remnants of that organization finally gave up in 1923, there was little problem with organized labor until 1935. Social legislation had caused M & O to consider withdrawing from its woods activities, but the real spark came when unions revived their recruiting in 1935.

Union activity was stepped up in the fall of 1936 with a strike that lasted until February 2, 1937, when a collective bargaining arrangement was concluded. A short truck drivers' strike in January 1937 halted all pulp shipments from south of the border, because the lumberjacks had also closed down the camps. The two strikes caught M & O at a crucial time, because heavy snowfall that winter necessitated hiring many extra workers to remove the snow before the log drive and to retrieve the timber left on the banks following the floods.

Independent farmer/loggers, who relied on family labor or one or two other workers, felt compelled to join the union, but other than paying dues, they "were not too affected." One worker felt that the greatest benefit he had from joining the union was protection from being fired. He was particularly affected because he drank, and the "union guard" kept him from getting into camp until he sobered up. The independent contractors, however, watched that 1936–37 strike with interest, because they knew they would be targets for the union when the lumber camps disappeared. They were not directly bothered that year, because the unions were chiefly interested in the M & O camp workers. Another short strike in the fall of 1937 was effective enough to cause some of the independents to stop working while it was in progress.

The story was different in 1938, when a contractor's camp along the old Galvin Line south of the Falls was caught in a struggle between the AFL and the Congress of Industrial Organizations (CIO). That inter-union struggle lasted for over two weeks before the AFL won the right to continue to represent the woods workers. Most contractors initially avoided any union problems. In Carl Dahlberg's 55 years as an independent contractor, he had little union trouble and was proud of his crew, which voted down unions twice. He felt that he had excellent workers, and the only serious problem he had with any of them was over liquor.[4]

The Last Log Drives

In some respects log drives were the biggest event of the year for woods communities located along a stream or a river. Walter Paul wrote that when people in the area heard the muffled roar of distant thunder, they knew that logs had struck rocks in the river bed. Everyone rushed to watch the log drivers attempt to break the jam. If the jam could not be broken with peavies or pike poles, dynamite was used.

The river drives were not an inexpensive way to move timber, for between 15 and 25 percent of the pulpwood and logs were lost on a drive from sinkers (logs stuck in the river or lake bed) or strays (logs on dry land along the stream). Laborwise, they were expensive. For example, it took up to three weeks for a drive on the Black River, which went 21 miles as the crow flies, to get to the Loman hoist. The interest bill was another major cost, for timber harvested in the fall could not be driven down the river until the following spring and was not used until that fall. By contrast, timber that went by rail could be processed within a few days after it was cut. When trucks were used, the time span was reduced to hours.

Yet another factor that was more of a problem occurred when there was not enough rain and snow to fill the rivers to float the timber. If a dry spell lasted more than one year, the cut timber might decay, which added to the loss. In the meantime, the sawmill stood idle for part of the season or, in an extreme case, all season. In the early 1920s, ILC had over $1 million invested in timber in western Koochiching and Lake of the Woods counties for three years before the rains came. This led to an early use of trucks in the Rapid and Baudette river valleys. When rain or snow did come, it often was in excess, which caused timber to be washed up on the land and created the added expense of putting it back in the river. Every drive had three crews: the watering crew, which got the logs moving as soon as the river started to flow; the bends and rapids crew, which kept the timber moving; and the rear crew, which cleaned the timber lying along the banks.

The last drive the full length of the Big Fork River had 2.8 million feet of pine and spruce logs, 60,937 cords of pulpwood, 11,521 railroad ties, plus a few thousand cedar poles and posts. Pay for the crew started at Wirt on March 28, 1928, but the river did not break up until April 17; on July 1 the drive reached the Rainy River, after covering a straight-line distance of 58 miles at a total cost of $13,067.46, of which $8,861.33 was for labor. There were four shorter drives down the Big Fork—the final one in 1932 marked the end of the virgin timber in that valley.

The last big pocket of virgin timber lay near the southeastern portion of Koochiching County within the Nett Lake Reservation, adjacent to the Little Fork and Nett Lake rivers. Backus secured title to that timber in the early 1900s and expected to enter the area with the Galvin Line, but that never materialized. M & O planned to harvest timber there in 1935–1936, but labor problems upset the time schedule. It became so dry that all workers were prohibited from smoking, but by January 1937, there was an accumulation of 4 feet of snow on the ground, which necessitated hiring extra workers to shovel and extra tractors to skid and to sleigh haul the timber. By the last week in March, 30,000 cords of pulpwood and 13 million feet of pine logs were on the river landings. Most of the pulpwood was piled on the frozen river. Heavy rains began April 15, and the river broke April 23. The river rose 15 feet, floating much of the timber onto the banks and even into the trees.

The water rose above the boom timbers and pilings at the Loman hoist. To prevent losing the drive, it had to be jammed upstream. The point selected was the Nett River Bridge, where Highway No. 65 crossed the Little Fork River. The jam was successful, causing a backup of logs for six miles. Over 150 workers were employed on the drive, which did not reach Loman until July 15. The total cost of that drive was $59,821.76, of which $51,662.60 was for labor. The drive from Wirt on the Big Fork had cost about $0.185 per cord. The final Little Fork drive cost was $1.20 per cord, of which about $0.40 was attributed to the flood and the rest to increased wages as a result of the new contract.

This marked the end of the virgin forest in Koochiching County. It was the final log drive and the end of the lumber camps. When the last timbers were sawed, the big ILC sawmill in the Falls was closed and removed, marking the end of an era.[5]

The Fate of the Lumber Camp Towns

A traveler through the northern border country in the 1990s would find only a small portion of the communities that once existed there. As the large lumber companies moved through the virgin timber forest at a rapid pace during the two decades from 1910 to 1930, they built transitory logging camps. Small service communities of a very temporary nature quickly sprang up in the logging areas. In some respects, the buildings in those villages were not any more permanent than the lumber camps themselves.

People who lived in the wilderness at the turn of the century saw a rapid migration into the area and by 1920 watched the persons who had come there start to leave. In the late 1930s, some of the original communities reminiscent of the hastily built frontier towns were still there, but many had disappeared.

Probably no community had a shorter life span than Grand Falls, just across the Big Fork River from Big Falls. It had a small school building, a two-story building that became a hotel, a small depot that was never used, and a small railroad water tank. When the only business—a small steam-powered sawmill—failed after one year, the town was doomed. Grand Falls was a community that died "almost as soon as it was born."

Between 1907 and 1916, Gemmell was known as the Cedar Capital of the World. It had two sawmills, a large cedar yard, the National Pole Company, and Ross and Ross, another lumber firm. Mizpah started at the same time as Gemmell, but the sawmill there did not reach its peak of production until after 1940. A 1912 article in *The Journal* stated that lumber camps in and around Margie would soon be a thing of the past. Shortly thereafter, the Margie Village Council accepted a bid of $220 for a three-cell jail.

In 1913 it was announced that twice-weekly mail service would commence between Rauch and Greany—Rauch's contact with the outside world. Bramble and Silverdale had the same service.

The citizens around Ray were elated when it was announced in 1910 that iron ore deposits had been located in the vicinity. R. K. Watt sunk a shaft and retrieved ore that indicated 70 percent iron. In late 1911, the Ray Iron Mining Company was incorporated by several persons, nearly all from the Falls. It was claimed in early 1912 that the firm owned 15,000 acres in Koochiching and St. Louis counties, and a boom was expected in the area.

An iron ore scheme around Northome reached even greater proportions when it was announced in 1911 that The Northern Minnesota Iron Mining Company was being formed with a capitalization of $1 million. Iron ore samples as produced by an expert from Minneapolis yielded 45 to 68 percent iron. Shortly thereafter, The Koochiching-Vermilion Iron Company announced that they had hit gold-bearing rock 140 feet down while searching for iron. The president of still another company was convinced that northern Minnesota was destined to be one of the "greatest gold-producing regions in the United States." Iron ore attracted attention again in 1922 when a process requiring peat for refining the ore was discovered.

Northome grew slowly, for the iron ore boom never materialized there. The town did not expand until 1915, when the Crookston Lumber Company started a lumber camp nearby. In 1920 it became sufficiently prosperous to justify a telephone company. In 1921 the Scenic Hotel opened, as did a combination men's clothing, furniture, and shoe store. Northome boomed in the 1920s, but when the camps were removed from the area after 1929, it stabilized. In 1935 the local economy received a reprieve with a $5,000 grant from the federal government to build a municipal liquor store.

The Big Falls mill reopened in 1915 after being closed for a year because of bankruptcy. Shortly thereafter a young attorney, J. J. Hadler, came to town. Prior to his marriage to Myrtle Jensen, he lived in the three-story Robinson Hotel, which was heated by a pot-bellied stove on the first floor. Toilet facilities included a two-story outhouse—the second story was connected to the second floor of the hotel. Big Falls had a population of about 400 people. A fire in 1932 destroyed 18 commercial buildings, which burned more "like haystacks than like buildings."

Only six commercial buildings remained, and the town never rebuilt to any extent. In 1935 water mains and fire hydrants were constructed with a federal government grant. A power plant was built in 1938.

Littlefork fared slightly better than some of the communities farther south, for it was fortunate to have a hospital. Its liquor store produced enough revenue by 1937 to get the village out of debt and finance new sidewalks. Littlefork stayed alive to a great extent because Vic Mannila and partners moved a sawmill there. They were "impressed with the local people." Within a year they were operating at full capacity and had six trucks on the road delivering their products.

Ericsburg, along the DW & P south of the Falls, had two three-story hotels in 1918. In 1933 Frank Keyes dismantled one of the hotels, which had not been used for several years. Ericsburg survived as a bedroom community to the Falls.

Ranier, named by M. S. Cook, civil engineer for the DWRL (later the DW & P), was established because it was the site of the rail crossing into Canada. It did not have cement sidewalks and street lights until the mid-1920s. When the bank went broke in 1930, and the Ranier European Hotel burned, the town's population stabilized. A community hall was built in 1939, and Ranier became another bedroom community for the Falls.

Loman, on the Rainy River, was the western terminus of the MD & W. The M & O hoist there captured timber that floated out of the Little Fork, Big Fork, and Black rivers, which was then loaded onto train cars. Camp 6, at Loman, housed the workers for the hoist. Loman Mercantile, incorporated by Frank Keyes and I. W. Hinckley in 1909, was the major local firm. The town's fate was sealed in 1937 when Camp 6 closed and the MD & W tracks were removed. Trucks hauled the timber directly from the woods to the mill.

Many communities located along the Rainy River and in the Pine Island and Beltrami Island areas were doomed by the resettlement project of the 1930s. These communities were Indus, Manitou, Birchdale, Frontier, Central, Bannock, Border, Clementson, Fairdale, Wayland, McClellan, Norden, Fairland, Stals, Carp, Bauldus, Hiwood, Bankton, Fruitland, Lovedale, Rako, Faunce, Pilgrim Hall, Dutchie, Clover Point, Roosevelt, Pitt, Hackett, Zippel, Williams, Graceton, Wabanica, Spooner, and Baudette. Many of them never had more than a few families.

Pitt is a typical example of a town whose economy relied on

the timber industry. In 1908 the CN built a depot there to serve the logging business. For a few years the depot was open 24 hours a day during the woods season. Pitt also had three stores, three timber yards, two blacksmith shops, and a blind pig. Only 17 years later the CN closed the depot, because it was no longer a profitable center.

Faunce, which was never more than a one-building village, was established during the rush of immigrants after 1910. The building was a combination store and home for the Vic Crabtree family. In the 1920s, gasoline pumps were added, and after Prohibition ended, a bar was installed. Faunce's boom years occurred when the CCC camp was located 1½ miles from the store. The schoolhouse was a mile north of the store. In 1930 Crabtree became county highway engineer for Lake of the Woods County and moved to Baudette. Mrs. Crabtree tried to manage the store for a period of time, but 33 miles from Baudette on dirt roads was too great an obstacle, so the couple sold it. The Crabtrees' successor was lucky, for his business was purchased by the government as part of the resettlement project in 1936. In 1984 Marian Crabtree Peterson tried to find where the store building was once located. She found only the cement slabs where the gasoline pumps had sat.

In 1914 Williams had a building boom that was probably second only to that of Baudette. A 26-room hotel, a brick store, a full business block, and several residences were built. There was talk of a $10,000 school because the original structure was too small. But by the 1920s, when most of the timber was gone, Williams stopped growing.

The need for many of these small communities diminished as the lumber camps disappeared and the homesteaders were relocated by the resettlement project. Those that survived were primarily service centers for contract loggers.[6]

A County Seat Survives

The establishment of a sawmill at Kenora in 1889 provided a market for timber along the northward-flowing rivers in Minnesota. In 1890 a sawmill was erected at Beaver Mills (later Rainy River), and in 1905 Shevlin-Clark-Mathieu also built a mill there. In 1896 the first land was patented in what later became Lake of the Woods County. A lumber mill was started in 1906 on the east side of the Baudette River by Shevlin-Clark-Mathieu in the village of Spooner, which was established to provide quarters for the mill workers. In 1909 Edward Engler built a sawmill at Baudette; this was smaller than the Spooner mill.

Baudette and Spooner, separated by the Baudette River, were the chief communities on the western edge of the territory under study. Their growth was limited as soon as the Loman hoist was established, for it cut off their greatest source of supply and left them with timber only from the Baudette and Rapid river valleys. But that was not immediately obvious, for Baudette rebounded quickly after the October 1910 fire. By December, nearly 200 buildings were erected. The last tent which had served as shelter after the fire was packed.

Backus planned the fate of Baudette and Spooner, for in 1912–13 he purchased the Shevlin sawmill at Spooner to use as a backup for his big sawmill at the Falls. In 1921 he purchased the Engler sawmill and closed it within a year. The sawmills in both communities suffered from labor disputes and repeated fires, several of which were caused by arson. Even though there was an outmigration during 1913 because many were disturbed by the labor disputes, 1913 and 1914 were boom years. By 1915 a second school (after the fire), requiring nine teachers, was constructed. The CN ran through Baudette, and there was talk of two other railroads. In 1915 Baudette had a population of 1,312 and Spooner about 500. The mills in the two villages flourished during World War I, when they employed over 750 people in addition to the woods workers.

As in Koochiching County, many of the early residents of northern Beltrami County felt that as soon as the virgin timber was gone, the area would turn to farming. There was talk of sending promoters to central states to extol the virtues of the region for agriculture. When lumbering tapered off after the war and the sawmills were closed, the residents had to turn to agriculture. A canning factory for berries and vegetables was planned, but dry weather halted further discussion of the project.

The 1913–14 boom caused residents in the 40 northern townships of Beltrami County to promote dividing the county. The first obstacle arose via a bill that would have prohibited counties under 50,000 population from being divided. A state law required that the area being considered as a new county have at least $4 million in valuation. In 1917 the 40 townships in question had a valuation of $1.4 million, but the local citizens were sure that would increase. The legislature agreed that if the valuation reached $3 million, county division could proceed. By 1917 Baudette and Spooner realized that if they wanted to make the county division plan work, they first would have to agree on where the county courthouse would be located. That was overcome when Spooner agreed to merge with Baudette if a new county was created. Reaching the agreement was easier than getting the job done.

In 1919 the legislature agreed that the northern 40 townships could become a separate county. A county convention was called in June 1922, and the vote for division was 200 to 18. On the matter of the county seat location, Baudette won over Spooner 114 to 104. On September 7, 8, and 9, 1922, a County Division Carnival was held. The money raised by that event was used to gravel streets for three blocks, and install cement curbing in Baudette. On November 28, 1922, Lake of the Woods County became official, but no final settlement was made regarding the county seat. After the resettlement project reduced the local population, the Spooner school closed, and the building was sold to the county for $1. Several years later Baudette and Spooner merged, and the building became the courthouse.

Shortly after Lake of the Woods County was established, *The Baudette Region* and *The Northern News*, of Spooner, consolidated, and W. T. Noonan became the sole owner. The region could not support two newspapers.

In 1925 the CN served notice that all the houses on CN property in what was called Old Baudette had to be removed by July 1. It took repeated notices from the sheriff to convince homeowners that they must move their houses. But by January 1927, Noonan noted that Old Baudette was "almost as deserted as a schoolhouse in summer time."

The year 1927 closed on a down note when the sawmill at Spooner was set on fire three times in six weeks by arsonists before it was finally destroyed on December 15. The mill was closed in 1922, but Backus kept it in reserve in case of a fire or a strike at the big sawmill in the Falls. That put the finishing touches on any hopes of continuing the timber industry, just as the resettlement project closed the door on most farming. The usual government projects of the 1930s, including a municipal building and, much later, a hospital, helped the county-seat town stem the tide.[7]

The Wilderness in 1939

When Leonard Costley, who spent his life working in the woods and in the mill, was asked in 1957 how he felt the virgin forest had been handled, he replied, "They logged the best they knew how but they had the mistaken idea that you never could use up all the timber . . . in the United States. In later years the companies began to realize that you couldn't slaughter timber that way and they had reforestation." Improved technology pointed the direction by the late 1930s to prove that the forest could be rehabilitated and would last forever if it were handled properly.

In the 30 years covered by this history, the massive power of Koochiching Falls was harnessed. Then came droves of unskilled workers, who labored in the primitive wilderness in a manner not much different from what had been done for centuries. Their days were numbered, but they did not understand that until the aftermath of World War I caused changing technology to penetrate the densest forest.

A new look at the world caused the environmentalists to stand their ground against the industrialists, who first opened the wilderness. A collapse in the world economy brought workers into new camps for the purpose of learning to cope with nature. From that experience, creative concepts of forest management proved the value of rehabilitating the wilderness to satisfy both economic and recreational needs.

Individuals came and left; homesteads were created and abandoned; villages boomed and withered; only the massive paper mills remained as a monument to a man of vision. Lessons were learned, and the stage was set for a brighter future relying on the rejuvenated, but still untamed, wilderness to serve generations yet to come.[8]

ENDNOTES FOR CHAPTER XIII

1. ILC Camp file; Ryan, I, p. 5; Costley interview; *The Baudette Region*, November 22, 1917; *The Northome Record*, September 17, October 29, 1920; Schneider interview; Pollard interview; correspondence between various individuals regarding tractor operations, Bussman file; Sedore file; Alfred Johnson interview.

2. ILC file; Pollard interview; *The Chronicle*, March 17, 1974; M & O Logging file; Gerber interview; Dahlberg interview; Mannausau interview; Alfred Johnson interview; Pollard-Pearson interview; Pollard, "Logging Railroad"; Ettestad interview; Henrickson interview; Bussman file.

3. *The Baudette Region*, February 20, 1925; Dahlberg interview; *The Journal*, January 20, March 6, 1930, December 19, 1935, April 30, 1936; Pollard interview; Tone interview; Plummer diary; Alfred Johnson interview; *The Mandonian*, Vol. I, No. 6 (March–April), No. 8 (July–August 1947), p. 10; M & O Logging file; Bergstrom interview; Bussman file; Mannila interview.

4. Pollard interview; Plummer diary; Alfred Johnson interview; Ettestad interview; H. Johnson interview; Pollard, "Logging Railroad"; *The Journal*, November 23, December 10, 1938; Henrickson interview; Miller interview; Dahlberg interview.

5. Pollard interview; ILC file; Kohlhase, *Spruce*, pp. 41–42; Paul, "Memories"; Bussman file; Ryan, II, p. 10; M & O Logging file; Dahlberg interview; *The Baudette Region*, May 31, 1917, March 20, 27, April 24, 1925; Lester E. Pollard, "Cost of Logging Operations and the Little Fork River Drive 1936–37," a typed manuscript in Pollard file, KCHS; Lester E. Pollard, "Recollections by L. E. Pollard of the International Lumber Company Logging Operations on the Nett Lake Indian Reservation 1935–36 and 1936–37 and the Little Fork River Drive of 1937," May 3, 1975, Pollard file, KCHS; Gorden interview; H. Johnson interview; Alfred Johnson interview.

6. Paul, "Memories"; Rogers interview; Hist. Res. Inv., p. 17; *The Press*, July 18, 1906, November 3, 24, 1910, January 19, August 10, 1911; *The Journal*, November 9, 1911, January 11, 25, March 14, 28, April 4, 11, 18, July 4, 1912, May 15, 1913, August 17, 1922, August 28, 1924, December 10, 1925, September 30, 1926, April 28, 1933, September 5, October 24, December 5, 1935, January 14, 1937, November 9, 1938, October 18, 1939; Albrecht & Thomas, pp. 31, 43; *The Mandonian*, Vol. I, No. 4 (July–August), No. 6 (November–December 1946); *The Chronicle*, June 23, 1974; *The Baudette Region*, April 2, 1914, March 29, 1917; Clarence H. Peterson, "My Memories of Bygone Days and an Account of the 1910 Fire," a manuscript in the Lake of the Woods County Historical Society, Baudette, Minn., no date; Marian Peterson interview; *The Northome News*, March 3, 1905; *The Northome Record*, December 10, 1915, April 23, July 23, 1920; interview of J. J. Hadler by Hiram M. Drache and Mary Lou Pearson, International Falls, June 7, 1976. Hadler was born May 3, 1888, and came to Big Falls in 1915. Gorden interview; Big Falls Community file, KCHS; Mannila interview.

7. Beck file; LOW Co. Hist.; *The Press*, December 22, 1910; *The Journal*, April 10, 1913; Pollard interview; *The Baudette Region*, March 26, April 2, 23, 30, December 10, 1914, February 18, September 2, 9, 1915, January 11, 18, February 1, April 26, 1917, March 21, 1919, May 28, August 6, 1920, June 9, August 25, 1922, July 25, 1924, May 22, 1925, August 13, 20, November 26, 1926, January 7, November 26, December 16, 23, 1927, April 8, December 2, 1938, January 6, 1939; Anderson, "Beltrami Island", p. 8; Sherwin Skaar, "Border Pines: A History of the Lumber Industry in the Vicinity of Baudette, Minnesota," a research paper, Department of History, Gustavus Adolphus College, St. Peter, Minnesota, March 15, 1968, LOW Co. Hist., pp. 12, 28, 34, 43, 44, 51. This is an excellent student paper on the lumber industry in the region.

8. Costley interview.

Appendix

TABLE I[1]

MEN HIRED BY AGENCIES AND FARES ADVANCED, 1927–28

Location	Men Hired	Fares Adv.	Cost of Fares
International Falls	2,360	1,210	$ 1,938.05
Duluth	3,442	3,263	21,106.15
Bemidji	999	747	2,214.11
Fargo	87	72	452.84
Grand Forks	16	13	96.51
Minneapolis	28	26	159.62
	6,932	5,331	$25,967.28

[1]ILC Camp file.

TABLE II[1]

FOOD COST AND AMOUNT PER MAN DAY
FOR VARIOUS ILC CAMPS

Year	Man Days	Food Cost Only	Total Cost[2]	Lbs./Day
1917	27,800	$0.5448	—	7.0190
1920	20,839	0.4764	$0.7931	—
1923	25,480	0.7105	0.9543	—
1928	262,990	0.4974	0.7423	6.5658
1929	227,228	0.4959	0.7500	6.3076
1931	29,692	0.3580	0.5116	6.6661
1932	145,181	0.3120	0.4770	7.3393
1933	246,861	0.3534	0.5545	—

[1]ILC Camp file.

[2]Total cost included labor, fuel, and supplies needed by the food service.

TABLE III[1]

MINNESOTA AND INTERNATIONAL RAILROAD
SCOPE OF OPERATION

Year	1905	1910	1912	1917
Miles of Line	125	—	192	204
Gross Earnings	$494,713	$770,042	$834,637	$862,531
Net Income	$30,000	$81,545	$132,336	$81,270
Passengers	126,091	265,216	212,397	258,283
Passenger Revenue	$111,610	$199,564	$234,202	$261,689
Total Tons	762,974	676,510	761,820	1,090,791
Forest Products	722,803	574,477	612,386	828,036
Avg. Distance Hauled (miles)	—	—	81.75	76.2
Employees[2]	514	778	695	612 (est.)
Avg. Daily Wage	$2.04	$2.23	$2.36	$3.67

[1]M & I files, MHS.

[2]Except for the eight general officers, whose daily wage varied from $1.25 to $14.70
during these years.

INSTRUCTIONS FOR BUTLER

[These instructions were provided to the butler at Redcrest, the summer home of Bror and Mary Dahlberg.]

Come in at 7:30 A.M.

Clean dining room, living room, and music room. Vacuum rug twice weekly (power plant will be turned on by Don or Omer to attach vacuum cleaner). Once a week vacuum furniture—furniture oil on furniture once a week.

Set breakfast table with colored cloths and paper napkins on screened porch, except when it is cold and cloudy—use dining room then. For breakfast have jelly in two dishes, plenty of butter, all the coffee cups and full coffee pot on small table by Mrs. Dahlberg's place. Have a pitcher of hot milk and two pitchers of cream on table, also . . . cold milk in pitcher that has cat for decoration. Have fruit juice or fruit in front of each place before we sit down. Bring on two plates of buttered toast wrapped in napkins and put on table as we eat fruit. Then two platters of whatever we are having are placed on the table and we help ourselves. Answer promptly when Mrs. Dahlberg rings bell so as to refill coffee pot and platters. Have flowers on breakfast table.

After breakfast do dishes and then come to Master bedroom and get Mr. Dahlberg's shoes to clean and clothes to press. Also do Mrs. Dahlberg's shoes. Finish these, straighten out Mr. Dahlberg's closet and his bureau drawers.

Get things ready for lunch which we usually have on the dock. Bring down cloth, paper napkins, paper plates, non-breakable glasses for beverage, silver, butter, bread, etc. Bring down food on trays covered with clean napkins, beverages, etc. and help serve them. Clear away after lunch and clean up pantry, dishes, etc. Go over to your room and straighten it out and take a little time for rest or amusement.

Fix cocktails or highballs before dinner and if we have company have a plate of hors d'oeuvres to serve with them.

Set table with four candles, two plates of jelly, two green cut glass dishes of raw vegetables, two green glass plates of bread, centerpiece of flowers, butter plates, etc. If there are more than six people for dinner, serve two plates of soup at a time, then two platters of meat or fowl, one for each side of the table. Follow with two vegetable dishes, one in each hand, etc. Quick prompt service is necessary. Keep water glasses filled and if we have wine, fill glasses twice.

Be sure large candles in stands are lit for dinner and blown out directly when we leave the table.

Just before we leave the table, go into living room and music room and straighten out, empty ash trays, fill cigarette boxes, etc.

After dinner come into living room and ask Mrs. Dahlberg if we will have a liqueur.

(Dahlberg files, KCHS)

Bibliography

Public Documents

Annual Report for 1939 of Land Use Planning Rural Zoning Ordinance for Koochiching County, Minnesota.

County of Koochiching v. *George A. Elder, Commercial Investment Co., John Nuveen & Co., R. S. McDonald, William Durrin, Harold Royem, and L. H. Slocum, Defendants,* Transcript of Testimony of Trial at Brainerd, District Court, 15th Judicial District, commenced January 17, 1919.

Historical Resources Inventory: Koochiching County, Minnesota. Prepared for Koochiching County Planning Advisory Commission by Aguar, Jyring, Whitman, and Moser, Duluth, Minn., August 1967. 1–23.

H.R. 19541, "An Act to Authorize the Drainage of Certain Lands in the State of Minnesota," 60th Congress, 1st Session, March 20, 1908. Chapter 181, Public Document 125.

Koochiching County Agricultural Extension Records, August 15, 1913–December 31, 1937.

Over-all Economic Development Program, Koochiching County, Minn., 1964. 1–23.

Preliminary Report to International Joint Boundary Commission Re: Levels of Rainy Lake and Other Upper Waters. P. C. Bullard and S. S. Scovil, Ottawa, Canada, 1930.

Proceedings of the Board of Commissioners, Koochiching County, Minn., January 2, 1907–May 19, 1921.

Proceedings of the City Council of International Falls, Minn., October 10, 1910–June 3, 1940.

Proceedings of the Municipal Court of International Falls, Minn., October 12, 1910–December 31, 1916.

Register of Inmates of the Poor Farm, Koochiching County, Minn., 1909–1952.

Report of the International Joint Commission, Hearing, Fort Frances, Ontario, June 1941. Ottawa, Canada, January 1942. 1–58.

Report of the International Joint Commission in the Matter of the Application of Watrous Island Boom Co. for Approval Plans for a Boom in Rainy River. Washington, D.C., 1909. 1–89.

349

Report of the International Joint Commission on Rainy Lake Reference: Final Report. Ottawa, Canada, and Washington, D.C., 1934. 1–82.

Report to the International Joint Commission: Relation to Official Reference Re: Lake of the Woods Levels. Adolph F. Meyer, Arthur V. White, Consulting Engineers. Washington, D.C., and Ottawa, Canada, 1916. 10255.

State of Minnesota v. *The Aitkin County Land Company,* Chapter 278, Laws of Minnesota, 1935.

State of Minnesota No. 31980, in the Supreme Court, 1939, *State of Minnesota* v. *Aitkin County Farm Land Company, a corporation.* Brief of J. J. Hadler, Koochiching County attorney for other county attorneys AMICI CURIAE.

Transcript of Testimony in Case 21492, January 19, 1917, *County of Koochiching* v. *George A. Elder, et al.*

Transcript of Testimony, *United States* v. *Dennis Baker,* March 30, 1931.

Articles, Bulletins, Periodicals, Newspapers, Dissertations

Alexander, W. W. "Overcrowded Farms." *Farmers in a Changing World: The Yearbook of Agriculture 1940,* ed. Gove Hambidge (Washington, 1940), 870–886.

Anderson, Alton A. R. "A Study of the Beltrami Island Resettlement Project." Master's thesis, University of Minnesota, St. Paul, July 1937, 1–95.

Baudette (Minn.) *Region.* February 2, 1914–December 31, 1939.

Blandin, C. K. "Edward W. Backus, The Last of the Lumber Barons." *Blandin Broke Pile* IV, No. 8, August 1951, 6–7.

"A Brief History of Lake of the Woods County, Minnesota, Early 1900s." Published by Lake of the Woods County Historical Society. 1980.

"Clearing Land in Northern Minnesota." *The Farmer* XXIX, No. 3, January 21, 1911, 82.

"County Drainage Work in Northern Minnesota." *The Farmer* XXIX, No. 28, July 15, 1911, 861–862.

"Farm Development Studies in Northern Minnesota." University of Minnesota Agricultural Experiment Station Bulletin No. 196 (St. Paul, August 1921), 1–44.

Fort Frances (Ontario) *Times.* April 19, 1906–April 18, 1912.

Hartley, G. G. "Northern Development Association Meeting." *The Farmer* XXIX, No. 24, June 17, 1911, 781, 785.

Hinckley, I. W. "Rainy Lake Legends: Recollections of Pioneer Days in Koochiching County." Privately published. 1942.

———. "Way Back When." Published as a supplement to "Rainy Lake Legends." Published by KCHS. 1949.

"How One County Cut School Costs: Koochiching Is Operating This Year at a 33 Percent Savings." *The Farmer* L, No. 6, March 19, 1932, 7.

International Falls (Minn.) *Daily Journal.* November 9, 1911–June 1, 1950.

International Falls (Minn.) *Press.* March 22, 1905–November 8, 1911.

International Falls, Minnesota: A Presentation of Its Commercial Future and Scenic Beauty. Privately published promotional booklet by the Koochiching Company (Minneapolis, 1909). In possession of Mrs. Mark Abbott.

Lesher, Everett. "Congregation Pioneering in Northern Minnesota: A History of the Rainy River Association." *Congregational Minnesota* XII, No. 4, December 1918 through XIII, No. 2, October 1919. A series of ten articles.

Liggett, Mrs. William M. "The Needs of Northern Minnesota." *The Farmer* XXVII, No. 4, February 15, 1909, 142–143.

The Mandonian: A Magazine for All Mando Employees XXI, No. 4, July–August 1946 through No. 8, July–August 1947.

Murchie, R. W. "Minnesota Rural Rehabilitation Corporation." *Minnesota Municipalities*, July 1935, 286–289.

Murchie, R. W., and C. R. Wasson. "Areas of Rural Distress in Minnesota." Cooperative Plan of Rural Research, Agricultural Experiment Station of University of Minnesota and Federal Works Progress Administration (St. Paul, December 20, 1936).

_____. "Beltrami Island Minnesota: Resettlement Project." University of Minnesota Research Bulletin No. 334 (St. Paul, December 1937) 1–45.

Newspaper clippings, KCHS, from *Bemidji Daily Pioneer, The Chicago Tribune, Duluth Herald, Duluth Tribune, Laurel* (Minn.) *Press, Minneapolis Journal, Minneapolis Tribune, New York Tribune, St. Paul Pioneer Press, Toronto Globe.* In many cases the dates were missing. If the date was available, it was used in the endnote.

Northome (Minn.) *News.* July 3, 1903–October 6, 1905.

Northome (Minn.) *Record.* August 13, 1915–December 31, 1930.

Rainy Lake (Ranier, Minn.) *Chronicle.* November 4, 1973–August 18, 1977.

Books

Drache, Hiram M. *The Challenge of the Prairie.* Fargo: North Dakota Institute of Regional Studies, 1970.

_____. *Koochiching.* Danville, Ill.: Interstate Publishers, Inc., 1983.

History of Koochiching County: Where the Trees Make a Difference. Koochiching County Historical Society, 1983.

Jesness, Oscar B., and Reynold I. Nowell. *A Program for Land Use in Northern Minnesota: A Type Study in Land Utilization.* Minneapolis: University of Minnesota Press, 1935.

Kohlhase, Sylvia. *In the Shadow of the Spruce: Recollections of Homestead Days on the Black River.* International Falls, Minn., 1974. (Privately printed.)

Larson, Agnes M. *History of the White Pine Industry in Minnesota*. Minneapolis: University of Minnesota Press, 1949.

Northome, Mizpah, Gemmell, Minnesota History 1903–1977, compilers Lorraine Albrecht and Dolly Thomas. Northome Bicentennial Committee, 1977.

Nute, Grace Lee. *Rainy River Country*. St. Paul: Minnesota Historical Society, 1950.

Oehler, C. M. *Time in the Timber*. St. Paul: Forest Products History Foundation and Minnesota Historical Society, 1948.

Ryan, J. C. *Early Loggers in Minnesota I & II*. Duluth: Minnesota Timber Producers Association, 1975.

Unpublished Material

Beck, Bill. Typed manuscript on lectures on the region, in possession of the author. 1–30.

Kerr, George C. "A Brief History of Northern Minnesota Railroads." A manuscript dated 1961. Beltrami County Historical Society.

Skaar, Sherwin. "Border Pines: A History of the Lumber Industry in the Vicinity of Baudette, Minnesota." A research paper, Department of History, Gustavus Adolphus College, St. Peter, Minn. March 15, 1968. Lake of the Woods County Historical Society.

Watson, Emma (Mrs. George) Andersen. Ericsburg, Minn. Eight cassette tapes made in 1965, in possession of the family.

Materials in Koochiching County Historical Society, Minnesota Historical Society, and Other Archives

Abbott, Mark M. "Fifty Years in Koochiching County." A speech given to the Koochiching County Historical Society, February 10, 1969. KCHS.

Abbott, Mark M., C. A. Anderson, and Clarence Rogers. "Presentation to the Rainy Lake Women's Club," 1967. KCHS.

Ayer, Lyman Warren. Cruiser Book covering his exploits from August 14, 1902, to July 1904. KCHS.

Backus, E. W., file, KCHS.

Backus, S. W., file, KCHS.

Barkovic, Joan. "The Sacred Heart Chapel in Cingmars." KCHS.

Big Falls file. KCHS.

Border Cooperative Telephone Co. records. KCHS.

Braaten, Elmer. "History, Service, and Scope, MD 7 W Railway Co." November 1984. KCHS.

Brown, Florence Howard. A memorial letter to May Smart, July 25, 1930. KCHS.

Bussman, Frank L. Forest manager for ILC. Bussman file. KCHS.

Camp Book Logging Accounts for M & O Camps file. KCHS.

Christie, James C. Letters of correspondence. MHS.

Crane Lake Portage. Manuscript. KCHS.

Echo Lake Timber Co. file. KCHS.

Enzman, Alex. "Pulling Koochiching County Out of the Financial Mud." Manuscript by former county treasurer. June 15, 1942. KCHS.

Enzman, Nancy Arleen. "Annie Shelland Williams: Pioneer Educator of Koochiching County, Minnesota." Research paper, University of Minnesota, 1976. KCHS.

Ericsburg (Minn.) Telephone Co. records. KCHS.

Evans, Rudolph. Letter of July 9, 1924, from the Ku Klux Klan, in possession of Robert Evans, St. Paul.

Frankel, Hiram D. "Report on Labor Disturbances in Northern Minnesota, December 1919–January 6, 1920." Report of the Adjutant of the Minnesota National Guard. MHS.

Fritzen, John. "The Cunningham-McGinty Gun Fight." Manuscript. KCHS.

Green, Frank. County Investigation of Finances, 1917–1918. KCHS.

Hadler, J. J. Address to the Rainy Lake Women's Club, November 9, 1967. Hadler file. KCHS.

_____. Booster Program of Kiwanis Club of International Falls. A speech on WCCO, May 18, 1925. Hadler file. KCHS.

_____. "Sketches of Koochiching County Finances, from January 1931 to October 1945." A speech to the KCHS, April 9, 1973. Hadler file. KCHS.

Hadler, J. J., file. KCHS.

"History of St. Michael's Church, Northome." KCHS.

Holmstrom, Gust, file. KCHS.

Howard, Elizabeth. A tribute to her father. Howard file, KCHS.

"Instructions 1917–1918 to Camp Foremen." ILC file. KCHS.

"Insulite History." A manuscript produced from an interview of Paul H. Kinports. KCHS.

International Lumber Company. Camp costs and correspondence, 1921–1948. KCHS.

_____. Railroad files. KCHS.

Johnson, Arnold R. Manuscript on land surveying. June 1966. KCHS.

Knoblauch, Charles. "Forest Service and Civilian Conservation Corps." Manuscript prepared by request of Mary Hilke, curator. KCHS.

Koochiching Chronicle (aka *Gesundheit*). The Koochiching County Historical Society Newsletter. Articles taken from the files of the society. KCHS.

Koochiching County Auditor's Books. KCHS.

Mayer, H. A. "History of St. Paul's Evangelical Lutheran Church, International Falls." Undated manuscript. KCHS.

Minnesota and International Railway Co. Includes records of the Big Fork and International Falls Railway Company. MHS.

Minnesota, Dakota, and Western Railroad records. KCHS.

Minnesota Loggers Association file. KCHS.

Northern Logging Congress file. KCHS.

Northern Minnesota Hospital Association records. KCHS.

Oberholtzer, Ernest. Clipping file. KCHS.

Old Settlers' Picnic file. KCHS.

Palm, Gust. Letters to Annie Shelland Williams. Williams file. KCHS.

Paper Mill and Wood Pulp News. March 29, 1913. KCHS.

Paul, Walter W. "Memories of the Minnesota and International Railway." Manuscript. April 1966. KCHS.

Pearson, Mary Lou. "The Kettle Falls Hotel and Dam." KCHS.

Peterson, Clarence H. "My Memories of Bygone Days and an Account of the 1910 Fire." LOWCHS.

Plummer, Samuel F. Diary, January 1, 1905–December 1948. Plummer was an active person in the Loman area—teacher, farmer, logger, township officer, notary, and community leader. His daily diary is one of the best primary sources uncovered by this author.

Pollard, Lester E. "Cost of Logging Operations and Little Fork River Drive, 1936–1937." Manuscript. KCHS.

_____. "Logging Railroad Development and Camp Organization and Operation." Manuscript. January 26, 1979. KCHS.

_____. "Recollections by L. E. Pollard of the International Lumber Company Logging Operations on the Nett Lake Reservation 1935–36 and 1936–37, and the Little Fork River Drive of 1937." Manuscript. May 3, 1975. KCHS.

Reich, Harold. American Federation of Labor organizer at the Falls. The Reich file is the best single source of local labor activity. KCHS.

Russian Orthodox Church, Bramble, Minn. Record of organization and by-laws. May 15, 1932. KCHS.

"St. Thomas Parish, International Falls." KCHS.

Sedore, Jim, file. KCHS.

Smart, May (Mrs. George). "1904 at Howard's Landing." Also extensive newspaper clippings on the Birchdale area. File. KCHS.

"Synopsis of Events Leading to the Creation of the Beltrami Island and Pine Island Resettlement Areas." Minnesota Conservation Department. MHS.

"Taxpayers League of Koochiching County." A 31-page promotion brochure. KCHS.

Telephones file. KCHS.

Virginia and Rainy Lake Company file. KCHS.

Williams, Annie Shelland. A massive file resulting from over 20 years of research and collecting by this pioneer educator. Williams file. KCHS.

"Zion Lutheran Church, A History." File. KCHS.

Interviews

Alexander, Frank F. International Falls, Minn., June 11, 1976. Mr. Alexander was born in Michigan on July 1, 1893, and came to Koochiching with his parents in March 1896.

Anderson, Paul. International Falls, Minn., June 8, 1976. Mr. Anderson was born August 24, 1907, and came to the Falls in 1934.

Austin, Grace (Mrs. Harold) Plummer. Emo, Ontario, April 12, 1990. Mrs. Austin, daughter of Samuel and Nellie Plummer, was born in Loman on May 22, 1915.

Barber, Harold D. Littlefork, Minn., July 24, 1989. Mr. Barber was born August 13, 1902, at Bertha, Minn., and came to Littlefork in 1910.

Bergstrom, Oscar. Loman, Minn., July 22, 1976. Mr. Bergstrom was born May 31, 1918, at Loman.

Carlson, Ellen M. (Mrs. Ernest). International Falls, Minn., August 19, 1976. Mrs. Carlson was born April 30, 1893, at Grasston, Minn., and came to the Wildwood area about 1910.

Carlson, Katie. Interviewed by Don Johnson and Mary Hilke, curator, KCHS. No date.

Costley, Leonard. International Falls, Minn., August 3, 1957. Interviewed by Bruce C. Harding, of the Forest History Foundation. On file KCHS and MHS.

Dahlberg, Carl J. Marcell, Minn., July 7, 1989. Mr. Dahlberg was born December 31, 1905, at Effie, Minn., and worked as a logging contractor for 55 years.

Eastman, Welles. Wayzata, Minn., July 16, 1974. Mr. Eastman was a great outdoor fan who traveled the wilderness area of northern Minnesota for many years in the early 1900s and kept extensive journals of his observations.

Erickson, Anna C. (Mrs. Harold); Harold M.; James L. Littlefork, Minn., June 10, 1976. The Ericksons were born March 10, 1910, June 13, 1913, and November 12, 1911, respectively. They farmed and logged at Littlefork.

Erickson, Gina (Mrs. John) Finstad. Ranier, Minn., June 3, 1976. Mrs. Erickson was born September 24, 1892, at Superior, Wisc., and her parents homesteaded at Buyck ca. 1905.

Erickson, Ruby (Mrs. Rudolph) Olson. International Falls, Minn., June 8, 1976. Mrs. Erickson was born February 6, 1907. Her father, Nels L. Olson, was a pioneer merchant, banker, and automobile dealer. He came to Littlefork in 1898 and later to the Falls.

Erickson, Scott W. Orr, Minn., June 20, 1976. Mr. Erickson was born September 17, 1899, at Clintonville, Wisc., and came to Orr ca. 1915.

Ettestad, John. International Falls, Minn., August 4, 1989. Mr. Ettestad was born June 26, 1914, at Northome, Minn.

Fraser, Ann (Mrs. Ronald C.) Stone. International Falls, Minn., June 3,

1976. Mrs. Fraser was born March 23, 1882, at Edmore, Mich., and accompanied her parents, the John J. Stones, to Koochiching in 1898.

Fritz, Robert F. Fargo, N.D., January 30, 1991. Mr. Fritz was born July 29, 1909, at Winton, Minn. His father came to the Falls in 1911 and was the only manager of the ILC sawmill there.

Gerber, Alex T. Orr, Minn., July 21, 1976. Mr. Gerber was born December 16, 1895, at Chippewa Falls, Wisc. He came to Cusson as an employee of VRL Co. ca. 1913.

Gorden, Owen L. Big Falls, Minn., July 24, 1989. Mr. Gorden was born September 14, 1914, at Big Falls and was involved in various businesses in the area.

Gustafson, E. R. International Falls, Minn., June 10, 1976. Mr. Gustafson was born July 19, 1902, at Hancock, Mich., and came to the area in 1926 as a member of a U.S. government surveying team.

Hadler, J. J. International Falls, Minn., June 7, 1976. Interviewed by the author and Mary Lou Pearson. Mr. Hadler was born May 3, 1888, at Ada, Minn., and came to Big Falls in 1919.

Hage, Ann Adams. Minneapolis, Minn., October 5, 1989. Mrs. Hage is the archivist for the Congregational Church of Minnesota.

Hanover, Effie (Mrs. Ralph). International Falls, Minn., July 22, 1989. Mrs. Hanover was born in 1910 in Lac qui Parle County and came to Littlefork as a nurse in 1933.

Hardina, Neil. International Falls, Minn., June 19, 1979.

Hemstad, Peter. International Falls, Minn., July 20, 1979.

Hendee, Fred. International Falls, Minn., August 12, 1976. Mr. Hendee was born December 9, 1913, and came to the Falls in 1945.

Henrickson, Elmer. International Falls, Minn., August 4, 1989. Mr. Henrickson was born June 15, 1914, at Baudette, Minn.

Hilden, Fred. International Falls, Minn., January 13, 1966. Interviewed by Arnold R. Johnson. Mr. Hilden was a scaler and buyer for M & O from 1915 to 1958.

Hilke, Robert. International Falls, Minn., April 11, 1990.

Hnatiuk, George. International Falls, Minn., July 26, 1976. Mr. Hnatiuk was born April 10, 1915, at the Falls.

Johnson, Alfred J. International Falls, Minn., July 26, August 11, 17, 1976. Mr. Johnson was born December 13, 1912, at Baudette, Minn. He was a contract logger and commercial fisherman.

Johnson, Arnold R. Littlefork, Minn., July 25, 1989. Mr. Johnson was born December 16, 1925, at Fairfax, Minn. He was an Iron Range Resources Rehabilitation Commissioner.

Johnson, Bert. Island View, Minn., June 10, 1979. Mr. Johnson was born August 13, 1915, at Superior, Wisc.

Johnson, Byrne and Don. Ranier, Minn., April 12, 1990. Don Johnson was born on April 6, 1906, at Minneapolis, and Byrne on December 20, 1929, at Ranier.

Johnson, Hilford. International Falls, Minn., June 2, August 10, 1976. Mr. Johnson was born July 16, 1905, and arrived at Big Falls in 1909.

Johnson, Mary Knox. Crane Lake, Minn., July 26, 1976. Mrs. Johnson was born July 15, 1915.

Johnson, Melvin and Pearl. Littlefork, Minn., August 12, 1976. Melvin was born on April 15, 1903, at Canton, Minn., and Pearl on October 2, 1902, at Prosper, Minn. They came to Littlefork in 1934.

Johnson, Raymond. Littlefork, Minn., August 3, 1989. Mr. Johnson was a district forester.

Keyes, Monte F. International Falls, Minn., August 19, 1976. Mr. Keyes was born February 8, 1907. His father was a business and city leader for about 40 years.

Knox, Oliver. Crane Lake, Minn., July 26, 1976. Mr. Knox was born December 29, 1884, in eastern Ontario and came to Kettle Falls in 1904.

Kohlhase, Joyce C. International Falls, Minn., August 13, 1976. Mr. Kohlhase was born June 12, 1906, at Bertha, Minn., and came to Mizpah with his parents in 1914.

Koski, Andrew. International Falls, Minn., August 12, 1976. Mr. Koski was born March 3, 1884, in Finland and came to the area in 1905.

Kucera, Leonard J. Ericsburg, Minn., August 12, 1976. Mr. Kucera was born August 16, 1914, at Ericsburg.

Lloyd, William A. Fort Frances, Ontario, June 4, 1976. Mr. Lloyd was born in 1911 in Fort Frances to a pioneer family in the lakeboat and riverboat business.

Malerich, Mary (Mrs. Bernard) Curran. International Falls, Minn., June 11, 1976. Mrs. Malerich was born October 10, 1901, at Mayville, N.D. She was a long-time city employee.

Mannausau, Clarence A. and Joseph S. International Falls, Minn., July 21, 1976, and Joseph only, May 5, 1987. Clarence was born on November 5, 1911, and Joseph on August 18, 1904, both at Loman. They were contract loggers.

Mannila, Vic J. International Falls, Minn., August 11, 1976. Mr. Mannila was born August 16, 1906, at Chisholm, Minn. He operated sawmills in several locations.

McLinn, Ruth (Mrs. Eugene) Gowdy. International Falls, Minn., July 26, 1976. Mrs. McLinn was born October 9, 1923, in Gowdy Township.

Miller, Joseph. International Falls, Minn., August 20, 1976. Mr. Miller was born March 17, 1889, in Austria. He came to this country in 1908 and to the Falls in 1909. He spent most of his life as a lumberjack.

Monson, Ruth. Fargo, N.D., December 20, 1990. Conversation about her father's experiences as a minister at Mizpah in the 1930s.

Nagurski, Bronislaw "Bronko." Island View, Minn., August 16, 1976.

Mr. Nagurski was born November 3, 1908, at Rainy River, Ontario, and came to the Falls in 1911.

Nelson, John H. Crane Lake, Minn., July 26, 1976. Mr. Nelson was born April 2, 1893, at Njutamger, Sweden. He came to the United States ca. 1905 and to the area ca. 1920.

Niedzwiecki, Mr. and Mrs. Kajeten. International Falls, Minn., August 15, 1978. Interviewed by Pauline Musetta, of KCHS. Kozimiera (Mrs. Niedzwiecki) was born on March 7, 1885, and Kajeten on August 10, 1889, both in Poland.

Olson, Oliver. International Falls, Minn., August 15, 1976. Mr. Olson was born December 19, 1898, at Pelican Rapids, Minn., and came to this area with his parents, the Nels Olsons, in 1902.

Onstad, Peter E. Moorhead, Minn., May 24, 1989. Rev. Onstad was born March 12, 1903, at Ada, Minn., and was a minister at Littlefork from 1928 to 1937.

Pearson, Martin. Littlefork, Minn., June 12, 1976. Mr. Pearson was born October 10, 1889, at Lima, Sweden.

Pelland, Ed. International Falls, Minn., June 8, 1976. Mr. Pelland was born May 20, 1892, in Michigan and after 1895 lived on his parents' homestead near the Little Fork and Rainy rivers.

Pelland, Laura (Mrs. Elmer) Moulton. International Falls, Minn., August 11, 1976. Mrs. Pelland was born September 9, 1890, and came to the area in 1909.

Peterson, Arvid. Birchdale, Minn., June 23, 1979. Mr. Peterson was born August 26, 1888, in Sweden, came to the area in 1910, and homesteaded at Manitou in 1912.

Peterson, Marian (Mrs. Frank) Crabtree. Island View, Minn., May 20, 1989. Mrs. Peterson was born March 26, 1920, at Faunce, Minn.

Plummer, James O. International Falls, Minn., August 1, 1979, August 2, 1989, and Emo, Ontario, April 12, 1990. Mr. Plummer was born October 7, 1901, at Arkansaw, Wisc., and came to Loman with his parents, the Samuel Plummers, in 1904.

Pollard, Lester E. International Falls, Minn., June 25, 1976, by Mary Lou Pearson; June 25, July 20, August 13, 1976, August 3, 1989, April 11, 1990, by the author; and several telephone conversations with the author. Mr. Pollard was born October 4, 1907, at Graceton, Minn., and held various positions from camp clerk to woods superintendent with M & O between 1927 and his retirement in 1972.

Rasmussen, Jennie (Mrs. Fred) Baker. International Falls, Minn., June 5, August 16, 1976. Mrs. Rasmussen was born March 23, 1898, at Koochiching and was the grandniece of Alexander Baker, the first settler, and the daughter of Joseph Baker.

Richards, Ed. Big Falls, Minn., October 9, 1985. Interviewed by Arnold R. Johnson.

Robertson, Stuart. International Falls, Minn., October 13, 1977, by Mary

Hilke; July 10, 1980, by the author. Mr. Robertson was born in 1892 in Toronto, Ontario, and came to Indus in 1904.

Rogers, Clarence H. and Ernest E. Ericsburg, Minn., June 4, 1976. Clarence was born on November 3, 1901, and Ernest on July 2, 1903. They lived on the farm at Ericsburg their entire lives.

Rose, Jess A. International Falls, Minn., June 7, 1976. Mr. Rose was born August 29, 1887, and came to the area in 1910. He was a customs officer for 30 years at several locations along the border from Baudette to Ranier.

Schneider, Ray and Lillian (Mrs. Ray) Sagen. International Falls, Minn., June 11, 1976. Ray was born on May 27, 1901, at Odessa, Minn., and Lillian on March 18, 1905, at Edmore, N.D. Mr. Schneider came to the Falls ca. 1920.

Serdaris, James and Helga (Mrs. James) Browman. International Falls, Minn., June 12, 1976. James was born on October 15, 1895, at Corinth, Greece, and Helga on July 2, 1900, at Hazelhurst, Wisc. Mr. Serdaris came to the Falls in 1914.

Slick, Mary Dodge. International Falls, Minn., July 22, 1987. Interviewed by Harry Anderson.

Tive, Eric J. and Alice Marie (Mrs. Eric) Peterson. International Falls, Minn., May 20, 1989. Eric was born on June 3, 1892, in Sweden, and Alice on June 13, 1901, at Cokato, Minn. Eric came to the Falls in 1915.

Tone, Aad. International Falls, Minn., July 24, 1976. Mr. Tone was born April 17, 1909, at Northome, the son of a pioneer attorney, teacher, and farmer/logger.

Watson, Emma (Mrs. George) Andersen. Ericsburg, Minn., June 20, 1976. Mrs. Watson was born May 25, 1882, in Denmark. She spent her first years in the United States in Minneapolis, and visited Ericsburg for the first time in 1905. In 1907 she married George Watson and settled there.

Watson, T. Neil and Edith (Mrs. T. Neil) Gorden. International Falls, Minn., July 28, 1989. T. Neil was born on August 16, 1905, at Minneapolis, and Edith on October 25, 1912, at Big Falls.

Williams, Charlie R. International Falls, Minn., August 15, 1976. Mr. Williams was born June 10, 1908. He spent most his working life as operator of the Kettle Falls Hotel.

Zatochill, Walter L. Owatonna, Minn., June 20, 1989. Mr. Zatochill was born October 18, 1913, at Owatonna.

Index

ABOUT THE AUTHOR

Hiram M. Drache's roots are in rural Minnesota. He delivered milk to customers in the village of Meriden in the 1930s, first with a sled or a bicycle with a sidecar and finally a 1927 Studebaker. While working on an uncle's farm, he milked by hand, shocked grain beside his aunt, and did other chores. His first field work was driving a single-row two-horse cultivator. During two threshing seasons he drove a bundle team. With those experiences behind him, he has never understood the strong feelings many people have about labor-intense farming of the past.

Drache's college career was interrupted by service in the Air Force during World War II, after which he received his B.A. from Gustavus Adolphus College, his M.A. from the University of Minnesota, and his Ph.D. from the University of North Dakota. He taught high school, worked in various businesses, and purchased his first farm in 1950. Since 1952 he has been a professor of history at Concordia College, Moorhead, Minnesota, where he specializes in European and economic history. Because of several innovations, his farming operation was the subject of many articles in regional and national farm periodicals. In 1962 he developed a computer record system for the farm and his cattle feeding business. After 31 years of farming, the Draches have rented out their farms.

Over three decades he has spoken to hundreds of audiences in 35 states, 6 provinces of Canada, Australia, and Germany.

This is Dr. Drache's seventh book. Previous volumes have dealt with the settlement of the agricultural frontier, contemporary mechanized farming, and farm management.

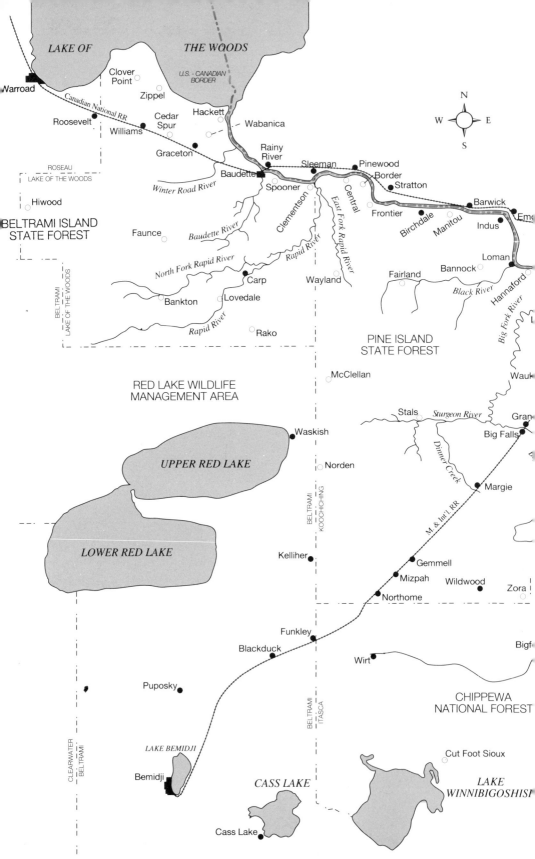